Where earth meets heaven

A COMMENTARY ON REVELATION

Where earth meets heaven

A COMMENTARY ON REVELATION

John G Strelan

The Bible version used in this commentary is the New Revised Standard Version (copyright 1989, Division of Christian Education of the National Council of the Churches of Christ in the United States of America). The biblical text is printed in full at the beginning of each section. Words and phrases from the text that are being commented on in the commentary are set in bold type. Numbers in bold type at the beginning of paragraphs refer to the verse or verses of the biblical text that are dealt with in that section of the commentary.

The following abbreviations are used for the various translations referred to in the commentary:

AV (King James or Authorised Version)
JB (Jerusalem Bible)
NASB (New American Standard Bible)
NEB (New English Bible)
NIV (New International Version)
NRSV (New Revised Standard Version)
RSV (Revised Standard Version)
TEV (Good News Bible — Today's English Version).

Wipf and Stock Publishers
199 W 8th Ave, Suite 3
Eugene, OR 97401

Where Earth Meets Heaven
A Commentary on Revelation
By Strelan, John G.

ISBN 13: 978-1-55635-439-7
ISBN 10: 1-55635-439-8
Publication date: 4/23/2007
Previously published by Open Book Publishers, 1997

To

Victor Pfitzner and John Kleinig,

partners in dialogue in
the preparation of this
commentary and in many
other contexts,

and

the students at Luther Seminary,
North Adelaide, who contributed
to the subject
UEB. 288B Revelation.

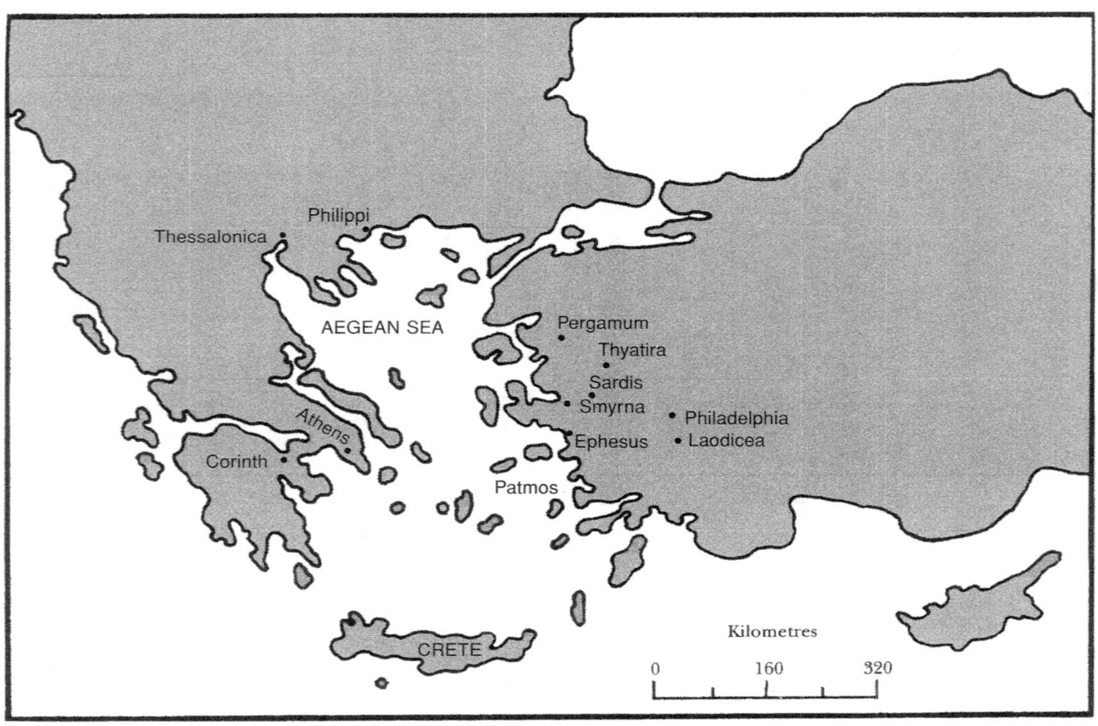
Philippi
Thessalonica
AEGEAN SEA
Pergamum
Thyatira
Sardis
Smyrna
Philadelphia
Athens
Ephesus
Laodicea
Corinth
Patmos
CRETE
Kilometres
0
160
320

CONTENTS

INTRODUCTION

Attempts to decode Revelation

> MELBOURNE: More than 40 000 fans witnessed the return of the Messiah at the MCG yesterday — but Geelong full forward Bill Brownless stole the show from the great Gary Ablett.
> Ablett booted two goals in a quiet return.

It is a sign of the times that the football reporter could take for granted that his readers would understand the reference to 'the Messiah'. In this respect at least we are back to the days of the New Testament, when messianic expectations were high, and promises of the return of a messiah were two-a-penny.

When an Australian weekly news magazine advertised a cover story on popular views of Christ and his second coming, it raised hackles or prompted smug smiles — but sold many copies — with its ad in national dailies:

> JESUS
> IS
> COMING
>
> LAST

Some people go to the sports pages of their newspapers, while some look to the news magazines, to keep them informed on the return of their favourite 'messiah'.

Christians, however, go to the Bible to learn of the return of the Messiah, the Lord Jesus Christ.

The last book of the Bible, in particular, has been the favourite of generations of Christians who want to satisfy their curiosity about the timetable of events associated with the return of Christ, the end of history, and the fate of the universe. The author of Revelation is hailed as a kind of divinely inspired Nostradamus. He is said to have foreseen world events at the end of the twentieth century, and to have written them down in a special code. All you need is a wise interpreter who has the key to the code, and all will be clear.

Hal Lindsey, author of the 1970s best-seller, *The Late Great Planet Earth*, evidently convinced millions of people that he is such a wise interpreter. Lindsey tried to show that the events which were occurring in Russia and the USA and other parts of the world had been predicted by the biblical prophets, including the prophet John. In 1980 Lindsey produced an updated edition of his earlier work. In this book he announced his conviction that 'the decade of the 1980s could very well be the last decade of history as we know it'. Study of the biblical prophets, especially of the book of Revelation, led Lindsey to this conviction. He was wrong.

The history of the church is littered with the remains of those who have thought that if only they could decode Revelation, they would be able to explain the inexplicable, know the unknowable, and answer questions about current affairs — questions to which the uninformed seek answers in vain. In his book, *Name of the Rose*, Umberto Eco tells of a conversation between two monks who are trying to unravel a complex murder mystery in a monastery:

> I asked him why he thought the key to the sequence of crimes lay in the Book of Revelation. He looked at me, amazed: 'The book of John offers the key to everything', he said.

In this spirit, a reader of the news magazine referred to earlier responded to the rather frivolous cover story by appealing to the book of Revelation for an explanation of the magazine's perceived impiety:

> It was interesting to note that your cover story 'He's Back!' had a tell-tale and most symbolic mark attached. On the front cover, the bar code was nicely positioned. Many serious Bible commentators are saying that the bar code is indeed linked to the anti-Christ's soon coming 'Mark of the Beast' mentioned in Revelation, Chapter 13. Perhaps this reveals the origin of your article.

How sad that this beautiful book has been so abused and misused by Christian people. Questions have been addressed to it that it was never intended to answer. The fact is that only half a dozen verses actually describe the Lord's return. Revelation is much more concerned with the present situation of its hearers or readers than it is with the future. Whatever information Revelation gives on the future it gives because in Christian thought the future makes sense of the present; it endows life with purpose and direction.

An alternative view of reality

In Revelation, God speaks of everyday things which are not at all secret, things such as political realities, economics, and daily living in an environment in which Christians are a minority. The book reveals these ordinary, everyday things in a new light, but there is nothing secret or mysterious about them.

John offers his hearers an alternative view of reality, an all-embracing view which includes the social, economic, and political realities of life in the Roman province of Asia in the second half of the first century of the Christian era.

One view, the natural human view, is that the Roman emperor, or the goddess Artemis, or a local deity — or all three — are in charge of life and death, sickness and health, blessing and destruction. Roman and provincial values, customs, and religious practices shape and control one's lifestyle. Life in the 'great city' is the only way of life. The philosophy of pluralism means that compromise is the only realistic option available to Christians. Cultural conformity is a 'must' if you want to survive economically and socially. And if you want to do more than just be a survivor, if you want to prosper, well . . .

Revelation urges Christians to put on God's glasses, to take another look at reality, to see things as God sees them.

The world according to God.

Christians are invited to recognise the copycat nature of all human power structures which pretend to be ultimates. Christians are urged to see the presence of Satan and his agents lurking behind all persons and powers and authorities who have rebelled against God.

The fundamental reality which Revelation reveals is that since the death and resurrection of Christ ('the Lamb who was slain'!), God is creating all things new (21:5). The old is being dismantled, unmasked, and stripped of its power. This is God's judging activity. At the same time, the new is being put in place. This is God's saving work.

Divine judgment and divine salvation: these twin activities of God are disclosed in a series of four revelations which the prophet John received while he was 'in the Spirit' (1:10;4:2;17:3;21:10).

The *first revelation* (1:9 – 3:22) was given to John when he was on the island of Patmos. It was the Lord's day. John was at worship, and under the control of the Spirit. While in this state, John received a vision of the risen Lord. Jesus commissioned John for his literary task, and through him issued to his church seven prophetic proclamations. When Jesus spoke, the Spirit was speaking. All who had ears to hear were to listen carefully to 'what the Spirit says'.

The *second revelation* is reported at some length in 4:1 – 16:21. The Spirit took John from Patmos to 'heaven', where the prophet was given a view of God in action, judging 'the inhabitants of the earth', and vindicating and saving his people. Included in this revelation was a view of the true state of the church, an unmasking of the enemies of the church, and a report of the ultimate end of both.

The *third revelation* is recorded in 17:1 – 21:8. The Spirit transported John to the desert, a place of safety. It is a suitable place from which to view the final destruction of the great city called Babylon, the human and demonic opponents of God and his people. John is shown, too, the final deliverance and vindication of the faithful followers of the Lamb, and the unveiling of the new heaven and new earth which God is creating.

The *fourth revelation*, reported in 21:9 – 22:9, is of another city, the new Jerusalem, the city of God and his people. The Spirit takes John to see this city from the top of the very mountain upon which the city descends from heaven. There on the mountain, heaven and earth meet — and John, in the power of the Spirit, is part of it.

In the sphere of the Spirit

The fourfold repetition of the words, 'I was in the Spirit', serves not only to designate the start of each revelation, but also to remind John's hearers or readers that when he received these revelations he was controlled by the Spirit, and he had entered the sphere of the Spirit. That sphere is outside the boundaries of space and time. In such a state, John was shown things which normally are not seen or known by human beings (hence, a 'revelation', that is, an unveiling). John was given God's glasses, so to speak. He saw things as they really are and really will be.

The New Testament gives few hints about what happens when a person escapes the limitations of space and time. Two passages are of some help in understanding John's experience.

First, when Satan tempted Jesus, he took him to a high mountain and 'in a moment' showed him all the kingdoms of the world (Luke 4:5; Matt 4:8). Clearly, this is not normal. The limitations of our existence are such that you just cannot see the world and all its power structures in one grand glance. What Satan did was to break through the barriers of time and space. By way of an aside: here is a case of an unholy spirit mimicking what the Holy Spirit does (see Exod 7:10-12).

The second relevant New Testament passage speaks of the transformation of the earthly body on the Last Day (1 Cor 15:52). The change will occur in an *atom*, the Greek says. Literally, the word means 'uncut'. The thought is of a moment of time so small that it cannot be divided. So Paul is talking not even of a split second. In short, time will have no meaning when our bodies are changed, when we move from one kind of existence, the 'earthly', to another, the 'heavenly'.

These two New Testament passages highlight a major difficulty which John faced when he came to write down the revelations which he had received. These revelations were given to him when he was outside the parameters set by time and space. He was in 'heaven', in God's 'space'. And he was in God's 'time', which is less than a split second and more than a thousand years.

In a nutshell, John's problem was: how 'on earth' was he to report all these things which he saw and heard 'in heaven'? He saw and experienced God's view of reality all at once. There was for him no 'first this, then that'. But when he comes to *report* his revelatory experiences, he cannot say everything at once. One sentence must follow another. It takes time and it takes space.

Perhaps a simple analogy will help to throw light on the unusual challenge which John faced. Suppose you sit on top of the Centrepoint Tower in Sydney on a Sunday, and you survey the city. You see the buildings, the harbours, the tennis courts, the parks, and the streets . . . the cars and trains rushing by below, a traffic accident, a robbery, a high-speed police chase . . . You see the people strolling to the local deli, the painted prostitutes, the playing children, the sun-bathers on the polluted beaches . . . families driving to worship in mosque and church, synagogue and football field.

You see all this in one sweep, in the space of a minute. Now you have to report what you have seen, to people who have never had that God-like experience of seeing the whole picture at once: Sydney alive on a Sunday morning. You must interpret what you saw, make sense of it all. You must show how these sights and sounds and happenings make up the city called Sydney.

That is your task. What will you do? What will you describe first? then? then? How will you link everything up, so that your readers get the same panoramic view that you had? What language will you use? How will you convey the feeling, the spirit which is Sydney town?

So you begin. 'First I saw this . . . then I looked around and saw that . . . next I saw something else . . . and I heard the police siren and the cheers of the crowd . . .' You will simply recognise the limitations of story-telling, and first tell of one part of what you saw, then another part. You will have a central theme to keep your story together, and perhaps you will set the mood by supplying background music which captures somewhat the geist and flavour of Sydney. So you will give your hearers the whole picture.

That is something like what John did. Failure to understand that has led to much misunderstanding of the book of Revelation. When John set down his report he used phrases such as 'Then I saw', 'After this I looked and saw', and 'I saw' or 'I heard'. These phrases do not mark off movements of time; they do not signal a temporal or linear order of events in the revelations which John was given.

When John received his revelations he was 'in the Spirit', under the control of the Spirit and in the sphere of the Spirit. So he was outside the restrictions of space and time, for God is Lord of space and time. These things are at his disposal; they do not limit or restrict him in any way. When John entered God's sphere of existence, he saw and experienced everything 'in a moment' (see Luke 4:5).

But when John came to report what he had seen and experienced, he had to write in some sort of order. He had to establish a movement from one episode to another, link everything, and interpret it all in such a way that it communicated clearly and made sense. *The apparent 'time markers' indicate movement in the progress of the report, not of the revelation which John is reporting.*

John's hearers have to imagine that John is saying: 'I have reported one part of the whole revelation; now let me repeat what I have said, but I'll use different words or images'. Or: 'Now I will tell you what else I saw and heard'. So John strives to describe in earthly, human words and symbols, events and scenes which belong to another dimension of existence. It's a bit like talking to a resident of Marble Bar about winter in Anchorage.

We never simply 'see' something. We always 'perceive' it, that is, we automatically interpret what we see, interpret it within the grid of our own knowledge and experience. If we have to tell others about what we have seen, we do so in a way which fits in with our audience's frame of reference. We want to describe and interpret what we have seen in such a way that it makes sense to our hearers. So John, as he reports the various revelations which he was given, uses language and symbols from his Bible and his world. He holds this Bible and this world in common with his audience.

The appropriate literary form of the first revelation (1:9 – 3:22) was determined directly by Jesus Christ: he gave John seven prophetic proclamations. John just had to write them down. In the case of the three other revelations (4:1 – 16:21;17:1 – 21:8;21:9 – 22:9), John was provided with a host of different symbols to use in his reports. But for the actual form of communication, the Holy Spirit led the seer to use the narrative or story as the main vehicle for conveying to hearers or readers the things which he saw and heard. The story or narrative sections of Revelation (for example, 8:6 –9:21;16:1–21) often use strange and even bizarre symbols and images. But sometimes the only way to express reality accurately is by means of symbols or poetry or music.

The main narrative sections are sometimes linked by means of smaller narrative segments in the form of dialogues which John has with an angel-guide or another heavenly figure, or even with Jesus himself (for example, 5:1–5;17:7–18). These dialogues or conversations serve to interpret a previous narrative, or to introduce a new one.

The context: worship

Surrounding the narratives, interwoven with them, indeed, permeating the whole book of Revelation, are accounts of heavenly worship. Worship is the context for all that John sees and hears in the four revelations which were given to him while he himself was at worship (1:10).

Worship is commonly thought of as a response to God's activity. This is correct as far as it goes, but it tends to establish or assume a division between God's actions and human responses in worship. John, however, observes no such boundaries or distinctions. Worship is God's work, in which people participate. By means of worship, people share in God's creative work; they even function as God's agents in this work. In short, worship is creative and constitutive.

Worship defines the church. By means of worship the church is continually renewed and reformed. Without divine worship, the church is dead.

Worship also defines and reveals reality. Since God's acts of revelation are always dynamic, creative, saving, and judging activities (see Rom 1:18;3:21), any revelation of reality which takes place in worship actually creates or constitutes that reality. Worship, then, establishes what is really true and what is false and a lie, what is truly real and what is counterfeit.

Worship is certainly the appropriate context in which to speak of reality as God sees it. For in the liturgy God provides a way of changing our 'world' so that it becomes a mirror of his 'world'. Liturgy has its own rhythm, its own sense of time and space, which matches that of God himself.

John, then, reports what he has seen and heard and experienced of the realities of time and eternity by means of narrative which flows out of worship, and which ends up in worship. The worship scenes which John describes are not interludes or interruptions to the story line. Rather, heavenly worship goes on all the time; it is prior to narrative or story; it provides the impetus and creates the context for the events of the subsequent dramatic narrative.

God shapes reality, our world, human history, and human destiny. But these things are shaped through human actions which God has authorised and empowered, and in which God is known to be present. This activity we call 'liturgy'. Liturgy says what 'is'.

Dramatic narrative is God achieving that 'is'. By means of worship, Christians participate in God's judging and saving activity which determines the basic contours of human existence now and in the future (see 1 Cor 6:2). Liturgy creates history. (For further discussion of the place of worship and narrative in the structure of Revelation, see the introduction to the report of the second revelation, pages 95-7.)

In view of the centrality of worship in Revelation, it is not surprising that the whole book is liturgical in character, from the opening sentences to the closing eucharistic prayer. The book is an apocalypse or revelation for use in the worship service as a prophetic proclamation (see 1 Cor 14:6,26,30). John received his revelation in sacred time, on the Lord's Day (1:10), at the time for worship. Since he could not be present in the worship services in person to share his revelation with his people, he wrote it down so that someone else (known as the *lector*) could read it for him during the sacred time of worship.

While Revelation was being read and heard, worship was taking place, worship on earth and worship in heaven. In worship, the barriers of time and space are broken down. By means of worship, people can match John's own experience when he received the revelations which are being read in the worship service. So the time of worship is certainly the best time to listen to the book of Revelation.

'A church', said a little altar boy, 'is like a reproduction of heaven — only not as good'. He was on the right track. The church's worship is more than just an earthly, human happening; it has a heavenly counterpart. The angels, creation, and Christian people who died in the Lord join with the worshipping community on earth to make the liturgy of the church a *public* liturgy. In worship, heaven and earth meet. And so we sing in the great *Te Deum*:

> We praise you, O God, we acknowledge you
> to be the Lord.
> All the earth now worships you . . .
> To you all angels cry aloud, the heavens
> and all the powers therein.

To you cherubim and seraphim continually do
cry . . .
The glorious company of the apostles praise you.
The goodly fellowship of the prophets praise you.
The noble army of martyrs praise you.
The holy church throughout all the world
does acknowledge you.

The book of Revelation was meant to be read aloud in a worship service. That is to say, one person (the lector) read the written revelation while the congregation listened (they did not follow in their pew Bible as we might do today). Listening was an art. A trained reciter could repeat after one hearing a lengthy poem of several hundred lines. John's hearers would not have had such highly developed skills; but they would have been accustomed to listening to long readings.

Written works were produced with an eye to how the material would sound when read aloud, and how the subject matter could best be followed and retained in the memory. So the writer supplied special clues and memory aids for the hearers.

For example, in Revelation John provides several sets of seven: seven letters, seven seals, seven trumpets, seven bowls, seven angels. These, together with subsets of four and three, and of the half of seven, provide signposts for the listeners to help them stay on track as they listen to the lector.

Another example: in chapters 17–21 John develops fully an image which is one of the dominant images in Revelation, that of the city. On the one hand, there is the city described as a rich prostitute; her name is Babylon. She is Satan's mistress. Like him, she and her citizens are heading for judgment and destruction. On the other hand, there is the city which has its origin in heaven. It, too, is a woman — a bride, the bride of the Lamb. Her name is New Jerusalem. She and her citizens share in Christ's victory, and her future is life with him forever. It would be very hard for hearers to forget these two vivid images; repeatedly they would have to ask themselves: 'To which city do I belong?'

That question would lead them to reflect on another, the central question of the book: 'Whom do I worship?' That question matches the central symbol of the book: the throne. God is the-one-who-sits-on-the-throne. Satan, who can only ape God, also has a throne (2:13). The question put to Christians is: only one king is to be honoured and obeyed and worshipped. Who is it? The evidence for where you stand, whose side you are on in the power struggle which Satan is doomed to lose — and has already lost — is given in the act of worship. The heavenly liturgy, which is a crucial part of the movement of Revelation, is directed only to God who sits on the throne, and to the Lamb (7:10).

Worship on earth is a confession of allegiance, a divine service, a participation with all the saints and angels in the victory of the Lamb. Worship on earth is an act of assembling before and around the throne, a turning of your back on Satan, the beasts, and all who worship these blasphemous parodies of the Triune God (13:3–8). Worship on earth — and specifically the acts of worship which include the hearing of this book, and the responses to it — is participation in God's acts of judgment and salvation, an announcement and an actualising of the kingdom of God, a direct attack on Satan and all his works and all his ways. Praise of God dethrones all idols.

A further example of the way in which John organises his material to help his hearers to follow and remember the reports, is found in the arrangement of the four revelations. The first (1:9–3:22) finds its match and its fulfilment in the fourth (21:9–22:9), while the second (4:1–16:21) and the third (17:1–21:8) belong together as symbol is related to the reality it symbolises.

But the most impressive aspect of the way the four revelations are structured is found in the second revelation (4:1–16:21). Built into John's report of that revelation is a miniature Book of Revelation (10:1-14:20). In these five chapters, which form the heart of the whole of Revelation, John gives his hearers a summary or precis of the total picture which the four revelations convey. In this central mini-report, there is a vision of Christ, a commissioning, a statement regarding the state of the church, an unveiling of the true nature of the enemies of the church, both human and demonic, and, finally, a picture of God at work, judging the wicked and delivering the faithful.

Listening to Revelation

So the first *hearers* of John's book had a number of clues and helps to assist them in understanding and remembering what they heard. Modern readers should make things easier for themselves by listening to the book as it is read in one sitting. One should listen to Revelation as one listens to a piece of music, to a Mozart symphony or a Bach cantata or an INXS track. Listen to the whole book, and don't try to isolate and explain every separate piece of information.

Revelation is like a video, with replays, slow-motions, close-ups, and stills. Revelation is a film which captures reality through the lens of the cross.

The outline of Revelation which is given on the next page is intended to help the reader of this commentary to visualise the basic shape of John's book. Whether it faithfully reflects the outline which John had in mind when he wrote, only God knows.

THE SHAPE OF REVELATION

Narrative		Worship
	prologue	
	opening liturgical sentences	
	commissioning of the prophet (1)	
	vision of Christ (1)	
state of the church (2,3)		
scroll (5)		acclamation (4,5)
seals (6,7)		lamentation (6)
		processional (7)
trumpets (8,9)		intercession (8)
	vision of Christ (10)	
	commissioning of the prophet (10)	
scroll (10)		
state of the church (11-13)		thanksgiving (11)
		acclamation (12)
judgment and salvation (14)		the new song (14)
bowls (16)		victory song (15,16)
Babylon (17,18)		lamentation (18)
	vision of Christ (19)	
judgment (19,20)		hallelujah chorus (19)
state of the church: new Jerusalem (21,22)		acclamation (21)
	epilogue	
	closing liturgical sentences	

THE COMMENTARY

PROLOGUE, 1:1–3

1 1 The revelation of Jesus Christ, which God gave him
to show his servants[a] what must soon take place; he made[b]
it known by sending his angel to his servant[c] John, 2 who
testified to the word of God and to the testimony of Jesus
Christ, even to all that he saw.
3 Blessed is the one who reads aloud the words of the
prophecy, and blessed are those who hear and who keep
what is written in it; for the time is near.

[a] Gk *slaves*

[b] Gk *and he made*

[c] Gk *slave*

1 The title given in some English Bibles ('The Revelation to John') is a translation of Greek words which were added many years after the book was written.

Some versions (for example, NEB, AV) translate the Greek title as 'The Revelation of John'. However, the author himself makes it very clear that his writing is not his, but it is the **revelation of Jesus Christ**. In biblical terms, a divine **revelation** involves both an uncovering of something which was hidden from human minds and experience, and the actual working out of that which is uncovered. For example, when Paul in Romans 1:18 says that 'the wrath of God is revealed . . .', he is saying not simply that people know about God's wrath, but that God's wrath is actually at work. We learn from God's doing. His **revelation** is powerful, both informative and performative.

The revelation or activity which John is reporting is indeed God's revelation, or, as John calls it, the **revelation of Jesus Christ**. A thought which is repeated throughout Revelation is that God's actions are carried out through agents. Here John records a five-stage transmission of the revelation: **God gave** it to his Son **Jesus Christ** who sent his **angel** or messenger to give it **to his servant John**, who wrote it down for his hearers, God's **servants**. The title 'servant' (literally 'slave') is given to all those who serve and obey God, no matter whether they are heavenly or earthly beings, no matter whether they belong to the old covenant (for example, Moses, Rev 15:3) or to the new covenant (22:3).

The servant is not the master; the two should not be confused one with the other (19:10). When the servants of God gathered in the sacred hour on Sunday to hear John's prophetic revelation, they heard not the words of the reader, nor of John, nor of an angel. They heard the word of God, an authoritative word which can be neither avoided nor contradicted. It is to be heard and accepted (22:7,18,19).

The revelation is given for the express purpose of showing God's people, **his servants, what must soon take place**. The Greek word translated here 'soon' has built into it the idea of 'quickly', 'shortly', and 'at the ordained time'. Ever since the death and resurrection of Christ, Christians have been living in God's 'soon'. They have been waiting for their Lord, who is 'coming soon' (22:7,12,20). Troubled and oppressed Christians, tempted to think that maybe they have misplaced their allegiance, join the cry of the martyrs for vindication and justice: 'How long, O Lord?' (6:10). The answer of the whole book of Revelation is that already now God is active, judging and saving. Present appearances are deceptive. The time is coming, and that time is **soon**, when God's justice and his salvation will be visible not only to the eyes of faith, but to the whole world (15:4;16:5,6;19:1-3).

The vindication and liberation of Christians is at hand. Of this they can be certain. For God is faithful. Just as the Lord Jesus said that he *must* suffer and die and rise again for the salvation and liberation of his people (Luke 24:26,46), so there are things which *must* happen for that salvation to be realised fully and finally. This is not blind fate; this is God at work (see comments on 20:3).

God disclosed his judging and saving activity by means of signs and symbols — a feature not unknown to New Testament prophecy (John 12:33;21:19; Acts 21:11) —

and **made it known** to John **by sending his angel** as the authorised agent, speaking and acting on God's behalf.

Angels have a very important role in the book of Revelation. An angel communicates the revelation to John; an angel commentates on the visions which John sees, and is John's companion on the way. Angels bear the bowls of God's wrath, and pour them out on the earth (16:1–21); an angel or an angelic figure functions as an intercessor for the saints, bringing their prayers into the presence of God (8:3–5). Sometimes, as in the last chapter of Revelation, it is hard to know whether Jesus is speaking or an angel. In fact, on many occasions in Revelation it is possible that for 'angel' we should read: 'an angelic representation of Christ', or 'Christ in angel form' (for example, 10:1-7;14:14–20).

An angel, for all his importance as God's agent, is nevertheless a slave, a **servant** of God and of the Lamb, and therefore John's fellow servant (19:10;22:9). John and his hearers should not forget this as they view the events in which the servant-angels play such a prominent part.

2,3 What John and the angel have in common is that they both serve as agents and spokespersons of God and the Lamb. Specifically, they both bear witness **to the word of God**, which is here defined as **the testimony of Jesus** (see 19:10). The phrase could mean: 'the witness or testimony of the word of God which has Jesus as its subject and centre', or it could mean: 'the witness or testimony which Jesus made in his life and work, his death and resurrection, to the judging and saving activity of God'. This testimony is the heart and soul of the word of God. The phrase has an ambiguity about it, perhaps intentionally reflecting the fact that in relation to the word of God, Jesus is both subject and object: he speaks the word of God and he is the centre and heart of the word, he gives the word its meaning and purpose. He *is* Word of God (19:13).

John uses several different phrases to characterise the revelation which God gives him: it is **the word of God**; it is the witness (**testimony**) which **Jesus Christ** gives in the word and to the word through his life, death, and resurrection; it is **the words of the prophecy** or **what is**

written in John's book which records **all that he saw**, and which is endorsed by Jesus himself (22:20). Let hearers and readers of all times note that the things which John saw and recorded are themselves **the word of God** and **the testimony of Jesus**. They are God and the Lamb in action, judging and saving, destroying and restoring, condemning and vindicating. When the words of the prophet John are read aloud in the worship service, the words do what they say.

So **those who hear** the words of this book should receive them as **prophecy**, given by the same Spirit who inspired the Old Testament prophets when they cried, 'Thus says the Lord!', or, 'The word of the Lord came to me'. The prophetic word is an authoritative word. It is a solemn moment: lector and hearers are bound by a common object, **the words of the prophecy**.

The beatitude or blessing which is pronounced upon lector and hearer underscores the solemnity of the hour. In content and purpose the blessing is similar to the one which Jesus pronounced upon all who 'hear the word of God and keep it' (Luke 11:27), that is, upon all who believe and obey his word. The beatitude recorded here is the first of seven which occur in Revelation (see 14:13;16:15;19:9;20:6;22:7;22:14).

Beatitudes are not platitudes. They are urgent calls to hearers to examine themselves and ask: 'Am I hearing and keeping the words of the prophecy of this book?' Beatitudes sound a warning to some and give assurance to others. So when both the lector and **those who hear** are said to be blessed, they are given a promise and a warning, one which should be taken with the utmost seriousness, for **the time is near**. God's judging and saving activity has been revealed and is at work now (see Rom 1:18;3:21); the time for repentance is now (22:10; see Heb 3:7–15).

The prologue or introduction to the book has summed up the source, the contents, and the purpose of the revelation. It closes in solemn vein, with a liturgical blessing pronounced upon all involved in the worship service. It prepares the way for the impressive opening sentences with which the worship in Revelation begins.

Worship then was prefaced by a beatitude, just as it is today in every Slavonic liturgy.

Opening liturgical sentences, 1:4–8

4 John to the seven churches that are in Asia:
Grace to you and peace from him who is and who was
and who is to come, and from the seven spirits who are
before his throne, 5 and from Jesus Christ, the faithful
witness, the firstborn of the dead, and the ruler of the
kings of the earth.
To him who loves us and freed[d] us from our sins by his
blood, 6 and made[b] us to be a kingdom, priests serving[e]
his God and Father, to him be glory and dominion forever
and ever. Amen.
7 Look! He is coming with the
clouds:
every eye will see him,
even those who pierced him;
and on his account all the tribes
of the earth will wail.
So it is to be. Amen.
8 So 'I am the Alpha and the Omega,' says the Lord
God, who is and who was and who is to come, the
Almighty.

[d] Other ancient authorities read *washed*

[e] Gk *priests to*

The combination of liturgical and 'letter' forms in these verses serves to underscore the divine authority of the whole book. It was not unusual for apostolic letters to be read in worship services (see Col 4:16; 1 Thess 5:27). In one of the earliest extant reports of Christian worship, Justin Martyr (about AD 100–165) writes:

> The memoirs of the apostles or the writings of the prophets are read for as long as time allows.
>
> When the lector [reader] has finished, the president addresses us and exhorts us to imitate the splendid things we have heard.

Conscious that he is writing for a worship situation, John has arranged the opening verses (1:4–8) into a kind of liturgical conversation. It could serve as a model of what should happen every time John's book is read aloud in the Christian assembly.

The movement of 'conversation' between the reader (who also speaks for John and God) and the hearers is as follows:

4,5a	**John**: trinitarian greeting
5b,6	**Hearers**: doxological response
7a	**Lector**: prophetic proclamation of Christ's coming
7b	**Hearers**: response: Yes! Amen!
8	**God**: self-presentation
	Hearers: silence

4 The greeting sets out the characteristic relationship between the author and the intended hearers. The author is identified simply as **John**. The lack of further identification, reminiscent of 2 and 3 John, suggests that the writer is well known in Christian circles. What is more important, the address sets the tone for John's role throughout the book: John is the viewer, the hearer, the writer, God's slave and instrument. Like his namesake, the Baptist, he is only a voice (heard via the lector); he is a prophet of the Lord, not the Lord. (For further discussion of the author, and the time of writing, see the commentary on 1:9.)

John has a message which he has written down (1:11), for **the seven churches that are in Asia**. The Roman province of **Asia** was the western part of what is often called Asia Minor (modern Turkey). When John wrote his prophecy, there were at least ten Christian congregations in that region, so **the seven churches**, who are identified later in this chapter (verse 11), probably are meant to symbolise or represent the total Christian community in Asia Minor, and perhaps even beyond. John's writing is directed to an ecumenical audience; it is intended to be read as word of God wherever Christians gather for worship.

The impersonal 'the seven churches' changes to the personal 'you' in the greeting. This is not a wish but a benediction in the usual Christian way, reflecting both Greek and Hebrew usage. **Grace**, the undeserved favour of God in Jesus Christ, and **peace** (Hebrew: *shalom*), the harmony and wholeness which is ours in and through Christ, come from the Triune God, Father, Spirit, and Son.

Grace and **peace** come
from him who is and who
was and who is to come; and
from the seven spirits; and
from Jesus Christ,
the faithful witness,
the firstborn of the dead, and
the ruler of the kings . . .

Grace and **peace** come, first, from God the Father. He is given titles which acknowledge his active, creative eternalness, in direct challenge to the title 'eternal' which on Roman coins was claimed by the Roman emperor. In what is probably a paraphrase of Exodus 3:14, God is described as the one **who is and who was and who is to come**. From everlasting to everlasting, he is God. He is not static but active, always creating, sustaining, and, in the mystery of his hidden ways, always making new all things (21:5).

Grace and **peace** come also **from the seven spirits who are before** God's **throne**, that is, from the Holy Spirit in the fullness of his person and power (see Isa 11:2).

And **grace** and **peace** come **from Jesus Christ**. About him three things are said: first, he is the **faithful witness** to the ways of God in defeating evil, the strange way of obedience and death. Christians are to follow that way (see 2:10).

Secondly, Jesus is the **firstborn of the dead** (see Col 1:18; 1 Cor 15:20). As such he is the Lord of both the dead and the living. He gives his people hope and courage, for he has gone before them into the future, where he rules over all. Thus he is the goal of our lives, the end to which we are heading (22:13). He sends the present out of the future, and it all comes with his compliments.

Jesus Christ is, thirdly, the **ruler of the kings of the earth**, those very authorities who oppose Christ and try to persuade Christians to worship the one whom the kings worship, the Antichrist called the Beast (16:14;19:19).

There are echoes here of Psalm 89:27, and especially of Psalm 2:2, which announces God's victory over those who set themselves against God and his Messiah (Christ). Although Psalm 2 is often referred to in Revelation, it is never actually quoted. In fact, of the 404 verses in Revelation, 275 contain one or more Old Testament allusions. There are more Old Testament references in Revelation than there are in any other New Testament book. But there are no exact or explicit quotations from the Old Testament.

5b,6 The response of the hearers to the magnificent trinitarian benediction with which John, through the lector, greets them, is to burst into a hymn of praise which celebrates the work of Christ. The benediction had concluded by confessing who Christ is. The response of the hearers focuses on the name of Christ, but it celebrates not who he is but what he has done (although his person and his work cannot, of course, be separated).

The hearers' praise is addressed

> **to him who loves us**; and
> to him who **freed us** . . .
> **to him be glory** and power . . .

Three works of Jesus Christ are celebrated. First, Jesus is the one who loves us, now and always; through thick and thin, he loves us. He loves us, and we should not let suffering or persecution or even death tell us otherwise. He loves us, always has, always will.

Once and for all, in the past, Jesus **freed us from our sins**. The price he paid was not 'gold or silver, but his holy precious blood and his innocent suffering and death', as Luther confessed in his *Small Catechism.* The Passover lamb foreshadowed what Jesus did: he gave his life so that we might be freed from slavery. Now he assures his people over and over again: 'This is my blood of the covenant, which is poured out for many for the forgiveness of sins' (Matt 26:28). Through the shedding of **blood** there is forgiveness of sins. The favourite name for Christ in the book of Revelation is The Lamb Who Was Slain.

To faithful Israel, who had been rescued from the slavery of Egypt at the first Passover, and baptised in the Red Sea (1 Cor 10:1,2), God gave the promise: 'You shall be my treasured possession . . . and you shall be for me a priestly kingdom and a holy nation' (Exod 19:5,6). Likewise we who through baptism share in Christ's death and resurrection (Rom 6:1–3), confess that he has created us a **kingdom** which is made up of **priests** who offer spiritual sacrifices to his God and Father (Rom 12:1,2; compare 1 Pet 2:9 and the context of baptism there). The church is already now 'a priestly community and an alternative kingdom to Caesar's idolatrous empire' (Krodel).

'Lost in wonder, love, and praise' as it contemplates Christ's saving work, the worshipping community breaks out into a final doxology: **to him be glory and dominion for ever and ever**. Christians in all times and places add their voices to the chorus of praise, and say: **Amen**!, that is, may it be so now and always.

7 The confession of the hearers concerning the power of the risen Christ, effective throughout the ages of the ages (1:6b), is picked up by the lector as he speaks of the end of time which is brought about by Christ's coming. John had described his message as one of prophecy (1:3); here is a typical prophetic oracle delivered in liturgical style. It begins with a weighty exclamation: **Look**! John uses this exclamation twenty-seven times in his book, always in key places to draw attention to an important statement (for example, 1:18;5:5;16:15;21:5). Jesus **is coming**, as he said he would, **with the clouds** (Matt 24:30; compare Dan 7:13; Zech 12:10–12). In the Old Testament, clouds were associated with divine activity: they symbolised God's power and majesty (Exod 16:10; Num 11:25; Ps 104:3).

Jesus' coming is a divine activity: it is the triumph of the slain Lamb. In Jesus' first coming, God was hidden in the lowliness of the manger, the ordinariness of the carpenter's son, the ugliness and lovelessness of the cross. God was visible only to the eyes of faith. Jesus' second coming, however, will be so open and obvious that **every eye will see him**. Those who will see him are defined more closely as those **who pierced him**. It is noticeable that John does not speak here of Christians. That is because Revelation tells of a *resurrection* of Christians and a *judgment* of unbelievers (see the commentary on 20:4-6).

Those who rejected Jesus are those **who pierced him**: they joined his executioners in putting him on the cross. These people, who come from **all the tribes of the earth**, will **wail** when they see him. They will beat their breasts in sorrow, not for what they did to Jesus (if only they *would* repent!), but for what they have done to themselves. They have brought upon themselves God's judgment because of their rejection of the salvation which is offered them in Christ, and because of their rebellion against him who is King of kings and Lord of lords (John 3:36; 1 John 5:11,12).

The worshipping community indicates its acceptance of the prophetic words concerning Christ's return by speaking a simple 'Yes' and 'Amen'. In Revelation, the responsive 'Yes' (*So it is to be*) expresses the endorsement of something that has been said (for example, 14:13;16:7;22:20). The responsive **Amen**, however, has the idea of 'May it happen'.

So here the people of God articulate both their acceptance of the words about Christ's coming (*So it is to be*), and their deep longing and sure hope that the coming of Christ will in fact take place (**Amen**).

8 The **Amen** with which verse 7 concludes is like a prayer that the Lord would come quickly (see 22:20). The final verse in this opening liturgy records the comforting response from God to the prayer expressed in the 'Amen' of his people. Now God himself speaks. He reveals himself, presents himself to the people who are prostrated before him.

In the worship book of Israel, the book of Psalms, God often presents himself to his people, reminding them of who he is and what he has done or will do for them (for example, Ps 50:7–20;81:8–16; compare Exod 34:6,7). In Revelation, although worship is clearly God's work and always takes place around the throne, direct divine self-presentation is rare. The two occasions on which God does speak directly are intimately connected: 21:6–8 fills out what God says in 1:8.

What a God! He is the **Alpha and the Omega**. Various magical formulas of the time used this expression to speak of the gods who supposedly held in their hands the power to bless or to curse. John's God is the great 'I am' (Exod 3:15), the one **who is and who was and who is to come**; the only one with power to bless and to curse (see Matt 10:28–33). He embraces and guides not just the beginning, but also the middle and the end of all history.

God reminds his worshippers that he is **the Almighty**, the *Pantocrator*, the 'sovereign Lord of all' (NEB). The emperor called himself *Autocrator* (ruler with absolute power). No! say the people of God. The God and Father of our Lord Jesus Christ (Eph 1:3) is the *Pantocrator* and the *Autocrator*; to him belongs all power in heaven and on earth. He controls all things.

In Revelation, Jesus is given many divine titles (for example, 1:17;22:13). But two titles are reserved for God in his Triune majesty and power: He Who Sits on the Throne (for example, 4:9;5:7) and *Pantocrator* (for example, 4:8;11:17). God alone controls history and the cosmos; he alone is its beginning and goal. Astrologists ancient and modern pretend to know what the future holds, and powerbrokers ancient and modern pretend to know where the power lies. Christians, however, confess not a 'what' or a 'where' but 'who': He who came once and who will come again to reveal his new heaven and his new earth which even now he is creating. Included in this new creation are all those who worship him as God and Lord; excluded are all those who refuse him the honour due to his name (21:5–8).

The opening sentence of this liturgical conversation began with a confession to God as the one who is and was and is to come. That is how it ends, with God confirming that confession, as it were. So the conversation is whole, complete. God has the last word, naturally. The only appropriate response to God's self-presentation is silence (see 8:1).

FIRST REVELATION, 1:9 – 3:22

The report of the first revelation which John received consists in the main of a long speech of the Lord Jesus (1:17b – 3:22), put in the form of a prophetic proclamation to the church.

These messages to the seven churches have the important function of mooring Revelation in the specific social, political, and cultural context of first century urban Christianity in the Roman province of Asia. These messages supply most of the key words and symbols which are used throughout Revelation. They provide the 'home base' to which the narratives and worship of the three other revelations constantly return.

In short, the first revelation (1:9 – 3:22) anchors Revelation in a concrete historical and geographic situation. It is concerned with Christian life and confession in a specific location in the eastern part of the Roman empire, that is, in the cities of the province of Asia. John's purpose is to ensure that his hearers understand that his report of the revelations which God gave him are meant for them, then and there. They are involved, crucially and critically, in what John has seen and heard.

John's commissioning and the vision of Christ, 1:9–20

**9 I, John, your brother who share with you in Jesus the
persecution and the kingdom and the patient endurance,
was on the island called Patmos because of the word of
God and the testimony of Jesus.[f] 10 I was in the spirit[g] on
the Lord's day, and I heard behind me a loud voice like a
trumpet 11 saying, 'Write in a book what you see and send
it to the seven churches, to Ephesus, to Smyrna, to
Pergamum, to Thyatira, to Sardis, to Philadelphia, and
to Laodicea.'**

**12 Then I turned to see whose voice it was that spoke to
me, and on turning I saw seven golden lampstands, 13 and
in the midst of the lampstands I saw one like a Son of
Man, clothed with a long robe and with a golden sash**

across his chest. [14] His head and his hair were white as
white wool, white as snow; his eyes were like a flame of
fire, [15] his feet were like burnished bronze, refined as in
a furnace, and his voice was like the sound of many waters.
[16] In his right hand he held seven stars, and from his
mouth came a sharp, two-edged sword, and his face was
like the sun shining with full force.

[17] When I saw him, I fell at his feet as though dead. But
he placed his right hand on me, saying, 'Do not be afraid;
I am the first and the last, [18] and the living one. I was
dead, and see, I am alive forever and ever; and I have the
keys of Death and of Hades. [19] Now write what you have
seen, what is, and what is to take place after this. [20] As for
the mystery of the seven stars that you saw in my right
hand, and the seven golden lampstands: the seven stars
are the angels of the seven churches, and the seven
lampstands are the seven churches.

[f] Or *testimony to Jesus*

[g] Or *in the Spirit*

The prophets of old sometimes received their commission in the context of a glorious vision of God in his majesty (for example, Isa 6:1–8; Ezek 1:1–28). John, too, is given such a vision when he is summoned to witness the opening of the seven-sealed scroll (4:1-6).

But here, at his commissioning to **write in a book** all that he sees and hears, John is granted a vision of the Lord and Judge of all, the Son of Man, Jesus Christ. This vision says clearly and unambiguously that the 'Lamb who was slain' is God indeed. Everything that is said about God can properly be said about Christ. As Son of Man he is the revelation of God. In him God has made himself known to human beings in a way which means that they can see God and live.

9 In verse 8 the Almighty God had presented himself to his people. Now John — rather diffidently, it seems — presents himself to his hearers: **I, John**.

The simplicity of the self-presentation suggests that John is well known to his hearers. He is their **brother** and fellow sufferer **in Jesus**. They knew him. The trouble is, *we* don't know for sure who he was. We know his name.

We know that he was a prophet who could write with the expectation that his words would be accepted as the authoritative word of God by the Christians in the Roman province of Asia. We know, too, that when he received his revelations he was on the **island called Patmos**. But we do not know if the author of Revelation is the same person as the anonymous author(s) of the fourth gospel and the Johannine letters. Nor do we know if the 'John' of Revelation is the apostle John.

Furthermore, no-one knows for sure when Revelation was written. The early tradition is that it was composed during the reign of Domitian, Roman emperor from AD 81–96. In the nineteenth century, however, most scholars favoured an earlier date for Revelation: they placed it to within a few years after the death of Nero (AD 68). Today a late date, towards the end of Domitian's reign, is favoured by the majority of commentators.

In recent times, students of the history of early Christianity have become more conscious of the flimsy evidence which is available, outside of Christian tradition, for a persecution of Christians by Domitian or during his reign. Furthermore, there is no evidence that emperor worship was promoted with greater vigour during the reign of Domitian than at other times. The imperial cult was strong in Asia Minor in the first century, but its strength was due to an unbroken tradition and development going back several centuries before Domitian.

On the other hand, there is no doubt that Christians were persecuted during the reign of Nero, emperor from AD 54–68. This persecution was demonic in its intensity; it did not, however, extend much beyond Rome and its environs.

Revelation itself gives two pictures: one is of a church situation in the Roman province of Asia. Christians there seem to have experienced nothing more than harassment from local authorities, and niggles and digs and maybe ostracism by their fellow citizens because of the stand-offish ways of Christians. For these Christians, the temptation to forsake Christ stemmed not from persecution, but from the attractiveness and ease of compromise.

The other picture which is given in Revelation is of a situation in which the Christian church has recently passed through severe persecution (see 6:9,10; 16:6;17:6;18:20,24;19:2;20:4). John says that he shares with Christians their **persecution** and their **patient endurance**. This statement is usually taken to mean that John had been exiled to Patmos because of his faithful witness.

We are looking for a time in the first century when Christians had just come through a period of persecution, but the Christians of Asia had hardly been touched by it. In fact, they were becoming complacent about their relationship with government and society. The period immediately after the death of Nero (AD 68) seems to fit the bill. The view taken in this commentary is that Revelation was written by a prophet or church leader named John in the late sixties or early seventies. Further evidence in support of this position will be offered in the commentary on chapters 13 and 17.

Christian existence, John confesses, has certain built-in tensions, well expressed in the coupling of **persecution** with **kingdom** and **patient endurance**. That these three belong together in the Christian life is indicated by the fact that in Greek one definite article ('the') links all three nouns, and all three terms are qualified as being **in Jesus**. To be a Christian is to share in the life of Jesus; his life was one of **persecution** and **patient endurance** as he bore faithful witness to the **kingdom** of God which he was ushering in. To be a Christian is to enter a fellowship of suffering (2 Cor 1:7; Phil 3:10;4:14).

The word which is translated as 'persecution' means the pressures, strains, and stresses which come to Christians who refuse to compromise. John shares their lot **in Jesus**, the Lamb who was slain. But this Lamb is also the one who conquers and has conquered; he rules, and his people rule with him (1:6;20:4–6). Theirs, then, is the **kingdom** of Christ; and since this kingdom is locked in a mortal struggle with the copycat kingdom of Satan, it is inevitable that Christians will suffer **persecution** for the sake of the **kingdom**. South African author Allan Boesak writes:

> Those who do not know this suffering through oppression, who do not struggle together with God's people for the sake of the gospel, and who do not feel in their own bodies the meaning of oppression and the freedom and joy of fighting against it, shall have grave difficulty in understanding this letter from Patmos. (*Comfort and Protest,* p 5)

The special gift from God which enables those who belong to the **kingdom** to endure **persecution**, is **patient endurance**. This is a rather bland translation of a word which signifies 'intestinal fortitude', 'guts', the creative use of trouble for purposes of growth towards maturity. **Patient endurance** is not the head-in-the-sand ostrich, but it is the bruised and bloodied boxer, who looks forward to the next round, because he's learning all the time; the longer the fight lasts, the more he learns and the better he gets. **Patient endurance** is the lone tree standing defiant on the windswept hilltop. **Patient endurance** is the calm, unruffled expectation of God's salvation, realised when Christ returns (1 Thess 1:2,3; 2 Thess 3:5).

John has said who he is; now he says where he is: on the **island called Patmos. Patmos** was a crescent-shaped, pocket-sized island in the Sporades group, lying in the Aegean Sea about fifty kilometres south-west of Miletus on the western coast of Asia Minor. It came within the jurisdiction of the city of Miletus, and was often used as a place to which to banish political undesirables. Contrary to popular ideas it was not a deserted, barren island; it had sufficient population to support a gymnasium and the cult of the goddess Artemis.

John says that he was on Patmos **because of the word of God**. This could mean that he was on the island because he had been preaching the word of God and was, therefore, banished to the island. Or it could mean he was on Patmos because he wanted to preach the word of God there; in other words, he was on Patmos voluntarily, for the sake of the gospel.

Tradition favours the first interpretation, and John's self-description (a sharer in the persecution and patient endurance) tends to support the traditional view. The second possibility, that John was on Patmos voluntarily, for missionary purposes, should not be dismissed out of hand. John describes the word of God as the witness (**testimony**) of Jesus. The word which John proclaimed was identical with that which Jesus himself proclaimed when 'the Word became flesh' (John 1:14). Jesus' testimony in word and action served as a guide and model for John's testimony in word and action. Such testimony involved both missionary endeavour (John 20:21) and suffering, persecution, and patient endurance.

10,11 Physically and spatially John was on Patmos **on the Lord's day**, the day of worship, when prophetic revelations were both received and proclaimed (see 1 Cor 14:26,30). To call a particular day 'the Lord's day' was to make a profession of faith. The people of the Roman province of Asia changed their calendar so that the year began on 23 September, the birthday of Caesar Augustus; this date, they said, marked the beginning of all things. Well, Christians said, the week begins with the day of *our* Lord, our king, the day on which our Lord celebrated his triumph, his resurrection.

Sunday, **the Lord's day**, was not a substitute for Israel's Sabbath. The **Lord's day** was the Eighth Day, which 'overcame' the week; it broke the boundaries of the old seven-day week. In Christ a new age has dawned. God has done a new thing: on Sunday a resurrection is encountered; the future enters the present, and all the old times and places belong to God in quite a new sense. All this was embraced in the thought of Sunday as the Eighth Day, **the Lord's day**.

At worship **on the Lord's day**, John found himself **in the spirit**. This translation ('spirit') would mean that John had an out-of-body experience. Possibly that is what happened. More likely, however, is the translation 'in the Spirit' (TEV,NEB,NIV), referring to the prophetic activity in which John is about to engage (4:2;17:3;21:10); it is an activity which can be done only within the sphere and under the inspiration of the Spirit. When John speaks, it is God the Son and the Spirit speaking for the Father (see 1:1;2:1,7). In short, John says he was 'on Patmos' and 'in the Spirit' at the same time. In worship, time and space, heaven and earth, meet.

John is told to **write in a book** what he sees. He did not seek the task; God gave it to him. The command to write was spoken by a **loud voice** coming from **behind** John. The voice is not identified at this point; but verse 12 indicates that the voice belonged to Jesus Christ, the 'one like the Son of Man' (see 1:19).

The voice was **loud** (literally 'great'). It sounded like a trumpet. That's the closest John could come to describing the sound. Igor Stravinsky once said that 'some sounds cannot be described, but they can be remembered'. John certainly would never forget the voice of his Lord. The trumpet-like blast would have reminded him of stories of God's dramatic appearances to his people, heralding marvellous deeds (for example, Exod 19:16; 1 Thess 4:16).

The **book** (literally 'scroll') which John was to write was to be addressed **to the seven churches** which serve as representatives of all churches. They are probably named in the order in which a messenger would visit them, beginning at Ephesus and moving clockwise through Pergamum to Laodicea. The fact that seven churches are named and located in seven cities, each of which has its own historical, cultural, and sociological profile, is a reminder that the word of God which is addressed to these churches must be interpreted within the context of earthly, temporal, ecclesial, and political realities. The Lord Jesus is speaking to real, flesh-and-blood people, who have neighbours to live with, governments to obey, children to educate, and enemies to resist. The situation of each church is described in some detail in the commentary on chapters 2 and 3.

12,13 John **turned** to look behind him **to see** who it was who was speaking to him in such a trumpet-like voice, and he sees a sight which must have left him breathless: a vision of the Lord Jesus Christ and his church as they really are, not as they appear to earthly eyes, bound by time and space, and shaped by earthly ideas of power and might, glory and wisdom. This vision of Christ, coming as it does at the beginning of the prophetic book, is determinative for all that follows. When Jesus Christ is seen as he really is, then everything else is seen in its proper perspective.

The **seven golden lampstands** are reminiscent of the seven-branched lampstand known as the menorah, which stood in the tabernacle (Exod 37:17–24). But the two are not identical. The menorah had three pairs of branches on a central stand. John's **seven golden lampstands** are individual, free-standing lamps, more like the ten golden lampstands in the main sanctuary of Solomon's temple (1 Kings 7:49). The seven lampstands are held together by him who stands right in the middle of them, the **one like the Son of Man**. In his hand he holds the seven stars (1:16), which are 'the angels of the seven churches', while the lampstands, according to 1:20, are the seven churches. These matters are discussed further in the commentary on 1:16 and 1:20.

The description of the one who is **like the Son of Man** seems to have been influenced by the language of chapters 7 and 10 of the book of Daniel. But to dissect this wonderful image is like inspecting the separate notes of a Mozart concerto. God is present! Here is God! The proper response to God's revelation of himself is not analysis but worship (see 1:17a).

The figure in the vision is **clothed with a long robe**. The high priest wore such a robe (Exod 28:4;39:29); so did prophets (see Zech 3:4). The **golden sash across his chest** suggests the kingly function ofjudge (see Rev 15:6). So the dress of this person speaks of great dignity, as befits a prophet, priest, or king.

14,15 The clothes match the man. His **head** is, like that of the Ancient of Days (Dan 7:9; compare 1 Enoch 46:1), **white as white wool, white as snow**. John can't find a 'white' white enough. The evangelist Mark also hunted for words to describe the 'white' of the transfigured Lord (Mark 9:3). Here is glory and wisdom and dignity without parallel in human experience.

But Christ is no disinterested, distant guru. **His eyes** flashed with energy and power, flame-like in their intensity (see 2:18;19:12; Dan 10:6). They were matched by his feet, which were of **bronze** polished to such a finish that they glowed as if they were still in the furnace. They speak of righteous action, holiness, truth.

The Lord's voice (see v 11) is a niagara of sound (compare Ezek 1:24;43:2). It mocked the feeble voices of the false prophets and the self-proclaimed 'lords' whom they served (compare 1 Kings 18:26–29). The babel and babble of false messiahs cannot drown the voice of Christ.

16 **In his right hand**, the hand of power and protection and honour, the glorious figure holds safe and secure **seven stars** which are 'the angels of the seven churches' (1:20). Whatever the meaning of the word 'angels' here (see commentary on verse 20), it is clear that John wants Christians to know that Christ is present among his people, and he is their supporter and protector. He is on their side. Even though his presence in their midst means that he knows all about them, and so has some very strong criticisms to make of them (see chapters 2 and 3), nevertheless he is on their side; he has not given them up. He holds them, grasps them in his strong right hand.

The phrase 'in his right hand' also denies to the Roman emperor any ultimate authority over the churches. Jesus rejects totally the emperor's claim to universal lordship, a claim exemplified in the coins of the time. These coins depict the emperor surrounded by the symbols of the planets.

Finally, John describes Christ's **face**. Two things stand out, both emphasising Christ's work as 'Judge eternal throned in splendour'. First, from his mouth comes a **sword**, two-edged and sharp (compare Heb 4:12; 2 Thess 2:8). Christ is judge of his church (2:16) and of the world (19:15). The instrument of judgment is that by which people live or die: the word of God (see Matt 4:4; John 5:24,38,45–48;8:51). This word is sharp, discerning, and penetrating; it makes no mistakes as it divides sheep from goats, and identifies accurately those who wear the robe of Christ's righteousness.

The other aspect of Christ's appearance which astounded John was the fact that the **face** out of which protruded the sharp sword was **like the sun shining with full force**. The vision took place on the Lord's day, which, fittingly enough, we call *Sun*day. However, the Son, not the sun, is the true light of the world. From his light the lamps and stars which are the church get their light (John 12:36; Matt 5:15; Eph 5:8-14). In his light the so-called great lights of the world (the sun, the moon, the emperors, kings, and other luminaries) pale into insignificance, just as the glory of Moses, the greatest of the prophets, was nothing compared with the glory of Christ (2 Cor 3:7 - 4:6; Matt 17:4,5). Indeed, so bright is the glory of the risen Christ that it outshines the midday sun (Acts 26:13). It is the creative light which first pierced the primeval gloom and brought life to the world; it is the redemptive light which cleaved the darkness of sin and brought eternal life to the world (John 1:1–18).

17 No human being can look upon the face of God and live (Exod 33:20; Isa 6:5). Little wonder, then, that John, like the guards at the tomb on Easter morning (Matt 28:4), **fell at [Jesus'] feet as though dead**. Fear and trembling, and a great sense of unworthiness and awe, take hold of those who get a glimpse of Jesus in his divine majesty (compare Peter, Luke 5:1–8).

But from the mouth which has the fearsome two-edged sword there come beautiful words of comfort and reassurance: **Do not be afraid**, 'Stop being afraid'. With these words, women and men were calmed and cheered by the Lord on several occasions (Matt 28:10; Luke 5:10; Acts 27:24). The one who speaks is he who holds in his right hand the seven stars, guarding them and keeping them safe. Since John belongs to that cluster of stars (see 1:20), it is not surprising that Christ places **his right hand** on John in order to calm his fears.

Who is this Christ who speaks the majestic 'Fear not!'? His self-description is sheer good news for his people. It shows how it is possible for us to look fully upon the glory of God which is revealed in the face of Christ, and yet live. Who is this Christ who speaks this majestic 'Fear not!'? For the second time in the first chapter of Revelation the great 'I am' is uttered. In 1:8 God himself speaks. He gives the divine guarantee to the announcement which stands at the heart of this book (1:7).

Now in 1:17 the same 'I am' speaks, this time in the person of Jesus Christ. He is **the first and the last** (see Isa 41:4;44:6;48:12). He is **the first**, because all things are from him; he is the **last** because to him are all things (Col 1:16–18).

18 Jesus is, furthermore, **the living one**, the one who has life in himself (John 1:4; 14:6). He once 'became dead', as the Greek puts it, but now lives **forever and ever**. This 'one like the Son of Man' (1:13) is a true human being: he died as do all humans. But he broke the pattern. He died, but now he is **alive**. Death could not hold him; it had no dominion over him. He conquered death. So he can say that he holds **the keys of Death and of Hades**.

Christ alone has the power to unlock Hades, the place of the dead (20:13); he alone is the master of Death (20:14). Christians, therefore, need have no fear: the last great enemy, Death, has been overcome by their Lord Jesus (1 Cor 15:26,56,57). He not only broke out of prison, but he took the keys with him.

19 The Christ who is giving this revelation is a conquering, glorious king. In him all things begin; in him all things have their present and their future. John should, therefore, confidently take up his commission to write (1:11). He should set down what he has **seen, what is, and what is to take place after this**.

Some commentators take these words to be an outline of the structure of Revelation, covering the past (1:12–18), the present (2:1 – 3:22), and the future (4:1 – 22:21). Against this view stands the fact that most of the reports in 4:1–22:21 focus on the present situation of the people of God, and on what God is doing now in terms of his work of judging and saving. In short, the primary focus is on the present, seen from God's point of view.

The verb 'I saw' (occasionally translated, 'I looked', for example 4:1;7:9) is used throughout Revelation to introduce a further stage in the report of the revelation which John had been given (for example, 5:1;6:1;7:1;10:1). This suggests that the phrase 'the things which you saw' (**what you have seen**) refers to the revelations John was given. The verb is in the past tense because John, of course, wrote the book *after* he had received his four revelations.

The second half of verse 19 (**what is, and what is to take place after this**) is best taken as a statement of what the revelations are: unveilings or disclosures of what is and what will be. Jesus, then, is saying to John: 'In writing down what you see, you are recording reality; you are reporting what really is and what really will be. Here is the truth of your present and your future. Write it down for all Christians to hear and to take to heart' (1:3,NIV). Verse 19 could be paraphrased: 'Write what you see, that is, record things as they are from God's perspective, and what they will be'.

In this way, Christians will see the world through fresh eyes. They will have an alternative view of reality, an all-embracing vision of their present and their future, seen through God's glasses. Such a view gives a sure hope, and provides a firm basis for resisting all temptations to compromise, to forsake the worship of God for the worship of the antigod. Satan pretends to offer a future. In reality he has no future; he is heading for annihilation (17:8,11).

US engineer and inventor Charles Franklin Kettering once observed that 'we should all be concerned about the future because we will have to spend the rest of our lives there'. True. But who has a future? Hollywood actor and producer Woody Allen eloquently articulated the hopelessness of a present and a future without God when he told a group of college graduates:

> More than any other time in history, humankind faces a crossroads. One path leads to despair and utter hopelessness. The other to total extinction. Let us pray that we have the wisdom to choose correctly.

To which cynicism we can only say: Thank God for his alternative vision!

20 Jesus himself interprets two symbols which John had seen in his commissioning vision: the seven golden lampstands (1:12,13) and the seven stars which Christ held in his hand (1:16). Inasmuch as human beings could not have worked out for themselves the meaning of these symbols, they belong to the category of 'mystery'.

In the case of the **lampstands** the interpretation is clear enough: **the seven lampstands are the seven churches**, the churches to whom Jesus is about to address words of commendation, censure, encouragement, and warning.

The interpretation of the **seven stars** as **the angels of the seven churches** was no doubt clear to the original hearers, but it is by no means clear to us. The interpretation of the mystery has created another mystery!

Who are 'the angels' of the churches? The traditional answer is that the 'angels' are the chief ministers or presiding elders of the congregations to whom John is writing. This view has been challenged on various grounds, such as: 1) there is no other New Testament instance of congregational leaders being called 'angels'; and 2) in Revelation 'angel' always refers to heavenly beings, not to human beings.

The view which is currently in favour is based on the Jewish idea that every nation had its angelic representative in heaven who supervised its fortunes and took the blame for its wrong actions. John, it is said, adapted this thought and applied it to the congregations of Asia. The 'angels' of the seven churches are 'the spiritual counterparts of human individuals or communities, dwelling in heaven, but subject to changes depending on the good or evil behaviour of their complementary beings on earth' (Moulton).

But there are arguments in favour of the traditional view that 'the angels' are flesh-and-blood people, leaders of congregations.

1) It is true that in chapters 4–22 angels are heavenly, 'spiritual' beings. They are agents, slaves, servants, representatives of either God or of Satan. But in chapters 2 and 3 they are clearly connected with Christian congregations; they do not represent God or Satan.

2) 'Angels' in chapters 4–22 simply act on behalf of God (or Satan). They are never warned, reprimanded, praised, or blessed; they are simply agents. They live or die with the one they serve. The 'angels' of the churches, however, are censured, commended, called to repent, urged to be faithful, and so forth. These are all human

activities, performed while earthly history runs its course.

3) In the structure of Revelation, chapters 2 and 3 have the important function of grounding in time and space the worship and narrative visions of chapters 4-22. Many things in chapters 2 and 3 have their counterparts or oppositions or fulfilment in the later visions. A consistent interpretation of chapters 2 and 3 takes the 'angel' of each church as a human being, rooted in earthly history and geography, as is the congregation he leads. **The angels of the seven churches** have their heavenly counterparts in the 'seven angels who stand before God' (8:2) and the 'seven angels with seven plagues' who come out of the sanctuary (15:1,6).

4) If the 'angels of the churches' are indeed leaders and teachers in the churches, then the notice that Jesus touched John with his right hand (1:17) assumes special significance. The right hand is the hand in which Jesus holds the seven stars (1:16), which represent the seven angels of the churches. John, too, was an 'angel'; he, too, feels the assuring touch of Jesus' right hand.

In summary: the view taken in this commentary is that **the angels of the seven churches** are the prophet-leaders of local Christian communities. John himself was such a prophet-leader (22:9). He was commissioned to record the prophetic proclamations of his Lord, words meant for John, for his prophet colleagues, and for all Christians in their care.

Debate concerning the identity of **the angels of the seven churches** should not distract us from praising and glorifying the Lord Jesus for what he does in verse 20. Before he tells his people how God sees them, 'warts and all', he assures them that he has not deserted them: he walks among them and holds them securely in his right hand (compare Matt 1:23;28:20). He speaks to them, then, not as their enemy but as their friend, not as their accuser but as their advocate. He speaks to them, not to break their hearts, but to encourage and strengthen them, and to warn them and call them to repentance, as necessary. He is for them, not against them (Rom 8:31).

State of the church, 2:1 – 3:22

Jesus is still the speaker; he continues a speech which began in 1:17 and concludes at 3:22. It is one of the longest of Jesus' speeches recorded in the New Testament.

Jesus has revealed himself as the sovereign Lord (1:9–16); he has assured congregational leaders and people that he is with them, that he holds them securely in his hand. Now he addresses seven solemn proclamations to them, in which he reveals the realities of their existence as Christian communities. Here is no idealising; here is rather a realistic description and evaluation of life in the congregations, what the members are doing and what they are leaving undone.

It is not surprising that in these two chapters Jesus urges the Christian communities to take a good look at themselves through God's glasses, so that they see things as they really are. That is what all of Revelation does: reveals God's view of reality, shows what is really true and truly real. Chapters 2 and 3 set the pattern and provide the moorings by which John secures the worship and narrative visions of the later chapters.

It is also not surprising that these proclamations are addressed to the prophet-leaders (the 'angels') of the seven churches. For Jesus usually speaks to his people through his servants the prophets, apostles, and pastors (compare 1:1).

The seven churches are addressed in a way which makes them, collectively, representative of the life and faith of every church of every age. However, they are not imaginary churches in invented situations. Jesus is speaking to responsible human beings living at a particular time and in particular places. Thus Revelation is anchored in the social context of first century Asian urban Christianity.

In speaking to his churches, Jesus draws on the history, geography, economy, politics, and culture of the cities in which the Christian communities live. It is as if the Lord Jesus were to write a pastoral letter to the people of Melbourne, and use the John Batman story, the state of the Yarra, the building of the temple known as the

Melbourne Cricket Ground, the Westgate Bridge disaster, and the Hoddle street massacre, to sheet home his message and anchor it in *this* life, not never-never land.

What was the environment in which Christians in Asia Minor lived in the late 60s and early 70s of the first century? What were their challenges and temptations? Each community was different; but some general observations may be made.

The western part of Asia Minor was one of the most significant areas in the development of early Christianity. Paul had been active there in the fifties (see 1 Cor 16:19), and his influence was still strong. The apostle John was said to have been associated with the area, especially with the city of Ephesus. The author of 1 Peter wrote to the churches of Asia Minor (and elsewhere), as did Ignatius, bishop of Antioch. Ignatius, who died about AD 107, addressed letters to five churches in western Asia Minor: Ephesus, Magnesia, Tralles, Philadelphia, and Smyrna.

At least eleven urban Christian communities are known to have been in existence when John wrote Revelation, and three major apostolic figures are known to have been associated with those communities: Paul, Peter, and John.

Asia was one of the more important provinces in the Roman empire. It supported a wide range of primary and secondary industries; it paid huge amounts of taxes into the Roman treasury; and it was a major peace-time source of slaves. It was also of strategic military and commercial importance.

Ambitious Roman civil servants regarded an appointment to the province of Asia as a step up the social and political ladder. The same could not be said for, say, an appointment to the province of Judea.

The culture of provincial Asia was Greek. The main language was Greek. The basic unit of political organisation was the city. The three hundred or more cities in the province were far more important to its people than was Rome. The cities nurtured the arts and culture, and provided the focal point and arena for religious cults and festivals.

In the cities of provincial Asia, Christians lived a basically quiet and peaceable life. They enjoyed the social and material benefits of being part of a great empire. Rome itself took very little direct interest in provincial affairs, so if Asian Christians had problems, they were local, not universal. The provinces enjoyed a great measure of autonomy and independence. In the first century no Roman emperor visited the province of Asia; no Roman legion was stationed there.

Religious cults and festivals were an important part of communal Greek culture in both rural and urban areas. The cult of the goddess Artemis, centred in Ephesus, dominated the religious life of many communities in Asia Minor and elsewhere. Archaeological evidence attests the presence of the cult in all parts of Asia Minor, the Greek mainland and islands, Italy, France, Spain, the north coast of the Black Sea, Phoenicia, and Palestine.

But probably the most important cult in provincial Asia was the imperial cult. This was a genuine religious phenomenon, not just a political activity in religious dress. Indeed, the reality which was the Roman empire has been said to have been constituted by three things: politics, diplomacy, and the imperial cult (S.R. Price).

The cult of the emperor was deeply entrenched in the Roman provinces: the further from Rome, the stronger the cult. Temples and sanctuaries were dedicated to the emperor, and festivals were held in his name. Inscriptions on public buildings and monuments hailed him as 'God and Lord', and gave him other divine titles.

In Asia Minor the emperor cult had been gathering momentum for several centuries before Christianity entered the public square. The cult had become part of the warp and woof of public and private life. There is, however, no evidence that people in Asia Minor in John's day had publicly to affirm their loyalty to Rome by worshipping before an image of the emperor. There might have been local outbreaks of discriminatory action and even persecution (see 2:13), but this was because Christians were Christians, and not necessarily because they refused to participate in the imperial cult.

The real problem for Christians would have arisen in connection with religious activities associated with public festivals, trade guilds, and local celebrations and customs. In many situations Christians would have been required by convention to sacrifice to Artemis or to a local deity or to the emperor. The Christians' reluctance to participate fully in public and semi-private functions with a religious component would have attracted the attention of their fellow citizens, and raised in people's minds suspicions of disloyalty and impiety.

Another relevant factor in the socio-religious profile of Asian urban communities was the presence of Jews. As a group they were well established and well connected in the cities. They had earned the right to practise their religion freely. In some cities Jew and Christian lived together in peace. In other cities there was often overt or covert hostility from the Jews. Christians resented the fact that they were not accorded the same privileges and given the same public recognition as were the Jews.

Christians, then, ran the risk of being treated with suspicion by both their Jewish and heathen neighbours. They were out in the cold. What to do? Some Christian prophets, known as 'the Nicolaitans' or the 'followers of Jezebel', seem to have taught that Christians had to learn to adapt to society. They have to compromise (see 2:5,14,20). A Christian, they said, cannot avoid being a citizen in a pagan society. Paul said that we have to honour and obey the state; Peter said the same thing. That means that Christians should take an active part in the commercial, social, and political life of the city. Why worry about a prayer here, a sacrifice there? Such token acts of worship of the gods does not involve a denial of God or the Lord Jesus.

The other response to this situation is the one given by Jesus himself throughout the book of Revelation. Put simply, Jesus says: No compromise, no both/and is possible. The claim which God makes on a Christian is total; it leaves no room for divided loyalty. Now is the time to stand up and be counted. Lukewarmness is capitulation.

The reality of the current situation is as it was in the time of Elijah: 'If the Lord is God, follow him; but if Baal, then follow him' (1 Kings 18:21). The visions in Revelation are meant to unveil the realities of the kingdom of Satan, to show the derived, copycat nature of all false gods and powers, to help Christians to see clearly the consequences of compromise.

This situation, this difficult situation, is familiar to Western Christians who also find themselves enchained by cultural and social values and lifestyles. We are losing our critical faculties; we are unable or unwilling to withdraw, to protest, to offer an alternative. Churches are so keen to 'belong' that they are seen by non-Christians as little more than social clubs. Among us the gospel has lost its cutting edge; it has been domesticated, and we with it. Compromise is the Christian's deadly and besetting sin.

We need to hear the message of Revelation. Especially do we need to listen to the words which Jesus, the caring Shepherd, addresses to flesh-and-blood Christian communities.

Traditionally, the material in chapters 2 and 3 has been called 'letters': 'The Letters to the Seven Churches' is the usual heading for these two chapters. In fact, however, the *form* which Jesus used to speak to the churches is less like an ancient letter and more like a royal or imperial edict or proclamation. It is like a proclamation made by a magistrate to regulate the thinking and behaviour of the community.

In terms of *content*, the material in chapters 2 and 3 is like the judgment and salvation oracles spoken by the Old Testament and early Christian prophets. So we could properly speak of prophetic proclamations issued to his subjects by the King of kings and Lord of lords. Pretenders to his throne, false clones of Christ — like local rulers or emperors, or the beast of chapter 13 — might issue all kinds of edicts and demand (and even get) obedience, adoration, and worship. But only one, the Lord God Almighty and the Lamb who was slain, is worthy to receive *all* honour and glory and might for ever and ever (5:13).

The seven prophetic proclamations have a similar structure:

— a command to write is followed by a self-description which usually picks up a feature from the vision in 1:9–16;
— the church is praised, rebuked, or exhorted;
— all hearers are called to take to heart Christ's words;
— promises are given to 'those who conquer', that is, to the repentant and believing followers of the Lamb.

a) To Ephesus, 2:1–7

2 'To the angel of the church in Ephesus write: These are the words of him who holds the seven stars in his right hand, who walks among the seven golden lampstands:
2 'I know your works, your toil and your patient endurance. I know that you cannot tolerate evildoers; you have tested those who claim to be apostles but are not, and have found them to be false. 3 I also know that you are enduring patiently and bearing up for the sake of my name, and that you have not grown weary. 4 But I have this against you, that you have abandoned the love you had at first. 5 Remember then from what you have fallen; repent, and do the works you did at first. If not, I will come to you and remove your lampstand from its place, unless you repent. 6 Yet this is to your credit: you hate the works of the Nicolaitans, which I also hate. 7 Let anyone who has an ear listen to what the Spirit is saying to the churches. To everyone who conquers, I will give permission to eat from the tree of life that is in the paradise of God.

1 Jesus is still the speaker. Twice already he had commanded John to **write** what he sees (1:11,19); now John is to **write** what he hears from the Lord. The words are addressed to **the angel of the church**, that is, to the prophet-leader of the Christian community **in Ephesus** (see the commentary on 1:19 for a discussion of the

meaning of 'angel' here). Christ's words are addressed to the prophet-leader, but they are meant for all members of the Ephesian congregation, and, indeed, for all Christians, as the exhortations in 1:7 and 1:11, for example, indicate.

The city of **Ephesus**, one of the largest and most famous of ancient cities, was old already in John's time. A majestic mall, eleven metres wide and lined with columns, ran through the middle of the city to the harbour, which served as a base for international trade. Ephesus was also the terminus of the great Royal Road, which led from Persia westward and served as an important caravan route.

Ephesus was also an important religious centre. The temple of Artemis, known as the Artemision, was one of the wonders of the ancient world. Artemis (Latin: Diana) and Ephesus were inseparable. A unique bond existed between the city and the goddess. There is evidence to suggest that the Ephesians believed that Artemis was even older than ancient Ephesus, and that the city owed its existence to the continued presence of Artemis in the environs of Ephesus.

In the Greco-Roman world, Artemis meant different things to different people. In the eyes of the citizen of Ephesus, Artemis was the deity who helped in time of life's transitions. Artemis was honoured as the eternal virgin. She had a special empathy with virgins and unmarried women. She herself did not menstruate, but she caused menstruation and guided girls through puberty. In brief, Artemis presided over the creation of Woman, that is, she led young girls into womanhood.

To a lesser extent, Artemis was regarded as the protector of young men.

Parents dedicated their children to the goddess, believing that her protection and blessing would follow them throughout their young lives. For many people, Artemis was worthy of praise and thanks because of her role as saviour and helper. She heard prayers and granted healing to the sick.

In summary:

> the main function and role of Artemis was that of protectress and savior. Artemis provides safety — for the

> city, for those who flee to her for sanctuary, for young men and women in particular. She was equally important as the goddess who helped and protected those in transition. At a political level, Artemis was the symbol of Ephesus, ancient, respected and honored even by political opponents in the city, and enduring in power and status. (R. Strelan, *Paul, Artemis, and the Jews in Ephesus,* p 52)

The two hundred thousand citizens of Ephesus looked upon the Artemision (the temple of Artemis) as one of the most sacred sites on earth. Philo Byzantius, who lived about two hundred years before John, wrote:

> The temple of Artemis in Ephesus is the only house of the gods. For whoever examines it will believe that the gods exchanged the heavenly regions of immortality to have a place upon earth.

Hundreds, even thousands, of cult functionaries served the goddess in the temple ritual and on special festival occasions. There was also a large staff of vergers, cleaners, attendants, and officials called 'theologi' who transcribed, interpreted, and recited the sacred stories. There were hymn writers to compose music, and boys choirs to perform it. Elders or presbyters handled financial matters. There is no evidence that the cult of Artemis was linked with sexual orgies. Quite the opposite, in fact: there was almost a sexual asceticism associated with Artemis, her temple, and her cult.

The imperial cult was also active in Ephesus: at one time in its history the city boasted three officially sanctioned imperial temples. But in Ephesus itself Artemis was supreme. Her cult took pride of place over any other cult, including emperor worship. The cult of Artemis was central to the whole fabric of life in the city of Ephesus.

With the cult of Artemis on one side, and vigorous emperor worship on the other, Christians in Ephesus must often have found themselves between a rock and a hard place. The presence of a large colony of Jews, with special and guaranteed privileges, would have done nothing to ease the Christians' situation. In all, the temptation to compromise must have been chronically attractive.

The **church in Ephesus** dates back to at least AD 52, when Paul made a brief visit and left Aquila and Priscilla there (Acts 18:18–21). Later Paul himself lived in Ephesus for two or three years, and his young offsider, Timothy, was 'pastor' there for some time (1 Tim 1:3). Early tradition associates both Paul and the apostle John with Ephesus; it is possible that with the fall of Jerusalem, Ephesus became the temporary headquarters of the church.

The Lord Jesus begins his address to the Ephesian Christians with the phrase, 'the words of'. That is exactly how an edict from a Roman king or emperor began. The eternal King identifies himself as the one who **holds the seven stars in his right hand, who walks among the seven golden lampstands**. These words come from the description of Christ in the inaugural vision (1:9–16), with two small but important variations. First, in 1:16 John said that Jesus 'held' (literally 'had') seven stars; here Jesus says that he grasps seven stars, **holds** firmly in his hand the prophet-leaders of the congregations. Secondly, in 1:13 John spoke of Jesus being 'in the midst of the lampstands'; here Jesus says that he **walks among** them, moves about in the midst of the churches. Without a doubt, Jesus Christ is alive and well and active in his church. He is no disinterested spectator or absentee lord. He dwells with his people (21:3), and knows them intimately, for better or for worse (see John 10:14).

2 Since he truly knows his people, Jesus can insist that he knows also the **works** which they perform as the fruits of faith, fruits expected of those who are joined to Christ and remain in him (see John 15:1–8). The **works** of the Ephesian Christians are specified as **toil** and **patient endurance**. Their **toil** is a combination of hard work and spiritual insight, in a hostile environment. It is exemplified in their unwillingness to **tolerate evildoers**, especially those **who claim to be apostles but are not**. These pretend apostles have been **tested** (compare 1 John 4:1) and exposed for what they are: **false**. Who were these people? Some say they were travelling evangelists; some say they were agents from Jerusalem (see 2 Cor 11:12–15); some say they were disciples of Paul;

some say they were associated with the Nicolaitans (see 2:6). We don't know who they were exactly; we can only assume they were potential troublemakers whom the Ephesian Christians identified and opposed. For this the Lord commends his faithful people.

3 The Ephesians' 'patient endurance' (2:2) is described more fully as **bearing up** for Christ's sake (**for the sake of my name**), and not growing weary. The idea inherent in the phrase 'patient endurance' was discussed in the comments on 1:9. Evidently the Ephesians are under threat, perhaps of persecution or economic discrimination, or the temptation to compromise, or all of these. The Lord Jesus is pleased with the way they are handling the situation. He praises them by repeating in verse 3 what he said he 'knows' about them in verse 2:

verse 2	**verse 3**
toil	not grown weary
patient endurance	enduring patiently
cannot tolerate	bearing up

4 As is usually the case in the Christian life, commendations are followed by a 'but', in this case a very strong 'but': **But I have this against you, that you have abandoned the love you had at first**. This is a shocking indictment, for it means that all their 'works' (2:2), their patient endurance, their concern for orthodoxy, their bearing up in the face of adversity — all are worthless, for they are done without love, love for God and love for the brother and sister (compare 1 Cor 13:5-7). Enthusiasm for the truth is nothing if one lacks love. True love for the truth is expressed in love for God's children (see 1 John 3:8–20; 4:20). Conversely, lack of love is one of the marks of the great apostasy of the Last Days (Matt 24:12).

5 The church in Ephesus was in a sorry state. It was near death. Hence the Lord's admonition is sharp and urgent. He urges them to **remember** and to continue to remember their first state, how things were in the first flush of faith. For they **have fallen**; indeed, 'fallenness' is their present condition. The only way out is to observe the three great imperatives of the Christian life: **remember** . . . **repent** . . . **do**.

When Christians **remember**, they bring the past into the present, they re-present it. So in the eucharist they 'remember' the Lord's death. When they 'remember' their baptism they apply to themselves today that which baptism works and accomplishes. When they 'remember' their sins, they own and acknowledge their condition before God. We are sinners, they say; we have sinned.

'Remembering' leads to repentance, a complete turn around, a turning to Christ in faith, and a turning away from sin and Satan and self. By way of contrast, in the cult of Artemis criminals were given immunity within the boundaries of the temple; they did not have to repent or change their ways.

With Christians, however, repentance is a necessary part of daily life. It is the first of those **works** which flow from faith. These **works** do not make faith faith, but faith makes these **works** 'complete in the sight of my God', as Jesus says (3:2).

The alternative to remembering, repenting, and doing is to have Christ **come** in judgment and **remove** the **lampstand from its place**, blow out the candle, extinguish the light altogether. For both Jews and Christians, 'the place' was the place of worship, where God is present, where people call on the name of the Lord (see Gen 26:25; Ps 116:12–19; 1 Cor 1:2) and remember his mighty acts as they worship him (see Ps 105:1–5; Isa 40:25–31). Jesus' threat to take the **lampstand from its place** means that God's servant, the prophet-leader, would be removed; the word of God would not be proclaimed; worship would cease. There would be no more calling on the name of the Lord in that 'place'. In short, God would withdraw his presence, and the people of God would be no more. The unrepentant people of Ephesus would be treated like those 'outside' (Rev 21:15) who have no place in the new city of God.

6 Another strong 'but' holds out a spark of hope: the Ephesians have **this** to their **credit**, they continue to **hate**, not the Nicolaitans, but **the works of the Nicolaitans**. In this they have the mind of the Lord, for he, too, hates their works. Typically, love which has its origin in God, and which is directed to God and the things of God, carries with it a corresponding hatred for that which is false and evil.

The **Nicolaitans** are a puzzle. Apart from what is said in 2:6,15 nothing is known of them. Perhaps the churches in Ephesus, Pergamum, and Thyatira were all troubled by similar groups with similar teachings. Locally they were known as **Nicolaitans** (2:6,15), followers of Balaam (2:14) or of Jezebel (2:20). Vague hints in chapter 2 suggest that these people had perverted Paul's teaching on responsible Christian freedom into a kind of free-for-all: you are free from the restraints and controls of God's law and you can do what you like. Certainly, cultural accommodation is the only way for Christians in the circumstances of the time, they said. Such teachings would strike responsive chords in the hearts of Christians today. Permissive society has invaded the church to such an extent that what we accept without turning a hair would have been violently rejected by the Ephesian Christians. They hated **the works of the Nicolaitans**. They were not, thank God, quite dead.

7 The first prophetic proclamation of the Lord Jesus closes with an encouragement and an invitation to 'hear'. This 'hearing formula', repeated seven times, calls the hearer to attention (see Mark 4:9). It underlines what should be heard, how it should be heard, and what follows from proper hearing. To hear is to obey; in this case, to remember, repent, and do (2:5).

Although Jesus Christ is the author of the prophetic proclamation, and although it is addressed in the first instance to the 'angel' of the Ephesian congregation, Jesus urges his hearers to **listen to what the *Spirit* is** continually **saying to the *churches*.** When Christ speaks, the Spirit speaks (John 14:26;15:26;16:13). And when the Spirit speaks the word of Christ to one congregation, it is to be heard as a message for the **churches**. It is an ecumenical message. The church acknowledged this truth when it recognised certain writings as authoritative Scripture in what we today call the written word of God, the Bible.

The threat in verse 6 is balanced by a promise in verse 7. The promise is directed to **everyone who conquers**, that is, to all who are faithful even to the point of death.

Christians conquer by their authentic witness to the truth, a witness validated, if necessary, by death (12:11). This fact stands in stark contrast to the violence, lies, and deceits by which Satan appears to conquer (11:7;13:7).

God's true people will live and rule with Christ in the new creation in the new Jerusalem, from which flows the river of life on the banks of which grows the **tree of life** (22:1,2). In the old, sin-ruined creation, Adam and Eve and their descendants were denied access to the **tree of life** (Gen 3:22–24). In the new creation the descendants of the last Adam (1 Cor 15:45–50) have full access to the tree of life in God's royal garden, his **paradise** (Rev 21:25 – 22:5, and see further comments there on 'the tree of life').

The **tree** was an important symbol in the cult of Artemis. It was thought to be a place of safety and salvation for the suppliant. This Artemis tree was surrounded by an enclosed garden (**paradise**), within which a criminal could find asylum.

Criminals do indeed find asylum, safety, and salvation at that 'tree' of which the tree of Artemis was a wicked parody: the cross of Christ. But asylum is granted so that the criminal, the sinner, will 'go and sin no more' (John 8:11). Remembering and repenting are the proper actions of those who have eaten of the fruit of Christ's Tree of Life. Christians anticipate their future eating in the new Jerusalem in their sacramental eating and drinking, as they remember the Lord's death 'until he comes'. They do not fear his coming, but they await it with eagerness as they pray: 'Come, Lord Jesus' (22:20).

b) To Smyrna, 2:8–11

[8] **'And to the angel of the church in Smyrna write: These are the words of the first and the last, who was dead and came to life:**

[9] **'I know your affliction and your poverty, even though you are rich. I know the slander on the part of those who say that they are Jews and are not, but are a synagogue of Satan.** [10] **Do not fear what you are about to suffer. Beware,**

the devil is about to throw some of you into prison so that you may be tested, and for ten days you will have affliction. Be faithful until death, and I will give you the crown of life. [11] **Let anyone who has an ear listen to what the Spirit is saying to the churches. Whoever conquers will not be harmed by the second death.**

Smyrna, which claimed the honour of being the birthplace of the poet Homer, had died and then been brought to life: it had been destroyed seven hundred years before John wrote and rebuilt four hundred years later. A fertile hinterland and a natural port on an ancient trade route enabled Smyrna to grow to be one of the richest cities in Asia Minor. It was also one of the most beautiful: the 'Glory of Asia' it was called. A model of town planning, it boasted the temples of Apollo, Aesclepius, Cybele, Aphrodite, and Zeus; a famous stadium; a library; and the largest public theatre in Asia.

Politically, Smyrna was noted for its faithfulness to Rome. Long before Rome became the dominant power in that part of the world, Smyrna had thrown in her lot with the young empire. As a reward, Smyrna had been declared a free city.

Today Smyrna is a thriving port named Izmyr, in Turkey.

It is not known when the gospel first came to Smyrna. Presumably it was at an early date, via Ephesus (see Acts 19:10). Constantly Christians had to battle against the hostility of the large Jewish population, as well as against the pressures which arose from the fact that Smyrna was an important centre for several flourishing cults, including the imperial cult. Today a large proportion of the population of Izmyr belongs to the Eastern Orthodox church.

8 The Lord Jesus uses two titles from the inaugural vision to identify himself (1:17,18). There the titles were meant to comfort and reassure John, who had been awestruck by the visions of 'one like the Son of Man'. Here they serve the same purpose. In both cases the hearers are told: 'Fear not' (1:17;2:10). The **words** which are addressed to Smyrna come from the Son of God who is **the first and the last**. This is a title of God himself according to Isaiah 44:6 and 48:12 (see Rev 22:13). The speaker is also the one **who was dead and came to life**. The focus of this title is slightly different from that in 1:18. There the emphasis was on continuity: Jesus is the one who lives, now and always. Here the emphasis is on the fact of the resurrection: Jesus 'became dead' (as the Greek puts it) and then sprang to life.

Taken together, the two titles of Jesus stress the truth that he who holds the church and its leaders in his strong right hand and moves freely among the churches is the Lord of the present and the future. Smyrnan Christians will have to endure slander, persecution, perhaps even death because of this Jesus, but faith in this same Jesus makes it possible for them not to fear.

9 Jesus knows the **affliction**, the stresses and strains, which make up the daily grind of the Christians at Smyrna. This **affliction** was probably due in no small measure to the **slander on the part of those who say they are Jews and are not**. It seems that the church was subjected to considerable opposition from the large and influential Jewish population in Smyrna.

The true people of God is a spiritual nation, not a particular ethnic group. True Jews, true sons and daughters of Abraham, are those who trust in God's forgiveness and look to God's Messiah for life and salvation (see John 8:33–47; Rom 2:25–29; Gal 3:29). Jews in Smyrna, who had rejected the Messiah Jesus and who had forgotten the injunction of God to deal with all people in kindness and justice, had forfeited their membership in the 'synagogue of the Lord' (Num 16:3;20:4;26:9). They belonged to another, a rival group, the **synagogue of Satan**.

The **poverty** of the Smyrnan Christians might have been caused by the attacks on property which usually accompanies persecution of minority groups — as the Jews in Germany and elsewhere in Europe experienced during the pogroms of the Third Reich. Or perhaps these Christians came from the poorer classes, and the fact that they were Christians made it even harder for them to survive or to change their economic status. Whatever the reason, the Christians in

Smyrna were poor; they lived on the bottom of the heap in one of the wealthiest of cities.

10 According to the values which dominate Australian culture, it is not possible to be poor and yet **rich** (contrast 2 Cor 6:10;8:9; James 2:5). But the poor Smyrnans were rich in faith and fidelity to Christ. These riches would be **tested** during the further affliction (v 9) which they were **about to suffer** at the hands of their enemies, who acted in obedience to **Satan**. Some would be imprisoned. This was not punishment; it was either a period of detention prior to a trial, or the time immediately after sentencing. Imprisonment led either to acquittal or banishment or execution.

During the legal proceedings, Christians would be sorely **tested** by God, and tempted by **the devil** to renounce the faith, deny their Lord, compromise, and in this way rescue themselves from a miserable situation. But this time of affliction, which might well move from interrogation to an appearance in the arena, would be limited by God to **ten days**. This is a complete period of time, but it is limited nonetheless. Even if this experience ended in a sentence of death, it would mean victory and life for the Christian. The precedent established by the resurrection Christ makes that a certainty (1:8).

The poor, afflicted Christians of Smyrna will find that for them, as true followers of the Lamb who was slain, life comes through death, victory through seeming defeat, power through being powerless (5:6-9). To those who continue to be **faithful** even to the point of dying for the faith, to them is promised the **crown** which consists of life. The reference here is not to the diadem, the kingly crown, but to the victor's wreath, frequently used in the New Testament as a symbol of the salvation which is gifted to the faithful (see, for example, 1 Cor 9:5; 2 Tim 4:8; 1 Pet 5:4).

So, despite the fact that Christians might die in the arena, and thus appear to have been conquered, the reality is that they are victors, more than conquerors (Rom 8:37), for the **second death** will not harm them. Jewish teachers used the term 'second death' to speak of eternal punishment, exclusion from life in the new creation. John uses the phrase again in 20:6,14 and 21:8 when he speaks of the ultimate fate of the wicked. This is another link of these early chapters with the final visions concerning the salvation of God's people and the fate of the wicked.

The faithful Christians in Smyrna are the paradigm of all Christians, who put their trust in the one who is the beginning and the end, the one who died and is alive. They stand their ground on the side of Christ against Satan and all his allies. The martyr Polycarp, bishop of Smyrna, was born about the time when John wrote Revelation. As he was led to the stake for burning, he was urged to save himself by denying Christ. He confessed: 'Eighty-six years I have served Christ, and he has never done me wrong. How can I blaspheme my king who saved me?' To which all Christians everywhere say: 'Amen!'.

c) To Pergamum, 2:12–17

12 'And to the angel of the church in Pergamum write: These are the words of him who has the sharp two-edged sword:

13 'I know where you are living, where Satan's throne is. Yet you are holding fast to my name, and you did not deny your faith in me[h] **even in the days of Antipas my witness, my faithful one, who was killed among you, where Satan lives. 14 But I have a few things against you: you have some there who hold to the teaching of Balaam, who taught Balak to put a stumbling block before the people of Israel, so that they would eat food sacrificed to idols and practice fornication. 15 So you also have some who hold to the teaching of the Nicolaitans. 16 Repent then. If not, I will come to you soon and make war against them with the sword of my mouth. 17 Let anyone who has an ear listen to what the Spirit is saying to the churches. To everyone who conquers I will give some of the hidden manna, and I will give a white stone, and on the white stone is written a new name that no one knows except the one who receives it.**

[h] Or *deny my faith*

Pergamum is Canberra. When in 133 BC the province of Asia was established as part of the Roman empire, Pergamum was named the provincial capital. In John's day it was probably the official residence of the Roman proconsul. It was regarded as the last outpost of Greek civilisation, and a great religious centre. The cult of Aesclepius attracted hordes of pilgrims, much as Lourdes attracts thousands today. Aesclepius, the god of healing, was symbolised by a snake. Any sick person who was touched by one of the tame snakes in the temple of Aesclepius was said to be healed instantly. This 'snake god' was given the title: Aesclepius Saviour. He is often depicted as a snake twined around a dead tree.

The god Zeus was also called 'Saviour'; he, too, was identified by the snake symbol. An imposing temple to Zeus Saviour sat 275 metres above the city on a rocky mountain. Its major feature was a huge white marble altar, set on a platform cut into the face of the rock. This temple was one of the wonders of the ancient world.

For Christians, Pergamum symbolised not only secular power but also civil religion. It was the administrative centre for the imperial cult. The temple dedicated to the emperor Augustus had been consecrated in 29 BC. It served as a model, and set the pace, for the cult in other provinces. In Pergamum, religion was used for political purposes; one's politics were a test of one's religious convictions.

Pergamum was noted also for its library of over two hundred thousand parchment scrolls; only Alexandria in Egypt had a larger collection. The word 'parchment' is derived from the name 'Pergamum'. In the first century, parchment had begun to replace papyrus as the common 'writing paper' of the Greco-Roman world.

The modern-day Bergama stands on the site of ancient Pergamum. Bergama's main street is lined with carpet shops where young women work at hand looms. In the centre of the town are the ruins of a large red-brick heathen temple, which once served as a Christian church. Bergama also contains the ruins of a huge outdoor theatre, palaces of priest-kings, and temples for Athena, Dionysius, and Trajan. The altar of Zeus has been found;

it is displayed in the Pergamom Museum in eastern Berlin.

12 The words of Christ are addressed to the spiritual leader or **the angel of the church in Pergamum**. Jesus describes himself as the one **who has the sharp two-edged sword** (see 1:16; Isa 11:4;49:2). He is apparently presenting himself in opposition and in contrast to the Roman proconsul who resided in Pergamum and had the power of life and death in his hands, symbolised by a two-edged sword (compare Rom 13:4).

Christ's power far far outstrips that of any earthly ruler. His **sword** comes out of his mouth (see 2:16); it is the powerful, creative word of God (19:13,15) which speaks dynamic, effective words of judgment and deliverance. So powerful is Christ's **two-edged sword** that it overcomes the power of Satan himself (Luke 4:12; Eph 6:17) and all who in rebellion against God dare to sit on **Satan's throne**.

13 The Christians in Pergamum are living in a situation of chronic seduction and impending persecution. The Lord **knows** it; that is why he focuses his message on the dangers of compromise and apostasy.

The Christians of Pergamum **are living . . . where Satan lives**. Both Satan and God's people had permanent residence in Pergamum; they had the same postcode. Neither Christians nor Satan were tourists. It must have come as a terrible shock to the Christians to be told that when the Lord looked at their city, he saw not a beautiful jewel but an ugly, hostile place where Satan lived and where, in fact, he 'sits enthroned' (J.B. Phillips; Moffatt). Life in Pergamum was life on the edge, a spiritual health-hazard.

The precise significance of the reference to **Satan's throne** is not easy to determine. But the reference is important, because 'throne' (meaning, God's throne) is a central symbol in Revelation. There is something about Pergamum which makes it a direct and obvious enemy of God. The city is the home of the antigod, the 'throne' which symbolises rebellion against the true 'throne'.

Perhaps **Satan's throne** refers to the throne-like altar of Zeus Saviour which dominated the cityscape. Perhaps the Aesclepius cult, with its promise of healing and salvation, was seen to be in direct conflict with the exclusive claims of Christ. Perhaps the imperial cult, which was centred on Pergamum, was especially fostered by the Roman proconsul who had his official seat in Pergamum. Maybe all these things together moved Christ to designate Pergamum as **Satan's throne**. It was the power centre of the enemies of God and of his people who bear faithful witness to Christ each time they join the heavenly hosts in worship around the throne of God (4:6–11).

At some point in recent history one man had been put to death by the authorities because of his **witness** to Christ. **Antipas** had been loyal to Christ even unto death (see 2:10), just as Christ himself had been loyal to his Father (1 Tim 6:13). Like his Lord in both life and death, Antipas was a 'true witness' (1:5;3:14). Legend has it that Antipas was roasted to death inside a brass bull.

One cannot properly deduce from this brief reference that there was an official policy of persecution of Christians at this time. It is not even clear that **Antipas** was a native Pergamese. He might have been brought in from outside to the earthly headquarters of Satan. He might have been a test case, a warning to all who chose not to support the local cults, especially the imperial cult.

As yet, no threats had been able to faze the Christians at Pergamum. They were **holding fast**, hanging on tight to the **name** of Christ, just as during the crisis **in the days of Antipas** they **did not deny** Christ, but steadfastly confessed their **faith** that Jesus (not Caesar or Zeus or Aesclepius) is Saviour and Lord.

14 There are, however, a **few things** which the Lord has **against** the Pergamene Christians. **Some** members of the church were not hanging on to the name of Christ (v 13); instead, they were embracing the **teaching of Balaam**. Balaam was the Old Testament prophet who advised **Balak**, king of Moab, that Israel would be stripped of God's protection if the people could be persuaded to **eat** food **sacrificed to idols**, and to practise fornication (Num 25:1 – 3;31:16).

'Fornication' sometimes is used in Scripture as another word for idolatry (for example, Isa 57:3; Jer 7:9); here it could have that meaning, or it could refer to sexual immorality in general (which is, in the end, idolatry; see 1 Cor 6:9; Eph 5:5).

Things sacrificed to idols covers a wide range of foodstuffs: meal, honey, cheese, various liquids, and animals. Only animals were so large that something might be left over from the sacrifice. The meat of sacrificed animals was often sold in the public market. Christians debated whether it was proper for them to eat such meat in their own home or in anyone's home. Paul discusses the problem in 1 Corinthians 8:1–13.

15 The Apostolic Council set as basic conditions for Gentile membership in mixed Christian communities abstinence from food sacrificed to idols and the avoidance of fornication (Acts 15:20,29). In Greece, the apostle Paul had not imposed the terms of the Council's decision on the Gentile churches; he left it up to Christian judgment and social responsibility.

It seems that a liberal party, known as **the Nicolaitans**, and headed by a prophet called Jezebel (2:20), taught a perverted version of the Pauline gospel. These people encouraged Christians to adopt a low profile in the urban communities. Instead of drawing attention to themselves by refusing to sacrifice to the gods, and so forth, Christians were advised to take part in the various religious activities of the city, the cult festivals, the rites associated with the trade guilds, and the ritual greeting to the emperor. The Nicolaitans taught that cultural accommodation was the name of the game; religious compromise was a valid option for Christians.

This teaching, to which Jesus gives the derogatory label 'Balaam', was widespread and popular. Apparently some Christians at Ephesus (2:6), as well as at Pergamum, held to the **teaching of the Nicolaitans**. So the Lord makes the direct accusation: 'You Pergamese **also** (that is, as well as some at Ephesus) follow the Nicolaitan heresy. Possibly also some Thyatirans were involved (see 2:20).

16 The Lord of the church issues a sharp call to repentance. Even th!ough only 'some' have been led astray by the Nicolaitans, the call to repentance is addressed to the whole community. The Lord's intention, like his intention with Nineveh of old, is that people should repent and live. Failure to listen to his call will mean that when he returns — as he will soon — he will deal with the disobedient ones with the sharp **sword** of his word, a word meant for salvation, but a word which can bring also judgment. Thus those who refuse to make use of the word of God as a defence and weapon against the tricks of Satan, and simply go along with his suggestions, will find themselves being judged by that very same word.

To debate whether the words, 'I will come soon', refer to a particular act of judgment upon compromising Christians at Pergamum or to the final judgment which takes place at Christ's return, is to set up a false either/or. In the light of Revelation 19:11-15, where the language of 2:16 is echoed, it is clear that judgment, like salvation, is taking place now (compare John 3:36); it is both a present and a future divine activity. The final judgment is constantly being anticipated in present experience. The unbelieving Albert Camus recognised this when he pointed out that there is no need to look to the future for God's judgment; it is taking place all around us.

17 To those who resist the temptation to compromise and to join the worshippers at Satan's throne (13:12) the Lord Jesus gives a twofold promise. First, they will receive a portion of the **manna** which, according to Exodus 16 and later rabbinic embroidery, was set aside as a memorial for future generations, was lost, and would be restored to the temple in Jerusalem only in the days of the Messiah. **Manna** is the food which is eaten in the new Jerusalem (22:1–5); those who feast on it are those who chose to starve at the pagan feasts, who chose to lose their job rather than take part in the trade union liturgies, who chose to go without food rather than perform an idolatrous act to get into the marketplace (see 13:17 and comments). Already now these faithful Christians enjoy a 'foretaste of the feast to come' when they celebrate the eucharist and remember the Lord's death 'until he comes'.

The second promise given to those who hold on to the name of Christ (2:13) is that Jesus **will give** them a **white stone** upon which their **new name** has been inscribed. In some tribal societies a **new name** is taken at every rite of passage, to symbolise the new person who has been created by that rite. Christians living in these tribal societies tend to take a **new name** at their baptism.

The name is the person. It is entirely appropriate that when the Holy Spirit creates us anew, we new people are given a **new name**, one which is known only to us and the Lord, and therefore one which no-one can take from us. The strange and wonderful thing is that we are all given the same name: son (or daughter) of God. Only those who are children of God truly 'know' that name.

This **new name** will be etched on a **white stone**. In John's day, white stones were used for all sorts of things: jurors cast black or white stones (white meant 'Not guilty!'); white stones were admission tickets to a banquet (the host knew you, you belonged); white stones with a divine name inscribed on them were used as bracelets to fend off evil spirits and to protect the wearer in time of danger. In verse 17 the most relevant cultural practice is that of using a white stone as a token of admission to a banquet: it was a sign of recognition; you knew the host and he knew you.

To faithful Christians the Lord Jesus Christ promises to **give**, as a free, undeserved gift, a place at the heavenly feast. The symbol of this is the white stone with my own new name written on it, given to me by my Lord himself, establishing my identity as his child and as a citizen of the new Jerusalem. Those who have this white stone will never have the gates of the city shut against them (21:25; compare Isa 65:15–25).

d) To Thyatira, 2:18–28

18 'And to the angel of the church in Thyatira write: These are the words of the Son of God, who has eyes like a flame of fire, and whose feet are like burnished bronze:

19 'I know your works — your love, faith, service, and patient endurance. I know that your last works are greater
than the first. 20 But I have this against you: you tolerate that woman Jezebel, who calls herself a prophet and is teaching and beguiling my servants[i] to practice fornication

and to eat food sacrificed to idols. 21 I gave her time to
repent, but she refuses to repent of her fornication.
22 Beware, I am throwing her on a bed, and those who
commit adultery with her I am throwing into great distress,
unless they repent of her doings; 23 and I will strike her
children dead. And all the churches will know that I am
the one who searches minds and hearts, and I will give to
each of you as your works deserve. 24 But to the rest of
you in Thyatira, who did not hold this teaching, who have
not learned what some call 'the deep things of Satan,' to
you I say, I do not lay on you any other burden; 25 only
hold fast to what you have until I come. 26 To everyone
who conquers and continues to do my works to the end,
I will give authority over the
nations;
27 to rule[j] them with an iron rod,
as when clay pots are
shattered —
28 even as I also received authority from my Father. To
the one who conquers I will also give the morning star.
29 Let anyone who has an ear listen to what the Spirit is
saying to the churches.

[i] Gk *slaves*

[j] Or *to shepherd*

The smallest of the seven cities receives the longest proclamation. **Thyatira** was situated on the great trade route which ran from Byzantium to the great cities of commerce along the coast of Asia Minor. Besides its strategic importance in the Roman road system, Thyatira was a commercial city: it dealt in dyes, wool, leather, linen, bronze, pottery, and the slave trade.

In a city like Thyatira, trade guilds and trade unions flourished and gained a lot of influence in the life of the city. There were trade guilds for just about every kind of business. The patron of the guilds was the god Apollo Tyrimnaeus, son of Zeus. Each guild, however, had its own guardian deity. These guilds posed serious problems for Christian traders and business people. You could hardly survive in business if you didn't belong to a guild. But the guild meetings included banquets in the temple of the patron deity; these feasts often ended in debauchery and immoral acts of the grossest kind. Furthermore, business meetings routinely began and ended with formal sacrifices to the deity.

Christians had to make some hard decisions. Just as today a Christian newsagent, for example, has to decide whether he or she is going to sell salacious and pornographic magazines and books, as well as the family-type material produced by the same publishers, or whether to refuse to sell the rubbish and smut and run the risk of losing the franchise.

18 The **words** which are addressed to the Christians at Thyatira come from **the Son of God**. This is the only place in Revelation that the title is used of Christ. Clearly it is meant to challenge directly the other 'son of god' who was so revered in the city: Apollo, son of Zeus. That Jesus is **Son of God** means that he is king over all the nations (see Ps 2:6–9); this kingship is his because of his obedient sonship (Phil 2:9,10; Rev 5:9,10).

The **eyes** of the Son of God are like a **flame of fire**, like the white-hot flame of a welder's torch (compare Heb 4:13). The same thing was said about the eyes of 'one like the Son of Man' in the inaugural vision (1:14), and about the eyes of the rider on a white horse who appears in the first of the final visions of judgment, victory, and salvation at the end of Revelation (19:11–16). In all three cases, of course, the reference is to the same Lord Jesus. He sees clearly, with 20/20 vision; his perceptions are accurate; his searching analysis of the Thyatiran situation penetrates like a laser beam through the outer appearances to the underlying realities.

His **feet are like burnished bronze** (see 1:15), flashing like the refined metal from the city's furnaces, whose fiery light would have been fixed on the retinas of every citizen. The fire and the shining bronze linked the local industry with the local god, the patron Apollo Tyrimnaeus. In his prophetic proclamation, Jesus claims the fire and the burnished bronze for himself. He sets himself against all opposing religious claims and false gods. Christ's authority and lordship are at stake here. People were being led to observe 'the deep things of Satan' (v 24) rather than the deep things of Christ (see 1 Cor 2:10). Such a challenge to his rule, and such a threat to his people, Christ will not tolerate.

19 The Son of God's piercing eyes light up the darkest corners of the community. So he, of course, **knows** all their **works**, all that they are doing by way of living the Christian life. Jesus is aware that the congregation is making progress; it is growing towards maturity (Eph 4:13,15). In particular the Lord notes their **love** for both God and each other, fruit and evidence of their **faith** in the Son of God as true Saviour and Lord. Their **faith** includes, as it usually does in Revelation, their fidelity to Christ and his word.

Furthermore, Jesus commends their **service** to each other, a natural working out of their love and their faithfulness. Finally, the Lord assures his loyal people that he is well aware of their patient endurance, their fortitude, their sheer 'guts'. In the face of all pagan pressures to compromise, they stand like a well-rooted tree, enduring the storm and even growing stronger because of the storm. In sharp contrast to the Ephesian Christians (2:4,5), their **last works are greater than the first**.

20 **But** — sadly, there is usually a 'but' in the Christian life — the Thyatirans **tolerate** and refuse to reject a false prophet known as **Jezebel**. This brings upon them the severe censure of the Lord. Toleration of false doctrine and false teachers, and faithfulness to Christ and love for him and his people, are mutually exclusive. If you cannot condemn falsehood you cannot confess truth.

In some early Greek manuscripts, **Jezebel** is regarded as the wife of the 'angel' or prophet-leader of the church in Thyatira. Far more likely, however, 'Jezebel' is a symbolic name. It calls up memories of the Gentile queen Jezebel (2 Kings 9:22; 1 Kings 16:31), who introduced sorcery, magic, and idolatry into Israel. The Thyatiran **Jezebel**, who presented herself to the Christian community as a Spirit-filled **prophet**, boldly solved the 'Christ versus Culture' problem which Christians faced daily in the marketplace, the workplace, and in social relations. She encouraged her fellow Christians to eat **food** which had been sacrificed to **idols**, and to **practice**

fornication, that is, to engage in spiritual unfaithfulness, which could involve also physical fornication (compare the Nicolaitans, 2:6 and 'the teaching of Balaam', 2:14).

So, like an attractive witch, Jezebel succeeded in **beguiling** the leaders of the congregation who were responsible for proclaiming the word and will of God, the Christian prophets who are called the **servants** of Christ (see 1:1). There is nothing more damnable than a person who claims to speak with the authority of the Spirit of God, but who speaks lies. Such people do so much damage to the trusting children of God and to the cause of the gospel. They are agents of Satan and the beast (12:9;13:14;20:10), and will share the fate of their masters, unless they repent.

21,22 God is surely a gracious God! Just as he called Jonah a second time, just as repeatedly he called Israel to repentance, so he gives Jezebel **time to repent**. Sadly, **she refuses**, she does not *want* to change her immoral ways and false teachings. She spurns the God of grace. So she draws upon herself the fearful word of the God of judgment: she will be thrown upon **a bed** of pain and sickness. Those who flirt with her teachings (**commit adultery with her**) still have before them the golden bridge of repentance. But **unless they** do in fact **repent** of following her teachings, they too will suffer **great** trouble and **distress**.

23 As for Jezebel's **children**, those who have committed themselves totally to her words and ways, they shall be struck **dead**, or, as the Greek text says: they shall be killed by means of the plague (see 6:8; Jer 21:7).

The punishment of the 'children' of Jezebel shall stand as a grim warning to every member of **all the churches** in Asia Minor. All **will know** that Jesus is not an ignorant, uncaring landlord, but he is the Lord, the one with eyes like flames of fire (v 18; compare John 21:17; Acts 1:24). Continually he scrutinises the **minds and hearts** of his people, by letting the searing searchlight of his word play upon them and their lives. As a consequence of the divine investigation, **each** member of the Thyatiran congregation will receive from Christ what his or her **works deserve**. It is a commonplace in the New Testament that **works** are a fruit of faith in Christ, and that your relationship to Christ is judged on the basis of your **works**.

24,25 Finally, the imperial Christ adds to his prophetic proclamation a few words of encouragement for the faithful people who have not been led astray by Jezebel and her disciples. Evidently she claimed that the gospel gave her such freedom and power that she could get involved with what she called **'the deep things of Satan'**. Christians who avoided the trade guilds and the heathen temple-feasts were poor, timid creatures, still drinking milk instead of tackling meat. Jezebel could take on Satan, move in the world of both good and evil, and engage in the sins of the flesh without being contaminated by them. Jezebel still has many followers among arrogant Christians who think they can explore unscathed **'the deep things of Satan'**. Not without reason does Paul warn against giving any space or opportunity to the devil (Eph 4:27).

Jesus has urged his faithful people at Thyatira to quit tolerating Jezebel and her ilk (v 20). Apart from this, he lays no **other burden** on them (see Acts 15:28,29 for a curious parallel). He simply admonishes and encourages them to **hold fast**, to take a firm grip and to hang on tight to what they have, until the glorious day of the Lord's appearing. What is it that they are to hang on to? Probably their 'love and faith and service and patient endurance' (v 19), for which they had been commended by their Lord.

26,27 The concluding promise is actually two promises, addressed to those who **conquer** by doing right to the end the **works** of Christ instead of the works of Jezebel (see vv 19,23). The first promise echoes the words of Psalm 2:8,9, but it also fits the situation at Thyatira like a glove, because the potters guild and other trade guilds were so powerful, and the Christians thought themselves to be so powerless. 'Impotent' Christians are promised **authority over the nations**. Their dynamic witness to Christ with their words and lifestyle is like a shepherd's staff to those who are moved to respond in repentance and faith (see 7:17), but it is like **an iron rod** to those who harden their hearts and reject the word (see Jer 18:1-11). So Christians exercise the same **authority** which the Son of

God (v 18) himself has **received** from his **Father** (see John 20:19–23; Rev 20:4–6).

28 The second promise to **the one who conquers** concerns the giving of the **morning star**. Venus was widely recognised as a symbol of authority; indeed, the Roman emperors claimed to be descendants of the goddess Venus. In direct contrast, Revelation says that Christ is the bright Morning Star (22:16), for he is the Emperor above all emperors, the King of kings and Lord of lords (19:16).

Faithful Christians are promised Christ himself, his authority, his power. But remember: the Morning Star is also the Lamb Who Was Slain. His power is the power of the gospel of Christ crucified; his presence with his people is in the proclaimed word, in the water and the bread and wine. Nothing spectacular, glorious, or flamboyant. Those who know what to look for behind the seeming simpleness and ordinariness of it all will **listen** carefully and hear **what the Spirit is saying to the churches** in this long prophetic imperial proclamation.

e) To Sardis, 3:1–6

3 'And to the angel of the church in Sardis write: These are the words of him who has the seven spirits of God and the seven stars:

'I know your works; you have a name of being alive,
but you are dead. 2 Wake up, and strengthen what remains
and is on the point of death, for I have not found your
works perfect in the sight of my God. 3 Remember then
what you received and heard; obey it, and repent. If you
do not wake up, I will come like a thief, and you will not
know at what hour I will come to you. 4 Yet you have still
a few persons in Sardis who have not soiled their clothes;
they will walk with me, dressed in white, for they are
worthy. 5 If you conquer, you will be clothed like them in
white robes, and I will not blot your name out of the book
of life; I will confess your name before my Father and
before his angels. 6 Let anyone who has an ear listen to
what the Spirit is saying to the churches.

Sardis rested on its laurels. It was once the capital of ancient Lydia and the residence of the king whose name became a byword for wealth: Croesus.

Sardis was said to be impregnable, totally safe from enemy attack, because it was surrounded by steep cliffs which were supposed to be impossible to climb. In fact, 'to capture Sardis' was a popular expression for doing the impossible. Alas, in 546 BC the soldiers of the Persian king Cyrus climbed the cliffs and captured the city. Three hundred years later Sardis had not learnt from history; but Antiochus the Great had: he captured Sardis by climbing the unclimbable cliffs.

Under Roman rule Sardis became famous for its luxury clothing trade, and for its magnificent temples dedicated to Artemis, Zeus, and the Roman emperor.

Archaeological work has uncovered the emperor's temple, a gymnasium, the council hall, shops, and a synagogue. From other sources we know that Sardis supported a well-integrated Jewish community; the first Christians there were probably of Jewish extraction. Today the small village of Sart stands on the site of a once great city.

1 Sardis the church had many of the characteristics of Sardis the city. It had a **name**, a reputation as an **alive**, active, vibrant congregation, but Sardis had become a secular church, a spiritual cemetery, 'the Church of the Holy Dry Rot', as someone named it. As a result of carelessness, lack of watchfulness, and forgetfulness of the word they had heard, the congregation was, in Jesus' judgment, **dead**.

Jesus addresses very harsh words to this congregation, but his self-designation, taken from Revelation 1:4,16,20 shows that he has not given up on them. For he, the Morning Star (22:16), holds in his hand (1:16,20) **the seven stars** who are the prophet-leaders ('the angels') of the seven churches; they are the ones who speak God's word of salvation and judgment. Jesus also **has the seven spirits of God**, that is, the Spirit of God in his fullness. He is the 'Lord and giver of life'; he works in and through the prophetic word to give new life to dry bones (see Ezek 37:1–14). The **seven spirits of God** alone can revive the

Sardisians who are so close to death. In short, the Lord Jesus has the only means of rescue. They had better listen to him!

2 'Wake up!' is the first admonition. A more literal translation is: 'Show yourself watchful'. The same sort of admonition was addressed to the disciples in Gethsemane. The word translated 'watchful' comes from the same word that is the basis for the name Gregory. All Christians should have Gregory as their second name: all are to be watchful, alert, on the ball (compare Rom 13:11; 1 Cor 16:13; 1 Thess 5:2–6).

The very command to 'awake' is a sign that all is not lost; death has not yet had the final say. The Lord never commands us to do something without giving us the necessary strength to do it. So 'you are dead' is not the last word which Jesus wants to speak over the Christian community at Sardis.

Secondly, the Christians at Sardis are to **strengthen what remains and is on the point of death**. Among the complacent and lazy Christians there remained only glimpses, bits and pieces, of the baptismal life, faint evidences of faith and love and obedience. These people fitted in well in the community; they had accommodated their faith so effectively to society that it roused no opposition. Like the Christians at Laodicea, they had become totally urbanised, at home in the city, physically, spiritually, and morally. When you looked at them and their lifestyle, you wouldn't guess that they were Christians.

Jesus tells them plainly that he has not **found** their **works perfect** (that is, complete) **in the sight of my God**. They are so incomplete as to be virtually non-existent. God has prepared the works for them to do (Eph 2:10), but these works have not characterised the Sardisian Christians' way of life. So when the God and Father of the Lord Jesus Christ (**my God**) looks at the **works** of the Christians, he finds them sadly deficient, poor, incomplete.

3 Jesus has given the diagnosis and the prognosis. Now comes the remedy in three brief imperial commands. First, Christians are to **remember** what they have **received**

and heard in their pre-baptismal instruction and on the day of their baptism. 'Remembering' is an important Christian activity: it involves not just calling to mind, recalling, but also re-enacting, reliving, and repeating in the present that which happened in the past. One of the words the Christians would have **received and heard** was the shout which greeted them as they arose from the waters of baptism:

Sleeper, awake!
Rise from the dead,
and Christ will shine on you. (Eph 5:14b)

Here is a word from the past which the somnolent Sardisians needed to re-present, hear again; and, having heard it, they needed to **obey and repent**. The only thing which could save them was a return to their baptism, to hear and heed again the cry: 'Sleeper, awake!'.

If they did not **wake up**, Christ would come, as Cyrus and Antiochus had come to their forebears, **like a thief** in the night, at an **hour** unknown and least expected (compare Matt 24:42; 1 Thess 5:2; Rev 16:15). A thief does not first send a fax. We cannot say with certainty that a thief *will* come (although these days the odds are that he/she will!). But in the case of our Lord, there is no question: he will come. The only question is when. The whole New Testament speaks of the unexpectedness and suddenness of his coming, despite the general warning signs.

4 There are a faithful **few** in Sardis to whom, no doubt, the Lord looks to spearhead the needed revival in the congregation. They have not **soiled their clothes**, the garments they put on at their baptism. These new, unspoiled clothes in which they were dressed symbolised the putting on of the Lord Jesus Christ, the receiving of his gift of cleansing, enlightenment, redemption, and righteousness (see Rom 13:14; Gal 3:27). For such people baptism is the beginning of a life lived in white, in the purity and holiness of the servants of God gathered before the throne and before the Lamb who was slain (Rev 7:13-17). They have 'walked worthy' of their calling and of their Lord (Eph 4:1; Col 1:10); they are considered **worthy** to **walk** with Christ as his servants, **dressed in white**

forever. To be adjudged worthy is a remarkable honour for Christians. In Revelation 'worthiness' is usually ascribed only to God and the Lamb who was slain (for example, 4:11;5:9). In 16:6 there is a remarkable and telling exception; the other exception is here.

5 Two promises are made to those who **conquer**, that is, to those whose garments are clean. They alone are ready for the Lord's coming; they alone will walk with Christ in his victory procession, dressed in the traditional **white robes** of the victor. These robes are supplied by Christ; they are robes of perfect righteousness and holiness, for they have been dyed white(!) in the blood of the Lamb (7:14). Christ's victory procession is their victory procession; his righteousness is their righteousness; his glory is their glory (20:4–6). That is the first promise.

The second promise is that the faithful will have their names preserved in the **book of life**, written not in wax, which can easily be erased, but etched, as it were, in steel. Not one name will be erased.

Moses once begged God either to forgive his people's sins or to remove Moses' name from the book of life which God had written (Exod 32:32). To ask for your name to be removed from the book of life was to ask to die. The idea of a book of life probably comes from the register of citizens, which was well known in the Roman world. If your name was on the register, you existed legally; if it was not there, you did not exist as far as the state was concerned. Today a social security or tax file number serves the same function: without a number you are nobody. So Jesus' assurance to the faithful few in Sardis means that they are known to him, they exist in his sight, their names (=they themselves; see 20:15;21:27) are written in indelible ink in his heavenly register, so they are safe. Jesus knows them; he will never let them go (compare John 10:28).

Jesus gives a solemn assurance to those who refuse to compromise, and who faithfully confess him before Jew and Gentile. He promises them that in the end he will publicly acknowledge them as his own (compare Matt 10:32; Luke 12:8). Their public recognition by God and the Lamb will contrast sharply with the fate of those who have denied Christ and worshipped the beast (13:11;14:9–11). These will have been 'forgotten' by God. To be remembered by God is heaven (Isa 44:21; Luke 23:42,43); to be forgotten by God is hell (Isa 23:15,16; Jer 23:39,40). 'He that is not with me is against me'.

6 Once again, the appeal to those who have ears to use their ears and listen to the Spirit, has about it a sense of urgency. The Lord is coming soon. Before you know it, he will be here. Wake up, church, wake up! Let the word of the Lord be heard once more. Repent and live!

f) To Philadelphia, 3:7–13

7 **'And to the angel of the church in Philadelphia write:**
These are the words of the holy
one, the true one,
who has the key of David,
who opens and no one will
shut,
who shuts and no one opens:
8 **'I know your works. Look, I have set before you an**
open door, which no one is able to shut. I know that you
have but little power, and yet you have kept my word and
have not denied my name. 9 **I will make those of the**
synagogue of Satan who say that they are Jews and are
not, but are lying — I will make them come and bow down
before your feet, and they will learn that I have loved
you. 10 **Because you have kept my word of patient**
endurance, I will keep you from the hour of trial that is
coming on the whole world to test the inhabitants of the
earth. 11 **I am coming soon; hold fast to what you have, so**
that no one may seize your crown. 12 **If you conquer, I**
will make you a pillar in the temple of my God; you will
never go out of it. I will write on you the name of my
God, and the name of the city of my God, the new
Jerusalem that comes down from my God out of heaven,
and my own new name. 13 **Let anyone who has an ear listen**
to what the Spirit is saying to the churches.

Philadelphia, about forty kilometres south-east of Sardis, was the gateway to a fertile volcanic region which accounted for much of the city's economic prosperity. The area was also an earthquake zone. In AD 17 a severe 'quake, said at the time to be the strongest in human history, flattened the city. Subsequent aftershocks persuaded many people to live outside the city and to commute to work.

Philadelphia (= 'brotherly love') was said to have taken its name from the legendary loyalty of the brothers Eumenes and Attalus; the latter was the reputed founder of the city. Later the name was changed to Neocaesarea; still later it was given the honour of being permitted to add an imperial title to its name: it became Philadelphia Flavia.

In later history, Christian Asia was overwhelmed by Islam. Philadelphia, however, remained a free and independent Christian city. It was the last Christian outpost in Asia Minor when it fell in 1390. Today the site of ancient Philadelphia is occupied by a town called Alashehir, meaning 'city of God'.

7 Jesus has no fault to find with **the angel** (the prophet-leader) and church at **Philadelphia**. He reminds them, by way of allusion and explicit statement, that the promises and privileges given to Israel of the old covenant have been inherited by the Christian community, the people of the new covenant.

The Lord Jesus describes himself in language which Israel reserved for Yahweh. God alone is the **holy one** of Israel; he alone is the **true one**: trustworthy, faithful, genuine, real (for example, Isa 5:19;43:3;65:16). These confessions to God are now transferred to Christ (compare Mark 1:24; John 6:69), the head of the new people of God.

Like Eliakim, the steward who controlled the entry to the palace of David (Isa 22:20–25), the Son of David **has the key of David**. And like Eliakim, he has the power to determine who is admitted to the house of David (of which he is head, Luke 1:32,33) and who will be excluded from the royal house in the new Jerusalem (see Rev 21:8,27;22:15).

The book of Revelation reminds us that all the keys that matter — the keys to life and death, to heaven and hell, to salvation and judgment — are held by the one who was 'despised and rejected by others' (Isa 53:3) but is the Judge and Saviour of all. So John records that Jesus has the keys of Death and of Hades (1:18); the keys to the house and city of David (3:7); and the key to the bottomless pit, the place of the devil himself (20:1).

8 Jesus assures the Philadelphians that he is fully aware of their **works**, their lives as Christians in a hostile and precarious world (see 2:2,19;3:2). Specifically, Jesus knows that even though they are only a handful, with no social status and no economic clout, they have **kept** his word (the positive act), and in so doing they have **not denied** him (the negative act). They are fruitful people, these Philadelphians. Their faithfulness corresponds to Christ's own: he has **set before** them a **door** which has been opened. What is this **open door which no-one is able to shut**? It is not, as some have suggested, a wide-open mission opportunity (see Acts 14:27;2 Cor 2:12). Nothing in the context supports that thought.

More plausible is the proposal that the **open door** symbolises the 'door' of salvation, that is, Jesus Christ himself, who is the only access to God (Eph 2:18; Acts 4:12). The assertion that 'no-one is able to shut' that door assures faithful Christians of their Saviour and their salvation. This interpretation fits the context, and might well be the correct one.

It is, however, possible that Jesus is here warning the Philadelphian Christians of their impending martyrdom, due to their fearless witness to the gospel (see comments on 6:11 and 11:7–10). In the Roman arenas, the *Porta Libitina* was the door through which were dragged the bodies of vanquished gladiators. Libitina was the goddess of corpses; in her temple were kept the death registers. To say that the *Porta Libitina* ('door of death') is **open** and that **no-one is able to shut** it, is to say that a violent death is inevitable.

This interpretation fits the context, especially in view of verse 10 and the reference to the 'crown' in verse 11 (victorious gladiators were given a wreath or crown to mark their triumph). For the Philadelphian Christians the immediate future looked bleak indeed; but that was not the whole story nor the end of the story.

9 The time is coming when roles will be reversed (compare Luke 16:19–31). The pseudo-Jews, that is, those who are Jews in the flesh but not in the spirit of faithful Abraham (see Rom 2:28,29), and hence belong not to the true synagogue of God but to the **synagogue of Satan** (see 2:9 and comments) — these Jews will one day acknowledge that they were wrong in their opposition to Christ and his people. They will come to **learn** that the Holy One of Israel (3:7) **loved** the Christians at Philadelphia as he always has loved the true Israel, and regarded them as precious above all nations (Isa 43:3,4).

Furthermore, in another unexpected reversal, instead of Gentiles paying homage to Israel in the age of the Messiah (as the Old Testament prophets had foretold, for example Isa 45:14;49:23;60:14), the Jews of Philadelphia would **come and bow down before** their Christian fellow citizens. Christians participate in Christ's reign (3:21;20:4–6); their right to reign will in the end be acknowledged by all, just as their Lord's right and worthiness to sit at God's right hand will be acknowledged by all (Phil 2:10; Rev 5:12–14).

10 The Philadelphians have been patient under pressure; they have **kept** Christ's **word** which calls for **patient endurance**, creative courage, tenacity, staying-power. They have confessed his name and not denied it. Since they have kept his word, Christ will **keep** them when the **hour of trial** arrives. The phrase, which echoes the sixth petition of the Lord's Prayer, speaks of not just a localised period of testing, but a universal one, designed to test **the inhabitants of the earth**, that is, the enemies of God and his people (see 6:10;8:13;11:10). The subsequent visions depict with increasing vividness this sifting and sorting out of those who refuse to worship God and the Lamb, and prefer to worship the beast. God's goal in so 'testing' them is to drive them to repentance; but the overwhelming response is to refuse the grace of God (see 9:20,21;16:11). That Christians will be safe during God's searching judging is certain; that they will be exempt from this time of **trial** is not said.

11 The time of trial is not open-ended: it has a limit, one determined by the return of Christ to final judgment and salvation (19:10–21). His **coming** is imminent and known to God (**soon**). For the Christians at Ephesus (2:5), Pergamum (2:16), and Sardis (3:3) the indisputable fact of Christ's return hung over them as a threat; for the Philadelphians, however, it is intended as comfort (see 22:7,20).

Knowing that Christ is **coming soon**, the Philadelphian Christians are to 'hang in there', **hold fast** to their salvation, so that no-one deprives them of the **crown**, the victor's wreath which is already now theirs as a certain gift from God. The admonition to 'hold on fast to what you have so that no-one can take your crown' must have made a deep impression on the early Christians, for it is often quoted in the literature of the young church. The admonition is especially significant in a situation where natural disasters and social and economic change made life precarious for everyone in Philadelphia.

12 The promise to those who **conquer** emphasises their stability and security as members of the household of God and citizens of the new Jerusalem. In the opening verse of this prophetic proclamation the Lord of the church invited the little flock at Philadelphia to see themselves as part of the new house of David, the new, true Israel. The promise which is given to the Philadelphians simply continues the encouragement.

First, Jesus says, each faithful person will be made a **pillar in the temple of my God** (three times in verse 12 Jesus speaks of 'my God'!). And they will never go out of that temple. Here is a good example of Revelation's freedom with symbols. Of course a pillar in a temple would never go out of it! But that is not the point. Pillars are essential to the very structure of a temple. The message is: God will not discard you; you are safe and secure in the temple of God.

The other part of the promise is about names being written on people. No wonder somebody was moved to remark that 'Revelation is a book filled with graffiti'! Christ says that he makes our safety and security triply sure by writing on each person **the name of my God, and the name of the city of my God . . . and my own new name**.

To have a name written on you establishes your identity; it says who you are and whose you are (13:16,17;22:4). To have God's **name** written on you means that you belong to him (see 14:1; Isa 43:1). To have **the name of the city of my God** written upon you means that you are a citizen of **the new Jerusalem**, the city whose origin is heavenly, not earthly (21:2 – 22:5). You have all the rights and privileges of citizenship. The ruler of the city is Jesus Christ. To have his **new name** written on you by Christ himself means that you belong to him for keeps:

As the branch is to the vine,
I am his and he is mine.

13 The urgent call **to listen to what the Spirit is saying to the churches** is intended once more to strengthen the community and to encourage it to hold fast to what it has. If in the other six Christian communities there are people who are keeping Christ's word and not denying his name, then the words addressed to the Philadelphians are meant also for them.

g) To Laodicea, 3:14–22

14 'And to the angel of the church in Laodicea write: The words of the Amen, the faithful and true witness, the origin[k] of God's creation:

15 'I know your works; you are neither cold nor hot. I wish that you were either cold or hot. 16 So, because you are lukewarm, and neither cold nor hot, I am about to spit you out of my mouth. 17 For you say, 'I am rich, I have prospered, and I need nothing.' You do not realize that you are wretched, pitiable, poor, blind, and naked.
18 Therefore I counsel you to buy from me gold refined by fire so that you may be rich; and white robes to clothe you and to keep the shame of your nakedness from being seen; and salve to anoint your eyes so that you may see.
19 I reprove and discipline those whom I love. Be earnest, therefore, and repent. 20 Listen! I am standing at the door,

knocking; if you hear my voice and open the door, I will come in to you and eat with you, and you with me. [21] To the one who conquers I will give a place with me on my throne, just as I myself conquered and sat down with my Father on his throne. [22] Let anyone who has an ear listen to what the Spirit is saying to the churches.'

[k] Or *beginning*

Laodicea, a city lying fifty-five kilometres south-east of Philadelphia, was named after Laodice, the wife of the city's founder. It was situated in the Lycus valley, not far from Hierapolis and Colossae (Col 4:13), where there were flourishing Christian communities. Hierapolis had hot springs, noted for their medicinal properties; Colossae had cold springs, famed for their purity. Laodicea's hot springs were outside the city. By the time the water travelled along the open channels to the homes of the citizens it was lukewarm.

Laodicea was a prosperous commercial centre, located on a major crossroad on the southern route from Ephesus through Anatolia. It boasted a flourishing CBD, as well as a medical establishment renowned for its skills in ophthalmology.

Laodicea, like Philadelphia, was in an earthquake zone. In AD 60 it was, in fact, destroyed by an earthquake. Laodicea was prosperous enough to be able to decline the emergency aid offered by emperor Nero.

Today the town of Denizli stands near the abandoned site of Laodicea. Its thermal springs attract tourists still.

14 The Lord's last prophetic proclamation is addressed, as were the other six, to **the angel of the church** — this time to **the angel of the church in Laodicea**, that is, to the prophet-leader of the Laodicean Christian community. As later verses show, this man's leadership left a lot to be desired. A document from the early church says that Archippus was the first bishop of Laodicea. Curiously, in his letter to Colossae (Laodicea's neighbour) the apostle Paul urges the Colossian Christians to 'say to Archippus, "Be sure to finish the task you were given in the Lord's service" ' (Col 4:17 TEV). Was leadership in Laodicea in need of a good shake-up already ten years or so before John recorded Jesus' words in Revelation?

The words with which Jesus identifies himself to the prophet-leader of the congregation are not drawn from the inaugural vision of 1:13–20, nor do they have obvious connections with the final visions of the new Jerusalem.

Jesus introduces himself as, first, **the Amen** (compare 2 Cor 1:20), just as God himself is the one 'whose name is Amen' (Isa 65:16,17 NEB). Secondly, Jesus is the **witness**, the **faithful and true** one who can be relied on as the **Amen** of God to all that God says and does and promises to do. He is the final and definitive word and revelation of God (see Heb 1:1), and the most dependable and trustworthy of witnesses to God's plans and purposes for the world.

Thirdly, Jesus is the **origin** or 'ultimate source' (JB, compare NEB) **of God's creation**. He is not the first being who was created; he is 'begotten, not made', as we confess in the Nicene Creed; he is 'before all things and in him all things hold together', as Paul confesses in a letter written to neighbouring Colossae not many years before (Col 1:15–20).

Since Jesus is the source of all creation, he is the one who rules the world, lights the world, interprets and makes sense of the world. He is also the one who redeems the world through his conquering death and resurrection (1:17,18;5:9,10; Col 1:20). So Christians who want to see the realities of the world, and how they are to relate to these realities, should listen carefully to what the Lord and Saviour of the world has to say. He knows all there is to be known about the realities of existence.

15,16 God knows the world of the Laodiceans; he **knows** them and their **works**, and he doesn't like what he knows. He finds that the Laodicean Christians have taken on the unpleasant characteristic of the local mineral water: they are tepid, **lukewarm**. 'You make me sick', Jesus says. It would be better if you were either **cold or hot**, then at least hypocrisy and compromise would not be involved. If you were genuine, Spirit-filled Christians or genuine, idol-worshipping heathen, things would be clear.

What the Lord abhors is hypocrisy, spinelessness, indecision and compromise, mouthed confessions and mechanical worship, and a barrenness in terms of fruit (**works**). His threat to **spit** the Laodiceans out of his **mouth** is his word of judgment upon them.

17 At this point Jesus quotes the Laodiceans and throws their own words back in their faces. They keep on saying that they are **rich**, as rich spiritually as they were, presumably, materially. They claim to have **prospered** spiritually as they had, no doubt, prospered materially. And they claim to **need nothing**: they are self-sufficient, they need nobody's help, and certainly they need no outside critique. Their self-assessment is, of course, sheer self-delusion. They are like the passengers on the *Titanic* as it sailed through thick fog with icebergs all around: they thought they were safe, secure, untouchable in the cosy confines of an 'unsinkable' ship.

The Lord shatters the Laodiceans' complacency in their make-believe world of dead works by itemising the symptoms of their true condition as seen through the X-ray eyes (2:18) of the one who is 'the faithful and true witness' (3:14). First, they are **wretched, pitiable**, or, as the NEB well translates: 'You are the most pitiful wretch'. The idea of the Greek is: 'If anyone is a pitiful wretch, you are'. The word translated 'wretch' is used by Paul in Romans 7:24 when he describes his miserable condition as a man caught between wanting to do one thing and doing the very opposite. And the word translated 'pitiful' is the same as that which Paul uses to describe the state of Christians if Christ has not been raised (1 Cor 15:19).

Why are the Laodiceans such pitiful wretches? Because they are **poor**, and they can't see it! They are **blind** to their own spiritual condition. And they are dressed in beggars rags (literally: **naked**). Very likely this description of their spiritual condition is meant to contrast with the material aspects of life in Laodicea, a city which prided itself on its financial institutions, its medical school, and its clothing industry.

18 The Lord's advice or **counsel** to the Laodiceans is really a call to repentance and faith. It begins with some wonderful promises which are meant to encourage the Laodiceans to turn to the Lord and live. To overcome their poverty they should **buy** from Christ refined **gold**, that is, in faith they should take hold of Christ and his righteousness: it is the only 'gold' which has currency in the new Jerusalem which is 'pure gold, clear as crystal' (21:18). Instead of priding themselves in the local clothing made from the glossy black wool for which Laodicea was famous, Christians should be clothed with garments made **white** in the blood of the Lamb (7:14). Clothed by God with divine forgiveness, the Laodiceans will, like Adam and Eve who were clothed by a gracious God (Gen 3:21), cover the **shame** of their **nakedness**.

For their blind eyes all the medical schools in Laodicea have nothing to offer. They will only truly **see** when their **eyes** are anointed with the **salve** which Christ has prepared for them: the medicine of the Holy Spirit, who opens blind eyes and turns our eyes from ourselves to see Christ and our neighbour (Eph 1:18; 1 John 2:10,11).

19 Jesus' words and the **discipline** which he administers here may seem to be harsh and hard. It is, however a sign, not of his hatred, but of his **love** for this wretched people (compare Heb 12:7; James 1:2). Anyone familiar with the Old Testament would know the saying:

My son, do not spurn the Lord's correction
  or take offence at this reproof;
for those whom he loves the Lord reproves,
  and he punishes a favourite son. (NEB)

So Christ disciplines his church for the sake of its rehabilitation, renewal, and life. The new life is to show itself in an earnestness, a zeal, a fervency of Spirit — the very opposite of the tepid, insipid character of their Christian lives up till now (3:15). And it is to be a life of repentance. As Luther said in the first of his Ninety-five Theses: 'Jesus Christ . . . willed the entire life of believers to be one of repentance'.

20 The word of encouragement with which the last proclamation concludes seems to be addressed to all seven churches. In it are words and ideas (for example, 'door', 'throne') which point to the next section of the book. This prophetic announcement concerns the coming of Christ. It is not a threat, but a promise meant for all who conquer, that is, all those who are loyal to their Lord Jesus.

The picture of Christ knocking at the door expresses in a vivid way the divine call to repentance, and the appropriate response. Always Jesus summons us to repentance. He stands at the door and knocks. He wants us to **open** to him, that is, to repent and turn to him in faith which will show itself in a life worthy of the gospel. Repentance is a characteristic of the Christian's daily life.

Such obedient servants of Christ will be ready for him when he comes in the end: they will respond to his final call, welcome him, and sit with him in the heavenly feast (Luke 12:35–40;22:29,30). Every time Christians celebrate the eucharist they anticipate this future feast. They pray

> . . . that each may be your welcome guest
> when you will spread your heavenly feast.

21 The final promise is given to the **one who conquers**. Christ, who sits with his **Father on his throne** (see 22:3), gathers his loyal people to be a 'kingdom, priests serving his God and Father' (1:6). The rest of the book is devoted to giving Christians a view of this ultimate reality, a present reality which will only be revealed to all in the future.

In subsequent revelations John is shown how verse 21 works out, a verse which summarises much of the contents of chapters 4–22:

> To the one who conquers I will give a place with me on my throne, just as I myself conquered and sat down with my Father on his throne.

The last prophetic proclamation to the churches concludes with a final call to all Christians to take urgent notice of what the **Spirit** of God is saying to them through the words of Jesus. Did Laodicea listen? We don't know. A church council was held in Laodicea about AD 370. At this council, so a curious tradition goes, the participants voted to exclude the book of Revelation from the collection of books to be included in what we call the New Testament. Revelation was rejected as an authoritative word of God.

Did Laodicea listen? A more important question is: Do we listen? Compromise and cultural accommodation is still the church's besetting sin. We still think that we can do the impossible: serve God and Mammon at the same time. We still persist in telling ourselves that we can worship God on Sunday and serve strange gods during the week. May we all listen carefully and urgently to **what the Spirit is saying to the churches!**

Where have we been? Where are we going?

The prophetic messages to the seven churches are grounded in the realities of first-century urban life in Asia Minor. These realities were experienced and interpreted in political, economic, and social terms. Our experience today is much the same, with one important difference: our perception of reality is shaped very much by radio, TV, films, and the print media.

Jesus calls Christians then and now to an alternative view, a minority and therefore unpopular view of reality. This view is the one which Jesus Christ, King of kings and Lord of lords, has of existence. It is an other-worldly view; nevertheless it is a view of *this* world, *this* existence, *present* reality. Thus the prophetic proclamations to the seven churches are rooted in time and place; they speak of real people in real situations: John, Patmos, seven cities each with a unique history, culture, politics, and economic environment. The rest of Revelation (chapters 4–22) constantly uses images and symbols which look back to chapters 2 and 3.

In short, chapters 4–22 of Revelation interpret the reality of the seven churches' situation. They provide Christians with a structure by means of which they can understand what is really going on in their world, what values they should hang on to, what matters and what does not matter, what is genuine and what is counterfeit, what is 'of God' and what is not, what is temporary and what is permanent. Above all, Christians learn to see and to know who is Lord and who is not, who alone is to be worshipped, and to whom worship is to be refused.

The transition from the first revelation (1:9 – 3:22) to the second (4:1 – 16:21) is facilitated by the reference in 3:20,21 to the open door and the throne. There the 'open door' referred to the salvation prepared by Christ. In 4:1, however, the 'open door' signals an act of revelation. A reference to something being 'opened' marks the major revelatory activities which are recorded in Revelation. Heaven is opened (4:1;19:11), or the seals of a book (6:1;8:1), or a book (10:1), or the temple (11:19;15:5).

These 'openings' are events of unveiling, revealing. Things happen as a consequence. In 4:1 heaven is opened, John moves into that other sphere of existence where the boundaries between time and space are fluid, and he sees 'what is, and what is to take place after this' (1:19), that is, present and future realities.

The first thing John sees is a *throne*, which was the last thing spoken of in the Lord's promise recorded in the prophetic announcement to the churches of Asia Minor (3:21). The 'throne' becomes the central image and focus of the book.

SECOND REVELATION, 4:1 – 16:21

In the Introduction to this commentary it was pointed out that two kinds of report dominate the book of Revelation: narratives, and accounts of heavenly worship. For a good understanding of Revelation it is vital to know how these two kinds of report function in the book, and how they relate one to the other.

Narratives are the powerful story of God in action, judging his enemies and delivering his people. Since they tell of divine actions, they break the barriers of space. God's judging and saving actions are cosmic in scope; they touch all that God has made, visible and invisible, 'all rule and authority and power and dominion, and . . . every name that is named, not only in this age but also in the age to come' (Eph 1:21).

That last phrase is a reminder that the narratives of Revelation break also the time barrier; they show that God's work of judgment and salvation is not only a future, end-time activity, but it is going on now, today. Because the narratives break the time barrier, it is proper to ask: *When* is this to happen? Answer: It is happening now and it will happen in the future. 'Those who believe in him are not condemned; those who do not believe are condemned already . . .' (John 3:18; see also 3:36).

The accounts of scenes of heavenly worship complement the narratives. They, too, cross the boundaries of space and time. They reveal that Christian worship is a participation in the heavenly liturgy, the worship of saints and angels around the throne of God. This is the reality of worship on earth, worship which seems to be so weak, so ineffective and impotent.

Worship is the source and dynamic for the divine judging and saving activity which is put into effect as the narrative unfolds. Hence Christian worship is a powerful activity; it is a sharing in the very work of God. For this reason, reports of heavenly worship are not scattered haphazardly throughout Revelation; on the contrary, they are carefully located in relation to the dramatic narratives, providing the impetus for the action of the narratives, and sometimes functioning as a response of praise for what God has done.

In short, heavenly worship and dramatic narrative relate as cause and effect: worship sets in motion the divine actions of the narrative. So, for example, the liturgy in praise of the victorious Lamb (5:9–14) is followed by the narrative of the opening of four seals. A liturgical response to these divine activities (6:9–11) leads on to the story of the opening of the sixth seal and the revelation of the protection which is guaranteed to God's people (6:12 – 7:8). This issues in further heavenly liturgy, a narrative dialogue, and the liturgical introduction to the next major narrative (7:9 – 9:21).

This same interplay between dramatic narrative and heavenly worship occurs throughout Revelation. It provides a major clue to understanding the contents of the book.

The heavenly worship scenes have another function in addition to that of launching and empowering the events of the narratives. The repeated accounts of heavenly worship are a constant reminder of who is the centre and focus of the events which are being narrated, who is doing the judging and saving, who is worthy of worship and praise.

George Bernard Shaw dismissed Revelation as 'a curious record of a drug addict's visions'. But in fact the book is speaking of realities, not fantasies and fancies. Revelation is describing life as it is and as it will be. The book accurately reflects our own experiences. Things happen to us, and we wonder whether God is still alive, or whether he is absent or dead. Perhaps Satan is in control, or some other power, human or demonic or both. Perhaps we create our own history. Are we captains of our own fate, or is history perhaps just one big machine, moving along in the oil of its own secretions?

The scenes of heavenly worship remind John's hearers that even though human or angelic agents figure prominently in the narratives they are not to be worshipped (see 19:10;22:8). This is especially true of the dragon and the two beasts. As a kind of unholy trinity, they give the impression that they control history and the future, and that they, therefore, are worthy of divine worship and praise (13:12–15). But the whole book of Revelation denies this premise. It is God who gives even the dragon and the beasts their limited powers and opportunities (13:5,7;17:17).

The only thing anyone in Revelation gives God is worship. Heavenly liturgy is a reminder that true worship is worship of the true God.

WORSHIP: liturgy of praise and acclamation, 4:1–11

**4 After this I looked, and there in heaven a door stood
open! And the first voice, which I had heard speaking to
me like a trumpet, said, 'Come up here, and I will show
you what must take place after this.' 2 At once I was in the
spirit,[l] and there in heaven stood a throne, with one seated
on the throne! 3 And the one seated there looks like jasper
and carnelian, and around the throne is a rainbow that
looks like an emerald. 4 Around the throne are twenty-
four thrones, and seated on the thrones are twenty-four
elders, dressed in white robes, with golden crowns on their
heads. 5 Coming from the throne are flashes of lightning,
and rumblings and peals of thunder, and in front of the
throne burn seven flaming torches, which are the seven
spirits of God; 6 and in front of the throne there is
something like a sea of glass, like crystal.**

**Around the throne, and on each side of the throne, are
four living creatures, full of eyes in front and behind:
7 the first living creature like a lion, the second living
creature like an ox, the third living creature with a face
like a human face, and the fourth living creature like a
flying eagle. 8 And the four living creatures, each of them
with six wings, are full of eyes all around and inside. Day
and night without ceasing they sing,**

'Holy, holy, holy,
the Lord God the Almighty,
who was and is and is to
come.'

**9 And whenever the living creatures give glory and honor
and thanks to the one who is seated on the throne, who**

lives forever and ever, [10] the twenty-four elders fall before the one who is seated on the throne and worship the one who lives forever and ever; they cast their crowns before the throne, singing,

11 **'You are worthy, our Lord and**
God,
to receive glory and honor and
power,
for you created all things,
and by your will they existed
and were created.'

[l] Or *in the Spirit*

1 The movement of Revelation is facilitated by a phrase which John likes to use to introduce the next part of his report: 'After this I looked and behold . . .' This could be translated simply as 'Next, I saw . . .' What John saw, while still on Patmos, was a **door** which had been opened **in heaven**.

'Heaven' is the sphere of existence where things are seen for what they really are: evil is seen as evil and good as good. It is a place where a fierce battle is fought between personal powers who are opposed to God and those who are on God's side. It is also, in Revelation, a shorthand for transcendence, for the 'otherness' of God in relation to his creatures and his creation. God dwells in heaven; he is, therefore, sometimes called 'the God of heaven' (11:13;16:11; compare Neh 1:4,2:20).

'Heaven' is a complex space. It contains the things we can see with normal vision (sun, moon, stars). But it also has things which can be seen only by 'going up' or by something being 'opened'.

John saw a door opened **in heaven**, and he heard the voice of the glorified Christ. He had heard this voice before (1:10). Now Jesus calls John to **come up** to heaven so that Jesus can **show** him what **must**, in God's work of judgment and salvation, **take place** next. **After this** means next in the story, not next in any supposed chronology of revelation. Readers of Revelation do well to repeat the salutary reminder of one commentator, that John is a lot less concerned with chronology than are some of his interpreters (Wilcock).

2 Since worship transcends space and time, the right time and the right way to 'go up' is in worship, where the Spirit of God is present and active among his people. John received his revelation on the Lord's day (1:10), the day of worship. In that sacred time the Spirit, who inspires the prophets and even moves them around bodily (for example, Ezek 11:1; Acts 8:39), took John to **heaven**, where he was able to see the whole panorama of events in heaven and on earth.

From this vantage point John sees many wonderful things and many remarkable events. He sees heavenly worship taking place 'day and night'. He sees God judging and saving. He sees the enemies of God and his people. Surely he is deeply impressed by all that he sees. But when he comes to put it all down in writing, he spotlights not an event, but a symbol: the **throne** of God.

He begins with God.

John does not see God; he sees only God's throne, the majestic radiance of God's presence, and the glory of God's court. John's description of the temple throne-room seems to have been influenced, positively, by the appointments in the Jerusalem temple, especially as described in Ezekiel 1:4–28, and negatively by the ceremonies associated with the Roman imperial court. It is as if John is saying: God and the Lamb rule; the Roman emperor and his court are a parody, a copy of the real thing.

The focal figure is God enthroned in glory. The **throne**, in Revelation, is the symbol of God ruling in splendour and might; hence it is the central object. Everything in the royal court is arranged in relation to the throne. Statistics serve to underline the centrality of the throne as symbol. Of the sixty-two occurrences of the word 'throne' in the New Testament, forty-seven occur in Revelation. The next most frequent usage is in Matthew's gospel (four times!).

In keeping with his reserve when speaking of God directly, or in recording God's direct speech, John does not depict God in human likeness. Instead, reflected light serves to evoke an image of the God of glory: the dazzle of translucent, diamond-like **jasper**; the brilliant glowing red of **carnelian**; and surrounding this light-display 'a halo like an emerald rainbow' (J.B. Phillips).

For the Romans, precious stones were the symbols of real authority; they were an important part of the emperor's robes and insignia. Here in heaven is the Emperor above all emperors, the only Lord God Almighty. The reference to the **rainbow** invites hearers to let their minds wander back through Ezekiel's vision (Ezek 1:28) to God's promise to Noah (Gen 9:13), and be reminded of God's everlasting covenant. The one who sits enthroned in splendour is the Saviour God.

4 **Around the throne** various beings are grouped in concentric circles. First is the rainbow of soft green. Next to the rainbow are the four living creatures (see comments on verse 6). Surrounding the throne, the rainbow, and the living creatures are twenty-four **thrones**, upon which are seated **twenty-four elders**. This is the only time in Revelation that the number twenty-four occurs. Roman emperors symbolised the fullness of their imperial authority by surrounding themselves with twelve *lictors* (a cross between bodyguard and press agent). The emperor Domitian is said to have doubled this number to twenty-four; in so doing he was unwittingly copying God, the true Emperor.

The **twenty-four elders** who surround the throne of the Emperor of all emperors have been variously identified as representatives of the twenty-four astral gods of the Babylonian collection of gods, or as a special class of angels, or — as seems most likely — the whole people of God (the twelve tribes of Israel and the twelve apostles).

As the faithful and victorious people of God, these **twenty-four elders** wear the symbols of their position: the **white robes** of those who have been made holy by Christ (see 3:4,5;6:11;7:9,13), and the **golden crowns** of those who have conquered in and with the Lamb (see 2:10;3:11). Both Romans and Jews knew the symbolic force of the golden crown. For Romans it was a standard award when honours were accorded a benefactor. As far as Jews were concerned, let the following inscription from about John's time speak:

> The synagogue of the Jews honoured Tatian, daughter of Straton, son of Empedon, with a gold crown and a seat of honour.

Normally, the place of honour in the synagogue was where the Torah was kept. In God's place of worship, the place of honour is around the throne of God.

5 The temple throne-room is such a kaleidoscope of movement and colour that John's eye seems to dart from one thing to another: he cannot take it all in at once. He gives no calm and methodical description. He shares a series of impressions, as if he is so overwhelmed that he doesn't know where to start. From the throne to the rainbow to the elders, he moves back to the throne and its immediate surrounds.

Emanating from the throne are **thunder** and **lightning**. Remember Sinai (Exod 19:16–18;20:18–20; compare Isa 29:6)! **In front of the throne** are **seven** torches of fire which, John explains, are the seven spirits of God (see 1:4). Christ himself is said to 'have' the seven spirits of God (3:1); they function as his 'eyes' (5:6). This symbol of the Holy Spirit in his sevenfold activity serves to complement the truth which has already been confessed, that the Holy Spirit is one with the Father and the Son. The **flashes of lightning**, the **rumblings and peals of thunder**, and the **flaming torches** all say: here is God; he is about to act. Worship him!

6 Also before the **throne**, extending beyond the burning lamps, is a **sea** so transparent that it reminds John of **crystal**. What is this sea? Some say it is the shiny pavement which, according to the *Koran*, was in front of Solomon's throne (compare Exod 24:10). Some say it is the great bronze cauldron in Solomon's temple, used for ritual washing (2 Chron 4:6). In this interpretation, the Spirit's fire and the washing in the 'sea' together suggest the rebirth of the Christian.

Others propose that the 'sea' is the Red Sea, through which the people of God pass. Their crossing of the sea is a conquest of the forces of evil, for the 'sea' is another name for the Abyss, the place of chaos from which the beast arises (13:1), and which is absent from the new order (21:1: 'and the sea was no more'). The psalmist confessed that the Abyss was troubled when God led Israel safely through the sea (Ps 77:16-20); and Isaiah praised God who took his people through the sea as one leads a horse to pasture (Isa 63:13). So easy was God's conquest of the sea, the symbol of evil and opposition to God!

Perhaps the 'sea' simply refers in a general way to the gulf which separates sinful creatures from the holy Creator. As John will show shortly, the Lamb of God has provided a way across that sea; he has bridged the gulf.

Certainly, it should be borne in mind that John's images are often polyvalent, that is, they can carry a variety of meanings. So 'sea' does not have to mean the same thing everywhere in Revelation.

The interpretation favoured in this commentary is that the 'sea' is the heavenly counterpart of the Red Sea (see 15:2). It serves as a symbol of the victory achieved by the new Exodus which is described so vividly throughout Revelation. It is very likely that the 'sea' of Solomon's temple (1 Kings 7:23–44) was the cultic replica of the Red Sea. The rabbis said that one of the ten miracles which God performed for Israel at the Red Sea was that he caused the sea to become congealed (see Exod 15:8) so that it was like a glass vessel.

Finally, John describes those beings who are nearest the throne of God: the **four living creatures**. Translators have a hard time trying to convey the exact relationship between these creatures and the throne. The Greek says that the creatures are around the throne and in the middle of the throne (compare the position of the Lamb in relation to the throne, 5:6).

The puzzle becomes less puzzling, however, if God's throne is seen as a typical oriental royal throne, which often had its arms and legs carved in the form of fantastic living creatures. For example, the back and sides of Solomon's throne were formed from sculptured lions and bulls (1 Kings 10:18,19 JB). So John can speak of the four living creatures as an integral part of the throne: they are **around the throne and on each side of the throne**, in the same way as the back, arms, and legs of a chair are an integral part of the space occupied by the chair.

7,8 These creatures, however, are not carved but **living**. They can fall down before the Lamb (5:8), or leave the throne-room to perform a task for God (15:7). Their six wings are reminiscent of the cherubim who form part of the throne-chariot in Ezekiel's vision (Ezek 1:4–21). John's hearers would think also of the cherubim who stood at each end of the mercy seat, of 'one piece' with the mercy seat, with wings spread to overshadow it (Exod 25:17-22;37:6–9). Since the mercy seat was thought of as God's throne (see Jer 3:16,17), the association of living creatures with mercy seat with throne of God would have come easily to John and his hearers.

The four creatures have **eyes** everywhere, it seems (compare Ezek 10:12). They are ever watchful, ever alert to do the will of him who sits on the throne and in whose presence they constantly live.

Three of the living creatures are said to be like a bird or beast, while the fourth has a **human face**. The rabbis had a saying:

> There are four lordly creatures. The lord among the birds is the eagle; the lord among the cattle is the ox; the lord among beasts is the lion; the lord over all of them is man. The Holy One, blessed be He, took them and engraved them on the Throne of Glory.

Early in the history of the church (by the end of the second century) the four creatures came to symbolise the four Evangelists: lion=Mark; ox=Luke; man=Matthew; eagle=John. But in Revelation the four creatures are meant to represent the whole created universe: the people, the animals, the hills, the seas, the rivers, the stars and space. The four creatures parallel the twenty-four elders, who represent the whole people of God.

It is worth noting that the four living creatures lead the heavenly worship. They are nearest the throne; fittingly, they lead the praise. The purpose of God's world is that it praises him. For that reason they praise him **day and night without ceasing**; their whole existence is one of praise. God's people respond with their own acclamation. This is the tremendous picture presented in the last verses of chapter 4.

Imagine the sights and sounds: the brilliant colours, the bolts of lightning and peals of thunder, the circles of worshippers around the throne, led by the four living creatures. The creatures sing the song which in Hebrew is called *Kadosh*, and in Latin, *Sanctus*. It is a modified version of the song of the six-winged seraphim in Isaiah 6:3. Praise is addressed to the thrice-holy God. In this evil and polluted world of sin, let no-one forget it: God, not evil, rules! Praise is addressed to the **Lord God the Almighty**. Thus the worshippers confess that real power and might in heaven and on earth rests, not with evil and the demonic, but with God.

Lastly, praise is addressed to the one **who was and is and is to come**. So the people of God confess that God's eternal power and being guarantees that his people will triumph over evil. Unlike the antigods, who are heading for destruction (17:8,11), God's future is always coming; it is not static or closed, but always open. God himself is always 'the coming one' (see 1:4,8; and 22:20!).

9–11 The **twenty-four elders** respond to the *Sanctus* of creation with a song of praise of their own. But first they prostrate themselves **before the one who is seated on the throne**. In Revelation, the people of God always prostrate themselves in the throne area (see 4:10;5:14; 11:1,16;19:4). True worship always takes place around the throne. That is to say, God is the centre of true worship.

The elders fall on their faces before God in an act of worship, and **cast their crowns before the throne** in homage and submission. They acclaim the worthiness of God to receive such adoration and praise. These elders are kings. They do what all kings should do: acknowledge that God alone is **worthy to receive** such **glory and honour and power**.

There is a political dimension to Christian worship. Not only does the worshipping community pray *for* kings and all who are in authority, but Christians also pray and worship *on behalf of* kings and political leaders. Christians do what earthly leaders should do: worship God.

God is worthy to receive these honours and acclamations because he is Creator of **all things**. His 'worth-ship' is clear; therefore he alone is to be the focus of all worship. Every person and being in the throne-room has no argument with this. But their approval does not create God's worthiness to receive heavenly praise.

In ancient times, the consent of the governed in the making of a ruler was taken very seriously. Without public acclamation no ruler could consider himself to be the legitimate ruler. This idea of 'by common consent' was important also when a ruler wanted to enter a city (known as his *adventus*, 'coming'). His right to enter and to function as a ruler had to be acknowledged by the shouts and acclaim of the citizens (see Jesus' entry into Jerusalem, Matt 21:1-11). God's cosmic rule, however, and his continued presence in the universe, needs no legitimation. The acclamation which God receives from his creatures is a response to his saving rule, not the cause of it.

DIALOGUE NARRATIVE: Who is worthy to open the scroll? 5:1–5

5 Then I saw in the right hand of the one seated on the
throne a scroll written on the inside and on the back,
sealed[m] with seven seals; 2 and I saw a mighty angel
proclaiming with a loud voice, 'Who is worthy to open
the scroll and break its seals?' 3 And no one in heaven or
on earth or under the earth was able to open the scroll or
to look into it. 4 And I began to weep bitterly because no
one was found worthy to open the scroll or to look into
it. 5 Then one of the elders said to me, 'Do not weep.
See, the Lion of the tribe of Judah, the Root of David,
has conquered, so that he can open the scroll and its seven
seals.'

[m] Or *written on the inside, and sealed on the back*

The shift to the next phase in the account of the revelation is signalled by the usual phrase, 'And I saw'. The dialogue narrative occurs occasionally in Revelation (for example, 7:13–17;17:7–18). Some of the prophets used this narrative form to convey an interpretation of what they had seen in a vision (for example, Amos 7:1–9;

8:1–3). Here, John inserts a dialogue narrative between a matching pair of worship scenes (4:1–11;5:6–14) in order to set the stage for the second of the two worship scenes, and to provide a framework for interpreting the worship scene properly. The dialogue narrative and the two worship scenes are linked by the common theme of 'worthiness' (see further the comments on 5:6).

1 A **scroll** is to be opened, a scroll which had writing on both sides, indicating the completeness of its contents. God holds this scroll in his **right hand**, the hand of power and might (Exod 15:6; Ps 44:3), and of righteousness and salvation (Ps 17:7;48:10). In his right hand, then, God holds the world's present and future. Will it be judgment or salvation, destruction or new creation, condemnation or vindication?

The scroll is **sealed with seven seals**. 'Sealing' is the opposite of 'revealing'. When something is sealed, there is no action, whereas, when something is opened (a door, a book), then revelation takes place: there is action, something happens. This scroll is well and truly **sealed** shut. None of its contents will be operative unless the seals are broken and the scroll or book is opened.

The scroll is no ordinary scroll. Not only does it contain the present and future of the universe, but it can be opened only by one who is 'worthy'. And that creates a serious problem. The heavenly worship which John has just described confessed that only God can properly be designated 'worthy'. Is there no-one else 'worthy'?

2 A mighty **angel** puts the question to the worshippers who are gathered in the temple throne-room. 'Who is worthy to open the scroll and break its seals?' It sounds like a replay of Goliath and Israel. Goliath challenged Israel to produce someone fit to fight him. But no-one could be found. Here in Revelation, the strong **angel** shouts with a Goliath-like voice and challenges the new Israel: Is there anyone among you who counts himself or herself worthy, as God is worthy?

3,4 The angel's challenge is greeted with unaccustomed silence. The twenty-four elders, the four living creatures, the countless hosts around the throne who sing their songs of praise 'without ceasing' (4:8) are silent. No-one was fit **to open the scroll** or **look into it**.

No wonder John wept **bitterly** (better: 'copiously'). If there is no-one to open the scroll and set in motion God's judging and saving activities, then the situation of John and of God's faithful people is hopeless. History is just a tale that is told. The last word is death. The devil has and deserves to have all the best tunes. We chose wrongly when we chose to worship and serve God and to reject the worship and service of Satan. If there is no judgment for those who rebel against God and mock and persecute his people, and if there is no salvation for the faithful, what is the point of perseverance, faithfulness, and confession to Christ? If there is no-one to unseal the scroll, then Julian Huxley is right: 'God is not a ruler but the last fading smile of a cosmic Cheshire cat'. And we Christians are of all people to be most pitied (1 Cor 15:19).

5 **One of** the twenty-four **elders** comforts John, urges him to stop sobbing (see Luke 7:13), and assures him that there is a David in the camp: there is someone who is worthy to open the seals of the scroll. This 'worthy one' is described in the political religious language of messianic prophecy: he is **the Lion of the tribe of Judah** (Gen 49:9) and the **Root of David**. He **has conquered**, this warrior of God (see 3:21), so he is worthy.

Let us, then, see this second David, this great Lion of Judah!

WORSHIP: Liturgy of praise and acclamation (continued), 5:6–14

6 Then I saw between the throne and the four living creatures and among the elders a Lamb standing as if it had been slaughtered, having seven horns and seven eyes, which are the seven spirits of God sent out into all the earth. 7 He went and took the scroll from the right hand of the one who was seated on the throne. 8 When he had taken the scroll, the four living creatures and the twenty-four elders fell before the Lamb, each holding a harp

and golden bowls full of incense, which are the prayers
of the saints. 9 They sing a new song:
'You are worthy to take the scroll
and to open its seals,
for you were slaughtered and by
your blood you ransomed
for God
saints from[n] every tribe and
language and people and
nation;
10 you have made them to be a
kingdom and priests
serving[o] our God,
and they will reign on earth.'
11 Then I looked, and I heard the voice of many angels
surrounding the throne and the living creatures and the
elders; they numbered myriads of myriads and thousands
of thousands, 12 singing with full voice,
'Worthy is the Lamb that was
slaughtered
to receive power and wealth and
wisdom and might
and honour and glory and
blessing!'
13 Then I heard every creature in heaven and on earth
and under the earth and in the sea, and all that is in them,
singing,
'To the one seated on the throne
and to the Lamb
be blessing and honour and glory
and might
forever and ever!'
14 And the four living creatures said, 'Amen!' And the
elders fell down and worshiped.

[n] Gk *ransomed for God from*

[o] Gk *priests to*

A little device which John often uses to make a point is the A B A' pattern. In 4:1–5:14 we have such a pattern:

A	4:1–11	Liturgy of praise and acclamation (God)
B	5:1–5	Who is worthy to open the scroll?
A'	5:6–14	Liturgy of praise and acclamation (the Lamb)

This arrangement helps to highlight the critical importance of the question concerning the unsealing of the scroll, and it sets the liturgical context for the opening of the scroll and the events which follow each act of opening (see also the comments on 5:1).

That the two accounts of worship (4:8–11;5:6–14) are a pair is evident from the parallels in form and content. Both begin with the focus on the throne (4:2;5:6). Seated on the throne is God (4:2,3) or the Lamb (5:6; see 22:3). The emphasis on the trinitarian nature of the worship is completed by the double reference to the Spirit (4:5;5:6). Both reports of heavenly worship locate the worshippers in relation to the throne (4:4;5:6), and in both cases the worshippers declare that the one who is on the throne is 'worthy' to receive all praise and honour (4:8-11;5:8-12). God is acknowledged as 'worthy' because of his work of creation (4:11); the Lamb's 'worthiness' is revealed in his work of redemption (5:9-12).

Finally, the theological necessity and rightness of this pairing of worship scenes is expressed in the ultimate sentence of praise:

> To the one seated on the throne and to the Lamb
> be blessing and honour and glory and might
> forever and ever! (5:13)

6 In one of the most dramatic and pivotal moments in the whole book, John tells of how he searched, searched, eager to set eyes on that which his ears had prepared him to see: a mighty lion (5:5).

He looks, and sees . . . a lamb!

Not a lion but a lamb! And not just any lamb, but a lamb which **had been slaughtered**, butchered (see 6:4,9;18:24), a sacrificial lamb. Is this the world's hope? This lamb? Lamb's have no future, except to become chops. Lambs are for death, not life.

But the lamb whom John sees is the Lamb of God who takes away the sin of the world (John 1:29), the Passover lamb to which all Passover lambs pointed (1 Cor 5:7; 1 Pet 1:19), the Lamb whose sacrificial death and triumphant resurrection meant victory over death and sin and all evil. All power belongs to him (he has **seven horns**), and all wisdom is his, the wisdom which belongs only to the one who is filled with the fullness of the Spirit of God (Isa 11:2). That Spirit is at work in **all the earth**, convincing men and women of sin, and gifting them with the rights of sons and daughters of God through faith in the Lamb of God (see John 16:7-11).

The Lamb is worthy, as God alone is worthy, because of who he is and because of what he has done. John very carefully describes the stance of the Lamb in relation to the throne. He is trying to distinguish between God and the Lamb, and yet confess their unity. The Lamb stands **between the throne and the four living creatures**. And yet the living creatures are themselves so close to the throne that they are said to occupy the same space as the throne (see comments on 4:6). The Lamb is also **among the elders**, and yet the elders stand around the throne. We know that the Lamb shares the throne with the Father (3:21). So probably the best we can do is the translation of the NEB: The Lamb stands 'in the very middle of the throne'; or, as the NIV has it: The Lamb 'is standing in the centre of the throne, encircled by the four living creatures and the elders' (compare J.B. Phillips).

This vision of the Lamb who was slain is the pivotal vision for the whole of Revelation.

John looks for a lion and sees a lamb.

Here is the epitome, the quintessential symbol of God's self-revelation, the heart of the gospel, the paradigm of how Christians are to view all of reality. God's revelation of his very own heart, of how he thinks of us, of what he has done for our salvation, comes in the very opposite of what we expect. It is a contradiction of our values and of our ideas of how things should be and should be done.

When we want to see who is worthy to execute God's judging and saving activity in the world, we look for a figure of power and might.

But we see a lamb, a slaughtered lamb at that. A victim.

Football teams proudly bear the name of 'The Hawks' and 'The Tigers', but whoever heard of a team called 'The Lambs'? But God's ways are not our ways. He reveals his total otherness by becoming a human being, a baby. In that baby God reveals his power by nursing at his mother's breast. God displays his majesty by appearing among us as a servant. He shows his glory by dying the death of a criminal between two criminals. And he shows us his love in that most shameful, that most unlovely of places, the cross.

John wants his fellow Christians, in danger of being mesmerised by the political-social view of reality, to read the signs — God's signs — and see things as they really are and will be. Where there is weakness, see strength; where there is poverty, see riches; where there is servanthood, see majesty; where there is defeat, see victory.

So don't be fooled: political power is not ultimate power; the glory of government of any stripe is not lasting glory; the values and attractions of society are not finally normative. At best, all these things are a parody, a distorted copy of reality where God sits on the throne and with the Lamb is worshipped.

7 Jesus Christ — for that is who the Lamb is — **took the scroll** from God. That means that Jesus, bone of our bone and flesh of our flesh, is Lord of life and death, present and future, salvation and judgment. In his hand he holds the world; but he also holds the church (1:13,16). So one thing is certain: as the great scroll is opened, and the events which it contains take place, Christ's people are safe. They know that the contents of the scroll are set in motion by Christian worship, where God's word and will for the world is heard, responded to, acclaimed, and done. And always at the centre of worship is the Lamb.

8 John now describes the act of worship which is the proper response to the action of the Lamb in taking the scroll and so revealing that he is 'worthy', just as God is 'worthy'. This worship is the dynamic for the opening of the scroll's seals, which sets in motion the divine activities of judgment and salvation described in the subsequent narratives (6:1 – 7:8).

The first and last action of the heavenly worshippers is an act of prostration before the Lamb. The physical gesture of humbling oneself in adoration before the Lamb comes before any speaking and singing, and it concludes the act of worship (5:14).

The **twenty-four elders** who lead the worship are described as temple functionaries. They are spoken of as if they were members of the Levitical choir which sang morning and evening on the top steps of the altar of burnt offering. The Levites represented the king, whose duty it was to praise God on behalf of the royal nation. So it is not surprising that the twenty-four royal elders (4:10) function as Levites: they lead the heavenly liturgy, each on his lyre (**harp**), the traditional instrument of psalmody (see Ps 33:2;98:5).

In addition to their levitical role (the Levites were a minor order of priests), the twenty-four elders functioned also as royal priests whose duty it was to offer incense. They held in their hands **golden bowls full of incense** (see Deut 33:10; Num 7:14). The bowls were probably broad flat disks shaped like saucers. They were **golden**, suggesting their freedom from any uncleanness or impurity.

The **incense** which these **golden bowls** contain are said to be the **prayers of the saints**, the people of God (see Rom 1:7 Eph 1:1). Later we learn that these prayers are offered on the altar of incense as the liturgical setting for the trumpet septet (8:2,3).

Like the Lamb during his earthly life, the **saints** are thought to be of no account, powerless, unimportant. But the prayers of the church ascend, like the sacrifices of the Head of the church himself (Eph 5:2), to the throne of God. They are accepted by him as a sweet-smelling offering (Ps 141:2), and they provide the dynamic for the divine judging and saving activity in the world. In short, 'the prayer of a righteous person has great power in its effects' (James 5:16).

9 The **song** which the heavenly worshippers **sing** is a **new** one. It corresponds to the new name (2:17;3:12), the new Jerusalem (3:12;21:2), the new heaven and earth (21:1), and the 'all things new' of the kingdom of the Lamb. Only a new song is appropriate. But the song is reminiscent of Psalm 33, where with a 'new song' the old people of God praised him for his righteousness, which was constant despite the opposition of the mightiest powers earth could muster. God's righteousness was that which rescued and delivered those to whom it was given. The **new song** of the heavenly liturgy is addressed to the Lamb; it tells why he is worthy to carry out God's acts of judgment and salvation, and to preside over the acts which connect his ascension with his return at the end of the ages.

Three reasons are given for the Lamb's worthiness **to take the scroll and to open its seals**. First, the Lamb has been **slaughtered** (there is a play on words in Greek between 'sealed' and 'slaughtered'). The Lamb had died a violent death: his throat was cut as the Paschal lamb (1 Cor 5:7). But his death meant liberation and redemption for all, just as the death of the Passover lamb led to liberation and rescue for ancient Israel (Exod 12:27).

Secondly, Jesus the Lamb is worthy because with his precious blood he purchased, or paid the ransom price for, prisoners of war who had been enslaved by the dragon, that is, by Satan and his earthly representatives. **For God**, the Lamb **ransomed** countless men, women, and children (of whom the one hundred and forty-four thousand of 14:3 are the sign and symbol) **from every tribe and language and people and nation**. Thus in his blood he broke down the barriers, removed the enmity and hostility between nation and nation, race and race, and formed from them one new international community (Gal 3:28; Eph 2:14–18). Their national anthem is the **new song**, known only to the people of the Lamb, 'the friends of the cross', as Luther calls them.

10 The third reason given for the Lamb's worthiness has to do with the purpose of his saving activity: people have been ransomed, redeemed, rescued in order to constitute God's **kingdom** which consists of **priests** (see 1:6). The emphasis is on kingship: **they will reign on earth**. Some manuscripts read: 'They reign on earth'. The copyist made an error, but the thought is correct: the people of God reign and will reign. Their reigning, however, consists in this, that they serve God and their fellow human beings. They do not lord it over them (see Matt 20:24-28).

11,12 In 4:11 God is acknowledged as the one who is worthy to receive glory, honour, and power, because he is the creator of all (see 10:5,6;14:7). Now the Lamb is said to be similarly worthy of royal acclamation and divine worship because he was slain and through his blood he created an ecumenical community. Creation and redemption are inseparable because the Creator and the Redeemer are one.

The 'new song' of the elders is not a solo piece; it is part of a great choral work. The elders (that is, the church) praise the Lamb for his creation of a new race of priestly kings. Now the countless number of **angels** who form the outer ring around **the throne** join their voices to those of **the living creatures and the elders**, in a shout of acclamation which greets the new community of the Lamb, and hails the Lamb as king, conqueror. He, they cry, is worthy to receive (or 'to take') those things which are his by right: **power and wealth and wisdom and might and honour and glory and blessing**.

Three points stand out here: 1) the scope of the universal acclamation of the Lamb far outstrips the range of people who ever acclaimed a Roman emperor, despite Rome's claim to be the hub of the nations. 2) The doxology offered to the Lamb is even fuller than that which in 4:11 was offered to the One on the throne (but compare 7:11). The listed attributes form a perfect septet, implying that the very fullness of divine honours is to be given to the Lamb. 3) The Lamb is designated as 'the Lamb who was slain'. Christians know of no other God, no other Saviour, no other Lamb than the 'Lamb-who-was-slain'. That has been his wondrous name from the foundation of the world (13:8 NIV), and that is his name in the eternal liturgy (1:5;5:6,12). Christ crucified, Paul names him (1 Cor 1:23). 'It is in the cross that God discloses the essence of what it is to be God' (A.M. Ramsey).

13 Finally, the mighty choir of angels has a counterpart choir which joins the heavenly liturgy and demonstrates clearly that here is a cosmic liturgy, one which breaks the barriers of time and space. This second great choir is made up of every created thing: the song of the land, the rhythm of the sea, the voices of the mountains, the music of the planets, the chorus of the great whales, the carols of the birds.

> The heavens are telling the glory of God;
> and the firmament proclaims his handiwork.
> (Ps 19:1)

In some esoteric systems, by the way, creation is said to sing in the key of D-flat. We who live in great cities are largely deaf to creation's chorus. But it is there, as surely as the church's liturgy is part of the great cosmic worship which celebrates the glory of **the one seated on the throne**, together with **the Lamb**.

Only one word remains to be spoken. It is uttered by the heavenly counterparts of all creation, that is, by the **four living creatures**. They began the heavenly liturgy with the *Sanctus* (4:8); now they bring it to a close with the **Amen!** No doubt John's own eucharistic thanksgiving ended with that same confident cry: **Amen!** (see 22:20).

If there are any doubts left, they are dispelled by the final wordless gesture by the twenty-four elders. With them, the church kneels before God and the Lamb, speechless, 'lost in wonder, love, and praise'. Silent adoration, face down before God, humbly receiving what God gives in worship — this is the proper posture of worship, a posture which, sad to say, is not often seen in worship today.

Where have we been? Where are we going?

The report which John gives of the throne room and heavenly temple has been full of wondrous sights and sounds and surprises. It is no surprise that God in all his glory should be the focus of all worship in heaven and on earth. That Jesus Christ, the victorious Son, shares centre stage with the Father, and shares with him the praise and adoration of all creation — that, too, is no surprise.

The surprise comes when John, who has been told that the Lion is the worthy one, looks for a lion and sees a lamb, the slain Lamb (5:6). Twenty-nine times in Revelation Jesus Christ is given the title 'the Lamb'; it is a key image in the book.

The conquering Lion-as-slain-Lamb is an image which reminds Christians that all reality is to be understood and interpreted in the light of the cross. There on the cross is revealed with piercing clarity the depth of human and cosmic sin and rebellion. There on the cross is revealed, with equal clarity, the wrath of God and the love of God. There in Christ, the Lamb of God, is God's victory over every power which wants to deprive us of our freedom and our future.

The word of the cross, then, is that word which uncovers the meaning of all existence. It alone enables Christian people to interpret the pain and suffering, the God-forsakenness and darkness, the rejection and persecution which are typical of the present order. When you live by the gospel you live by faith, not sight; you trust what you hear, not what you see.

In the series of events which are now to be set in motion (6:1 – 22:5), John sees some terrible things. It might seem that Satan is in control. But it is *the Lamb* who has opened the seals of the great scroll and set these events in motion. Jesus Christ the Lamb rules and exercises his sovereign power in acts of judgment and salvation. The Lamb is Lord.

NARRATIVE: The Lamb opens four seals, 6:1–8

6 Then I saw the Lamb open one of the seven seals, and I heard one of the four living creatures call out, as with a voice of thunder, 'Come!'[p] 2 I looked, and there was a white horse! Its rider had a bow; a crown was given to him, and he came out conquering and to conquer.
3 When he opened the second seal, I heard the second living creature call out, 'Come!'[p] 4 And out came[q] another horse, bright red; its rider was permitted to take peace from the earth, so that people would slaughter one another; and he was given a great sword.
5 When he opened the third seal, I heard the third living creature call out, 'Come!'[p] I looked, and there was a black horse! Its rider held a pair of scales in his hand, 6 and I heard what seemed to be a voice in the midst of the four living creatures saying, 'A quart of wheat for a day's pay,[r] and three quarts of barley for a day's pay,[r] but do not damage the olive oil and the wine!'
7 When he opened the fourth seal, I heard the voice of the fourth living creature call out, 'Come!'[p] 8 I looked and there was a pale green horse! Its rider's name was Death, and Hades followed with him; they were given authority over a fourth of the earth, to kill with sword, famine, and pestilence, and by the wild animals of the earth.

[p] Or *'Go!'*
[q] Or *went*
[r] Gk *a denarius*

The twin scenes of heavenly worship (4:1–11;5:6–14) which precede this narrative (6:1–8) do not form a pious introduction to the events which follow. Rather, they provide the setting for the drama of judgment and salvation, as well as being its dynamic and moving force. That is to say, the heavenly worship is the action from which the subsequent judging and saving activities flow.

Who participates in heavenly liturgy? God, the Lamb, all creation on earth, the angels, the saints, the church in heaven, and the church on earth. That means that when the word of the Lamb is sung, confessed, and proclaimed in earthly worship, then the world faces a crisis: is it to be judgment or salvation? In their worship the people of God on earth participate in God's judging and saving activity. In worship, idols are dethroned, the enemies of God are judged, and the 'friends of the cross' are rescued and forgiven.

Beware blinkered vision! Our first reaction to tragedies and catastrophes and disasters, such as those described in the seal septet, is to see in them evidences of God's *absence.* However, by placing these seal scenes in the setting of heavenly worship, John challenges us to see in these events evidence of God's *presence,* his involvement in our affairs. This is a unique view of reality, the 'alternative view' of existence which is offered in the book of Revelation.

The fact that it is God who initiates the acts of judgment and salvation described in 6:1–8 is symbolised in three ways. First, the Lamb opens the seals and so sets in motion the events which follow. Secondly, the command to the four horsemen comes from the four living creatures who form part of the actual throne of God. Thirdly, the worship scene in 6:9–11 provides the liturgical response to the narrative of 6:1–8; at the same time it supplies the spring out of which flow the events of the subsequent narrative (6:12–17). All true worship is directed to God and the Lamb, and directed by them. Such worship says to all who will listen: the narrative which flows out of worship is God in action.

1 John continues to report what he **saw**: the breaking of the seals which fasten the great scroll. As **the Lamb** breaks each seal, a lot of terrible, catastrophic things happen. They are the kind of things Christians were led to expect would happen in the final days of this world's history (see Mark 13:3–27; Luke 21:7–37). The events which occur at the opening of each seal are bad, but they are not as bad as those which they preview: the events which follow the blowing of the seven trumpets and the emptying of the seven bowls. There is in Revelation a kind of heightening or escalation of judgment as the book moves inevitably to its conclusion.

When **the Lamb** broke the first of **the seven seals** John heard **one of the four living creatures** issue a command. **'Come'!** says the living creature in a thunderous voice, indicating that he speaks with the voice of God (see John 12:29; Rev 10:3,4;14:2). Note that it is the living creatures who, together with the Lamb, put into effect the judging and saving activities which establish the reign of God in the universe.

The living creatures represent all of God's creation (see 4:6–8 and comments). The events which are unleashed by the opening of the first four seals are not 'natural' disasters, but they affect the environment. Creation is both God's instrument and the victim of the working out of God's judgments on a rebellious humanity.

Some commentators say that the summons (**Come!**) is addressed to Jesus by a creation which is longing and groaning for his return (see Rom 8:19–23). However, the role which the living creatures play in the bowls narrative of chapter 15 (15:7) speaks in favour of the interpretation which has been proposed here.

2 In response to the summons of the living creatures, a **white horse** appears. It is ridden by one who has a war **bow** in his hand. He has been authorised by God to exercise authority (**a crown was given to him**). Who is this first of four horsemen? In view of 19:11–16, some have suggested that the first horseman is the conquering Christ. Others point to Mark 13:10: the first horseman is the gospel which overcomes the world.

However, Albrecht Dürer, in his famous picture of the four horsemen of the Apocalypse, was right in grouping the first horseman with the other three.

The first horseman represents a counterfeit of the white horse of 19:11. A **crown** was worn by royalty, by prophets, and by those who received prophetic oracles. In the Greco-Roman world, the **bow** was associated with Apollo, the god who was thought to inspire prophecy.

The first rider, then, represents the false prophet and false prophecy which were traditionally associated with end-time plagues and disasters of cosmic proportions. Thus in Matthew 24:4–8, Jesus speaks of false prophets,

wars, famines, and earthquakes (the exact order followed in Revelation 6:1–13; contrast Mark 13:5–8).

The phrase, 'a crown was given to him', is a reminder that God is in control; he crowns kings and prophets and uses them for his purposes. They are instruments of his judgment and salvation. Not even a Pilate, the supreme authority in the Roman province of Judea, could lift a finger to touch Jesus without God's own empowering (see John 19:11). One of the most startling and reassuring truths expressed in this book is that it is God who 'gives' even to Satan the power and opportunity to do his satanic work, a work which, in the end, leads to his own destruction (for example, 20:7–10).

3,4 **Red** is the colour of bloodshed and also the colour of the Dragon (12:3). When Christ **opens the second seal**, another **living creature** summons a blood-red horse. God permits the rider on this horse **to take peace from the earth**. God gives him, furthermore, the means for doing this: **a great sword**, the symbol of civil war and strife. As Cain butchered Abel (1 John 3:12), so brother will butcher brother, citizen **slaughter** citizen. Blood will flow as God's judging activities bring an end to the pretence of 'peace on earth' (see Matt 10:34).

There is irony here. Rome was proud of the *Pax Romana*, the 'peace' which Rome had inaugurated. But one Roman writer had the honesty to record the bitter remark of a defeated tribal leader: 'They create a desert and call it peace'. Shortly before John wrote, the British queen Boudicca (Boadicea) had led a bloody revolt against Roman oppression. The death toll was seventy thousand. Suetonius Paulinus, the Roman general, restored peace by killing a hundred and fifty thousand Britons. Rome preserved a bloody peace. The *Pax Romana* really meant keeping Rome happy at all costs (see the comments on 18:9–11).

5 The **rider** of the **black horse** holds in his hands a **pair of scales**, a symbol of famine (see Lev 26:26; Ezek 4:16). When people must 'eat bread by weight . . . and drink water by measure' (Ezek 4:16), then there is a shortage, a famine which means food rationing. This is one result of the bloody activities of the rider on the red horse.

6 The rationing leads to the setting of a famine price, not a starvation one. But it's bad enough. By means of **a voice** which comes from **the middle of the four living creatures**, John registers creation's protest against the horrors of famine. For a full **day's pay** (a denarius) a person could usually buy about twelve quarts of wheat.

Now the famine conditions mean that the price of staples has soared — and, of course, the poor are hardest hit. Now a **day's pay** purchases only a **quart of wheat**, enough to feed the labourer, but not his family.

What would his family eat? Barley was cheaper than wheat; it was regarded as food for the poor. With his day's pay the labourer could buy **three quarts of barley**. His family would not starve to death. They had barley, and the other two staples, **olive oil and wine**.

The command not to **damage the olive oil and wine** is another indication that God on his throne is controlling and containing also these situations which are caused by the inhumanity of human beings to human beings, by human greed and human thirst for blood. It is also a reminder that even when God judges he does not always destroy. He still leaves time and space for repentance, which, as long as this earth remains, is the goal of even his judging activities (see 9:20,21).

7,8 The last rider of this grim quartet sits on a **pale green** horse. The colour is the deathly pallor of a corpse. An appropriate colour, for its rider is **Death** whose henchman is **Hades**, the place of the dead (see 1:18;20:13,14). The instruments which this awful duo use to satisfy their constant hunger are traditional (see Jer 14:12): the **sword** (compare the second horseman), **famine** (compare the third horseman), and **pestilence** ('pestilence' is the proper translation of a Greek word which is often translated as 'death').

To the traditional trio a fourth is added: **the wild animals of the earth**. Wild animals are the usual symbol for the demonic (see Mark 1:13).

The overall impression is of things out of control. Evil is self-destructive, and when evil runs riot everything is destroyed indiscriminately. The demonic seems to be in charge; chaos is king. But the impression is false. God is at work. He uses all kinds of agents, but the rule of the universe is firmly in his hands. Jesus did not merely defeat the powers of evil; he made them agents of his own victory and instruments of his will. So John reminds his hearers that it was the Lamb who **opened the fourth seal**, and it was the **fourth living creature**, speaking from the centre of the throne-room, who summoned the fourth horseman with the imperious 'Come!'.

God gives Death and Hades only limited authority: only **a fourth of the earth** will experience their power of destruction. In the end, Death and Hades will themselves be destroyed (20:14) by him who holds in his hand the key to their destruction (1:18).

WORSHIP: The fifth seal lamentation, 6:9–11

[9] **When he opened the fifth seal, I saw under the altar the souls of those who had been slaughtered for the word of God and for the testimony they had given;** [10] **they cried out with a loud voice, 'Sovereign Lord, holy and true, how long will it be before you judge and avenge our blood on the inhabitants of the earth?'** [11] **They were each given a white robe and told to rest a little longer, until the number would be complete both of their fellow servants**[s] **and of their brothers and sisters,**[t] **who were soon to be killed as they themselves had been killed.**

[s] Gk *slaves*
[t] Gk *brothers*

The opening of the **fifth seal** reveals the church at worship. It is a suffering church, and, like suffering Israel of all times, its worship consists of both praise and lament.

In its laments, ancient Israel directed to God accusatory questions: Why? and How long? (for example, Ps 74:1; Lam 5:20; Ps 44:23; Jer 14:19). The nation had experienced the apparent absence of God. This was an unnerving and inexplicable experience. Like people groping in the dark when the light fails, Israel asks: Why? Why? Why? How long? How long?

But these laments *are* addressed to God. They express hope despite the seeming absence of God, and in spite of his silence. The lament is directed to God, the one who alone can do something about the catastrophes and suffering which have come upon his people.

In the psalms of Israel, the lament ends in praise of God (note especially Psalm 22). Lamentation is the voice of suffering; praise is the voice of joy. Both suffering and joy are part of the experience of the children of God.

The Old Testament scholar Claus Westermann once wrote:

> Just as joy and sorrow in alternation are part of the finitude of human existence (Genesis 2–3), so praise and lamentation are a part of man's [sic] relationship to God. Hence, something must be amiss if praise of God has a place in Christian worship but lamentation does not. Praise can retain its authenticity and naturalness only in polarity with lamentation. (*Praise and Lament in the Psalms*, p 267)

9 When the four horsemen ride the earth, times are particularly hard for Christians. They really do have to live by faith and not by sight. What they see suggests that the demonic, not God, is in control. It's not easy for Christians to maintain their confession to Christ, to stand by their conviction that God is near, that he has not deserted the world and left it to its own devices.

The temptation to despair, to give up on God, is great, and made even greater by the taunts and scorn of the enemies of the church. Harder yet to handle are the thoughtful questions and challenges of sensitive people: Where was God in the Holocaust, in Hiroshima and Vietnam, in Somalia and Ethiopia, in every human tragedy? It's difficult enough for Christians themselves to wrestle with these questions, let alone answer God's critics.

How do you hold together these two: God . . . and human suffering? If only God would come out from behind his masks, reveal himself, show us and the world that he is God, that he is in control, that we were not deluded in our worship of him as Lord and King!

The cry for God to show his hand is uttered by the martyrs on behalf of all the people of God. Like their Lord (5:6), the martyrs had been butchered because of their witness to God's word, that is, their **testimony** to the Lamb-who-was-slain. Their place is **under the altar**. In Revelation 'the altar' is always the altar of incense. In Solomon's temple it was located in the Holy Place, but it was thought of as being part of the Holy of Holies, where was God's throne (it bridged the space through the curtain between the Holy Place and the Holy of Holies).

Twice daily, incense was offered on this altar, and once a year the High Priest sprinkled on this altar the blood of atonement (Exod 30:10; Lev 16:18,19).

The martyrs, then, rest right next to the throne of God; they are in God's presence, 'safe in Jehovah's keeping'.

10 The lamentation of the martyrs under the altar of incense is joined with the prayers of the worshipping community in heaven and on earth (8:1-5). To God, the **holy and true** one, the only **Sovereign Lord**, they address the age-old question: 'How long, O Lord, how long?' **How long** does the suffering and discredited church have to wait before God judges **the inhabitants of the earth**, that is, those who actively oppose God and his people (see 13:8)? The martyrs saw themselves as true descendants of ancient Israel who looked to king Jehu for deliverance from the ravages of Queen Jezebel. God commanded Jehu:

You shall strike down the house of your master Ahab, so that I may avenge on Jezebel the blood of my servants the prophets, and the blood of all the servants of the LORD. (2 Kings 9:7)

The fifth seal, like the other seals, still has to do with judgment. But it raises again the question of the Christian's involvement in this judgment. And the answer is the same as before: in their prayers and worship Christians participate in both the saving and the judging work of God. So, for example, a sermon in which God's word and will is truly proclaimed is a dynamic, active work which confronts people with God's judgment and his salvation. 'Those who have ears to hear, let them hear'. The same truth applies to the whole liturgy, including the hymns and the prayers, the confession of sins, the absolution, and the eucharist itself.

Armchair Christians and critics regard the anguished plea for the judgment of the wicked as unchristian and immoral, quite out of keeping with the gentle spirit of the gospel. But the cry of the martyrs is 'the language not of private revenge but of public justice' (Caird). Their concern is for God's vindication, not their own. For they know that when God and the Lamb are revealed to be all in all, then it will also become clear to everyone who and whose these martyrs are: they are God's own portion (Eph 1:14), sealed with the seal of God on their foreheads (Rev 7:3). Then they, too, will be vindicated.

The martyrs' prayer is, in fact, answered in the judgment visions of the sixth seal, the seven trumpets, the seven bowls, the series of events surrounding the final judgment, and in the place which the martyrs occupy in the new heaven and the new earth.

11 But the martyrs must wait for their *public* rehabilitation until their **number** is **complete**. Although the churches in the Roman province of Asia had experienced only localised and individual acts of persecution, their **brothers and sisters** in and near Rome had just come through a severe time of persecution, and the indications were that if John's people resisted compromise and stood up for what they believed, persecution was inevitable, sooner rather than later. Before the great Day of the Lord came, there would be a number of Christians — **fellow servants** and **brothers and sisters** — who would add considerably to the number of souls 'under the altar'. The history of the church shows this to be true: still today Christians are being **killed** for the faith, just as those early martyrs **had been killed**.

So the saints in heaven are told to be patient, to **rest** just **a little longer**. But as a sure sign and assurance that they do indeed have a place at the marriage feast of the Lamb (19:7,8; compare Matt 22:11–14), **they were each given a white robe**. White is the symbol of purity, but also of victory. They have conquered, as Christ has conquered, in the most unlikely way: through death they gained life; through defeat they in Christ achieved victory; through weakness they demonstrated the power of God; through shame they have come to glory. Their salvation is a reality; all that remains is the unveiling, their vindication before the world. 'Will not God grant justice to his chosen ones who cry to him day and night? . . . I tell you, he will quickly grant justice to them' (Luke 18:7,8).

The lamentations of Israel always expressed the hope that God would deliver them; so they concluded with expressions of praise in confident anticipation of such deliverance. The lamentation which John records in 6:9–

11 certainly expresses a hope. But where is the praise? In Revelation, John often presents his account of an event in two parts. For example, the opening worship scene (4:1 – 5:14) is broken into twin scenes by the dialogue narrative of 5:1–5 (see commentary). Likewise, the account of the judgment and punishment of Satan and his hordes (20:1–10) is divided into two parts by the report concerning the reign of the saints (20:4–6).

In keeping with this pattern of pairs, John presents the lamentation of God's people in 6:9–11, and concludes the worship scene with the song of praise sung in the processional liturgy recorded in 7:9–12. Later on in Revelation, John gives this same pattern an ironic twist: he records three lamentations by worshippers of the beast (18:9–19). They sing no song of praise, for they have no hope. The praise is sung in the great hallelujah chorus of God's people, recorded in 19:1–8.

NARRATIVE: The Lamb opens the sixth seal, 6:12 – 7:8

12 When he opened the sixth seal, I looked, and there
came a great earthquake; the sun became black as
sackcloth, the full moon became like blood, 13 and the
stars of the sky fell to the earth as the fig tree drops its
winter fruit when shaken by a gale. 14 The sky vanished
like a scroll rolling itself up, and every mountain and
island was removed from its place. 15 Then the kings of
the earth and the magnates and the generals and the rich
and the powerful, and everyone, slave and free, hid in
the caves and among the rocks of the mountains, 16 calling
to the mountains and rocks, 'Fall on us and hide us from
the face of the one seated on the throne and from the
wrath of the Lamb; 17 for the great day of their wrath has
come, and who is able to stand?'

7 After this I saw four angels standing at the four
corners of the earth, holding back the four winds of the
earth so that no wind could blow on earth or sea or against
any tree. 2 I saw another angel ascending from the rising
of the sun, having the seal of the living God, and he called
with a loud voice to the four angels who had been given
power to damage earth and sea, 3 saying, 'Do not damage

the earth or the sea or the trees, until we have marked the servants[u] of our God with a seal on their foreheads.'

4 And I heard the number of those who were sealed, one hundred forty-four thousand, sealed out of every tribe of the people of Israel:

5 From the tribe of Judah twelve
thousand sealed,
from the tribe of Reuben twelve
thousand,
from the tribe of Gad twelve
thousand,
6 from the tribe of Asher twelve
thousand,
from the tribe of Naphtali twelve
thousand,
from the tribe of Manasseh twelve
thousand,
7 from the tribe of Simeon twelve
thousand,
from the tribe of Levi twelve
thousand,
from the tribe of Issachar twelve
thousand,
8 from the tribe of Zebulum twelve
thousand,
from the tribe of Joseph twelve
thousand,
from the tribe of Benjamin twelve
thousand sealed.

[u] Gk *slaves*

The opening of the **sixth seal** (like the blowing of the sixth trumpet, 9:13–21) introduces 'that day of wrath, that dreadful day when heaven and earth shall pass away'. It is the day when all who are to be judged shall stand before the 'Judge eternal, throned in splendour'.

When the **sixth seal** is **opened**, an **earthquake** shakes the earth as a terrier shakes a rat. Earthquakes were not uncommon in the region of the seven cities, but this one breaks the Richter scale. It is, however, only one of several cosmic disturbances which signal the end of a world opposed to God, and the coming of the supreme Judge and Lord. There is a solar and lunar eclipse: the **sun** goes into mourning; it puts on black **sackcloth** (compare Isa 50:3; Matt 24:29; Luke 23:45). The moon turns to blood (compare Joel 2:31; Mark 13:24). So those heavenly bodies which were thought to be the powers behind the powers are rendered useless.

13 Even the **stars**, the celestial lights which were believed to control human destiny ('Your Week by the Stars'!), **fall** helplessly from the sky as green **figs** fall from a tree when it is **shaken by a gale** (compare Mark 13:28).

14 To complete the picture of the total dissolution of the present universe, John sees the sky disappear as if God rolls up a blind; more exactly, he sees God crack open the vault of heaven and roll up the two halves (compare Isa 34:4). And the very foundations of the earth, **every mountain and island**, are moved. The impossible happens (Mark 11:23; 1 Cor 13:2)!

The terrible catastrophes which occur when the sixth seal is opened are not so much descriptive as symbolic of the activities of God at the end of history. The early Christians had been told to expect such activities, and they had been warned to be watchful and ready for the return of the Lord which these activities heralded (for example, Mark 13:4–36; 1 Thess 5:1–11; 2 Pet 3:1–13). For with the death and resurrection of the Lamb, the countdown to the Day of the Lord has begun. We are living in the last times. Soon God will publicly be seen to respond to the cry of his people (6:10); he will vindicate himself and them, and let his wrath fall upon 'the inhabitants of the earth' and all dehumanising and oppressive powers.

15,16 The list of those who imitate their ancestor Adam in trying to flee from the wrath of God (Gen 3:8) contains seven kinds of people, suggesting a complete listing. Every stratum of society is involved, from emperor to slave. The political structures are there: **the kings of the earth**; the politicians and civil officials (**the magnates**); and the military. They, for all their power and authority, will be helpless in the face of God's wrath.

Likewise, economic status will be worth zilch. The **rich and the powerful** will be unable to bribe God or manipulate him. And social standing will be forgotten as **everyone, slave and free** (the major social distinction at that time) will be joined at last in common fear of the wrath to come. They will beg the mountains to fall on them and so hide them from the **face** of God and **from the wrath of the Lamb** (compare Hos 10:8; Luke 23:28–31).

To speak of 'the face of God' is to speak of God's presence (see Gen 4:16; Ps 95:2; Matt 18:10). To 'seek God's face' (Ps 27:8) is to gain admission to the royal presence; to 'hide from God's face' is the very opposite: to try to avoid God, dodge him, flee from him (see Jonah 1:3,10). In the presence of God, the wicked perish 'as wax melts before the fire' (Ps 68:2), whereas the righteous give thanks to him and live in his presence (Ps 140:13; see Rev 7:9–12).

The thought of God's wrath, and especially of the **wrath of the Lamb**, is a difficult one for those who want God to fit their own idea of how God should be. They don't want God to be God. However, Christians cannot avoid the truth that Jesus Christ, the *crucified* Christ, is the revelation of God in both his love and his wrath. God made him to be sin for us, and so treated him as The Sinner: God's wrath focused with laser-like sharpness on Jesus Christ, there on the cross. God did this, and Christ bore this, for us. And therein lies the revelation of his love; there in that most loveless of places we see the love of God.

The love of the Lamb is proclaimed over and over again in the gospels (although the usual word is not 'love' but 'compassion'). However, the gospels also reveal to us the Lamb as a righteous judge whose face is turned against those who reject him, seek to dethrone him, and oppress his people. The Lamb's **wrath** is not arbitrary, a blind lashing out in frustration and rage (as ours is so often). On the contrary, the **wrath of the Lamb** is his holy, righteous, steady response to sin and evil.

17 But, as the book of Revelation shows, even the exercise of divine wrath has as its goal the repentance of the sinner — until the time for repentance is finished, the 'day of salvation' (2 Cor 6:1,2) has passed, and the lines are drawn forever. That time comes on the Day of the Lord. On that day, **who is able to stand**? This fateful question is asked over and over again by the prophets who contemplated the Day (for example, Nah 1:6; Mal 3:2). The answer is given in the next two scenes, which show the people of God, sealed and safe, at worship 'before the throne and before the Lamb' (7:9,15), unafraid, unashamed, and full of joy.

7:1 The narrative which follows (7:1–8) is not an interlude nor an interruption nor a new story. It is a continuation of the narrative begun at 6:1. Specifically, it is a continuation of the account of what happened when the Lamb opened the sixth seal. He had spoken of judgment; but several times in the seal septet God's people had asked questions: How long will God wait before he shows himself to be just, right, and in charge? Who is able to survive when God pours out his wrath on an unbelieving world?

Who can stand? Who is safe? Is anyone safe from the wrath of God? Specifically, are we safe? There is a lot of evidence around today to support the thought that evil has triumphed, that God's people are naive fools, quite out of touch with reality. The world is going down the drain, and God's people with it.

The reality, God's reality, however, is that God's people always have been, always are, and always will be secure, protected, unharmed by the wrath of God. In the name of the Lamb they have fled from the God of wrath to the God of salvation, and there they are safe. This view of reality is portrayed in the continuation of the sixth seal vision in 7:1–8.

In Haggai 2:21,22 God announces:

I am about to shake the heavens and the earth, and to overthrow the throne of kingdoms; I am about to destroy the strength of the kingdoms of the nations . . .

But in verse 23 God also promises:

On that day . . .I will take you, O Zerubbabel my servant . . . and make you like a signet ring; for I have chosen you, says the LORD of hosts.

The narrative of the opening of the six seals (6:1–17) stands in the same relation to the narrative and worship described in 7:1–17 as verses 21 and 22 stand in relation to verse 23 of the second chapter of Haggai. While he is judging and destroying the wicked, God makes sure that his people are safe.

This divine concern for the safety of the church is brought out in the narrative of the four wind-angels (7:1–3). Even though, in terms of John's report, this story comes *after* the narrative of the opening of the six seals (6:1–8;12–17), in terms of John's theological and pastoral message it must be thought of as coinciding with God's acts of judgment. While seals are being opened and God's judging actions are taking place, God's people are being sealed, that is, they are being saved and kept safe. When God acts, it is to judge or to save.

So John, having reported the opening of six seals, goes back in his narrative to tell of something else he saw in the second revelation which God gave him (4:1 – 16:21). The connecting phrase, **after this**, indicates 'next' in order of the narrative, not in chronological order. What John wants to report next concerns the **four angels** whom he saw **standing at the four corners of the earth**. John follows the geography of his times when he speaks of the earth as if it were a square. According to the Old Testament, God sends winds from each corner of the earth; these winds are agents of destruction (see Jer 49:36; Dan 7:2).

2,3 The four wind-angels match the four horsemen of the first four seals (6:1–8; see Zech 6:5). But an even closer pairing is that of the four wind-angels with the 'four angels who are bound at the great river Euphrates' (9:14). The similarities between the four angels who are summoned to action after the opening of the sixth seal (7:1–3) and the four angels who move into action after the blowing of the sixth trumpet are detailed in the commentary on 9:15–17.

This pairing of angel quartets is another indication that John is reporting the same revelatory events under different symbols: the seven seals narrative and the seven trumpets narrative speak of one and the same divine judging and saving activity.

The four angels whom John saw are not permitted to go about their destructive work until the **servants of God** are securely protected. This protection was set in place by an **angel**. We are not told who this angel is, but there are indications that, as in several other places in Revelation, the 'angel' is Jesus himself (see 8:3–5;10:1–7). The evidence is as follows: The angel comes from the east, the point from which, according to Jewish tradition, the Messiah was to come. The east was also the direction from which the glory of God comes to the temple. In the New Testament, one of the messianic titles given to Jesus is The Glory (see Eph 1:17; James 2:1; 1 Pet 4:14).

Furthermore, the angel from the east is not *given* the seal of God, he *has* it. John is careful in Revelation to distinguish between what God 'has' and what he 'gives' to others. God often 'gives' divine power and authority to his agents, who act on his behalf, or who act under his direction and control. But this angel 'has' the seal of God with which to seal the servants of God.

According to the apostle Paul, the Holy Spirit is the seal of God (2 Cor 1:22; Eph 1:13; 4:30). Paul teaches that where the Spirit is, there the risen Christ is truly present among his people (2 Cor 3:17,18; 1 Cor 15:45, and note especially the interrelationship implied in Romans 8:9–11). In John's gospel, Jesus posits such a close relationship between himself and the Spirit that, even though he is absent from his disciples, his presence with them is as certain as the presence of the Spirit (John 14:16; 15:26; 16:7; compare Rom 8:9–11). In Revelation, the seal is placed upon the foreheads of the faithful; it consists of the name of the Lamb and of God (22:4; 14:1). The seal, then, has to do with the 'name', that is, the very essence, nature, and activity of Father, Son, and Holy Spirit.

All this suggests that the 'angel' who speaks with such authority to the four wind-angels not only 'has' the **seal of the living God**, but *is* himself the seal. The 'angel' here is the Lamb, the one who secured for all his people safety in the time of God's wrath, and peace for evermore (see 7:15–17).

It should be noted that, in a sick copy of the sealing of God's people, the followers of the beast also have a mark on their foreheads (13:16,17). This gives them special privileges, and distinguishes them from Christians. But it gives them no protection from the wrath of God and the Lamb; indeed, it serves to identify them as people who deserve God's wrath and punishment (19:20).

4–8 John did not *see* the host of **those who were sealed**, but he *heard* their **number**. This is the clue to interpreting verses 4–8: the focus is on what the number stands for, not on what it adds up to. According to verse 3, those who are sealed are 'the servants of God'. There are one hundred and forty-four thousand of them, **twelve thousand** from each of the tribes of Israel, except for Dan.

The people of Israel were known as the 'servants of God' (see Deut 32:36,43; Ps 79:10). Are, then, exactly one hundred and forty-four thousand Israelites preserved and protected from the wrath of God? Such a suggestion flies in the face of all of Scripture, and especially in the face of Revelation, which consistently uses numbers as symbols, not statistics.

When John recorded his vision, the 'twelve tribes of Israel' were not a physical, historical entity; the phrase was a theological construct meaning 'the people of God'. Repeatedly New Testament writers use the phrase as a synonym for 'the church' (see James 1:1; Gal 6:16; 1 Pet 2:9,10; Gal 3:29). In Revelation itself, the city of which Christians are citizens — the new Jerusalem (21:2) — has on its gates the names of the twelve tribes (21:12).

The list of the tribes in 7:4–8 is not in fact an exact list of the twelve tribes of Israel, nor does it match any other known list. Judah precedes Reuben (the oldest brother), perhaps because the new Israel is led by the Lamb, 'the Lion of the tribe of Judah' (5:5; see Gen 49:10). Dan is replaced by Manasseh, the firstborn of Joseph. The omission of Dan reflects, perhaps, a tradition that Dan marched at the edge of the people of Israel during the wilderness wanderings, and was unprotected by the 'cloud of glory'. Without divine protection they fell away, and never entered Canaan. Since the 'Exodus' theme recurs in Revelation, this explanation fits the context (see 7:15–17); it might well be the correct one.

The number, one hundred and forty-four thousand, expresses totality and completeness. It corresponds to the perfect dimensions of the wall of the new Jerusalem (one hundred and forty-four cubits, Rev 21:17). Here the number symbolises the sum total of all believers from every nation and tribe and people and language (see 7:9), who battle along in the middle of the testing and suffering and temptations to compromise which comprise life in this world. They are the church of God, the people of God, sealed, protected, authenticated as God's very own possession, his signet ring (Haggai 2:23). God's wrath and his judgment will not concern them; they are protected by the saving seal of the Lamb (see 7:2; and see the comments on 20:4–6).

WORSHIP (continued): The processional liturgy, 7:9–12

9 After this I looked, and there was a great multitude that no one could count, from every nation, from all tribes and peoples and languages, standing before the throne and before the Lamb, robed in white, with palm branches in their hands. 10 They cried out in a loud voice, saying,

'Salvation belongs to our God
who is seated on the
throne, and to the Lamb!'

11 And all the angels stood around the throne and around the elders and the four living creatures, and they fell on their faces before the throne and worshiped God, 12 singing,

'Amen! Blessing and glory and
wisdom
and thanksgiving and honor
and power and might
be to our God forever and ever!
Amen.'

The narrative which began at 6:1 was preceded by a report of heavenly worship. This worship was the dynamic for the events of the narrative. In 6:9–11 John reported that the opening of the fifth seal disclosed heavenly worship in the form of lamentation. The lament was atypical in that it lacked the usual element of praise (see comments on 6:9–11). John now makes up for that 'lack' by concluding his account of the worship scene which he had begun in 6:9–11. The great processional liturgy of 7:9–12 is the 'praise' ending of the worship begun in 6:9–11.

True worship is service of God, meaning first and foremost service by God. Worship re-establishes divine order in a chaotic universe. All divine actions in which Christians participate begin, continue, and end in worship.

In his description of heavenly worship John speaks again of one hundred and forty-four thousand. These are the same people about whom he has spoken in the narrative of 7:1–8. They celebrate as they march in procession up to new Jerusalem and into the temple of their God. The one hundred and forty-four thousand is a much larger group than the people of God on earth. John is shown the full reality of the people of God, not as we see it, but as God sees it, and as Satan knows it to be. C.S. Lewis placed these words into the mouth of a senior devil. He spoke of

> the Church as we see her spread out through all time and space and rooted in eternity, terrible as an army with banners. That, I confess, is a spectacle which makes our boldest tempters uneasy. (*The Screwtape Letters*, p 15)

John saw the church of God at worship; worship always transcends time and space (cf comments on pages 17-19).

9 Once again John says, **I looked**; that is to say: 'Here is something else I saw in the amazing revelation of everything present and future which God enabled me to see. I have to tell you that I saw the same worshipping community which I told you about in chapters 4 and 5, but I saw them walking in procession . . .' Same worship; same worshipping community; different perspective.

John did not 'hear' a symbolic number (see 7:4) but he sees an actual number, 'an enormous crowd — no one could count all the people' (TEV). Here is the statistical figure of those who are sealed, not the symbolic figure (7:4). How many are there? So many that it is impossible to count them. And, as was prefigured on the day of Pentecost (Acts 2:5–11), the people of God are made up of men and women and children **from every nation** and from every ethnic group and every linguistic family. In short, they come from every part of the world: a cosmopolitan, multicultural, multilingual multitude (see 5:9).

The worshipping community is **constantly standing before the throne and before the Lamb**. Unlike the enemies of God who try to flee from his presence and hide themselves from him (6:15,16), the people of God 'come into his presence with thanksgiving and . . . make a joyful noise to him with songs of praise' (Ps 95:2). Already now they spend their lives in the presence of God and of the Lamb.

They can stand in such a position without fear because, like the Exodus people of old at Sinai (Exod 19:10), they wear **white robes** of purity and righteousness, made for them by Christ. And just as Israel of old celebrated the Exodus event at the Feast of Tabernacles with ceremonies which included the waving of palm branches and the reciting of Psalm 118, so the new people of God celebrate their Exodus, their deliverance, salvation, and lasting shelter in God's presence (7:15;21:3) with a heavenly Feast of Tabernacles. They ascribe salvation to **God** and to **the Lamb** (see Ps 118:25; John 12:13).

Salvation should be understood in its fullest sense, as is done especially in the Old Testament (for example, Ps 18:27,28;22:19–21;69:1,2). Salvation is not only deliverance from sin and death and other evils of body and soul; it is not only security and protection from the wrath of God; but it also has to do with the quality of life, the fullness of the life of those who stand continually in the presence of the living God (7:9). Salvation includes the restoration of relationships, a putting-back-together-again of things as they should be. Salvation is God saying 'Good, very good' once more over his creation.

11,12 When the people of God are at worship, it is not only those on earth who are worshipping. The acclamation which is repeatedly offered to God and the Lamb by the palm-waving procession draws a shout of agreement (**Amen!**) from '**angels** and archangels and all the company of heaven'. They 'threw themselves face downward in front of the throne, and worshipped God' (TEV).

Their song of praise consists of seven ascriptions, all of which were featured in the worship described in chapters 4 and 5. In the Greek, each word is emphasised by putting a 'the' in front of it: 'To our God be *the* blessing and *the* glory and *the* wisdom . . .' The meaning is that if there is any glory it belongs to God, if there is any wisdom it comes from God, and so forth. Even salvation, which those involved in the imperial cult said was found in the Roman emperor, comes from God. The sevenfold doxology denotes completeness; all there is belongs to God:

For from him and through him and to him are all things. To him be the glory forever. Amen. (Rom 11:36)

The concluding **Amen!** expresses the fervent desire and hope of the worshipping community for the complete realisation in the future of that which they confess now in their worship. This is taken up in the next stage of John's report. It is a dialogue narrative, in which the worship scene of 7:9–12 is commented on and a picture of God's future is painted for John and his hearers to imprint on their hearts.

Before we leave the worship scene of 7:9–12, an important point needs to be repeated. This report of the victorious people of God, celebrating life and salvation around the throne of God, is the completion of the report of worship which began in 6:9–11. There John recorded a lamentation in which the people of God asked the 'Why?' question. In 7:9–12 the worshipping community answers its own question as it praises God for the liberation and rescue he has achieved for them.

Here is comfort and assurance for Christians who experience oppression and injustice of a political, social, or economic kind. Things will not always be as they are now; indeed, God has sown the seeds of change; he is making all things new (21:5). Wait for it!

In the fight against *apartheid* in South Africa, Archbishop Desmond Tutu has testified to the sustaining power of this vision of God's victorious and liberated people celebrating in the full dignity of children of God.

DIALOGUE NARRATIVE: 'Who are these, clothed in white?' 7:13–17

13 Then one of the elders addressed me, saying, 'Who are these, robed in white, and where have they come from?' 14 I said to him, 'Sir, you are the one that knows.' Then he said to me, 'These are they who have come out of the great ordeal; they have washed their robes and made them white in the blood of the Lamb.

15 For this reason they are before the
throne of God,
and worship him day and night
within his temple,
and the one who is seated on
the throne will shelter
them.
16 They will hunger no more, and
thirst no more;
the sun will not strike them,
nor any scorching heat;
17 for the Lamb at the centre of the
throne will be their
shepherd,
and he will guide them to
springs of the water of life,
and God will wipe away every
tear from their eyes.'

13,14 John uses the occasional dialogue narrative to keep his story moving, or to set the stage for the next scene, or to explain and interpret a previous scene (see comments on pages 105-6). Here it is important to John that his hearers are clear about the realities, both present and future, which were revealed in the scene of heavenly worship (7:9–12). So he repeats a conversation that he had with **one of the elders** (see 4:10). All the time, John must have been full of questions, just as we are as we become involved in John's experience through reading aloud his report in the context of worship. In this instance an **elder** anticipates John's question by asking one of his own — a familiar game between teacher and student. John knows how to play; he immediately bats the ball back into the elder's court: 'Sir, you know the answer to your own question; now please teach me, help me to be sure that I have properly understood what I've seen'. And so the elder explains.

Where have those who are robed in white come from? They are characterised as people who are coming **out of the great ordeal**. They have not merely *passed through* the great ordeal, but they have their origins, their roots, in the great ordeal, just as the new Jerusalem is characterised as always 'coming down from heaven', that is, having its roots and origin in God.

The **great ordeal** is the afflictions, troubles, tensions, stresses, testing which Christians experience because they are followers of the Lamb who was slain. The **great ordeal** is the evidence for the presence of the kingdom of God in the world. That is how God works: he reveals victory and lordship in the midst of tribulation and patient endurance (1:9). The cross is a throne; power is revealed in weakness. If you split these divine pairings, you conceal the view of reality which God wants us to have: victory, salvation, and life is in the Lamb who was slaughtered, not in the emperor or any other human or demonic power.

The paradoxical nature of the realities of Christian existence is heightened by the elder's statement explaining how the multitudes got their white robes: **they have washed** them, whitened them, **in the blood of the Lamb**. How can red blood make robes white? The riddle is solved when we remember that, according to the Scriptures, sin makes people and things unclean. Sin pollutes. If anyone is to stand in the presence of the holy God they must be cleansed. Strangely enough, the Old Testament sacrifices and ceremonies provided for the use of blood (itself a pollutant) to symbolise purification from sin (Lev 8:14–30;14:6–8; compare Isa 1:16–20; Haggai 2:10–19).

The purification rituals of the old covenant, however, pointed to Christ, and received their power from his death. He is the Lamb Who Was Slain, the Son of God whose blood 'purifies us from every sin' (1 John 1:7 NIV; compare Rev 1:5;5:9).

15 Freshly washed and cleansed (Eph 5:26,27), and wearing the white robes of purity provided by the shameful, sin-laden, sacrificial, self-polluting death of Christ, Christians are fit to stand **before the throne of God** (that is, in his presence) and do what they do every day of their lives: **worship him** (Rom 12:1–3).

To describe this life of worship, present and future, John draws on the Exodus image of God's people being kept safe during their journeyings, and he links this image with another, that of life in the new Jerusalem. God's saved and redeemed people spend their days **within his temple**, and there God spreads his 'tent' over them, he shelters them with his presence, just as he always has done with his people (see Zech 2:10; Isa 4:5,6; Psalm 91).

16 Life in the temple, safe in the shelter which God provides, is like that idyllic existence which was promised to the exiled people of God in Babylon:

They shall not hunger or thirst, neither scorching wind nor sun shall strike them down, for he who has pity on them will lead them, and by springs of water will guide them. (Isa 49:10)

The salvation, which is a present possession of God's people but whose fullness they await, is described as the absence of **hunger** and **thirst** and of any physical hardship or deprivation — the very opposite, in fact, of whatever was experienced in the 'great ordeal' in which the people of God were formed as his people (7:14).

17 The reason for this wonderful state of affairs is that **the Lamb at the centre of the throne** (see 5:6), the Lamb Who Was Slain and who gave up his life for his sheep (John 10:11,28), **will be their shepherd**. Here is another startling combination, like that of the Lion and the Lamb of chapter 5. Whoever heard of a lamb leading a flock of sheep! Lambs frolic and gambol; they do not act as shepherds and leaders of the flock.

But Jesus Christ is indeed the Lamb who guides his flock to **springs of the water of life**, and feeds them with the bread of life, precisely by dying and becoming the Lamb Who Was Slain (see John 4:14;6:51;7:37,38). That is why the Lamb came into the world: that his sheep 'may have life, and have it abundantly' (John 10:10). When this abundant life is fully entered, then there will be no more pain and sorrow, no grief and heartache. No more tears. **God** himself will see to that.

So the people of God are safe. In this life their safety and security is a faith-conviction rather than something that can be demonstrated. The people of God are a people on the way, a people 'coming out of the great ordeal' (7:14). But their health and wholeness, their salvation, is a reality which interprets all their earthly experiences. In the end, when the new heaven and new earth which God is creating are unveiled (21:1–5), then the Christian's safety and security will be both an experienced and a seen reality.

Where have we been? Where are we going?

John began his account of what he saw and heard in the second revelation (4:1 – 16:21) with a magnificent throne-room scene in the heavenly temple. He told of God who sits on the throne, of the Lamb who was slain, and of the worship which takes place 'day and night' around the throne of God (4:1 – 5:14).

John also told the story of the divine judging and saving activities which this heavenly worship set in train. To tell the story he used the image of a book (scroll) which was sealed with seven seals. If this book remains sealed, then Christians have no hope, for sin and evil and the triumph of Satan would be God's last word to us. If this book remains sealed, then there is no sense in talking about the human condition and rescue from that condition, for there is no rescue. Then Alan Moir's question, 'Why do people behave like this?' can best be answered by the sociologists and behavioural scientists. Theology has no answer. Alan Moir's explanation is as good as any: blame it on the violent videos.

Alan Moir, *The Sydney Morning Herald*

But the Lamb who was slain has changed the whole course of human history. He went to the heart of the human condition, took it upon himself, experienced the emptiness of life without God, paid the penalty for humanity's rejection of God, and changed the whole pattern of human existence. He gave it a goal and a purpose which means life, not death.

Because the Lamb did this, he is worthy, and he has the authority to execute divine judgment and divine salvation. This is what John speaks of in his narrative of the Lamb opening the seals of the scroll (6:1 – 7:8).

This same divine activity is pictured again in John's account of the blowing of seven trumpets (8:6 - 11:15). Repetition is the mother of learning. People who cannot read, and can only listen to a reader, need stories to be repeated in order to grasp the message fully.

The narrative of the seven trumpet blasts is set in the context of worship. It is preceded by worship (8:1-5) and it ends with worship (11:15–19). Thus John's hearers are reminded that when they pray, sing hymns, and proclaim the Word, they are participating in divine service.

THE SEVENTH SEAL WORSHIP: Liturgy of intercession, 8:1–5

**8 When the Lamb opened the seventh seal, there was
silence in heaven for about half an hour. 2 And I saw the
seven angels who stand before God, and seven trumpets
were given to them.**

**3 Another angel with a golden censer came and stood
at the altar; he was given a great quantity of incense to
offer with the prayers of all the saints on the golden altar
that is before the throne. 4 And the smoke of the incense,
with the prayers of the saints, rose before God from the
hand of the angel. 5 Then the angel took the censer and
filled it with fire from the altar and threw it on the earth;
and there were peals of thunder, rumblings, flashes of
lightning, and an earthquake.**

When the **seventh seal** is opened, there is no narrative action. John has nothing to narrate. In fact, no-one anywhere has anything to say. There is simply **silence in heaven**. This silence is, as we shall see, the beginning of worship. The opening of the seventh seal, like the opening of the fifth seal (6:9–11), discloses heavenly worship, worship which begins with silence.

This silence is awesome. The four living creatures who praise God 'without ceasing' (4:8); the white-robed chorus who worship God 'day and night' in his temple (7:15); the myriad angels who worship before the throne (7:11); the thunder and lightning (4:5) — all are silent before the Lord (compare Zech 2:13; Hab 2:20).

What is the meaning of this heavenly silence? Among the many answers which have been given, the following warrant careful consideration:

1) The silence signals that the seals narrative is complete; it prepares the hearer for the next narrative event: the seven trumpets. 'It is as though there is one bar's rest for the whole orchestra and choir of heaven before they launch into the second of John's symphonic variations' (Caird).

2) The silence in heaven means that 'God is listening to us, to our prayers, groans, helpless cries' (Krodel). In the heavenly worship the prayers of the saints rise before God with the smoke of incense; heaven is hushed so that the prayers of *all* the saints may be heard before the throne of God.

3) The silence corresponds to the 'time of prayer' (Luke 1:10) in the ritual of the daily sacrifice in the temple; it came between the pouring of the blood at the base of the altar (see Rev 6:9) and the burnt and drink offerings which were accompanied by the blowing of trumpets (see 8:2).

All these suggestions have something to commend them, especially the last two. The view taken in this commentary is that the **silence in heaven** is to be explained by the pattern of the book. Dramatic narration and heavenly liturgy belong together. Heavenly worship is both the launching pad and the climax of the story which is told, the events which occur. The opening of the seventh seal leads to no dramatic narration. Instead, the hearers are left to contemplate what is *not* narrated: the final judging and saving actions of God on the Last Day. This impressive, pregnant, narrative silence is matched by liturgical silence.

Liturgical silence is worship. Here, it is the opening act in the worship which is described in 8:1–5. Such silence has about it a sacramental quality; by it the worshippers wait on God to speak and act when humans have reached the limits of speech. 'Silence is God's friend', said Mother Teresa. Silence speaks when speech is beyond us. Sometimes, as we contemplate the work of our God in creation and redemption we are so 'lost in wonder, love and praise' that we are speechless: we can't find words to express our feelings of awe and adoration.

Geoffrey Wainwright, in *The Study of Liturgy*, summed up this situation well when he wrote:

> The language of adoration pays homage to the surpassing majesty of God and sings his amazing love for his creatures and his unexampled grace for sinners. At times, adoration will pass over the linguistic horizon into eloquent silence. (467)

The time span — **about half an hour** — probably indicates a period which is relatively short (one twenty-fourth of a natural day), and yet long enough to impress those who are listening to the divine drama, long enough for all of John's hearers to ponder deeply on the events in which they are caught up as they listen to John's account.

The scene is set in heaven, viewed as a temple corresponding to Solomon's temple. John reports that he **saw the seven angels who stand before God**. The definite article 'the' suggests that John has in mind a definite group of seven angels. In Revelation, the only seven angels who have been spoken of previously are the angels of the seven churches. These angels, identified in this commentary as the prophet-leaders of the congregations, certainly 'stood before God' as they led their people in worship, adoration, and praise of God. Perhaps the **seven angels** here are to be seen as the heavenly counterparts of the seven angels of the churches. Since these are the angels who blow the trumpets which set in motion God's judging and saving activity, this might well be John's way of emphasising the truth that the church, through its worship, participates in God's work of judgment and salvation.

This point is developed in the next verses. They tell of how the high-priestly angel takes the censer filled with the prayers of God's people, mixes them with the incense which God has given him, adds fire from the altar, and then throws the censer on the earth. With this dramatic action the angel signifies that God is present, and that the actions which follow on the blowing of the trumpets are all divine actions in which the people of God participate.

Subsequent development of the same theme occurs in 15:5–8, where John again introduces *the* seven angels. These are dressed as royal priests; they are given golden bowls, filled with the wrath of God.

To each of the seven angels who **stand before** him as servants (see 1 Kings 17:1;18:15; 2 Kings 3:14) God gives a trumpet. Throughout this book, God's action of 'giving' is always worthy of special notice. Here he gives each angel a trumpet. This means that the plagues and the deliverance which take place when the trumpets are blown are all part of God's judging and saving activity; all are from him.

The blowing of **trumpets** is not part of the liturgy of intercession. John's hearers might have expected the trumpets to be blown, given the strong association which in the Old Testament and Judaism trumpets had with worship. Trumpets were blown at all Jewish feasts, at the daily sacrifice, and on the first day of each month. Most significant was the sounding of the trumpet on the first day of the seventh month (*Tishri*), the start of the penitential season, which concluded on the tenth day with the great Day of Atonement.

The rabbis regarded this ten-day period as a preview of the Day of the Lord and the last judgment. Not surprisingly, then, the New Testament tends to associate trumpets with the return of Christ to judgment and the recognition of God as sovereign Lord (Matt 24:31; 1 Thess 4:16,17).

Here the trumpets take part in the worship service by observing the silence with which the liturgy had begun.

3,4 The heavenly worship continues when another unidentified **angel** approaches the altar. Who is this angel? He is not one of the seven to whom God gave the trumpets (8:2). And yet he leads the worship of the saints, and he has a mediatorial role: the prayers of the worshippers come to God **from the hand of the angel**. The worship which this angel leads sets in motion the events of the trumpet septet. The same thing happened when the Lamb opened the seven seals in the context of heavenly worship (4:8-5:14; 6:9-11;7:9–12).

John calls this priest-angel 'another angel' (see 7:2 and comments). Could this angel who acts as a priest, leads the people in worship, and brings their prayers and petitions before God — could this angel be the Lord Jesus? According to the letter to the Hebrews, this 'angel' *can* be none other than Jesus Christ, for he and he alone is the only high priest of the new covenant who ministers in the Holy of Holies (Heb 8:1,2). This truth, which is summarised in the phrase, 'worship in the name of Jesus', is developed in detail by the writer of Hebrews (see Heb 2:11-18;7:25;8:1-3; 9:19-25;10:19-25).

In sum: the angel-priest in 8:1–5 is the Lamb Who Was Slain. He leads his people in worship. If it seems strange that Christ should be the one who is worshipped and the one who worships, consider a further mystery: God 'gives' Christ a **great quantity of incense** which he in turn offers back to God (for the significance of God 'giving', see commentary on 6:2 and 13:5). The importance of this notice cannot be overstressed. It points to God's seminal participation in worship. The Lord gathers people together; the Lord leads the divine service. Worship is always the result of God's initiative.

Swiss theologian Karl Barth expressed this truth well when he wrote:

> The church service is in the first instance . . . divine action . . . What a human being can and should do here is to serve. That this service is *divine* service is something which is brought about not by people but by God and God alone. It is *God* who wills that divine service be held. It is *God* who provides the media suitable for it. It is *God* who bears witness through them to his grace. It is *God* who by this means awakens, purifies and advances faith. All along the line it is God and not us. (*The Knowledge of God and the Service of God*, p 192)

God, then, provides the incense for the liturgy of intercession which his Son leads. Without this incense no act of worship would take place, for the **smoke of the incense** is the means by which the **prayers of all the saints**, which have been mixed with the incense, come to God.

In faith Christians pray at Vespers:

> Let my prayer be counted as incense before you:
> And the lifting up of my hands
> as an evening sacrifice.

John records how well that faith is grounded in reality: the prayers of the saints are placed on the **golden altar** which is **before the throne**. This can only be the altar of incense. In Solomon's temple it was made of cedar and overlaid with gold. It belonged to the Holy of Holies (1 Kings 6:22[RV]; Heb 9:3,4), but it stood in the Holy

Place, presumably to make possible the offering of *daily* sacrifices.

On the **golden altar** of incense the **prayers of the saints** are like glowing coals upon which Christ the priest sprinkles the granules of **incense** supplied by God himself. From Christ's **hand**, then, the intercessions of the saints come to God, for Jesus himself is **before God**. The fact that worship takes place in the presence of God is emphasised in these verses by the repetition of the phrase 'before God'. The seven angels are said to stand before God; the angel-priest (Christ) who leads the worship is said to stand before God. God is not absent from worship; all true worship takes place in his presence.

Another phrase which is used in these verses is 'before the throne'. To speak of the 'throne' in Revelation is to speak of God himself. So, 'before the throne' means 'before God'. The followers of the Lamb are often said to be 'before the throne' (for example, 7:9,11,15; 11:16;14:3,5). That simply means that they are in God's presence (see 20:12). That is where God's people worship; worship brings them into the presence of God. This truth is expressed in the beautiful picture of **the prayers of the saints** being placed on the **golden altar that is before the throne** of God.

In Solomon's temple, the ark of the covenant with the mercy seat above it was regarded as God's **throne**. In New Testament times, the ark was absent; the Holy of Holies was empty except for the rock upon which the ark was said to have rested. A censer with smoking incense was placed on this stone in the Holy of Holies, which was kept in total darkness.

In the heavenly temple, however, all is light. Jesus the great High Priest brings the prayers of his people to God, for he stands before God, just as the altar upon which he offers the prayers stands before the throne of God.

5 The awesome power of prayer is indicated by the action of the angel in throwing the prayer-filled censer **on the earth**: immediately there is a dramatic display of God's power and presence. The **thunder** and noise and **lightning** and **earthquake** summon up memories of Sinai, but the purpose here is to herald the divine activity which will take place when the trumpets are blown. All this happens as a consequence of the prayers of intercession of the saints. As in the seal septet (5:8;6:9–11), so here the church on earth and in heaven asks God to vindicate them and to reveal himself in judgment and mercy. Prayer might seem to be a lonely exercise of faith; in reality, it is part of the worship of heaven, and prayer 'in the name of Jesus' is not without effect (see James 5:16–18). In tune with the intercessory worship of the saints, God judges and saves, as the narrative of the trumpet septet depicts so vividly.

NARRATIVE: The five trumpets are sounded, 8:6 – 9:12

[6] Now the seven angels who had the seven trumpets made ready to blow them.

[7] The first angel blew his trumpet, and there came hail and fire, mixed with blood, and they were hurled to the earth; and a third of the earth was burned up, and a third of the trees were burned up, and all green grass was burned up.

**[8] The second angel blew his trumpet, and something
like a great mountain, burning with fire, was thrown into
the sea. [9] A third of the sea became blood, a third of the
living creatures in the sea died, and a third of the ships
were destroyed.**

**[10] The third angel blew his trumpet, and a great star
fell from heaven, blazing like a torch, and it fell on a
third of the rivers and on the springs of water. [11] The
name of the star is Wormwood. A third of the waters
became wormwood, and many died from the water,
because it was made bitter.**

[12] The fourth angel blew his trumpet, and a third of the sun was struck, and a third of the moon, and a third of the stars, so that a third of their light was darkened; a third of the day was kept from shining, and likewise the night.

13 Then I looked, and I heard an eagle crying with a
loud voice as it flew in midheaven, 'Woe, woe, woe to the
inhabitants of the earth, at the blasts of the other trumpets
that the three angels are about to blow!'
9 And the fifth angel blew his trumpet, and I saw a star
that had fallen from heaven to earth, and he was given
the key to the shaft of the bottomless pit; 2 he opened
the shaft of the bottomless pit, and from the shaft rose
smoke like the smoke of a great furnace, and the sun and
the air were darkened with the smoke from the shaft.
3 Then from the smoke came locusts on the earth, and
they were given authority like the authority of scorpions
of the earth. 4 They were told not to damage the grass of
the earth or any green growth or any tree, but only those
people who do not have the seal of God on their
foreheads. 5 They were allowed to torture them for five
months, but not to kill them, and their torture was like
the torture of a scorpion when it stings someone. 6 And
in those days people will seek death but will not find it;
they will long to die, but death will flee from them.

7 In appearance the locusts were like horses equipped
for battle. On their heads were what looked like crowns
of gold; their faces were like human faces, 8 their hair
like women's hair, and their teeth like lions' teeth; 9 they
had scales like iron breastplates, and the noise of their
wings was like the noise of many chariots with horses
rushing into battle. 10 They have tails like scorpions, with
stingers, and in their tails is their power to harm people
for five months. 11 They have as king over them the angel
of the bottomless pit; his name in Hebrew is Abaddon,[v]
and in Greek he is called Apollyon.[w]

12 The first woe has passed. There are still two woes to
come.

[v] That is, *Destruction*

[w] That is, *Destroyer*

The opening of the seven seals (6:1 – 8:1) was preceded and concluded by heavenly worship. The clear message was: the events which occur with the opening of the various seals are to be seen as divinely directed actions.

Hence Christian worship is to be addressed only to 'the one who sits on the throne and to the Lamb' (5:13).

Since in many ways the seal septet is paralleled by the trumpet septet, it is not surprising that the sounding of the seven trumpets is both preceded and succeeded by heavenly worship (8:1–5 and 11:15–19). Furthermore, in both septets the sixth seal and sixth trumpet disclose God's judging activity and God's care for, and protection of, his people (6:12–17 and 7:1–8; 9:13–21 and 10:1–11:13). And just as the opening of the seventh seal issued not in narrative but in worship (8:1–5), so does the sounding of the seventh trumpet (11:15–19).

Finally, it should be noted that although the trumpet septet looks back to the seal septet, it also looks forward to the bowl septet (16:1–21). Both the trumpets and the bowls narratives are reminders of the Egyptian plagues: all who have ears to hear should know that God executes his judgments in order to deliver his people. Christians are to view the realities of their situation through the wide-angle lens which God provides in this marvellous revelation to John.

6 The report of heavenly liturgy is finished. The report is finished, but not the liturgy. It is ongoing ('without ceasing', 'day and night'). It forms the soil, the context, the background music if you will, for the events which John narrates. He reports scenes of heavenly worship, not because they come and go, but because worship is always there: whatever he saw in the revelation, he heard always in worship. So it is in the context of worship that the **seven angels** prepare to **blow** the trumpets which God had given them (8:2).

Of the events which occur with the blowing of the six trumpets, the first four touch the sources of human life; the fifth and sixth affect people directly, and are identified with demonic forces. The report of the blowing of the seventh trumpet is followed by another account of heavenly worship.

John uses the paradigm of the Egyptian plagues to describe the events which follow on the blowing of the trumpets and the pouring out of the bowls. The parallel lies not in the fact that the church was oppressed as Israel was oppressed, but in that the Egyptian plagues marked the beginning of the deliverance of God's people.

Furthermore, the Egyptian plagues did not harm the people of Israel (compare Rev 7:1–8;9:4), and they were limited in their effect. Their purpose was to pierce the hard heart of Pharaoh and his people, and to induce them to change their minds and attitudes. In the same way, God's purpose in the trumpet blasts is to sound the warning of the impending judgment, and call the world to repentance (compare Amos 4:6). The fact that only a third of the world is affected shows that the trumpet events are a warning, just as every sickness is a little death, a reminder of the future awaiting us all.

7 The trumpet blast of the **first angel** brings disasters which resemble the effects of the seventh Egyptian plague (Exod 9:22–26) and the fourth and seventh bowls (Rev 16:8,9,19–21). There is 'fiery hail' (a better translation than **hail and fire**) which is **mixed with blood**, either in the sense that the colour of the hail was a blood-red (compare Joel 2:30), or that the result of God's act of hurling the fiery hail **to earth** was that blood was shed. Certainly the effect is cosmic in its devastation: **a third of the earth** and of the trees was **burned up**, together with all green grass. Scorched earth, as Napoleon — and the people of Vietnam — learnt, supports no life.

The fiery hail and the ecological disasters which followed call to mind our acid rain, the fallout from Chernobyl, and the other consequences of our exploitation of the environment for our selfish ends. We reap what we sow. But it would be wrong to say that only now are we feeling the effect of the first trumpet blast. The 'fiery hail mixed with blood' is a symbol for every kind of disaster which damages our natural environment.

8,9 When **the second angel blew his trumpet**, God caused **something like a great** burning **mountain** to be **thrown into the sea**. Since John is not here describing 'natural' happenings but an act of God, our focus, like his, should be on the effect not the cause (what kind of mountain-mass could create such havoc?). The effect is that **a third** of the world's seas turned to **blood** and a

third of all marine life **died**. The parallel with the first Egyptian plague is obvious (Exod 7:20,21).

This trumpet blast, like the first, damages the natural environment. But the addition of the words, 'a third of the ships were destroyed', suggests that the damage was not only environmental but also commercial (see 18:9–19). The **sea** (= the Mediterranean Sea) was the economic backbone of the Roman empire. Cripple the merchant fleet and you cripple Rome (see the comments on 18:9–19 for remarks on Rome's vast import network).

Even if the reference here is primarily commercial, the parallel with the Egyptian plague still holds, for the turning of the Nile to blood would have meant economic ruin for the Egyptians. As an aside we can note that it is curious that after the Lord's attack on the economic system of the temple Matthew records a saying concerning the throwing of a mountain into the sea (Matt 21:12–22).

10,11 The **third angel** causes a **third** of the earth's drinking water to become undrinkable and even poisonous. He does this by causing a **great** burning **star** to fall from **heaven**. The star is named **Wormwood**. No known star had or has that name; presumably it was so named for its poisonous effects.

The fall of a star seems to be an echo of the lament of the king of Babylon: 'How you are fallen from heaven, O Day Star, son of Dawn!' (Isa 14:12). Babylon and all those who share in her idolatry have poisoned their own drinking water and brought about their own destruction (compare Amos 5:6,7;6:12). That is to say, the consequences of the perversion of justice and the worship of false gods, including the imperial cult, is that God '[feeds] this people with wormwood, and [gives] them poisonous water to drink' (Jer 9:15).

This third plague has no parallel in the Exodus plagues, nor in the bowl septet. It is, perhaps, to be thought of as the reverse of the miracle at Marah (Exod 15:25), which took place after Israel had been rescued from Egypt and from the threat of Pharaoh's army.

12 The **fourth** trumpet blast had terrifying repercussions in the functioning of the heavenly bodies:

for one-third of the day and one-third of the night there was no light of any kind (compare Amos 8:9; Isa 13:10; Mark 13:24). Darkness was the last 'nature' plague to hit the Egyptians (Exod 10:21–29). It signals the time of demonic activity (see John 13:30) and the return of chaos (Gen 1:2). It is one of the things which will be 'no more' when the new heaven and new earth are unveiled (Rev 21:25;22:5).

To be in darkness is to be without God (see 'outer darkness', Matt 8:11,12;25:30). This fourth plague, which is only partial in its effects, is a preview of the total, perpetual darkness which is already now characteristic of the ungodly (Rom 1:21; Eph 4:18;5:11), and which will be theirs forever unless they repent — something which, alas, Pharaoh did not do.

13 In the seal cycle (6:1–17), the first four seals formed a single group. The trumpet cycle follows the same pattern. John indicates a break between the first four trumpets, which devastated the physical and economic environment, and the next three trumpet blasts, which will heap **woe** upon woe on those who 'do not have the seal of God on their foreheads' (9:4), that is, upon the stubborn and rebellious 'inhabitants of the earth', as John usually calls the worshippers of the dragon and his offsiders.

The triple 'woe' is a warning of impending judgment; the woes are addressed to all those who, like Chorazin, Bethsaida, and Capernaum, refuse to acknowledge God even when his judging and saving activities are done before their very eyes (see Matt 11:21–24). 'Watch out!', the woes say, 'the last lot of plagues are going to be even worse than the first'.

The threefold 'woe' is announced by a lone **eagle** which circles in the sky in plain view of all, up there where the sun reaches its highest point at noon. The bird might have been an **eagle** or a vulture (see Hos 8:1; Luke 17:37). 'Wherever the corpse is, there the vultures will gather', said Jesus concerning the coming of the Son of Man (Matt 24:28). The meaning of that proverbial saying is: Where there are sinners, there judgment from heaven will not be far behind.

The context, then, suggests that what John saw and heard was a vulture, a bird which everyone associates with death and decay. The alternative view is to see here 'an ironic reversal of an Exodus image. Yahweh bore the Israelites 'on eagles' wings' (Exod 19:4) . . . Hovering over prey that will soon be dead, the eagle is an ironic symbol of the inevitability of calamities to come' (Krodel).

9:1 The gods are just, and of our pleasant vices
Make instruments to plague us.

Shakespeare was echoing Solomon, who is reported to have said that 'the instruments of people's sin are the instruments of their punishment'. Both wise men have captured the central message of the ninth chapter of Revelation.

In this chapter John shows how ugly and horrible evil is. He does this for the sake of those who are dazzled by the things of Satan. John's purpose in Revelation is pastoral. He wants to present the facts of life so vividly that no-one will mistake that which masquerades as the real thing for the reality which is found in God alone. Chapter nine, then, is another exposé of Satan and all his forces.

When the **fifth angel blew his trumpet**, John **saw** 'a Star which had dropped from heaven to earth' (Moffatt). This star is an angel (see 1:20). The fact that it had **fallen from heaven** does not in itself mean that it was a 'bad' angel. 'Fallen' is used in a moral sense only once in Revelation (2:5). Good or evil, this angel is God's agent: to him God gives **the key to the shaft** which connects the earth to **the bottomless pit**, that is, the Abyss, the place where evil spirits live. Here is in-the-Spirit geography (4:2), the geography one becomes aware of when one moves outside of space and time, as John did.

The Greek Old Testament uses the word 'abyss' (**bottomless pit**) to translate the Hebrew word for the primeval Ocean, the personified Deep (Gen 1:2;7:11). The 'abyss' was thought of as a monster, crouching beneath the foundations of the earth (Deut 33:13). The crossing of the Red Sea made the Lord's name glorious, because he led his people through the monster as one leads a horse to pasture (Isa 63:13). The 'abyss' (**bottomless pit**) and the 'sea' are the same place.

2,3 When the star-angel unlocks the Abyss, a huge swarm of **locusts** fly up, like smoke from the belching chimney of a factory furnace. So huge and thick is the swarm that it darkens the **sun and the air** (see 8:12; Joel 2:10). There are echoes here of the sixth and eighth Egyptian plagues (Exod 9:8,9;10:12-20). The eighth plague is given a cosmic interpretation in Joel 1: on the great Day of the Lord a huge army of locusts leads the attack on 'all the inhabitants of the earth' (Joel 1:2).

4,5 The swarm of locusts, headed by Apollyon (see v 11), are not ordinary beasts, eating vegetation as real locusts do. They are, in fact, expressly forbidden to damage **the grass of the earth or any green growth or any tree**. Plant life is not to be harmed; that means that human life will still be sustainable. So the locusts are permitted ('allowed') to use their scorpion-like tails with 'stingers' (v 10) to **torture** people, **but not to kill them**.

Furthermore, a time limit is placed on their activity: **five months**, which is the normal life span of a locust. One further important restriction concerns the safety of God's people. In Egypt, the plagues did not touch the people of Israel (Exod 8:22;9:4;10:23). Now those with 'the seal of God on their foreheads' (see comments on 7:3) are safe, unlike those who were misled into having the mark of the beast placed on their foreheads (13:16,17; see also 14:9–11; 16:2–21).

The torment or the **torture** which the locust-demons inflict is not described in detail: it is simply said to be like the **torture of a scorpion when it stings someone**. But we don't need a description; it is all around us all the time. And in case we miss it, our TVs and newspapers and novels portray it all in lurid detail: the grim wages of chemical addiction; the dehumanising effects of modern technology; the sexual promiscuity and the mockery of marriage ('I now pronounce you pair-bonded for as long as your relationship remains mutually nourishing'); the child abuse and killing of embryos; the manic drive for success; the worship of money and power, status and leisure, sport and possessions.

If these things have any attraction at all, they surely lose their fatal fascination when we see what John saw: the ugly face of evil in all its forms.

6 The consequence? In his sovereign freedom God hands people over (Rom 1:24,26,28) to experience the results of their own rebellion. Albert Camus was right when he warned: 'Don't wait for the Last Judgment. It takes place every day.' So great is the torment, that people wish they were dead, but death keeps on eluding them. Life would be an eternity of hell if God in his mercy did not limit the suffering ('five months'). His purpose is not death, but life. He seeks not rebellion, but repentance (see 9:20).

7–10 Since the locusts represent demonic hordes, evil stripped of any attractive dress, it is not surprising that John describes them as bizarre, grotesque, repulsive creatures, horrors straight out of Hieronymus Bosch. They are long-haired, scaly, winged insects, shaped and equipped like war horses. They wear what seem to be **crowns of gold**, like great kings, or like the priests of the imperial cult who wore golden crowns inscribed with the imperial image. Sometimes these crowns displayed a dozen or so cameos of the emperor and his family.

These creatures, who seem to spring from the nightmares of the most imaginative of Hollywood's visual-effects artist, have faces like **human faces**, dominated by great protruding lion's fangs. A horrifying sight! But the most horrifying part is that these creatures *have human faces.* The worst evils in this world are perpetrated by people. And this human wrongdoing 'returns with demonic venom to torment either its perpetrators or his [her] associates or descendants' (Caird).

11 The focus on the evil which humanity generates is sharpened by the reminder that these are not ordinary locusts: locusts 'have no king', says the proverb (Prov 30:27). But these locusts do. He is a personal being; he is **the angel of the bottomless pit**. That is to say, he is the very personification, representative, and symbol of all that the bottomless pit is and stands for (contrast: 'the angel of the church at . . .' 2:1,8). He has a name: **Abaddon**. In Hebrew the name means 'destruction'; in Greek the name is **Apollyon**, which means 'the destroyer'.

The Greek **Apollyon** is not an accurate translation of the Hebrew **Abaddon**. Perhaps John chose this name to get people thinking of the god Apollo, one of whose symbols was the locust. What an irony! Your god rewards you by tormenting you and destroying you. The irony might be even greater: the emperors Caligula and Nero both mimicked the god Apollo. If this is what John had in mind, then he is reminding his hearers in a most dramatic way of two important truths: first, evil always destroys itself. This fact is developed at length in the third revelation (17:1 - 21:9). Secondly, the emperor, and all civil authorities for that matter, can only exercise the power which God gives them; they have no power and no authority in and of themselves. For, John says, the locusts **were given authority** (v 3). That is to say, God gave it to them (see Pilate, John 19:11).

12 With the appearance and activities of the beast, summoned by the blowing of the fifth trumpet, the **first woe** announced by the vulture ('eagle', 8:13) **has passed. Two** are yet **to come**. The second is announced after the events described in 9:13 – 11:13, and just before the blowing of the seventh trumpet. The third woe is never identified in this trumpet series, because instead of the third woe, which is expected with the blowing of the last trumpet, John records a further scene of heavenly worship (11:15–19 and comments).

The function of the announcement of the three woes is to form a link between the trumpet cycle (8:6-11:15) and the bowl cycle (16:1–21).

NARRATIVE: The sixth trumpet is sounded, 9:13–21

13 **Then the sixth angel blew his trumpet, and I heard a voice from the four**[x] **horns of the golden altar before God,** 14 **saying to the sixth angel who had the trumpet, 'Release the four angels who are bound at the great river Euphrates.'** 15 **So the four angels were released, who had been held ready for the hour, the day, the month, and the year, to kill a third of humankind.** 16 **The number of the troops of cavalry was two hundred million; I heard their**

number. [17] And this was how I saw the horses in my vision: the riders wore breastplates the color of fire and of sapphire[y] and of sulfur; the heads of the horses were like lions' heads, and fire and smoke and sulfur came out of their mouths. [18] By these three plagues a third of humankind was killed, by the fire and smoke and sulfur coming out of their mouths. [19] For the power of the horses is in their mouths and in their tails; their tails are like serpents, having heads; and with them they inflict harm.

[20] The rest of humankind, who were not killed by these plagues, did not repent of the works of their hands or give up worshiping demons and idols of gold and silver and bronze and stone and wood, which cannot see or hear or walk. [21] And they did not repent of their murders or their sorceries or their fornication or their thefts.

[x] Other ancient authorities lack *four*

[y] Gk *hyacinth*

13 The solitary **voice** which John hears when the **sixth angel** blows his **trumpet** is, like John the Baptist (John 1:22), just that: an unidentified voice. What is more important is where the voice comes from: **from the four horns of the golden altar before God**. This is the altar of incense with its **four horns** or pillars set at each corner (Exod 27:1,2). From this altar rose the prayers of God's people, prayers which precipitated the judgment activity of God which is recorded in chapters 8 and 9 (8:2–5). From this altar came the martyrs' plea to God to reveal his justice and to vindicate himself and his people (6:9–11). The events of the sixth trumpet are, then, God's response to the prayers of the church which are described simply as **a voice from . . . the altar**.

14 The voice from the altar orders the sixth trumpet angel to free **the four angels** who up to this point have been held in check by God **at the great river Euphrates**. For the pious Jew, the Euphrates marked the theological limits of the holy land. For the Romans, the river marked the eastern boundary of the empire; beyond the Euphrates lurked the feared Parthians. Historically and symbolically they were The Enemy. The bloodthirsty mounted archers of the Parthians were the stuff of nightmares for Roman general and Jewish leader alike.

The **four angels** who stand bound at the frontier represent these Parthian hordes. They point to the fact that the enemy behind the enemy is not human but demonic. The definite '*the* four angels' suggest a known group. They are, in fact, the mirror image of the four angels in 7:1,2. There a loud-voiced angel commands the four angels who stand at the four corners of the earth and hold back the winds, not to harm the earth, so that the safety of the saints is assured (7:1,2). Here in 9:15–17 a voice from the four corners ('horns') of the altar commands that the four angels in the east be released in order to harm the rebellious people of the earth. 'Reversal of subject and object of the command results in a reversal of consequence' (Thompson).

John reminds his hearers that saving and judging are twin activities of the one God, by putting together a neat set of parallels and contrasts:

7:1	four angels	from	four corners (of earth)	hold back four winds
9:13, 14	a voice	from	four corners (of altar)	says: Release!
7:2	a voice	from	East	says: Do not harm!
9:14, 15	four angels	from	East (Euphrates)	are released

Two further parallels follow: in both cases, John *heard* the number of those involved in the action, and then he *saw* them (7:4,9;9:16,17). Finally, the accounts end with a dramatic contrast: the multitudes in chapter 7 fall down and worship God (7:11), whereas the rebellious people of chapter 9 refuse to repent (9:21). In both cases, God's will is that all should repent and live; but the response to his judging and saving actions is very different.

15 The angels were released **to kill a third of humankind**. This is not total destruction of the human race, but a terrible warning and foretaste of the wrath to come, unless people repent (9:20). God commands that the angels be released at a time of his choosing, designated precisely to the very **hour**. This sense of the 'right' time refers here to God's judging activity, intended to bring people to their senses and hence to final salvation. The same concern for the right time is likewise shown when the Scriptures speak about God's acts to rescue, save, and bless his people (see Num 1:1; Hag 2:10,18), especially and above all in the sending of his Son, who is the full revelation of God and the mirror of the Father's heart (John 3:16; Luke 2:1,2; Gal 4:4).

16 The four angels become two hundred million 'mounted troops' (TEV). When John says that he 'heard' a number, he is signalling that the number is symbolic (see 7:4). Here he wants to convey some idea of the sheer size of the realm of evil and wickedness, and of the demonic forces who are released into the world (see Gog and Magog, Ezek 38:9). They are a mighty army, intent on opposing God and his people. But although in the book of Revelation armies are reported to have gathered for battle, there is never a battle (12:7–9 tells of a legal battle). Instead, the demonic armies are the instruments of God's judgment upon sin and evil. Ultimately, they gather together only to destroy themselves, or to make it 'more convenient' (if one may speak in very human terms) for God to destroy them.

Evil is self-destructive. This is surely the meaning of the 'release' of Satan, the gathering of the demonic forces, and the final judgment by God recounted in 20:1–10. C.S. Lewis portrays this truth graphically when he has Screwtape, the senior devil, in lip-licking raptures at the thought of devouring Wormwood, the not-so-bright junior devil (*The Screwtape Letters*).

17 The demonic army of mounted horsemen is just as repulsive as the beast-army described in 9:7–11. This is hardly surprising, since John is describing the same hostile forces. The horsemen wear **breastplates** which are similar to the colours of the three horses described in the 'seals' narrative (6:3–8): **fire** ('red', 6:3); **sapphire** ('a red colour bordering on black', 6:5); and **sulphur** (the yellowish-green of brimstone, see 6:8). Here is a small signal, reminding hearers at the end of the 'trumpet' sequence, that the whole series is a working out in detail of the seal septet.

The riders do not do the killing; they are mounted on horses who have leonine heads which breathe out **fire and smoke and sulphur**.

18,19 These monsters kill by the same means as God killed the inhabitants of Sodom and Gomorrah (see Gen 19:24–28). A **third of humankind** is killed. But many others ('the rest of humankind', verse 20), are wounded by the horses' tails, which are like writhing snakes which have poison in their **heads** (compare the beasts with 'tails like scorpions', 9:10).

Snakes have always been associated with the demonic, with magic, sorcery, and evil in many forms. The snakes which form the horses' tails act in a particularly antigodly way: the **harm** which they **inflict** is fatal. Their mesmeric ability causes those people who were not killed by the **plagues** which came from the mouth of the horses to continue their rebellion against God by continuing their false worship, their idolatry.

20 Here the matter at issue in the book of Revelation is stated starkly: the prayers and worship of God's people set in motion a series of divine judgments which are intended to bring to repentance those who worship **demons and idols of gold and silver and bronze and stone and wood, which cannot see or hear or walk** (compare Ps 135:15–17). Worship is the question. The book is a 'revelation of Jesus Christ' (1:1). At its heart is 'the one who sits on the throne' and 'the Lamb'. Whom do you worship? God or Satan? The Lamb or the dragon? The triune God or his parody, the dragon and the two beasts? It is impossible to try to 'hobble on one leg then on the other' (1 Kings 18:21, JB), or to 'sit on the fence' (NEB).

It is worth noting that the four angels of destruction are released with God's full knowledge and consent: the command comes from the altar which is before the throne (9:13,14). The terrible events which occur subsequently are God performing what Luther calls his 'alien work', his work of killing in order that he might give life, of judging in order that he might save. This fact is indicated in a number of little ways in 9:13–21. For example, in Revelation 'fire' is consistently associated with God (for example, 1:14;2:18;4:5;10:1; 18:8). The only time 'fire' is associated with the demonic is in 13:13, where the second beast imitates God in his attempt to persuade people to worship the first beast. Finally, 'fire' is associated with appropriate witness to God as Saviour and Judge (11:5; compare Luke 12:49).

21 The saddest word of all: **And they did not repent** (see v 20; Matt 11:20–24). God's will is a saving will (1 Tim 2:4). His goal in letting loose what *we* call good and evil is the repentance and the salvation of men and women (see Rom 2:4; Luke 13:1–9).

So in the last times God will speak to people in all sorts of ways: through the prophetic and apostolic word spoken by his worshipping church; through pains and joys; through nuclear threat and nuclear promise; through the death of a daughter and the birth of a baby; through the hoarse cry of the drought-stricken land and the cheers of a bumper harvest; through the devastation of war and the creative blossoming of peace — in all sorts of ways God calls people to repentance. Reflection on the word of God recorded in 2 Peter 3 is appropriate at this point.

God whispers, speaks, shouts, but so many refuse to leave their life of sin and disobedience. They continue, like old Pharaoh, to resist God and his call. So they continue in their **murders** (which in those days meant primarily the aborting of foetuses), their drug dependency (**sorceries**), their sexual immorality and infidelity, and their thievery. In short, they live out their idolatry. Jesus' message to John and his churches is the same as that which he spoke to and through the apostle Paul:

> Be sure of this, that no fornicator or impure person, or one who is greedy (that is, an idolater), has any inheritance in the kingdom of Christ and of God. Let no one deceive you with empty words, for because of these things the wrath of God comes on those who are disobedient. (Eph 5:5,6)

Where have we been? Where are we going?

At this point in his recounting of the things that he saw in the second revelation (4:1 – 16:21), John engages in a marvellous exercise in effective communication to those who hear but do not read. He continues to tell what happened when the sixth trumpet sounded; it is basically a repetition of what happened when the Lamb opened the sixth seal. Repetition aids the memory.

At the same time, John starts all over again, and right in the middle of Revelation he places a summary of the book. He does this by introducing the concept of a little book. What is written in this book (scroll; 10:1 – 14:20) is a precis of the book which John was told to write. It is a microcosm of a macrocosm.

Some commentators have called the section 10:1 - 14:20 an interlude. Others see it as an extended introduction to the second half of Revelation. It is neither of these. It is a book within the book.

The connection of the little book with John's book is indicated by means of several linking devices. For example, the completion of the trumpet septet comes as part of the activities which take place as John describes the contents of the little book (10:1 – 11:15). Reversals occur in the circumstances and events reported in chapters 5 and 10. The book in chapter 5 is sealed so tightly that no-one can open it except the mighty 'Lion of the tribe of Judah', who unseals it and so enables its contents to be revealed and activated. In chapter 10, however, a mighty angel (who is in fact the Christ), with a voice like a lion, holds open a scroll. Its contents are declared, presumably, by the angel and the seven thunders (10:3). John is told *not* to write anything down (contrast 4:1), and in fact to 'seal up' what the seven thunders said (10:4).

Finally, it should be noted that the judging and saving actions of God in chapters 10–14 are reported in the reverse order in 17:1 – 21:4, indicating a link with the following section of John's book.

Other links may be indicated briefly: John eats the bitter-sweet book, and is commanded to prophesy 'again'

(10:9–11). This takes the hearer back to the opening vision of 1:19,20, when John is directed to write what he sees, that is, what is reality and what will be reality. Both commissionings refer to a 'mystery' (1:20;10:7), and to things which are to come (1:19;10:7). Lastly, the 'mighty angel' of 10:1–3 is, as we shall see, the same person as the 'one like the Son of Man' in 1:12–16.

One difference between John's larger book and the smaller one is in the role which John plays: in the one case he is an observer, a recorder; in the other he is a participant (he 'eats' the book!).

NARRATIVE: The sixth trumpet (continued), 10:1 – 11:14

**10 And I saw another mighty angel coming down from
heaven, wrapped in a cloud, with a rainbow over his head;
his face was like the sun, and his legs like pillars of fire.
2 He held a little scroll open in his hand. Setting his right
foot on the sea and his left foot on the land, 3 he gave a
great shout, like a lion roaring. And when he shouted,
the seven thunders sounded. 4 And when the seven
thunders had sounded, I was about to write, but I heard a
voice from heaven saying, 'Seal up what the seven
thunders have said, and do not write it down.' 5 Then the
angel whom I saw standing on the sea and the land
raised his right hand to heaven
6 and swore by him who lives
forever and ever,
who created heaven and what is in it, the earth and what
is in it, and the sea and what is in it: 'There will be no
more delay, 7 but in the days when the seventh angel is to
blow his trumpet, the mystery of God will be fulfilled, as
he announced to his servants[z] the prophets.'**

**8 Then the voice that I had heard from heaven spoke
to me again, saying, 'Go, take the scroll that is open in
the hand of the angel who is standing on the sea and on
the land.' 9 So I went to the angel and told him to give me
the little scroll; and he said to me, 'Take it, and eat; it will
be bitter to your stomach, but sweet as honey in your
mouth.' 10 So I took the little scroll from the hand of the
angel and ate it; it was sweet as honey in my mouth, but
when I had eaten it, my stomach was made bitter.**

**11 Then they said to me, 'You must prophesy again about
many peoples and nations and languages and kings.'
11 Then I was given a measuring rod like a staff, and I
was told, 'Come and measure the temple of God and the
altar and those who worship there, 2 but do not measure
the court outside the temple; leave that out, for it is given
over to the nations, and they will trample over the holy
city for forty-two months. 3 And I will grant my two
witnesses authority to prophesy for one thousand two
hundred sixty days, wearing sackcloth.'**

4 These are the two olive trees and the two lampstands that stand before the Lord of the earth. 5 And if anyone wants to harm them, fire pours from their mouth and consumes their foes; anyone who wants to harm them must be killed in this manner. 6 They have authority to shut the sky, so that no rain may fall during the days of their prophesying, and they have authority over the waters to turn them into blood, and to strike the earth with every kind of plague, as often as they desire.

7 When they have finished their testimony, the beast that comes up from the bottomless pit will make war on them and conquer them and kill them, 8 and their dead bodies will lie in the street of the great city that is prophetically[a] called Sodom and Egypt, where also their Lord was crucified. 9 For three and a half days members of the peoples and tribes and languages and nations will gaze at their dead bodies and refuse to let them be placed in a tomb; 10 and the inhabitants of the earth will gloat over them and celebrate and exchange presents, because these two prophets had been a torment to the inhabitants of the earth.

11 But after the three and a half days, the breath[b] of life from God entered them, and they stood on their feet, and those who saw them were terrified. 12 Then they[c] heard a loud voice from heaven saying to them, 'Come up here!' And they went up to heaven in a cloud while their enemies watched them. 13 At that moment there was a great earthquake, and a tenth of the city fell; seven thousand people were killed in the earthquake, and the rest were terrified and gave glory to the God of heaven.

14 The second woe has passed. The third woe is coming very soon.

[z] Gk *slaves*

[a] Or *allegorically;* Gk *spiritually*

[b] Or *the spirit*

[c] Other ancient authorities read *I*

1 John continues his account of what he **saw** when the sixth trumpet was blown: he saw **another mighty angel**. The previous mention of a **mighty angel** was in 5:2, where such an angel challenged the heavenly assembly to

produce someone worthy to open the seven-sealed book. When John says that he saw 'another angel' he is indicating that he saw the Lord Jesus in the form of an angel (see 7:2;8:3). He is **wrapped in a cloud** (1:13;14:14; compare Dan 7:13) and, like the one who sits on the throne, he is surrounded by a **rainbow** (4:3). His **face** shines like the sun (1:16), as did his face on the mount of transfiguration (Matt 17:2). **His legs** are reminiscent of the pillar of **fire**, the sign of God's presence which accompanied Israel on its desert journey (1:15; see Exod 13:21,22). This angelic Christ speaks with a loud voice which is connected with thunder (see 4:5), and which is like a **lion roaring** (see the Lion of Judah, 5:5). This combination of divine attributes from accounts of visions of God and Jesus in chapters 4 and 1 suggests very strongly that the **mighty angel** whom John saw coming **down from heaven** is none other than Jesus Christ. He appears, as he does frequently in Revelation, in the form of an angel, a servant of God.

2 Jesus, the mighty angel, holds **in his hand** an **open** book. Unlike the great scroll which was so firmly sealed that only the Lamb (that is, Jesus) could open it, this **little scroll** (book) has already been opened. John's hearers are not immediately told what is in the little book, because instead of revealing its contents, John eats it (see comments on verses 9,10).

The subject matter of the book evidently has to do with the whole world, for the Christ-figure places **his right foot on the sea and his left foot on the land**. His message is universal in address, and his divine authority reaches into every corner of the earth (compare Heb 2:5). The **sea** and the **land** are the places from which arise the two beasts of the dragon (13:1,11). Jesus sets his feet on both places: even the domains of 'the strong one' are his (compare Mark 3:27). The church should recall this truth as it contemplates the face of the enemy unmasked in 12:1 – 13:18.

3 The demonic locusts had lions' teeth (9:18), and the snake-tailed horses had lions' heads (9:17). Christ has the **voice** of a roaring lion (as does the devil himself, who can only mimic Christ, never do anything original; 1 Pet 5:8).

In response to the loud shout of the Christ-angel (compare Amos 1:2;3:4–8), or maybe as an echo, **the seven thunders** sound. This is, perhaps, a reference to the sevenfold voice of God (Ps 29:3–9). Or it might be a more general allusion to the presence and the voice of God (Rev 4:5;8:5;11:19), as when the Father responded to the prayer of his Son and the listeners said it was thunder, or that an angel had spoken (John 12:27–29). Certainly the definite '*the* seven thunders' suggests a specific set of thunders. Psalm 29 seems to be the most likely reference.

4 Although it is not clearly stated, John's hearers are, it seems, to assume that the **seven thunders** (that is, God) revealed to John the contents of the little book. He was **about to write** down what he had heard — as he had been commanded to do in the inaugural vision (1:11,19; see also 14:13;22:10) — when an unidentified **voice from heaven** (presumably the voice of God) directed John not to write anything down. Instead, he was to **seal up** what the **seven thunders** had said (compare Dan 12:4,9).

Some commentators have called this a 'puzzling prohibition'; some have accused John of 'teasing the reader'. Why talk about the little book if the contents are not to be divulged? The simplest answer is the one suggested by verses 10 and 11. John is not to *record* the seven thunders' revelation of the contents of the little book, but he is to *enact* it. He does this by prophesying, participating with the church in God's judgments and his saving acts.

In the book of Revelation John faithfully records the things which he saw and heard, as well as what he did and said in response to those visions. Always, of course, John records only these things which God chose to reveal to him. After all, this 'revelation of Jesus Christ' (1:1) is revelation within limits. Some things Christians don't need to know; some things they are better off not knowing. The day and the hour of Christ's return, for example, are known only to God — thank God!

5,6 The saints beneath the altar had asked, 'How long?' (6:10), just as Daniel had asked, 'How long shall it be until the end of these wonders?' (Dan 12:6). The answers are given by an angel-figure: 'Michael' in Daniel,

Jesus Christ in Revelation. In both instances the angel-figure validates his answer by swearing with his **right hand** lifted in oath (compare Heb 6:13–17). **There will be no more delay**, Jesus promises. This is certain, guaranteed by the God who created the world as he willed (see Rev 4:9–11), and who will bring the world to its destiny, as he wills.

7 The vindication of the saints, the unveiling of all that is now hidden, the unmasking of the enemy, the revelation of Jesus Christ in judgment and deliverance — all this will take place **in the days when the seventh angel is to blow his trumpet** (11:15–19). We are living in those 'days' now. Christians participate in the heavenly worship which permeates these days and provides the context for the divine acts of judgment and salvation.

The worshipping people of God know **the mystery of God**, for they hear it in the words of the 'holy apostles and prophets' to whom the Spirit revealed it (Eph 3:5). That **mystery** or open secret is God's plan and purpose in Christ, to 'gather up all things in Christ, things in heaven and things on earth' (Eph 1:10). In short, the **mystery of God** is the gospel of Jesus Christ, the gospel which is the power of God to salvation, but also that word of God which brings judgment upon those who refuse to hear what the Spirit says to the church, and through the church to the world.

The blowing of the seventh trumpet will first disclose a scene of heavenly worship (11:15–19). Worship is the perpetual context of God's actions. Having reminded his hearers of this truth, John will proceed, in chapters 12–14, to describe the actors and events which are revealed when the seventh trumpet is sounded. This section, 12:1 - 14:22 is, then, an expansion of 11:7. It speaks of the reality of things present and of things to come.

The church has the task of proclaiming and modelling God's present and the future which he has in mind for the cosmos (Eph 1:9,10). For this task God gave to his church **his servants the prophets** (see Eph 4:12). He commissions and equips them for service.

8 John's commissioning, which he now reports (vv 8–11), is a paradigm of the commissioning of all Christian prophets, and of all Christian witnesses for that matter. The same heavenly **voice** (the voice of God or a voice speaking for God) which had commanded John not to exercise his prophetic role of writing things down (v 4), now tells him what his prophetic task will be: he is to take the **open** book (**scroll**) from the Christ-angel who straddles land and sea, that is, the whole earth.
9 When John asks Jesus for the book, he is told, in a replay of the commissioning of the prophet Ezekiel (Ezek 2:8 – 3:3), to **eat** the book. That is, he is to internalise the message, make it his own, 'own' it. Only those who have been grabbed and filled by the word of God can proclaim it to others. Only a rescued Jonah can preach rescue to Nineveh. All Christians speak to the world from between the jaws of the fish.
10 John had been warned by the angel-Christ that the little book would taste as **sweet as honey** (compare Ps 19:10), but it would become **bitter** in his belly as he digested it. That is in fact what happened. 'Sweetness' means life; 'bitterness' means death. That is the nature of God's word, as Paul says: to some the word of God is the aroma of death, for others it is the sweet smell of life (2 Cor 2:15,16). It is a powerful word, not to be underrated nor despised. It is the 'power of God unto salvation' for those who believe (Rom 1:16), but it is also 'sharper than any two-edged sword . . . able to judge the thoughts and intentions of the heart' (Heb 4:12). To the unbeliever it becomes their accuser and judge.

John, like all proclaimers of God's word, would experience the sweet and the sour of Christian witness. All Christians rejoice with the angels in heaven, when one sinner is turned by the word from death to life (see Luke 15:10,24). And all Christians are grieved when those who hear the word turn away from it, and remain dead in their sins (Eph 2:1). It leaves a bitter taste in their mouth, and causes them to join their Lord in weeping over an unrepentant people (Luke 19:41–44; Matt 23:37–39). 'Every person who struggles to preach and teach the word of God knows this taste, this satisfaction, and this sickness in the stomach' (Boring).

One further point needs to be made: In this world of sin, the word of God can mean death not only for those who hear it but also for those who proclaim it. The fate of the 'two witnesses' (who symbolise the witnessing people of God) bears testimony to this truth (11:6–10). Martyrdom is always one of the potential fates which awaits a faithful witness.

11 After making the message of the little book his own, John is given his mission. It is as broad as that which was given by the risen Lord to his disciples (Matt 28:18–20) and to Paul (Acts 9:15). The same Lord tells John that he **must** prophesy. The divine urgency and necessity which impelled Paul (1 Cor 9:16) now drives the prophet John.

John's prophetic activity is concerned with all sorts and conditions of men and women, with **peoples and nations and languages and kings**. He is not told to *go* to these groups, but he will speak **about** them as he recounts the events which unfold when he measures the temple and when the seventh trumpet is blown (11:1 – 14:21). He will reveal the true picture of all human society, divided any which way you like: ethnic divisions (**peoples**), religious groupings (**nations** = non-Christians as distinct from Christians), linguistic clusters, and political structures. **Kings** are mentioned especially, in view of the constant challenge to Christians to compromise by participating in worship of God and in the imperial cult. Willy-nilly, John will be speaking about political matters; they touch Christians where they are, therefore he must make sure his hearers know who are the powers behind the powers.

11:1 John had been told not to reveal the content of the little book, but to digest it and make it his own, so that he could participate in the events of which he is to speak. As a caring pastor, John concerns himself with the security and the mission of the church. First God gives him a God's-eye view of the state of the church, its safety, and the work which God calls the church to do. This is a reprise of what Jesus did in chapters 2 and 3.

Through an unidentified agent (probably an angel), God gives John a **measuring rod**. With this powerful, heavenly rod, John is to **measure the temple of God and the altar and those who** prostrate themselves in **worship there**.

In God's vocabulary, the act of measuring puts together things which belong together, and sets them apart from things which do not belong. So holy things (such as the temple, the altar, and the worshippers) cannot be included with unholy things in the same measurements. In other words, the extent of the measurement marks the boundaries of those things which are holy and therefore under God's care. God himself, who makes people holy, has set the boundaries, and indicated the lines of demarcation: this far and no further. Everyone and everything within the boundary lines are untouchable, protected, and inviolable.

When John wrote these words, the physical temple at Jerusalem was either under siege or already lay in ruins. John is speaking here symbolically of the people of God. In Revelation, **the altar** is always the altar of incense in the Holy Place (see 8:1,3;9:13). It is the place where the people of God prostrate themselves in worship before the throne of God. It is the place of God's presence. This 'place', where the worshipping community gathers, is the 'altar' and the 'temple' and even the 'holy city'. The comment in 11:19 indicates that the equation 'temple=holy place' is valid; and the fact that the Holy of Holies was a cube (1 Kings 6:20), as is the new Jerusalem (Rev 21:16), supports the equation: temple=holy place=holy city. In any case, in Revelation the **holy city** is always the new Jerusalem, the people of God.

In all, then, the divine command to John should read; 'Rise and measure the temple of God, that is, the altar and those who worship there'.

2 Excluded from the zone of holiness and divine protection is the **court outside the temple**. The inner court of Herod's temple in Jerusalem was divided into three sections; the outermost section was 'given over to the nations' (see Mark 11:17). This court was regarded as sacred, as part of the temple in the wider sense. But in the architecture of the new temple of God there is a very simple but very clear line of demarcation: between those who worship God and those who don't. So **the court outside the temple** is made up of people who worship other gods. As we shall see, they worship the beast; they have his mark upon them; and they, with him, are headed for destruction (14:9–11;19:20). John calls these people **the nations**; the same phrase is often translated in the New Testament as 'the Gentiles'. In Revelation John seems to divide all humanity into 'Christian' and 'Gentile'; other Christian writers followed the Jewish pattern of dividing humanity into either 'Jew' or 'Gentile'.

The **nations** demonstrate their idolatry and rebellion against God by trampling **over the holy city for forty-two months**. Since the holy city is the worshipping people of God, it is clear that John is saying here that God's people will experience a short period (**forty-two months**) of oppression and persecution at the hands of those who deny God's rule. That is what appears to be the reality of life as a follower of the Lamb. But there is an alternative view of reality which Christians should consider. In all the turmoil and stress and strain of trying to hold fast the faith and lift high the cross, God is keeping his people safe (they have been 'measured'). The opposition, however, has not been measured, and is therefore unprotected from the wrath of God and the Lamb (see Rev 6:16,17 and 7:3,4). Wait for the great reversal (Luke 16:19–31)!

3 While the oppression and persecution of the people of God is going on, the prophetic activity of the church is being carried out — indeed, precisely at that time. The activity of the 'two witnesses' is a symbolic expansion of the commissioning of John (10:11). These two witnesses share the burden of prophecy which was given to John (10:11;11:3); they are called 'prophets' (11:10) and 'witnesses' (11:3). This correlation reminds John's hearers that John's commissioning was a commissioning of the whole church to call all the people of the earth to repentance and faith, even while those same people were trampling on the church and trying to destroy it.

John tells four things about these two witnesses who represent all the people of God. First, the two have their prophetic **authority** directly from God. The church and its ministers have no authority other than that which God gives them. Theirs is a delegated authority, one which belongs to the proclaimed word, not intrinsically to the proclaimer.

The prophetic proclamation takes place during a limited time, symbolised as **one thousand two hundred and sixty days** (= forty-two months = three and a half years). It is the time of the beasts' reign of terror (13:5-7), the time the woman (=the church) is nourished in the desert, the place of safety. It is the period of oppression which the church experiences in the end-time (12:14).

So three and a half years is the divinely controlled time which marks the whole life of the church on earth. During this time the church, represented by the two witnesses, is to prophesy **wearing sackcloth** (compare 2 Kings 1:8; Mark 1:6). Sackcloth symbolises both the repentance which is the goal of the church's proclamation, and also the characteristic attitude of the life of the church. 'Jesus Christ . . . willed the entire life of believers to be one of repentance', said Martin Luther in the first of his 95 theses. A church which does not repent daily is in no position to call others to repentance. 'A church is powerful only when itself is penitent' (Sweet).

4 Secondly, by means of familiar symbols, John tells his hearers who these two witnesses are. They are **the two olive trees** which, in the vision of Zechariah, stand on either side of the lampstand with seven lamps (Zech 4:3;6:11–13). In Zechariah, the olive trees symbolised the high priesthood of Joshua and the kingship of Zerubbabel. The **two lampstands** recall not only Zechariah's vision, but also and especially the inaugural vision of John (1:12,20;2:5). Together, the olive trees and lampstands are symbols of the church, the witnessing and worshipping community, whom God has made a 'kingdom and priest' (1:6;5:10), and among whom the Lamb stands as Lord and Guardian (1:20;7:17).

5 Protection and power is the third aspect of John's description of the two witnesses (=the church). The number 'two', necessary for a valid witness (Deut 19:15), is reminiscent of Jesus' sending out of the seventy 'two by two' (Luke 10:1); he assured them that no-one would **harm** them; and he gave them authority 'to tread on snakes and scorpions, and over all the power of the enemy' (Luke 10:19).

One thing that John makes very clear in his book is that the church is safe; no enemy can harm the people of God. The gates of Hades itself will not prevail against the church of Jesus Christ (Matt 16:18), because Christ has broken open the gates and thrown away the key.

Protected . . . and powerful. The power of the two witnesses (=the church) is described in terms of the experiences of the two great witnesses of the Old Testament: Elijah and Moses (see the Transfiguration, Luke 9:30,31). When soldiers came to arrest Elijah, he called down fire from heaven (2 Kings 1:10–12). Later, Jesus rebuked James and John for wanting to 'do an Elijah' when the Samaritan villagers rejected Jesus (Luke 9:53–55). But now John transforms the image, and says that anyone who wants to harm the church **must** be destroyed by fire from the mouth of the two witnesses. The reference is to the word of the Spirit of God which the two witnesses speak: it is like fire (Jer 5:14) which judges and devours those who reject it (see 20:9).

Fire-from-the-mouth is a divine action; it signals the presence and power of God (see Ps 18:8). That these two witnesses perform this divine action is a clear sign that they are sent from God. However, it should be noted that fire issued also from the mouth of the demonic hordes described in 9:17. God uses even the demons, who in their arrogance mimic God and his servants, for his purposes (see the comments on 9:13-19).

6 Furthermore, the **prophesying** church (in the persons of the two witnesses) has been given by God the **authority** to emulate Elijah (1 Kings 17:1) in inducing droughts. This could refer to a drought of the word of God, when Christian witnesses shake the dust off their feet and declare that, since the proclaimed word has been rejected, they move on. Such a drought of hearing the word of God (see Amos 8:11) is an even worse catastrophe than a physical drought.

Alternatively, the ability to cause droughts could be a reference to the role which the worshipping church plays (see 8:1–5) in bringing about the events of the end-time, events intended by God to bring people to repentance (see the comments on chapter 8). In this vein, the two witnesses are said to be like Moses: they can turn water into **blood** and bring **every kind of plague** onto the earth.

The Egyptian plagues were intended to bring Pharaoh and his people to repentance. Likewise, the church at worship (8:1–5) is God's agent for helping people to reflect on the tragedies and catastrophes of life, and to face ultimate realities, to inquire after God's purposes, and to listen to what the Spirit is saying to them even in these terrible times (see comments on 9:20,21).

7 Finally, in verses 7–12, John describes the fate of the two witnesses, that is, the inevitable road upon which the church must travel.

The fate of the witnessing church, the church which refuses to compromise and elects to remain faithful to the word of God, is parallel to that of the Lord Jesus. At this point it is imperative that John's hearers learn to take the long view, the alternative view, God's view of reality. They need to remember that appearances are deceptive.

On earth, the church's immunity to attack and death is not unlimited. Whenever the witness of the church is done as it should be done, the church becomes vulnerable. When Christians give their testimony, declare clearly and publicly whose they are and whom they worship, they show their hand, put their cards on the table.

So Christians are exposed to attack: from the state, from society, from members of the trade unions or sporting associations or academic societies. But these groups may be 'fronts', masks behind which may lurk the ultimate enemy: **the beast that comes up from the bottomless pit**. He, his partners in evil, his activities, and his fate, are described more fully in chapters 12-14. For now, John gives his hearers a preview of the beast and his work.

Characteristic of the beast is that he is always ascending from the **bottomless pit**, that is, from the Abyss (9:1), which is also called the Sea (13:1). The abyss (=the Sea) is the beast's natural home, his place of origin (see Mark 5:13). Contrast this with the new Jerusalem, whose characteristic is that it is descending from heaven (3:12;21:2). The new Jerusalem is the natural home and origin of the Lamb and his people, for it is the city which God built (Heb 11:10).

The beast is really a bad copy or a cynical imitation of the Lamb (see the comments on 13:3,4). Here it is noticeable that whereas the Lamb conquers by dying — he is the Lamb Who Was Slain — the beast conquers by killing. In response to the witness of the church, the beast makes **war** on the witnessing people of God. He will **conquer them and kill them**. The beast wins; God loses. So it seems. What follows appears to confirm that seeming fact of life.

8–10 Shamed and disgraced, the **bodies** of the dead witnesses lie in the street of the city in which they were killed. It is the same city in which **also their Lord was crucified**. So the witnessing church follows its Lord along the road of rejection, suffering, and death (see John 15:20).

The question is: where is the **great city**? John's hearers are given a number of clues. It is a place where people from all parts of the known world can come and stare at the **dead bodies** of the two witnesses, and deny them the dignity of a decent burial. Lying there in the street, they become a source and symbol of pollution and uncleanness.

The **great city** is a place where the **inhabitants of the earth**, the ordinary citizens of the empire who reject the gospel and make life hard for God's people, can come and **gloat** over the humiliation and death of the church. They can put on a big party, **exchange presents**, and generally celebrate the demise of the church.

The **great city** has a long pedigree, but you won't find it on any map. For the **great city** is wherever people are gathered in rebellion against God; wherever the social and political structures oppose the church of

God; wherever wickedness and evil rules. The **great city** is the place where the voice of God is not heard, where the prophets are stoned, where the Lord is crucified, where the helpless embryos are murdered, the very old and the very young abused, where money and technology is lord, people are dehumanised, and the environment is raped.

The first **great city** is Babylon (16:19), also known as Babel (Gen 11:9); its successors are Nineveh (Jonah 1:2,3:2) and Rome. Christians today should have no trouble in recognising the **great city**. **Prophetically**, that is, using the symbolic language which is appropriate when God's Spirit moves the prophet to describe earthly things from God's point of view, the **great city** is called **Sodom and Egypt**. Sodom was the city of sin, the city which rejected God and which God rejected (Isa 1:9,10; Jer 23:14). Egypt was the place of slavery for God's people, the place of hardened hearts and of refusal to listen to the voice of God and his witnesses (Exod 11:9,10).

The **great city** and its inhabitants had found that the church's uncompromising witness made them uncomfortable, spoiled their fun, questioned their motives and morals, and challenged their whole way of life. The church's witness **had been a torment**, but now it was still. The nagging fools are dead. Let us eat, drink, and be merry! The verb 'to torment' is used in the New Testament of the condition of demons who react when they confront Jesus (for example, Matt 8:29). In Revelation its usage (apart from 12:2) is restricted to the fate of those who refuse to repent when God's wrath is revealed. When they silence the faithful witnesses, these people think that at last their torment is finished. Alas, the worst is yet to come:

> Those who worship the beast . . . will also drink the wine of God's wrath, poured unmixed into the cup of his anger, and they will be tormented with fire and sulphur in the presence of the holy angels and in the presence of the Lamb. And the smoke of their torment goes up forever and ever. There is no rest day and night for those who worship the beast. (14:9–11; compare 20:10)

Kyrie eleison! Lord have mercy!

11 The two witnesses (=the witnessing church) emulate their Lord not only in his death, but also in his resurrection. The **three and a half days** indicates a comparatively brief period of time, matching the three and a half years during which the witnesses witness and the enemies oppress the church (11:2,3). The number of days corresponds to our Lord's resurrection 'after three days' (Mark 9:31). In a new creative act, the Spirit of God, who is 'the Lord and giver of life', breathes life into the church which the 'inhabitants of the earth' think is dead, defeated, and defunct (see Ezek 37:10).

This is how God always acts with his church: he is always renewing it, giving it new life, in keeping with his declaration at the end of Revelation, a declaration which summarises the whole book: 'Behold, I am making all things new' (21:5).

The two witnesses stand up in full view of everyone. The reaction of those who see them is reminiscent of the reaction of those who saw the risen Lord: they **were terrified** (literally: 'great fear fell upon them'; see Matt 28:4).

12 Finally, the church joins its Lord in his exaltation (see Eph 2:6). An unidentified **loud voice**, which might well have been the voice of the Lord himself (see 1:10) summoned the two witnesses to come up to heaven (see 4:1). So they, like their Lord, ascended to heaven in *the* **cloud** — not just any old cloud, this, but the cloud of God's glory, the same cloud which took Jesus into heaven (Acts 1:9), and which overshadowed the Lord at his transfiguration (Matt 18:5), and in which he will come in glory at the End (Luke 21:27; see Rev 14:14).

When Jesus rose from the dead, no-one witnessed it. Early non-biblical accounts tell in detail how Jesus' enemies in particular witnessed the resurrection. But according to the biblical record, the Lord's resurrection was witnessed by no-one. When he ascended, only his disciples were witnesses to the event. But when God has finished renewing and creating his church (Eph 2:20), then everyone will see it, including the **enemies** (see Ps 23:5,6), whom John had earlier called 'the inhabitants of the earth' (Rev 6:10;8:13;11:10).

13 A further parallel with the death and resurrection and ascension of the Lord may be noted: when the two witnesses ascend in the cloud, **a great earthquake** occurs (compare Matt 27:51–54;28:2). As a result of this manifestation of God's presence in judgment or in deliverance (see 6:12;8:5;11:19), a small portion (**a tenth**) of the great **city** is destroyed. **Seven thousand** lose their lives in the earthquake. This is perhaps an ironic use of a number usually associated with the story of Elijah, who was assured that there were seven thousand in Israel who had not bowed in worship to the beast in the form of Baal (1 Kings 19:18). Earthquakes are the symbol of the shaking of the very foundations of the world of the beast and his worshippers.

One clear message of the book of Revelation is that Christians have to face the fact that in many instances the 'inhabitants of the earth' will refuse to respond to God's call to repentance (see 9:20,21). Here, however, John's hearers are told that the witness of the church, and the events associated with it (persecution and death; God's wrath against enemies; God's renewal of the church) will cause **the rest** of the people — those not killed by the earthquake — to fear greatly, and to give **glory to the God of heaven**. In 9:20, by way of contrast, John reports that 'the rest' did not repent.

This is a good example of how John in his revelation sees the whole picture at once, but he can only set it down one thing at a time. It seems that what in fact he was given to see was *a twofold response* to the witness of the church: repentance and a refusal to repent. The primary sin is the refusal to honour God and to give thanks to him (Rom 1:21). The proper response to God's self-revelation in word and action is to 'fear God and give him glory' (Rev 14:7; see 15:4).

The Philistines were told to 'give glory to the God of Israel', and not to harden their hearts (1 Sam 6:5–8). In the story of Jonah, the heathen sailors 'feared the LORD even more and offered a sacrifice' to him (1:16), while the inhabitants of the great city of Nineveh heard Jonah's message, 'believed God', and put on the sackcloth of repentance (Jonah 3:5), just as the two witnesses wore sackcloth in anticipation of the repentance which their message would effect. It is significant that the final parallel between the story of the two witnesses and the story of Jesus is found in the response by the observers. When Jesus died, the centurion, who was probably the legal witness to Jesus' death, 'gave glory to God, saying: "Certainly this was a righteous man" ' (Luke 23:47; compare Mark 15:39). The wife of the Roman governor made the same confession (Matt 27:19).

John's purpose in recording his revelation in the way that he does is surely not to join in the age-old speculation on the fate of the heathen. He wants, rather, to encourage his Christian people not to give in to the temptation to compromise and to worship the beast; they are, rather, to continue their faithful witness, knowing God's promise that his word does not return to him empty, but it accomplishes its purpose in God's own way and own time (Isa 55:10–13).

Where have we been? Where are we going?

In the narrative recorded in 10:1 – 11:13 John had two things going at once. On the one hand, he began a summary account of the whole book of Revelation. His precis opened with a vision of Christ (10:1–3) and a commissioning (10:8–11); then followed a description of the state of the church, its work in the world, and its enemies (11:1 – 13:18); the summary concluded with the story of the fate of the people of God (safe and saved) and of the enemies of God (judged and destroyed) (14:1–20).

At the same time, in 10:1 – 11:13, John continued his account of what he had seen when the sixth trumpet was blown. This account had begun at 9:13. Before that trumpet was blown, John had announced that two 'woes' were still to come. Now in 11:14 he announces that with the end of his story of what happened when the sixth trumpet was sounded, the **second woe has passed**. The **third woe** is, like the Lord himself, **coming very soon** (see 22:7,12,20). Indeed, John's hearers will look for the **third woe** to be unfolded when the seventh trumpet is blown by the angel. For the blowing of the seventh trumpet should unveil the events of the Last Day; when that is done, the 'woes' will be complete.

In fact, however, John repeats exactly what he did when he reported the opening of the seventh seal: he described a scene of heavenly worship (8:1–5). So here, instead of a narrative of the last judgment and the destruction of all evil and the triumph of the saints, the blowing of the seventh trumpet discloses heavenly worship, followed by a theophany, evidences of the presence of God as Saviour and Judge (11:15-19; see 8:5).

This really is a surprise, for the announcement had been made in 10:6,7 that, with the blowing of the seventh trumpet, this is it, there is nothing more to be said. With the blowing of the seventh trumpet, the End has arrived. But surprise! There is no terrible destruction, no terrible battle between God and Satan. There is no dramatic narration of end-time events. Instead, the blowing of the seventh trumpet leads to worship!

The hearer (and reader) must remember that everything that John records as happening, happens in the context of heavenly worship. John reminds us of this fundamental fact by starting his story with worship and continuing his story with worship and ending his story with worship. He is about to tell his hearers about the **third woe**, about what it means that 'the kingdom of the world *has become* the kingdom of the Lord' (11:15). In chapters 12–15 the hearers are told of the enemy, his followers, their fate, and the fate of the people of God. The story of the end of all things is all here, as it is told again in chapters 17–22. But it is a story of what is happening now; the story crosses the boundaries of space and time, and records how things are from God's eternal viewpoint. Worship is the only context in which such boundary-crossing can occur for the earth-bound people of God. If we are to see John's revelation as he saw it, we can do so only as worshippers of the one who sits on the throne, and of the Lamb.

THE SEVENTH TRUMPET WORSHIP: Liturgy of thanksgiving, 11:15–19

15 Then the seventh angel blew his trumpet, and there were loud voices in heaven, saying,
'The kingdom of the world has
become the kingdom of our
Lord
and of his Messiah,[d]
and he will reign forever and
ever.'
16 Then the twenty-four elders who sit on their thrones before God fell on their faces and worshiped God,
17 singing,
'We give you thanks, Lord God
Almighty,
who are and who were,
for you have taken your great
power
and begun to reign.
18 The nations raged,
but your wrath has come,
and the time for judging the
dead,
for rewarding your servants,[e] the
prophets
and saints and all who fear your
name,
both small and great,
and for destroying those who
destroy the earth.'
19 Then God's temple in heaven was opened, and the ark of his covenant was seen within his temple; and there were flashes of lightning, rumblings, peals of thunder, an earthquake, and heavy hail.

[d] GK *Christ*

[e] Gk *slaves*

One commentator has called this scene of heavenly worship, together with the ending to the narrative of the seal septet (8:1–5), examples of John's 'cancelled conclusions'. This can be a misleading phrase, for John does not in fact 'cancel conclusions'. On the contrary, the conclusion stands plain for all to see. John repeats this conclusion (and the events which lead to it) several times, so that his hearers and readers will be in no doubt whatsoever about the ultimate outcome of their lives of faithful witness on the one hand, and the lives of those who worship the beast on the other. This, John says, is how things end up.

15 How do things end up? In Jewish worship, the blowing of the seventh trumpet was a signal for the singing of a hymn of praise and thanksgiving. When the **seventh angel blew his trumpet**, John tells us he heard **loud voices in heaven**. The worship which followed the opening of the seventh seal began with silence (8:1). But now the hosts of heaven shout aloud for all to hear. They celebrate the salvation which was won by the Lamb who was slain, the only one worthy to open the sealed scroll (5:9,10).

The kingdom of the world, which so many thought was forever in the hands of Satan and his beastly agents (see Luke 4:5,6), was, in fact, never Satan's. God always has been king; but the acclamation and thanksgiving which should have been there when the six trumpets sounded, have been missing. Now, however, the last trumpet has sounded, and the mighty shout of acclaim goes up from those in heaven and on earth who worship God and the Lamb: 'God is King!'

As in Psalm 47:5–8, so also here and often in the New Testament, 'kingdom' is to be understood dynamically: it signifies God at work, ruling the world in justice and righteousness, and blessing his people with peace. Usually when the New Testament speaks of 'our Lord' it means the exalted Lord Jesus (for example, Rom 1:4; 1 Cor 1:9; Heb 7:14). In Revelation, the two other occurrences of the phrase 'our Lord' likewise refer to the Lord Jesus (11:8;22:21). This uniform usage, together with the clear reference to Psalm 2:2, suggests that the heavenly worshippers are celebrating the fact that 'all power in heaven and earth' (Matt 28:18) has been given to **our Lord** Jesus, that is, to the one whom the psalmist calls God's **Messiah** (=Christ).

So the Lamb Who Was Slain, the 'pierced one' (1:7) who was slaughtered before the foundation of the world (13:8), is now 'King of kings and Lord of lords' (19:16); he will **reign** as king for a thousand years (20:4–6), that is, **forever and ever** (22:5).

The kingship of the **Messiah** is a consequence of his work of redemption (5:9–14; see Phil 2:10). The fourth gospel in fact teaches that the throne from which Christ began his reign is the cross. His rule is a present fact. Heavenly liturgy unites past, present, and future in one present, eternal reality which leaps over space and time. This is *the* truth which Christians must write on their hearts: Jesus 'our Lord' reigns.

16,17 Because Jesus is Lord, the people of God of all ages and across all time and space — symbolised by **the twenty-four elders** (see 4:4) — prostrate themselves **before God** and break out in a song of thanksgiving. God is addressed as **Lord God Almighty, [you] who are and who were**, but not as the one 'who is to come' (compare 1:4,8;4:8). In this heavenly liturgy, which telescopes the future into the present, God *has* come. That's how certain is the future, thanks to the Lord Jesus.

God has come and has **begun to reign**. From the time of Christ's coming to earth, God's sovereign rule was seen to be exercised against all the powers of evil and the sinfulness of human beings. God in Christ took up his **great power** and began to rule. Not that God had not reigned before. He had. But in Christ the alternative, fake pretenders to God's throne are exposed, fought against, and defeated. Their power is broken on the tree of the cross (Col 2:15). The recognition, the acclamation of God as king has begun: now by the church, then by all, whether they like it or not (Phil 2:9–11).

18 The coming of the kingdom by means of the proclamation of the reign of God brings both judgment and salvation to the world. The presence of the reign of God causes the **nations** to rage, to trample on the proclaimers, and to kill them (Ps 2:1–5; Rev 11:1–13). Their raging John describes in more detail in subsequent chapters. The raging of the nations, however, is matched by God's anger, an anger which is not aimless or mindless, but a fitting response to the arrogant and rebellious raging of the enemies of God.

In a brief resumé of the events described in more detail in chapters 19 and 20, the heavenly liturgy speaks of those things which, from the perspective of earth, lie in the future. But God is not mastered nor dictated to by time. He chooses the *kairos*, the right **time for judging the dead**. The divine judgment will fit the crime. Human wrath and raging will be met by terrible divine wrath and raging. Those who **destroy the earth** will be utterly destroyed by God (see 18:1-16;19:15–21;20:9,10).

On the other hand, God's coming and reigning is a **time** for **rewarding** his people. The Greek reads: 'to give *the* reward'. The 'reward' which is granted when Christ returns is not something earned, but something granted graciously by God (Rom 4:4). The recipients are called God's slaves (**servants**), the usual name in Revelation for all who fear and worship God, both angel and human (note especially 19:10).

These **servants** of God are described in three groupings: first, **the prophets** such as John himself; the 'angels' of the seven churches; and the faithful witnesses (1:1;2:1;10:7;11:10). Secondly, there are the **saints**, the loyal people of God. Thirdly, those who **fear** the **name** of God. It is not clear who is meant by this last group. Among the Jews, 'God-fearers' were non-Jews who worshipped in the synagogues (see Acts 13:16,43).

Perhaps John uses the phrase here to speak of those who were not formally members of the church — maybe not even baptised — but who 'gave glory to the God of heaven' (see Mark 15:39; Luke 23:47; Rev 11:13).

In Melanesia, in the early days of the gospel, there were men and women who were friends of the cross, but whose polygamous state prior to the gospel was deemed by the church to exclude them from the church. Perhaps to these **small** ones God gives the reward of life as his gift, just as he gives it to the **great**. God looks not at the outward appearance but at the heart, and God is no respecter of persons (Rom 2:11; 1 Pet 1:17). The first are last, the last are first; the greatest is the least (Matt 11:11;20:16).

19 To open is to reveal, unveil. At the end of the account of heavenly worship John observes that the temple of God in heaven **was opened**, and **within** was revealed the ark of the covenant, which is elsewhere called the 'throne of God' (8:2–4). In short, the scene of heavenly worship in 8:1–5 is repeated, for the **temple** and the **ark** are John's symbol for the faithful people of God gathered in worship around the throne of God. The parallel with 8:1–5 is continued in the description of the signs of God's presence: the thunder and lightning and earthquake (see 8:5).

This scene is preparation and a presupposition for the events and persons described in chapters 12–14. John is going to speak about the church and its terrible opponents. He is going to speak about the 'trampling of the holy city' (11:2). John had reminded his hearers that the holy city, that is, the worshipping people of God, will be safe (11:1). Now, before he speaks of the dragon and the two beasts who oppose God and his church, John urges his hearers to remember the alternative view of reality. To this they must cling, come what may.

Three times John says that the temple and its contents belong to *God*. The temple has been **opened**, so it is revealed to all; it is also exposed and vulnerable. But remember: in the temple is the **ark** of God's **covenant**, the very throne of the mighty God. He displays the symbols of his majesty and might: **flashes of lightning, rumblings, peals of thunder, an earthquake, and heavy hail**. These are earthly phenomena, reminding God's people that his temple and his throne are not only 'in heaven', but his rule embraces also this earth: 'The kingdom of the world has become the kingdom of our Lord', God's people confess in worship (11:15).

The opening of the temple of God makes the worshipping people of God vulnerable to the enemies, but it also makes the enemy vulnerable to the awful activity of a majestic and holy God. By means of worship, God's harried and harassed people participate in God's actions against his enemies (see commentary on 5:8 and 6:10). This truth John's hearers (and readers) should write on their hearts as they continue to listen to John's narrative of what he saw in his second revelation (4:1 – 16:21): the unveiling of the situation of the church in the world today, the enemies who oppose it, and the fate of both church and opposition (12:1 – 14:20).

NARRATIVE: The dragon v the woman and her child, 12:1-9

**12 A great portent appeared in heaven: a woman clothed
with the sun, with the moon under her feet, and on her
head a crown of twelve stars. 2 She was pregnant and was
crying out in birthpangs, in the agony of giving birth.
3 Then another portent appeared in heaven: a great red
dragon, with seven heads and ten horns, and seven
diadems on his heads. 4 His tail swept down a third of the
stars of heaven and threw them to the earth. Then the
dragon stood before the woman who was about to bear a
child, so that he might devour her child as soon as it was
born. 5 And she gave birth to a son, a male child, who is
to rule[f] all the nations with a rod of iron. But her child
was snatched away and taken to God and to his throne;
6 and the woman fled into the wilderness, where she has
a place prepared by God, so that there she can be
nourished for one thousand two hundred sixty days.**

**7 And war broke out in heaven; Michael and his angels
fought against the dragon. The dragon and his angels
fought back, 8 but they were defeated, and there was no
longer any place for them in heaven. 9 The great dragon
was thrown down, that ancient serpent, who is called the
Devil and Satan, the deceiver of the whole world — he
was thrown down to the earth, and his angels were thrown
down with him.**

[f] Or *to shepherd*

1 John introduces the four protagonists in the events which he is about to recount. In order of mention: the church, Satan, Christ, and God.

First John sees in the sky a **great portent** or sign. In the gospel of John, the miracles of Jesus are called 'signs'. They point to Jesus' God-given role and dignity, and they challenge those who witness them to confess the lordship of him who performs the signs. The signs which Jesus gives in his actions, culminating in his rule from the throne of the cross, are portents, tokens of the inbreaking of the kingdom of God and the beginning of the End. They are end-time signs.

The sign (**portent**) which John sees in the sky is a symbol of an end-time reality. Which reality? John sees **a woman** dressed in the trappings of a being from heaven. She is **clothed with the sun; the moon** is her footstool, and on her head she wears a tiara of **twelve stars**. A beautiful and glorious figure. The woman is Zion, the mother of the faithful (see Isa 66:6–11), the one indivisible community of the old and new covenants. She is called the 'church' or the 'people of God' (see Gal 4:26;6:16).

Perhaps the glorious description of this woman (the church) is meant to contrast her with another woman, the primal Woman, venerated throughout Asia Minor: the goddess Artemis. She was often pictured clothed in her upper body with many breasts, which might easily be thought of as suns or moons. Artemis was the goddess who presided over birth and growth. Certainly the heavenly woman which John sees is meant to be compared and contrasted with yet another woman (a twin of Artemis), the whore named Babylon, who is one with the scarlet beast, the agent of the red dragon (17:3–6).

2 The woman is **pregnant**; indeed she is in labour. Her splendid dress contrasts with her agonised cries as the pains of childbirth bite into her. With this symbol of Israel, the covenant community, as a pregnant woman, John takes his hearers back to the birth of the Messiah. The prophets had consistently foretold that the Messiah would come from faithful Israel; God had promised that the Saviour of the world would be born of Abraham's seed; and Jesus himself said that 'salvation is from the Jews' (John 4:22).

3 Before saying more about the child who is born of this woman, John describes another sign or **portent** which appears in the sky. It is mind-boggling to imagine that great black screen up there, with those magnificent constellations appearing. John sees a **great red dragon**, as impressive in its way as was the woman. Nobody has to guess at the reality which the red dragon represents: he is 'that ancient serpent, who is called the Devil and Satan, the deceiver of the whole world' (v 9).

In the Old Testament the **dragon** is known by various names, including Leviathan, who is the beast defeated at the Exodus (Isa 51:9,10). In Ezekiel chapter 32, Pharaoh is spoken of as the dragon. In Revelation, Pharaoh and Egypt are symbols of evil, oppression, and the persecution of God's people. The dragon, then, is a 'natural' symbol for the prince of evil, the Devil or Satan.

The dragon is fiery **red** in colour, as befits his bloody work (see the beast, 17:3). He is huge, immensely powerful, and hard to defeat. Horns are symbols of power; the dragon has **ten horns**, that is, great power. The 'head' stands for the source and origin of something; **seven heads** suggest that the dragon is very fertile. We know that he produces henchmen in his own image (13:1;17:3).

The seven heads are crowned with the symbols of royal power and authority: they wear royal crowns, not a tiara or wreath of victory, which the woman wears (12:1). In all, the dragon is the epitome of evil which is powerful, persistent, and pervasive.

A modern equivalent to the symbol of the great red dragon would be the great white shark. This Leviathan rules the waves with ruthless efficiency; very few humans have survived unscathed an attack by this dragon of the deep.

Pastor Joel Bulu, a Tongan missionary to Fiji in the middle of the 19th century, did survive a shark attack. His account of that incident reads like a parable based on the book of Revelation:

> Suddenly something struck sharply against my thigh . . . and lo, it was a shark! Then it was with me as if my soul were clean gone out of my body. A great darkness fell upon my eyes, and I could no longer see the shore or the people or the houses: all was dark.
>
> One thing only I remembered — the lotu [Christian worship]; and I said, 'Today my life is at an end. Let me now pray once more to my God'. I prayed, and in one moment the darkness was gone, though still I could not

> see the shore or any earthly being; but as I looked upwards, it seemed to me that the heavens opened, and I saw the throne of God; and a great multitude clothed in white raiment, and shining with a blaze of light.
>
> Oh the glory of it, the wondrous glory! It was gone in a moment, like a flash of lightning on a dark night; but I saw it, I saw it! As plain as noonday I saw it, and my soul was glad and strong within me. I wished not to live. 'Let me die today,' said my heart rejoicing. I no longer feared the shark. It was nothing to me, though my flesh was torn, and my blood was flowing . . .

Bulu then tells of how the shark released his thigh in order to take another bite. Bulu became so enraged at what was happening to him that he thrust his arm into the shark's wide-open mouth and down the monster's throat. When the shark gagged and released his arm, Bulu grabbed the dazed creature round the body and tried to drag it to shore. But soon he felt faint from loss of blood:

> A deadly sickness crept upon my heart; a mist came over my eyes; there was a sound in my ears like the roaring of the surf; I fell down and knew no more. And this is how the Lord delivered me out of that fearful strife. (*Joel Bulu: The Autobiography of a Native Minister in the South Seas,* pp 29–31)

4 Like a hungry crocodile (Ezek 29:3–5), the dragon lashes out with his **tail**, scrapes from the sky a **third of the stars**, and throws them to earth. This could mean that 'the activities of the evil one in other spheres have their repercussions here on earth' (Morris); it could mean that the dragon is 'hostile to God's creation' (Krodel). Or it could simply mean that the dragon is so huge and powerful and evil that whenever he moves he wreaks havoc and contributes to conditions of chaos in the universe. A somewhat similar thought was expressed by people in Melanesia when they attributed an earthquake to the effects of their creator-ancestor turning over in his bed.

The dragon's destruction of the stars is a casual action. His real interest is the woman, and in particular the child she is about to birth. He wants to **devour the child** the moment it is born. The hatred which the dragon, the ancient serpent, has for the child is as old as sin itself

(Gen 3:15). Pharaoh the dragon (Ezek 32:2) tried to destroy Moses, the servant of God. And through his agent Herod, Satan tried to destroy the Christ-child (Matt 2:13). When he was thwarted, he killed all the little boys in Bethlehem and environs. Still today the children, unborn and new-born, are the focus of attacks from those who disregard the word and will of God.

5 In the fullness of time, when God was ready (Gal 4:4; see Rev 11:18) — not when the dragon decreed it — the Messiah was born: the woman **gives birth to a son, a male child**. John emphasises that the child is a male, perhaps to remind his hearers of the Egypt experience of Israel, who gave birth to male babies whose lives were threatened by Pharaoh (Exod 1:15 – 2:10). The child born of the woman who symbolises faithful Israel is also a male, and therefore vulnerable to the world powers (as the Herod episode demonstrated, Matt 2:13–15). This child, who later fled from one part of his land to another because of hounding by authorities (for example, Matt 4:12; 12:15; 14:13; Mark 3:7; see John 6:15), was destined to challenge all authorities, all rulers, all Pharaohs, Herods, and Caesars. He is King of kings and Lord of lords (Rev 19:16).

He will **rule** (literally 'shepherd') **the nations** firmly but with complete authority (see the comments on 2:27). At this point the kingly rule of the child is the focus of attention. So John moves directly from Christ's birth to his ascension. Our Lord's ascension to the right hand of God, that is, to the place of power and authority (Eph 1:19,20), is clear evidence that, despite all Satan's vigilance and all his cunning, he failed to 'devour' the child. Jesus' ascension is described in dramatic fashion: God **snatched** the child **away** and took him to his **throne**. There, as John has shown his hearers already (5:6–14), the child lives and reigns with God, and receives the acclamation and praise of the heavenly hosts.

Christians do well to reflect on the fact that two of the symbols chosen to present Christ to his people in Revelation are a slaughtered lamb and a new–born baby. It forces us again and again to rethink our ideas of power and potency, lordship and authority.

6 The child is safe; but what of the mother? She is left on earth, but she is not without protection. She has been given all the armour she needs to defend herself against the wiles and stratagems and attacks of Satan. She also has the sword of the Spirit, which is the word of God (Eph 6:17), with which to take the fight up to Satan. All the powers of sin and death and hell will not prevail against her (Matt 16:18; Rev 1:18).

This essential 'safeness' of the church is expressed in the declaration that God had prepared a **place** for her in the **wilderness**. A 'place' means here, as it does in 2:5, a place of worship. The **wilderness** (desert) here signifies a domain of safety, away from the great city, the home of the beast. The wilderness is the place to which Israel wanted to go so that she could worship God as she should (Exod 5:1–3). Israel was guided there by cloud and fire, and nourished by God with manna, after escaping from the dragon, Egypt. The wilderness is the place where Israel first loved God (Jer 2:2). The wilderness contrasts with the great city, where Jezebel, the great whore, tries to attract lovers to herself.

In the desert the church is protected and nourished for one thousand two hundred and sixty days. It is no coincidence that one thousand two hundred and sixty days is the time of prophecy of the two witnesses (11:2,3). During the time when the church is called by God to witness and make confession to her Lord; during the time before the Last Day, a time which will be kept short for the sake of the saints (Matt 24:22); during the time that the church is suffering and Christians are hurting and even dying for their faith; during the time when the temple is being trampled (11:1–15) — during this time the church is safe. 'My sheep will never perish. No-one will snatch them out of my hand' (John 10:28).

7–9 The section 12:7–9 fills in a gap which John left in his account of the conflict between Christ (the 'child') and Satan (the 'dragon'). He had moved directly from Christ's incarnation to his ascension and enthronement in heaven. Christ rules (12:5). But how did that happen? The usual New Testament answer is that Jesus atoned for sin, reconciled us to God, won forgiveness for us, gave us his righteousness in exchange for ours, liberated us from the power of sin and death, and so forth. That is the meaning of what Christ did for us; that is what happened in the time of his earthly ministry.

John does not deny or contradict any of these New Testament answers. He, however, answers by means of a most unusual image: he speaks of the earthly ministry of our Lord, including his death on the cross and his resurrection, as a **war** which took place **in heaven**. John was himself 'in the Spirit' and in the sphere of heavenly existence; he wants his hearers to view Christ's saving work in its cosmic dimensions. How did the cross affect the claims of Satan to be the rightful ruler of all people, since 'all have sinned and come short of the glory of God' (Rom 3:23)? Do we have any hope of standing firm in the face of temptations to compromise our faith and worship Satan? (see Luke 4:6,7).

John's answer? A **war** took place **in heaven**. This war does not involve guns or nuclear weapons or amputations or killings. It is a legal war, fought in the law court of heaven.

The prosecution is led by the **dragon**, known also as the **Devil** or **Satan**. The latter name is a Hebrew word which means 'accuser', in the legal sense of a person who lays charges in a court of law. The former name (**Devil**) is the word which the Greek translators of the Old Testament often used to render the Hebrew name 'Satan'. In Greek, the name 'Devil' means, actually, 'slanderer'. Satan not only accuses sinners before God, but he also instigates sin by slandering God and causing people to question God's words and his authority: 'Did God really say . . .' 'You certainly will not die . . .' (see Gen 3:1,4). The devil is a liar and a deceiver from the beginning. He is The Enemy. He leads people into sin, and then turns round and accuses them 'before God' (12:10) all the time. He is like a corrupt undercover police officer who gathers a gang to help him rob a bank, and then arrests them and charges them with committing a crime, while he pockets the proceeds of the robbery.

The leader of the defence team is called **Michael**. He is not said to be an angel, although he leads an army of

angels. Most modern commentators assume that John is referring here to the archangel Michael, who is mentioned in Jude 9, and described in the book of Daniel as the great prince who was the patron and protector of the Jewish nation (Dan 10:21).

There is, however, an ancient precedent for identifying **Michael** with the Lord Jesus Christ, the 'child' whom God snatched to heaven and set in his place of rulership. A number of factors speak in support of this identification:

1) Several times in Revelation John has portrayed Christ as an angel-like figure (see comments on 7:2;8:3;10:1–3). For readers familiar with the Old Testament, this would not have come as a shock. They would recall several stories in which the Lord God appeared in angelic form to people. Typically, the story tells of how a man addresses a question to an 'angel'. The account then continues: 'And Yahweh replied . . .' So, for example, in Judges 6:11–14 the narrator tells of how Gideon addresses a question to 'the angel of the LORD' (v 11), but then, the narrator says, 'the LORD turned to Gideon and said . . .' (v 14; compare Gen 18:9–13; 19:18–21).

Furthermore, in Daniel 10:5,6 an 'angel' is described as having attributes usually associated with God himself. Indeed, the description undoubtedly provided the model for John's description of the glorified Christ who appeared to the prophet in the first revelation (Rev 1:9–20).

2) The name 'Michael' means 'he who is like God'. Whoever bears this name represents the glory of God himself (see Exod 15:11; Ps 89:6,7). Only Jesus Christ can properly be said to be 'like God' (see John 5:18; Phil 2:6). It is worth noting that the beast, who always mimics Christ, is acclaimed by his worshippers with the cry: 'Who is like the beast, and who can fight against it?' (Rev 13:4).

3) In Revelation, Jesus often speaks and acts through his servants, his agents, including angels and prophets such as John (for example, 1:1;11:1; 15:6;19:9,10). The dragon, too, usually acts through agents, notably his servants the two beasts, the whore Babylon, and various earth rulers (for example, 13:1-18;17:1–18).

But twice in Revelation, we contend, Christ and the dragon come into direct contact (12:7–9 and 20:1–3). Both occasions mark a crucial stage in the story of judgment and salvation. In both instances the dragon is carefully identified as the devil and Satan. The view taken in this commentary is that in both instances the angelic figure who directly confronts Satan is the Lord Jesus himself (12:7,9 and 20:1,3).

4) It could be argued against the point made in 3) that Revelation 12:7–9 and 20:1–3 are both examples of Jesus acting through an agent. However, in both cases the 'angel' does that which, according to the New Testament, only Jesus Christ does and can do: enter Satan's house and plunder his goods (Matt 12:29; Luke 11:22); cast Satan out of heaven by the power of his name (Luke 10:17,18); and destroy him who has the power of death, and indeed all his evil works (Heb 2:14; 1 John 3:8). Only of Christ is it said that he 'disarmed the principalities and powers and made a public example of them, triumphing over them' (Col 2:15). Only of Christ is it said that he destroys 'every rule and every authority and power' (1 Cor 15:24). And only Christ judged the 'ruler of this world' and cast him out of his kingdom (John 12:31,32).

These things Christ accomplished through his obedient life, his suffering, death, and resurrection. His servants benefit from what he did, and proclaim and confess his saving lordship. But it is foreign to the whole tenor of biblical teaching to ascribe in any way the conquest of Satan and his forces to anyone other than to 'him who sits on the throne and to the Lamb'. Honour and glory and power and might and wisdom belong to God alone. He alone is worthy (Rev 4:11;5:2,9,12–14). Christians conquer by virtue of being 'in Christ'; he *gives* them victory; they cannot obtain it for themselves.

In short, only of Christ can it be said that he defeated Satan on earth and in heaven; only of Christ can it be said that he in the end judges and destroys Satan.

5) Lastly, two small points. First, John does not, in fact call **Michael** an 'angel'. Secondly, every name in the

revelations recorded in 4:1 – 22:9 is symbolic. For example, Babylon, New Jerusalem, Mount Zion, Armageddon, Gog and Magog. There is no compelling reason for assuming that in the case of the name 'Michael' John is breaking his pattern.

One unspoken reason for hesitation on the part of some commentators is the misuse of this text by a non-Christian religious group. This group teaches that Jesus is not God. They love this text because it seems to say that Jesus is Michael, the archangel. So they favour the identification Michael=Jesus, meaning that Jesus is only an angel; he is not God.

This conclusion can be rebutted on many grounds. There is no need to give up the identification of 'Michael' with Jesus because some people are drawing false conclusions from that interpretation. The abuse of something does not negate its proper use. The fact is that of all the books in the New Testament, the book of Revelation bears the most powerful testimony, and makes the most moving confession, to Jesus Christ as true God, the only Saviour and Lord.

While we cannot speak with absolute certainty, the view taken in this commentary is that it is the Lord Jesus Christ himself who, under the name of **Michael** ('he who is like God'), refuted the accusations of the dragon, won the legal battle, and drew from God a sentence of 'Not guilty' for all believers in Christ. **The dragon and his angels fought**, but they **were defeated**.

This defeat of **Satan** and his hosts by Michael Christ has important consequences, two of which can be noted here. First, because of Christ's victory, there is now 'no condemnation for those who are in Christ Jesus' (Rom 8:1). By virtue of their union with Christ, Christians have conquered their accuser by the 'blood of the Lamb' (12:11); indeed, they are more than conquerors through him who loved them (Rom 8:37).

The whole of Romans, especially chapters 1–8, is an excellent commentary on Rev 12:7–9. In Romans 1–3 Paul conducts a lawsuit against humanity, and concludes that all stand condemned before God. But in chapters 3–8 Paul shows how God acted in Christ to give believers peace, pardon, acquittal, and victory over all accusers and all enemies. He concludes: 'Who will bring any charge against God's elect?' His answer is: No-one, because it is 'Christ Jesus who died, yes, who was raised, who is at the right hand of God, who indeed intercedes for us'. So then, nothing 'in all creation will be able to separate us from the love of God in Christ Jesus our Lord' (Rom 8:33,34,39).

A second consequence of Christ's victory is that there is **no longer any place** for Satan **in heaven**. So he is thrown out. Before the throne of God, sinners plead Christ's blood and righteousness. In the face of such a plea, what can Satan say? His mouth has been shut; his power as both accuser and slanderer has been broken. He has no rightful place in heaven. So he is disbarred, expelled. He and his angels are **thrown down to the earth**. There, as he writhes in his death throes, he attacks the church, still thinking that he will live to fight another day. Such is the ultimate stupidity of evil.

WORSHIP: Liturgy of acclamation, 12:10–12

10 Then I heard a loud voice in heaven, proclaiming,
'Now have come the salvation
and the power
and the kingdom of our God
and the authority of his
Messiah,[g]
for the accuser of our comrades[h]
has been thrown down,
who accuses them day and night
before our God.
11 But they have conquered him by
the blood of the Lamb
and by the word of their
testimony,
for they did not cling to life even
in the face of death.

12 **Rejoice then, you heavens**
and those who dwell in them!
But woe to the earth and the sea,
for the devil has come down to you
with great wrath,
because he knows that his time is short!'

[g] Gk *Christ*

[h] Gk *brothers*

Jesus Christ, the Lamb of God who takes away the sin of the world, has triumphed. He has conquered the powers of sin and death and Satan and hell. In heaven, before the throne of God, Christ has resisted and rebuffed all the accusations which the Accuser makes against the people of God. He has won the lawsuit; Satan and his accusations have been thrown out of court, that is, out of heaven.

The Lamb has conquered. But what of his people on earth? Terrible forces are ranged against them. Do they, too, conquer in the Lamb?

Once again, as he has done so many times already in Revelation, John reminds his hearers that worship is the context in which everything in the book is happening. The Accuser might lay charges against God's people 'day and night' (v 10); but heavenly worship is also taking place 'day and night' (4:8;7:15). It is worship of the Lamb which determines reality and interprets all that happens. Worship reveals how things really are, it establishes what is genuine and what is imitation, it joins heaven and earth and present and future.

The reminder of the existence and potency of heavenly liturgy is particularly appropriate at this point in John's narrative. It provides a decisive interpretation of the scene of heavenly 'war' which John has just described (12:7–9), and it affirms the reality of Christ's victory in which Christians participate when they worship. Heavenly worship does what it says; God's mighty power to destroy and to save is released through worship.

As hearers listen to the narrative of 12:13 – 14:20, which includes a description of the terrible trinity that threatens God's servants, they should do so with this joyful acclamation ringing in their ears: 'Now have come the salvation and the power and the kingdom of our God and the authority of his Messiah!'

10 The **loud voice** of an unidentified person **in heaven** bursts into liturgical song which offers a prophetic interpretation of 12:7–9, and responds to the victory of Christ which John has described. The **voice** could belong to the angels in heaven, the fellow servants of Christians. More likely, the voice belongs to the whole heavenly worshipping community, which acknowledges the worshipping community on earth as their **comrades** (see 11:15–18).

Praise is the proper response to God's creating and saving actions (Rom 1:19,20). It is also the way to kick Satan in the head, and to actualise Christ's victory for the Christian. Praise of God dethrones all idols and repeats Christ's victory over Satan. Ignatius, an early Christian leader, wrote to his people:

> Make every effort to come together more often to give thanks and glory to God. For when you gather together frequently, the powers of Satan are demolished and his destructiveness is nullified by your common faith.

The song of praise which the heavenly liturgy hymns, announces that the conquest of Satan and his expulsion from heaven means that from **now** on (that is, from the cross and resurrection, the pivotal point in human history), God is making all things new (21:5). He is destroying the old, including the kingdom of Satan, that usurper and deceiver. Four synonyms celebrate the triumph of God through **his Messiah** (= Christ). The first is **salvation**, which here means victory, as in 7:10;19:1. **Power** is coupled with salvation, for God's saving actions are the supreme demonstration of his power (Eph 1:19–22). The second pair of phrases interpret each other: **the kingdom of our God** means in fact that God's **Messiah** (Christ) is exercising the **authority** which is his by right of obedience to the Father and conquest of Satan (Matt 28:28; 1 Cor 15:24–

28; Phil 2:6–11). The language here is reminiscent of the first and paradigmatic scene of heavenly worship described in chapters 4 and 5 — and why not, since all the various accounts of heavenly worship are simply recording the one grand liturgical celebration.

The reverse of the coming of God's salvation is that the one who works unceasingly to find ways of accusing God's people before God has been thrown out of the heavenly courtroom, out of the presence of God. His role as accuser is ended with the death and resurrection and ascension of Christ. In Roman law, a person who is found guilty of making false accusation receives the penalty which the accused would have received (compare Esther 5:13;7:10). So the dragon, Satan **the accuser** who seeks to devour and destroy God's people (11:7; 1 Pet 5:8), is himself heading for destruction. He will be destroyed by the Judge before whom he makes his accusations (Rev 17:8;20:10).

Twice the worshipping community use the word 'our' in this liturgy: **our God** and **our comrades** (literally 'brothers'). So the heavenly hosts identify with their worshipping brothers and sisters on earth who still have to bear the day-and-night accusations of Satan. However, heavenly worship, in which Christians on earth participate, is also a day-and-night activity (4:8;7:15), and it is led by the great High Priest and Mediator himself, the Lamb who was slain (8:1–4).

11 Christians conquer Satan; they answer his accusations by pleading the **blood of the Lamb**. That is, whenever Satan and the law and other powers uncover their unrighteousness, Christians plead Christ's righteousness:

> Jesus, thy blood and righteousness
> My beauty are, my glorious dress;
> 'Mid flaming worlds, in these arrayed,
> With joy shall I lift up my head.

The phrase 'the blood of the Lamb' is a shorthand for the obedient life, the suffering, death, and resurrection of Christ for us, in our place and on our behalf. Christians conquer by this 'blood' and **by the word of their testimony**. The redeemed bear witness to their Redeemer. All their worship is a **testimony**, a confession to him before the world. Such fearless and consistent confession of Christ is acknowledged by Christ when his faithful witnesses stand before God, accused by Satan of every sin in the book. Jesus promised: 'Those who declare publicly that they belong to me, I will do the same for them before my Father in heaven' (Matt 10:32). On this promise Christians can rely, for Jesus is himself 'the faithful witness' (Rev 1:5).

12 Little wonder, then, that the **heavens** (the only time the plural form is used in Revelation) and everyone tabernacling there in God's safekeeping, are urged to **rejoice** or celebrate. The 'inhabitants of the earth' (the enemies of God's people) celebrated when the faithful witnesses were put to death and their bodies were left to rot in the streets of the great city (11:10). But their celebrations were premature. The real, lasting merrymaking belongs to **those who dwell** in heaven. They rejoice at the victory of the Lamb, at their own triumph in him, and at every separate battle that is won when a sinner repents and returns home (Luke 15:23,24).

The thought of these verses is summed up in the words of Jesus as he greeted the seventy witnesses who returned exuberant from their mission of speaking and of casting out demons in Jesus' name:

> I watched Satan fall from heaven like a flash of lightning . . . Rejoice that your names are written in heaven. (Luke 10:18,20)

The victory of the Lamb, the acquittal of sinners, the expulsion of Satan from heaven and the drawing of his teeth — all this does not lead to an earthly paradise for the people of God. It, in fact, *seems* to result in continued pleasure for the worshippers of the great red dragon, at the expense of the worshippers of God and the Lamb.

But the apparent happiness and contentment is deceptive, like everything that the **Devil** does and achieves. Underneath every clown-face there is sadness; behind every laugh there are tears; after every godless party there is the emptiness of despair at the uselessness of it all. 'What does it profit people if they gain the whole world . . .?'

The heavenly liturgy concludes with a **woe** pronounced upon **the earth and the sea**, which is the home of the dragon and his offsiders, the two beasts (13:1,11). The fact that **the devil has come down** to the earth means trouble for everyone. Christians will bear the brunt of his **wrath** (12:17) as he lashes out in one last paroxysm of destruction in the short **time** left to him before the End (see Eph 5:15). But in contrast to the reign of the Lamb, which is forever and ever (11:15), Satan's time to exercise the limited power still granted him is confined to a **short** span of three and a half years. During this time the church witnesses, and suffers because of her witness (11:2,3).

The followers of the red dragon, and his henchmen the beasts, will also suffer as a result of the dragon's presence on earth. In his blind rage he will, in fact, destroy his followers; or they, in so blindly following him, will destroy themselves (see 17:16,7;19:19–21). Sin is self-destructive; evil is its own worst enemy. Punishment fits the crime. Yes, even the wrath of the devil is, in the end, used by God to work out his wrath against 'all ungodliness and wickedness of those who by their wickedness suppress the truth' (Rom 1:18; see also vv 24,26,28).

NARRATIVE: The enemies of the church, 12:13 – 13:18

**[13] So when the dragon saw that he had been thrown
down to the earth, he pursued[i] the woman who had given
birth to the male child. [14] But the woman was given the
two wings of the great eagle, so that she could fly from
the serpent into the wilderness, to her place where she is
nourished for a time, and times, and half a time. [15] Then
from his mouth the serpent poured water like a river after
the woman, to sweep her away with the flood. [16] But the
earth came to the help of the woman; it opened its mouth
and swallowed the river that the dragon had poured from
his mouth. [17] Then the dragon was angry with the woman,
and went off to make war on the rest of her children,
those who keep the commandments of God and hold the
testimony of Jesus.**

18 Then the dragon[j] took his stand on the sand of the
seashore.
13 And I saw a beast rising out of the sea; and on its
horns were ten diadems, and on its heads were
blasphemous names. 2 And the beast that I saw was like a
leopard, its feet were like a bear's, and its mouth was like
a lion's mouth. And the dragon gave it his power and his
throne and great authority. 3 One of its heads seemed to
have received a death-blow, but its mortal wound[k] had
been healed. In amazement the whole earth followed the
beast. 4 They worshiped the dragon, for he had given his
authority to the beast, and they worshiped the beast,
saying, 'Who is like the beast, and who can fight against
it?'
5 The beast was given a mouth uttering haughty and
blasphemous words, and it was allowed to exercise
authority for forty-two months. 6 It opened its mouth to
utter blasphemies against God, blaspheming his name and
his dwelling, that is, those who dwell in heaven. 7 Also it
was allowed to make war on the saints and to conquer
them.[l] It was given authority over every tribe and people
and language and nation, 8 and all the inhabitants of the
earth will worship it, everyone whose name has not been
written from the foundation of the world in the book of
life of the Lamb that was slaughtered.[m]
9 Let anyone who has an ear listen;
10 If you are to be taken captive,
into captivity you go;
if you kill with the sword,
with the sword you must be
killed.
Here is a call for the endurance and faith of the saints.
11 Then I saw another beast that rose out of the earth;
it had two horns like a lamb and it spoke like a dragon.
12 It exercises all the authority of the first beast on its
behalf, and it makes the earth and its inhabitants worship
the first beast, whose mortal wound[n] had been healed.
13 It performs great signs, even making fire come down
from heaven to earth in the sight of all; 14 and by the signs
that it is allowed to perform on behalf of the beast, it
deceives the inhabitants of earth, telling them to make

an image for the beast that had been wounded by the sword[o] and yet lived; 15 and it was allowed to give breath[p] to the image of the beast so that the image of the beast could even speak and cause those who would not worship the image of the beast to be killed. 16 Also it causes all, both small and great, both rich and poor, both free and slave, to be marked on the right hand or the forehead,
17 so that no one can buy or sell who does not have the mark, that is, the name of the beast or the number of its name. 18 This calls for wisdom: let anyone with understanding calculate the number of the beast, for it is the number of a person. Its number is six hundred sixty-six.[q]

[i] Or *persecuted*

[j] Gk *Then he*; other ancient authorities read *Then I stood*

[k] Gk *the plague of its death*

[l] Other ancient authorities lack this sentence

[m] Or *written in the book of life of the Lamb that was slaughtered from the foundation of the world*

[n] Gk *whose plague of its death*

[o] Or *that had received the plague of the sword*

[p] Or *spirit*

[q] Other ancient authorities read *six hundred sixteen*

Always in his book John is concerned with showing his Christian hearers how things really are. He wants them to see the substance not the shadow, the reality not the facade. His people are aware that there are visible forces which challenge the rule of God and the Lamb, and tempt Christians to compromise. These visible forces include the emperor and his local representatives and representations, the local religions and religious practitioners, the trade guilds and their patrons, the great city and its cultural and social life.

Behind these forces — the powers behind the powers — are the rulers, the authorities, the cosmic powers of this present darkness, the spiritual forces of evil, as Paul names them in Ephesians 6:12. The masks which these powers of evil wear are attractive and seductive (see 17:4). John, the faithful pastor, strips off the masks and says to his people: Are you tempted to forsake God for a god, to follow the social leader instead of the Lamb, to leave the church for the city? Then let me show you whom you are really worshipping, and what your end will be unless you repent and turn in faith once more to the Lamb (14:6–20).

The call in these chapters (12,13) is, as John says, 'for the endurance and faith of the saints' (13:10). Those who have the right perspective will see the seeming absence of God, and his apparent inability or unwillingness to control or prevent evil, as neither the whole story nor the end of the story. Faith sees that God actually *gives* the evil powers their power, in order to bring about their destruction. Faith sees that the counter-images and parodies and caricatures of God, which seem to be so wise and powerful, are actually foolish creatures who gather together and assemble themselves and make a big show of force, only so that God can destroy them 'more easily', to speak in human terms (see 19:17–21; 20:7–10).

Faith sees that the evil which is presently rampant in the world, and which we experience as a dread reality in our lives, is part of the last throes of an enemy which has been mortally wounded, defeated, and thrown off his throne (12:7,8). Divine worship in the name of Jesus is a constant opening of the enemy's mortal wounds, a constant dethronement of Satan, and a constant reminder of his ultimate and inevitable destruction (19:17 – 20:7).

13,14 Chapter 12 is arranged in a little pattern which is very common in Revelation:

A narrative of conflict (vv 1–9)
B heavenly worship (vv 10–12)
A' narrative of conflict (vv 13–17)

The central segment (B) reminds hearers that heavenly worship is the centre and circumference of all the activities which John narrates.

In verse 13, then, John resumes the account of conflict between the woman (the people of God) and the dragon (Satan). The detailed description which John gives in 12:13–17 and 13:1–18 is meant to help the church to see clearly the nature of the enemy. Christians are reminded that worship of the red dragon is attractive but fatal in its consequences. The dragon and the church are mortal enemies.

The dragon had failed to destroy the **male child**, the Christ who had been born of the **woman**. He then turned to persecute **the woman**, the church of God. But she fled, as Mary and Joseph fled from the wicked king Herod (Matt 2:13–15), to 'her place in the desert' (TEV), her very own place which God had prepared for her. In this she contrasts with Satan and his angels, for whom there is found no place with God (12:8).

God always looks after his own. Just as he cared for Israel when that people was forced to flee into the **wilderness** from the great dragon (Pharaoh), so now he provides asylum for God's people. He nourished Israel with heavenly food (1 Cor 10:3); he continues to nourish his people in their present wilderness with the food of his word and sacrament during the 'three and a half years' of their life in this world as his pilgrim people.

When Israel reflected on its deliverance from Egypt, it used the image of God bringing them on eagle's wings to a place of safety (Exod 19:4; Deut 32:11). John recalls this image as he speaks of a second Exodus of the people of God.

15 Up to this point, John has repeated in verses 13 and 14 what he had said in 12:1–6. Now he picks up the thread of the story to show the state of the church. In a nutshell, it is safe and yet constantly threatened. An example of the threat is the dragon's (= **the serpent**) attempt to drown the people of God in a sea of lies and deceits (see 2:2,6,13,14,20;13:11–17;16:13). This is a demonic mimicking of the way in which God destroyed the armies of the dragon (Pharaoh)in the sea (Exod 14:27,28;15:1,4–10). Satan threatens to drown the people of God in a sea of lies. To swallow, or rather be swallowed by, the lies of Satan leads inevitably to death and destruction.

16 But the flood of lies does not drown the people of God. In the song which Moses and the people sang after the crossing of the sea, they described God's victory over the Egyptians thus:

> You stretched out your right hand,
> the earth swallowed them. (Exod 15:12)

So John is continuing the Exodus motif when he reports that the earth once again comes to the rescue of God's people (Satan never learns!). The **earth opened its mouth and swallowed the river which had flowed from the mouth of the dragon**. There is a particular irony here: the earth is supposed to be Satan's domain, but it works to provide deliverance for the people of God. The earth is God's agent, both for destruction and for preservation. The earth is the Lord's (Ps 24:1;50:12; Rev 11:15).

17,18 Thwarted in his efforts to destroy the people of God as a worshipping community, the dragon in his wrath proceeds to marshal his forces in order to **make war** on the individual members of the church of God. John calls them **the rest of her children** (literally 'her seed'), recalling Genesis 3:15 and the prophesied conflict between two opposing forces.

Who are these people, called here 'the rest of her offspring'? They are further described as **those who keep the commandments of God and hold the testimony of Jesus**. This and similar phrases are used in Revelation to designate the faithful witnesses to God's word and to the testimony which Jesus gave to God in his own life and work, and in his confession even unto death (see 1:2,9;6:9;19:10;20:4). In short, these people are truly at odds with the dragon. They serve and obey and worship God, not the dragon nor the beast. In their witness unto death, they are true followers of the Lamb who was slain. Christians are people who keep God's commandments by walking as Jesus walked (1 John 2:6; see Rev 14:4). The prophet John himself is a good example of one of the faithful offspring of the church (1:2,9).

For reinforcements in his war against the people of God, the dragon goes to the edge of the sea, which is his native element. He waits there for his CEO to emerge. He takes his stand **on the sand of the seashore**; his conqueror, we shall see, takes his stand on the solid rock of Mount Zion (14:1; see Matt 7:24-27).

The unholy trinity, 13:1–18

Satan is a creature; he is not the Creator. As a perverse, rebellious creature Satan cannot create anything or do any new thing. Everything he does is a distortion, a twisted copy or imitation of the real thing. Behind all the glamour and glitz is not reality, but a parody of reality. The kingdom of Satan is like a Hollywood filmset, made up of magnificent buildings with false fronts. Behind the facade is nothing. Emptiness.

For his fight against the people of God the great red dragon is joined by two beasts. Most commentators agree that the beast from the sea represents the political and economic order of Rome, which is so corrupt that it could only be described as satanic. It is personified in Rome by the emperor, in the provinces by the proconsuls and local governors and magistrates.

The beast from the earth is the religious leaders, the priests and priestesses of the imperial cult, the functionaries and other officials in the temples dedicated to Artemis and other deities. He is the philosophers and theologians who are the custodians of the story, the myths which perpetuate the power of the cults.

Together these three — the dragon and the two beasts — form a satanic trinity. They parody in their person and work the holy Trinity.

1,2 The first **beast** characteristically rose **out of the sea**. The **sea**, which is here the Abyss, the bottomless pit (11:7), symbolises chaos and evil. It is the source and the natural habitat of this beast.

According to Jewish creation mythology, on the fifth day of creation God created two sea monsters, Leviathan and Behemoth (see Gen 1:21; Ps 74:13,14). Behemoth, the male monster, was confined to the desert (see Job 40:15–24), while Leviathan, his female counterpart, was confined to the sea (see Job 41:1–11). Jewish expectation in John's day was that after the Messiah had been revealed, the two monsters would appear, each from its own place.

Hence, for John and his hearers, the appearance of the **beast rising out of the sea** would have signalled: the Messiah (Christ) has come; here now comes the antichrist, the enemy of the Messiah and his people. Long before, Daniel had seen four beasts rising out of the sea (Dan 7:1–8). John's description of the one beast combines the bizarre features of all four of Daniel's beasts. The beast itself was **like a leopard**; its **feet** were like those of a bear;

and **its mouth** — strange that: it has one **mouth** and **seven heads**! — was **like a lion's mouth**. And it had ten **horns**.

In Daniel's vision, the four beasts represented four different empires and political powers. By combining all four beasts in one, John is saying that this beast epitomises all political power.

The beast's **power** and **authority** is indicated by his **horns** with **ten diadems**, which suggest universal sovereignty. Satan, it will be recalled, had also seven heads and ten horns (12:3). The beast from the sea is a clone of the dragon. But he is also an evil parody of Christ in his claim to universal sovereignty (see 19:12) and in the presence on his heads of **blasphemous names** (see 19:12). This is probably a reference to the divine titles such as 'Lord', 'God' 'Saviour' which were given to the emperors even when they were still living. The coins of the time bear witness to this practice.

This beast has received from its 'father' the dragon **his power and his throne and great authority**. The parody of Christ is obvious (see Matt 28:18; Rom 1:4; Eph 1:23).

3,4 The blasphemous mimicry continues with the description of **one of its heads**: it has been fatally wounded, but it has been healed. The parallel to the Lamb is indicated by the fact that the Lamb is described in 13:8 (see 5:6) in exactly the same language, as 'having been slaughtered'. And a death and resurrection of the beast is suggested by the language of 13:14: 'the beast had been wounded by the sword and yet lived'.

It is possible that John has in mind a legend concerning the emperor Nero, who had claimed divine honours, terrorised the infant church in Rome, and provided a model for all future attacks on the church everywhere. On June 8, AD 68, Nero committed suicide. But few people actually saw the body or witnessed his burial. It was rumoured that Nero had not really died, that he had joined the Parthians, the great enemy of Rome. He would return as head of the Parthian army and exact a terrible vengeance on Rome because of its hatred and rejection of him.

We cannot be certain that John had Nero in mind when he painted his portrait of the beast. What is certain is that the beast presents himself as an alternative to Christ, as Christ's *alter ego* who is to be worshipped instead of Christ.

Just as the faithful worshipping community of the Lamb comes from all nations and tribes (7:9), so the **whole earth** gapes in **amazement** at the beast, and prostrates itself in worship before the **dragon** and the **beast**. To the **beast**, that counterfeit god, they give the acclamation and praise which is due to God alone. 'Who is like the beast?' they ask, in mockery of the question, 'Who is a God like you?' (Ps 35:10; Exod 15:11). And the defiant question, 'Who can fight against the beast?' echoes the challenge issued by the infidel Goliath (1 Sam 17:10). The Philistine giant's challenge and boast were an attack on God by the gods. It was a test of who is worthy to be worshipped.

Demonic powers are unleashed when false gods are worshipped. Contrariwise, the powers of evil and the demonic are checked and destroyed when Christians maintain the 'testimony of Jesus', and worship God and the Lamb. With such worship the defeat of the beast which Christ achieved on the cross is repeated in the life of the church (see comments on 12:7-12).

5,6 The dragon gave the beast this or that. It seems that the dragon really does have the authority to say: 'To you I will give the glory of the kingdoms of this world and all this authority; for it has been given over to me, and I give it to anyone I please' (see Luke 4:6). But four times in Revelation 13:5–8 John says that the beast 'was given' or 'was allowed'. This way of speaking is called the 'divine passive'. It means: God gave or allowed.

In short, the beast can do no more and no less than what God allows. The beast's (and the dragon's) power and authority are not ultimate, nor are they equal to that of God. They are limited and controlled by God. God gives the beast **a mouth** so that it can betray its own rebellious nature by **uttering haughty and blasphemous words** (see Rom 3:13,14; Matt 15:18,19).

Furthermore, God puts a time limit on the beast's exercise of **authority**: **forty-two months**. This is the time of the church's witness, the time before the return of

Christ, when the people of God will be trampled on and persecuted and seemingly defeated (see 11:2–9;13:7).

During this limited period, defined symbolically as **forty-two months**, the beast blasphemes **God**, both **his name and his dwelling**. To blaspheme God's **name** is to blaspheme God himself, for God and his name cannot be separated. The imperial cult especially involved blasphemy, inasmuch as the emperors were given divine names which properly belong to God alone.

The blasphemy against God's **dwelling** (literally 'tabernacle') is explained by John as blasphemy against those who **dwell** (or tabernacle) **in heaven** These are the worshipping people of God (11:1,2;15-19) who prostrate themselves before God's throne. God dwells in their midst, together with the Lamb (7:15). An attack on God is an attack on his people; an attack on the people of God is an attack on God himself.

7 God permits such an attack on himself and on his **saints**. He even permits the beast to **conquer** his saints (see 11:7–10). What, then, of God's promises of protection (12:13–17), promises that the gates of Hades will not prevail against his church (Matt 16:18); promises that Christians are 'super-conquerors' in Christ (Rom 8:37)? The answer lies in Christ. Christ's death is his victory; the cross is his throne. By killing Christ, the powers of evil destroyed themselves; they snatched defeat from the jaws of victory. They wounded Christ's heel, but he crushed their head (Gen 3:15). Indeed, the wound which the beast displays (13:3) is truly mortal, for it is inflicted by Christ (see 12:7–9).

Those who are 'in Christ', and among whom God dwells, share in Christ's victory by virtue of their dying and rising with him in baptism (Rom 6:1–11). It is true, Christians still get sick, they still die, and death seems to be entitled to claim another victory. Certainly some Christians die as a direct result of their confession to Christ. We still have such martyrs today. The beast still seems to be winning the war. But Christians know which view of reality is the ultimate one, the one that matters.

Victory lies with the Lamb who was slain, not with the beast who in the end will be cast into the lake of fire, together with his fellow beast, and the dragon, and the worshippers of the beast (19:20,21;20:10–15).

8 The beast has a worldwide following, corresponding to the universal mission of the church (11:6–10). 'All the inhabitants of the earth' is John's usual phrase for men and women in active rebellion against God (for example, 3:10;6:10;8:13;11:10). The beast exercises authority over them, and they acknowledge and activate that authority by worshipping the beast. Such people cannot possibly have their names written by God in **the book of life of the Lamb that was slaughtered**. That is to say, they are not followers of the Lamb; they are not known to him; they do not worship and obey him (see John 10:14,27). (For comments on the phrase **book of life** see commentary on 3:5).

A note on verse 8 in the NRSV says that the verse may be translated: '. . . written in the book of life of the Lamb that was slaughtered from the foundation of the world' (compare NIV; Phillips). This translation is to be preferred. It is true that God 'chose us in Christ before the foundation of the world to be holy and blameless before him' (Eph 1:4). But John wants here to say something else; he wants to remind his hearers of the divine perspective on the battle that is going on between the dragon and the church.

The Lamb was not slain by the whim and will of Satan, but by the foreknowledge and will of God (see Acts 2:23; 1 Pet 1:19,20). There is something mysteriously constant about the crucified Christ which goes behind the spatial and temporal limitations implied in the phrase, 'he suffered under Pontius Pilate'. From the perspective of heaven, the crucifixion is not just a momentary event in history. In terms of victory over the beast, the Lamb always was, always is, and always will be the Lamb Who Was Slain. Ever since sin first came into the world, forgiveness of sins has been for the sake of this Lamb.

It is this theological perspective, one which crosses the boundaries of space and time, which John wants his hearers to make their own. They will then see things as they really are, not as Satan fakes them. The way to retain this perspective is to continue to worship, for worship enables Christians to participate in God's work, and to see the reality of their existence from the perspective of eternity.

9 The vision of the horrible beast ends with a warning: peaceful coexistence is impossible. It's an either/or situation. You worship either the beast or the Lamb.

For the last time in Revelation, **anyone who has an ear** is summoned urgently to **listen**. Unlike the calls which conclude the prophetic proclamations to the churches (2:1 – 3:22), the summons here functions as an introduction to the prophetic word. It resembles the prophetic preamble: 'Hear the word of the Lord!' *What* should be heard, and *how* it should be heard, is stated in verse 10.

10 Years before John wrote, the prophet Jeremiah had brought to Jerusalem a fearful message of judgment:

> Those who are for death shall go to their death,
> and those for the sword to the sword;
> those who are for famine to famine,
> and those for captivity to captivity. (Jer 15:2 NEB)

John echoes Jeremiah, but his thrust is somewhat different. The disciples' Gethsemane experience seems to have influenced the interpretation of Jeremiah's words. They are now thought to apply to Christians who are tempted to compromise, or to take vindicatory action against those who make life miserable.

The first couplet of verse 10a urges Christians to stand firm, to accept the facts of life. Unlike Peter, who said he'd go to prison for his Lord, but then denied that he even knew him, John's people are to recognise God's hand in whatever happens to them. They are to bear the stigma of Christ even to the point of imprisonment and death. Compromise is not part of the Christian's vocabulary.

The second couplet (verse 10b) speaks about paying back, taking vengeance. The one who takes the sword will die by that same sword (see Matt 26:51–56). You don't protect the church or the gospel by force of arms or with any earthly power. The gospel needs no defence, and God is the church's protection. God, of course, can look after himself.

God's way to victory was the way of the cross. His power is in the preaching of the word of the cross; it is the 'power of God to salvation' (Rom 1:16). God's way was to take all sin and evil upon himself, on the cross, and so break the power of Satan once and for all (Col 2:15). Two things there are which die when we don't pass them on: enmity and love. Love flourishes when you pass it on; enmity dies when you absorb it.

The final sentence of verse 10 says in the Greek: 'Here is the patience and the faith of the saints'. John seems to be speaking directly to his hearers: **Here** means, in this context, 'amid all this' (J.B. Phillips) talk of compromise and vengeance. 'Here those who understand the way of the cross exhibit the perseverance and faith which is characteristic of saints'. John's words are a challenge. He expects a response in the life of his hearers.

In summary: John warns his hearers that as they face the threat of the beast from the sea, their **patience**, that is their courage under pressure, will be given a good workout. As a pastor, John would be very happy if he could say of his people what Paul said of the Christians in Thessalonica:

> We boast of you among the churches of God for your patience and faith during all your persecutions and the afflictions that you are enduring. (2 Thess 1:4)

11 The parody of the blessed Trinity is completed with the arrival of the second beast, the one who later on is called the 'false prophet' (16:13;19:20;20:10). This beast apes the Holy Spirit. God's Spirit bears witness to Christ through signs and wonders (Acts 2:22; Rom 15:19). The third person in the unholy trinity is the mouthpiece of the dragon, and he, too, performs miracles (13:14; see 2 Thess 2:9).

Furthermore, just as the Holy Spirit inspires people to believe in Christ and to worship God in Jesus' name, so this beast is bent on establishing the universal worship of the dragon. In earthly terms, the second beast is the false preacher, the false priest, the false teacher. He is legion. He dominates the electronic media.

Characteristic of the second **beast** is that he rises **out of the earth**. The earth is a friend of God's people (12:16).

So this is the start of the beast's deception: his origins in 'the earth' might lead us to suppose that he, like the earth itself, is on our side. His appearance supports the supposition, for he looks **like a lamb**. He is not powerful: he has only **two horns**, in contrast to the first beast and the great red dragon, who each had ten horns (12:3;13:1). The impersonation of a lamb is devilishly deliberate. Christians will immediately think of The Lamb (5:6), their Lord Jesus. In all, the beast's origin and appearance are meant to give the impression that he is on the Lord's side and therefore on our side.

But, as frequently happens in Revelation, the appearance reflects the *apparent* reality; true reality is expressed in what is heard, especially in the liturgy of heavenly worship. In this case, the beast's own words betray him. He might look like a lamb and seem to belong to the Lamb, but he speaks **like a dragon**. Listen carefully, shut your eyes to the outward appearance, test what this lamb says against what the Lamb says, and you will discover that he is not on your side, not on the side of the Lamb. He is on the side of Satan. He is a wolf in lamb's clothing, a false prophet (Matt 7:15; Rev 16:13;19:20).

12 The beast's horns suggest that it wields the power of the Lamb. In fact, however, it **exercises all the authority of the first beast on its behalf**. The translation, 'on its behalf', is a legitimate rendering of the Greek. Preferable, however, is Moffatt's translation: 'He exerts the full authority of the beast *in his presence*' (compare NEB, TEV). A true prophet stands in God's presence, takes his orders from God, and serves him alone, like Elijah (1 Kings 17:1) and Gabriel (Luke 1:19). The false prophet stands in the presence of the beast and acts as his mouthpiece and servant. It must be remembered, of course, that the beast gets its authority from the dragon.

The specified task of the second beast is to act as the agent or publicity officer of the first beast; he is to plan and promote the worldwide worship of the beast. In plain language, the false prophet's brief is to persuade everyone to worship Satan in the person of Satan's earthly representative, the political and economic power structures of the empire, headed by the emperor.

What John is depicting to his hearers, then, is the enemy behind the attractive facade of the Roman provincial world. First there is the dragon. Secondly, there is the first beast, epitomised in the person of the emperor. Thirdly, there is the second beast, who represents human ideologies, religious movements (such as New Age), evangelists and so-called prophets who prey on people's fears and hopes. They proclaim, not the word of the Lord, but their own word, to their own advantage. Prophets for profit, they are.

Hearers and readers should keep in mind that the beasts represent the dragon; they are carbon copies of their master. What they do, he does; what he does, they do. So no attempt should be made neatly to divide up the work, so to speak. The total picture is of an evil trinity, three in one and one in three. The dragon (Satan) is a liar and deceiver, as is the second beast. The dragon (Satan) demands worship, just as does the first beast.

13 The true Lamb created a people for God, a worshipping community, a holy nation (7:15;11:1; 1 Peter 2:9). The beast who looks like a lamb plans likewise to create a community of people for Satan, consisting of all 'the inhabitants of the earth' (13:8). He achieves this goal by 1) performing miracles; 2) establishing the first beast as a cult figure; 3) creating what amounts to a membership list, with every member having his or her own badge of membership.

First of all, then, the beast (the false prophet) presents himself as a true prophet in the mould of Elijah. He performs all kinds of miracles; he even makes **fire come down from heaven to earth** (1 Kings 18:24–38). Miracles are ambiguous. They prove nothing about the genuineness of a prophet's or preacher's credentials. A miracle-worker could be from Satan or from God. Our Lord, who himself performed miracles, warned that in the last times false messiahs and false prophets would perform marvellous miracles (Mark 13:22; Matt 24:24; see 2 Thess 2:9). Miracles, then, are very unreliable tests of a prophet's authenticity. Listen to his or her confession to Christ; look at the fruit he or she bears! (see Deut 13:2–4; Matt 7:15–20; 1 John 4:1–6).

14 But 'by dint of the miracles he is allowed to perform in the presence of the beast' (Moffatt), the second beast is able to seduce the gullible and willing **inhabitants of the earth**. He is **allowed to perform** these miracles, permitted by God to do them. The phrase 'the inhabitants of the earth' is John's term for those who have already thumbed their noses at God, ignored him (Eph 4:17–19). They have deceived themselves into thinking that God can safely be written off. So that same God lets them experience the results of their own folly. Those who deceive themselves are easily deceived by others. They end up entrapped in a web of lies and deceit. You will never recognise a lie until you know what is the truth.

The second beast, the false prophet, has so dazzled his audience with his miracles that they eat out of his hand. He tells them to repeat the sin of Israel at Sinai (the golden bull, Exodus 32) and the sin of Nebuchadnezzar (the golden statue, Daniel 3), and to create an **image** or statue of (not: **for**) the **beast that had been wounded by the sword and yet lived** (see comments on 13:3).

15 After the image had been created, God permitted the false prophet to imitate the Holy Spirit himself. Just as God gave life to Adam, the image of God (Gen 2:7); just as the Holy Spirit gave life to the dry bones of Israel (Ezek 37:10) and to the two witnesses (Rev 11:11), so now the second beast mimics the Holy Spirit by giving **breath** (Greek: *pneuma* = spirit, wind, breath) or life **to the image of the beast**. The result? The image was able to speak.

Religious fraud is not a modern phenomenon. Trickery, deception, magic, and ventriloquism were par for the course in John's day among the priests and prophets of the various cults and temples. It is part of the deception of false religion; it is part of the self-deception of those who believe what they want to believe.

The significant aspect of this statue was not that it could talk — many religious statues could be made to appear to talk and even to move — but that it served as a means of identifying who is who in terms of religious commitment. In the days of Nebuchadnezzar, you either prostrated yourself before the golden statue and lived, or you stood up straight and died (Daniel 3:1-6). Now, once again, God's people are tested: **worship the image of the beast** and live, or refuse to worship and **be killed**. Thus the godless state, the parody of God, establishes order and conformity by killing. A government always becomes bestial when it demands absolute obedience, and denies freedom of worship to the people of God.

Christians in the Roman province of Asia were under enormous pressure to show that they were loyal, committed citizens of the city and the empire, by participating in the imperial cult, sacrificing to local deities, venerating Artemis, and generally being part of the religious life of the community. Life became economically and socially marginal for those who refused to conform to local religious patterns and practices.

Some people in the churches of Asia tried to persuade Christians that a compromise of sorts was not only advisable but also appropriate, since idols are really nothing (see 1 Cor 8:4–6). But John exposes the idolatrous nature of the worship of the emperor or Artemis, or of making sacrifices at meetings of the trade guilds. Compromise might be attractive, but it is a fatal attraction.

Once upon a time, Shadrach, Meshach and Abednego lived in the city of the beast. They had to choose: worship a statue of the beast and stay alive, or worship God and be put to death (Dan 3:1–7). In the case of Christians in Asia, the choice is: worship God and live, or worship the statue and die. That is the reality, as God sees it.

16,17 The counterfeit prophet (the second beast) has fascinated 'the inhabitants of the earth' with his miracles (v 13). He has persuaded people to make a cult figure out of the beast (13:14,15). In his efforts to introduce an alternative to the worship of God, the second beast causes all those who worship the beast to be marked with a distinctive mark.

The parody continues: just as God's people are marked with his seal (7:2), so the followers of Satan are given their mark. And just as God's people consist of men and women from every spectrum of humanity (7:9;11:18), so the followers of the beast and the dragon are said to represent humankind in all its diversity. The phrase 'both small and great' is a way of speaking about all kinds of people; it is shorthand for totality.

The followers of the beast are defined more closely in economic and social terms: **rich and poor, free and slave**. A totalitarian state is unendingly greedy. It demands absolute commitment on the part of its citizens, and it is not satisfied until it has sucked its people dry.

Those who acknowledge the beast's claims are **marked** in conspicuous places: on **their right hand** (or perhaps, 'wrist') **or forehead**. In John's day it was not unusual to mark people by tattooing or branding them to indicate ownership, or to protect someone. Thus God marked Cain with his protecting mark. The apostle Paul said that he bore the marks of suffering which indicated that he belonged to Christ. Readers of *Phantom* comics know of the 'good' mark of the Phantom; it protects all who live under its sign.

It is hard to know what kind of mark was placed upon those who worshipped the beast. Perhaps it was the mark which a slave received, or the mark stamped on a coin. In either case, the meaning would be: I belong to the beast, to the emperor, to Satan.

Another possibility is that the mark refers to the sealing of a contract. The mark, then, would confirm that the bearer accepts the rule and authority of the beast. Or perhaps the mark is something like the stamp which, in some countries, voters receive on their hand to indicate that they have voted as the law requires, and to stop them from breaking the law by voting more than once. In this case the mark would be a form of control and a form of recognition of an obedient citizen.

It is impossible to be certain about the meaning of the mark. The reference to the 'right hand' and to the economic sanctions which are directed against those who do not have the mark suggests a combination of ideas. To get into the local market you had to make a little sign of respect to the local god or to the image of the emperor. If you did that, you received a mark on your wrist or forehead.

In the market itself, you used imperial coinage. If you wanted to survive, and even flourish in the economic and social world of Asia, you had to use the coin of the realm. Those coins had stamped on them the imperial image (see Matt 22:21,22), often in the form of a divine or semi-divine being. Sometimes they bore the image of the goddess Roma.

Christians were between a rock and a hard place. The 'mark of the beast' did not mean death. On the contrary, it was the passport to operate in society. There was no coercion, apart from the fear of missing out on the goodies which society had to offer. Poverty is the inevitable price you pay for refusing to worship the gods of state and society. To avoid poverty and to grasp the good life, it is deceptively simple to move from wary participation in the life of the city to identifying yourself with the culture, to letting the city determine your values and set your priorities.

In the Roman province of Asia, the state did not threaten to imprison people or behead them for being nonconformists. It simply applied social and economic pressure to persuade people to accept the mark of the beast. The trouble was: to accept the mark was to accept the beast's name and authority.

The simplest solution for Christians was to tell 'silent lies', that is, do or say nothing which would publicise the fact that they were different. In short, the easy way out was compromise. John's point is simply that compromise is impossible for faithful Christians.

17,18 The attempts to discover the precise nature of the mark of the beast have not been helped by the information which John gives. He says that the mark is

- — the name of the beast
- — the number of its name
- — the number of a person (or: 'a human number' or: 'a man's number')
- — six hundred and sixty-six or six hundred and sixteen (depending on which manuscripts are correct).

A lot of attention has been devoted through the centuries to trying to discover the name of the person behind the number six hundred and sixty-six (or six hundred and sixteen). Among the candidates have been

Nero, several popes, Martin Luther, Napoleon, Hitler, Ronald Reagan, and Gorbachev. One thing is certain: if John had a person in mind, it would be someone from his own era, and not from a later age. He is talking about someone his own people knew. The best candidate is the emperor Nero.

Nero fits the bill well in terms of his character, his policies, his manner of death, and the legends surrounding him. Nero unleashed a bloodbath on Christians, just as Hitler, another monster, unleashed a bloodbath on Jews. Nero committed suicide, but, as also in Hitler's case, there was immediate speculation about his death, and talk about his return to establish his imperial rule once again. Nero fits well the image of the beast who had his throat cut, who was dead, and is now alive (13:3,14).

It so happens that the name *Neron Kesar* (an attested Hebrew version of Caesar Nero) has the numerical value of six hundred and sixty-six (n=50; r=200; o=6; k=100; s=60; the vowels 'e' and 'a' don't count). When the final 'n' is dropped the total value of *Nero Kesar* is six hundred and sixteen (see the footnote to v 18). So if John wanted his readers to recognise an individual whose name is coded six hundred and sixty-six (or six hundred and sixteen), Nero is the most likely candidate. And it does seem that John had Nero in mind. But why go about identifying Nero in such a roundabout way? It certainly was not the way to keep a secret, because any Roman official with some imagination could have worked out that John had Nero in mind. Using numbers as a kind of code was a common practice.

It seems that John was doing more than simply making the statement: the emperor Nero is the beast. He is saying something about the very nature of the beast. Notice that John does *not* say that **anyone with understanding** would be wise enough to work out the *name* of the beast; rather, he says that such a person could work out the **number of the beast**. The focus is more on the significance of the number itself than on who the number stands for.

Pick a number! What would be a good number, a human number, for a beast who is the symbol of all false religion and all anti-God and anti-Christ activities?

Christians who were accustomed to working with numbers as symbols were familiar with the idea of seven hundred and seventy-seven as the number for God in his perfection. So seven hundred and seventy-seven was a human number for God.

For the anti-God, for the beast, for the one who wanted to be given the worship which belongs to God alone (13:4), for this parody of God and the Lamb, what better number could there be than six hundred and sixty-six? John sees numbers (and measurements) as a means of access to the essential structure of a person or thing. Numbers reveal something fundamental, the essence.

Satan is essentially and fundamentally a fraud, a counterfeit 'God' who always falls short. He speaks lies, not the truth; he apes the triune God with his unholy trinity, but he never is, nor ever will be, God. His proper number is six hundred and sixty-six, the number which perpetually falls short of seven hundred and seventy-seven. It was a helpful happenstance that Nero's name could be so arranged that it added up numerically to six hundred and sixty-six. But John's primary focus is on the symbol of the number six hundred and sixty-six, not on whose name the number might represent.

Understanding that six hundred and sixty-six is the right number for the beast **calls for wisdom**. Wisdom, not smartness. True wisdom, that which begins with the fear of the Lord, is the wisdom of the cross of Christ crucified. It is a wisdom born of faith in Christ, the Lamb who was slain. Such wisdom, a gift of God, has no trouble in seeing the beast for what it is. Such God-given wisdom recognises that worship of the beast is worship not of the Creator but of the creature who has fallen short of the glory of God. True wisdom sees clearly that six hundred and sixty-six is the proper number for any person, power, or structure which is opposed to God and his people.

It is worth noting that the first known commentator on the number of the beast is Irenaeus of Lyons, who was born about sixty years after John wrote Revelation. Since he was much nearer to John's time and culture than we are, he deserves a hearing. Irenaeus sees the number six hundred and sixty-six as a symbol which interprets rather than identifies the beast. For Irenaeus the number six hundred and sixty-six evoked ideas of evil, human wickedness, idolatry, and rebellion against God. The number six hundred and sixty-six is a fitting number for the beast, the agent of Satan the arch-enemy of God and his people.

WORSHIP: The new song of the 'other' community, 14:1–5

14 Then I looked, and there was the Lamb, standing on
Mount Zion! And with him were one hundred forty-four
thousand who had his name and his Father's name written
on their foreheads. 2 And I heard a voice from heaven
like the sound of many waters and like the sound of loud
thunder; the voice I heard was like the sound of harpists
playing on their harps, 3 and they sing a new song before
the throne and before the four living creatures and before
the elders. No one could learn that song except the one
hundred forty-four thousand who have been redeemed
from the earth. 4 It is these who have not defiled
themselves with women, for they are virgins; these follow
the Lamb wherever he goes. They have been redeemed
from humankind as first fruits for God and the Lamb,
5 and in their mouth no lie was found; they are blameless.

Right in the middle of the worldwide community of those who worship the beast and have their mark of membership on their foreheads or right hands — right in the middle of this community there lives another community, the alternative community, the people of the Lamb.

John has described this community several times (for example, 7:4–17;11:1–3). But having just spoken of the community of the beast (in chapter 13), John's pastoral instincts impel him to remind his hearers that *they* belong to an alternative community, the fellowship of the Lamb. So he describes briefly this community, its worship, and essential characteristics.

1 John sees the Lamb, the Saviour Jesus Christ. In other reports of the revelations of Jesus which he receives,

John portrays Jesus as one who lives with and among his people. In the report of the inaugural vision (1:9–20), the 'one like the Son of Man' stands among the 'seven lampstands' which are the churches of the Roman province of Asia (1:12,13,20). In the throne-room scene of chapter 5, John saw the Lamb standing 'among the elders' (5:6), that is, among the worshipping people of God who sing a new song (5:9-14). The symbolic number of these worshippers is one hundred and forty-four thousand. They are marked with God's seal on their foreheads. Their shepherd is 'the Lamb at the centre of the throne' (7:17). Indeed, Jesus himself leads his people in worship before the throne (8:1–4), and sees to their safety as they live in the hostile community of the beast (11:1–3).

Now, once more, John reports that he saw **the Lamb**. Once more the Lamb is **standing** with and among his people, the one hundred and forty-four thousand who have on **their foreheads** the **name** of God and the Lamb (see 7:3). Names are written on people as a form of identification. Those who worship the beast have branded on them the name of the beast (13:17). There is no doubt as to who they are and to whom they belong. Likewise, the Lord knows those who are his. They have been sealed with the Holy Spirit (Eph 4:30) and marked with the name of the Lamb and with **his Father's name**. To be so known by God and to be given an identity by him is to have salvation in the fullest sense.

The Lamb and his people stand on **Mount Zion**. This is neither the geographical Mount Zion nor the heavenly Mount Zion, but the symbolic Mount Zion. It is the place of God's presence among his worshipping people, the place of freedom and safety for the children of God. It is the holy hill on which God has set his king (Ps 2:6). It is the place of salvation for all who call upon the name of the Lord in the Day of the Lord (Joel 2:28–32).

2,3 This communal 'calling on the name of the Lord', foretold by the prophet Joel, is heard by John as a single **voice from heaven**. There is no contradiction here. God is present among his people on earth, but they are part of the worshipping community around the **throne** of God. Mountains are the place where heaven and earth meet. Mount Zion is the place where God and his people meet; it is where the new Jerusalem comes down from heaven to earth. In that city there is no temple except God himself, who dwells in the middle of his people (11:2–4;21:10,11;22:3–5).

One of the major emphases in the book of Revelation is this: the small, weak, harried and harassed people of God on earth have received from him one mighty gift, the gift of worship. When they worship, they participate in heavenly worship which is performative, dynamic, and effective.

The heavenly liturgy which John hears reminds him of the **sound of many waters** (like Niagara Falls? see 1:15;19:6) or of **thunder** (see 6:1;19:6) or of **harpists playing on their harps** (better: 'lyres', see 5:9). So John draws on the sounds of nature and of instruments in an effort to capture the music of the liturgy. It's a new sound, proving that the devil has neither the best tunes nor the new ones.

The words of the heavenly liturgy are new too (see 5:9). They are new to human beings, they have not been composed by human beings, and they cannot be learnt by human beings unless God enables them to do so. For the **new song** is the song of the Lamb (5:9), the song of salvation and victory which has been won by the Lamb who was slain. By his death and resurrection he abolished death and brought life and immortality to light (2 Tim 1:10). He also destroyed him who had the power of death, the devil (Heb 2:14). By his blood Christ 'ransomed for God saints from every tribe and language and people and nation' (5:9).

No human being could dream up such a song. It has to be taught by God (Ps 25:12), for it does not come naturally. And once by faith it is learnt, it has to be practised. Every act of worship, every eucharist, every meditation upon the word, is an exercise of faith, a practising of the new song which only the **redeemed** can learn and sing. For they have been set free, separated out from **the earth**, that is, out from among the rest of humankind (14:4) who reject the Lamb, choose to be marked with the name of the beast, and worship him (13:4,12).

4,5 Four distinguishing marks identify these redeemed singers of the new song. First, **they are virgins**, that is, **they have not defiled themselves with women**. In a book which continually uses symbolic language, it is foolish to insist that these one hundred and forty-four thousand are unmarried males who have religiously refrained from sexual relationships with women. There is not a hint in Scripture that God regards sexual abstinence as a condition for membership in his community. In any case, where on earth do you find virginal males who meet another requirement: **in their mouth no lie was found; they are blameless**? If these characteristics are taken literally, we would have to conclude that nobody, male or female, belongs to the one hundred and forty-four thousand.

What, then, is the symbolism of this first characteristic: **they are virgins**? The simplest answer is that they are men and women who have not worshipped the beast; thus they have kept themselves clean from the pollution of idolatry, which is often spoken of in the language of sexual immorality (see Jer 3:8,9; Matt 12:39; James 4:4).

In this understanding, the one hundred and forty-four thousand 'virgins' are the 'bride of the Lamb', the new Jerusalem. She is 'holy' (21:9–11), not in herself, but because Christ has **redeemed** her, washed her and cleansed her, presented her to himself as a bride without spot or blemish (Eph 5:27). These 'virgins' are the opposite of the whore Babylon who corrupts the nations with her seductive power. She is the mother of all whores (17:5). Christians have not been seduced by the painted beauty of the prostitute Babylon; they have not 'drunk from the wine of her fornication' (17:2).

The second characteristic of the one hundred and forty-four thousand is that these holy people of God **follow the Lamb wherever he goes**. They are true disciples, true sheep of the Good Shepherd (John 1:37;10:27). Worshippers of the beast follow where he goes; he goes to destruction (17:18). Worshippers of the Lamb also follow where he goes; he goes through death to life (John

12:20–26). Once an eager would-be disciple of Jesus announced: 'I will follow you wherever you go'. Jesus responded by reminding him of the hard road he had to walk as the Son of Man, a road that must end in the cross. And he warned his followers not to be ashamed of him, but to be willing to lose their lives for him. Such faithful followers he will confess before his Father in heaven (Luke 9:22-27,57,58).

Those who follow the Lamb wherever he goes can expect to experience hard times, rejection, captivity, exile, even death (13:10). They can, however, also most certainly expect life and salvation (19:14).

Thirdly, the one hundred and forty-four thousand have been purchased with the blood of the Lamb. This sets them apart from the bulk of **humankind** who worship the beast. They are special, these one hundred and forty-four thousand. Like the **firstfruits** of the womb or of the crop, this new Israel of God is set aside, dedicated to the service of God (Lev 2:12; Ezek 45:1;48:9). They are a suitable offering in the service (=worship) of God, **for they are blameless**.

They are **blameless**. This fourth characteristic is not an innate one, but a gift of God. The Lamb was slain just so that his people could be spotless and blameless (Eph 1:4; Col 1:22), like the Lamb of God himself (1 Pet 1:19).

So as followers of the Lamb, Christians offer to God sacrifice and praise. Such worship is acceptable to God for Jesus' sake (Rom 12:1; Eph 4:28–5:2). This is so because they have washed their robes in the blood of the Lamb (7:14) and they come into God's presence as pure and holy people, spotless in his sight.

Such purity and holiness expresses itself in the foremost visible mark of the Christian: truthfulness. Lies and falsehoods are one of the dominant characteristics of the beast (16:13;19:20), his lord Satan (John 8:44), and his followers (Rev 3:9). In contrast, truthfulness in both word and action is what Jesus does and teaches (John 14:6; Eph 4:21). Such truthfulness has always been the mark of the people of God (Zech 8:16; Matt 5:17; Eph 4:15,25). In the new Jerusalem, there is no place for liars (Rev 21:7;22:15).

In summary: the picture of the one hundred and forty-four thousand worshipping people of God serves to remind John's hearers that the community of the beast is not the only option. There is another possibility, an alternative community: the people of the Lamb. Do not compromise, John says. Do not be misled. Remain in and with the Lamb.

The other function of this account of heavenly liturgy and of the worshipping community is to initiate the series of judgment activities which are reported in the rest of the chapter 14. This is a normal pattern in Revelation: God's acts of judgment and salvation flow out of heavenly liturgy, and take place in the context of heavenly worship (see commentary on 5:8 and 6:10).

NARRATIVE: The last gospel call; the last judgment, 14:6-20

**6 Then I saw another angel flying in midheaven, with
an eternal gospel to proclaim to those who live[r] on the
earth — to every nation and tribe and language and
people. 7 He said in a loud voice, 'Fear God and give him
glory, for the hour of his judgment has come; and worship
him who made heaven and earth, the sea and the springs
of water.'**

**8 Then another angel, a second, followed, saying,
'Fallen, fallen is Babylon the great! She has made all
nations drink of the wine of the wrath of her fornication.'**

**9 Then another angel, a third, followed them, crying with
a loud voice, 'Those who worship the beast and its image,
and receive a mark on their foreheads or on their hands,
10 they will also drink the wine of God's wrath, poured
unmixed into the cup of his anger, and they will be
tormented with fire and sulfur in the presence of the holy
angels and in the presence of the Lamb. 11 And the smoke
of their torment goes up forever and ever. There is no rest
day or night for those who worship the beast and its image
and for anyone who receives the mark of its name.'**

[12] Here is a call for the endurance of the saints, those who keep the commandments of God and hold fast to the faith of[s] Jesus.

[13] And I heard a voice from heaven saying, 'Write this: Blessed are the dead who from now on die in the Lord.' 'Yes,' says the Spirit, 'they will rest from their labors, for their deeds follow them.'

[14] Then I looked, and there was a white cloud, and seated on the cloud was one like the Son of Man, with a golden crown on his head, and a sharp sickle in his hand!
[15] Another angel came out of the temple, calling with a loud voice to the one who sat on the cloud, 'Use your sickle and reap, for the hour to reap has come, because the harvest of the earth is fully ripe.' [16] So the one who sat on the cloud swung his sickle over the earth, and the earth was reaped.

[17] Then another angel came out of the temple in heaven, and he too had a sharp sickle. [18] Then another angel came out from the altar, the angel who has authority over fire, and he called with a loud voice to him who had the sharp sickle, 'Use your sharp sickle and gather the clusters of the vine of the earth, for its grapes are ripe.'
[19] So the angel swung his sickle over the earth and gathered the vintage of the earth, and he threw it into the great wine press of the wrath of God. [20] And the wine press was trodden outside the city, and blood flowed from the wine press, as high as a horse's bridle, for a distance of about two hundred miles.[t]

[r] Gk *sit*

[s] Or *to their faith in*

[t] Gk *one thousand six hundred stadia*

The three 'woes' which John had talked about earlier (9:12;11:14) are now matched by three pronouncements which are good news and assurance to the faithful. They contain, however, implicit notes of warning against compromise and apostasy. The angels who deliver the three messages are the first in a group of seven who are involved in the end-time activities which are reported here. John's report of these activities culminates in twin accounts of the harvest of the wicked (14:14–20).

6 The reference to **another angel flying in midheaven** is a hint to hearers that they should recall the three 'woes' which were announced by an eagle who 'flew in midheaven' (8:13). The message of the angel is not, however, a 'woe', but **an eternal gospel**. Eternal, because it has to do with the age to come as well as with the present age (2 Cor 4:17,18). This gospel contrasts sharply with the 'gospels' of the prophets and priests of the imperial and local cults. These so-called gospels are transient, but they lead, if followed, to eternal condemnation (14:11).

The angel is concerned with the evangelisation of the whole world, or, as John puts it, 'all those who "sit" on the earth': **every nation and tribe and language and people**. These 'inhabitants of the earth' (17:2) have turned away from God. They have brought upon themselves the wrath of God, because they have failed to honour God as God, and refused to worship him. This is the primal sin (Rom 1:18–23).

7 The invitation of the angel includes the announcement that **the hour of [God's] judgment has come**. Good news? Yes. The very fact that God still addresses his rebellious creatures, that he has not given up on them, this is good news. It is good news that God calls people to **fear** him, that is, to put their hope and trust in him. It is good news that God urges people to prostrate themselves before him and to **worship him** who is the Maker of all things, including **heaven and earth, the sea and the springs of water**. These, by the way, are the elements of creation which are terribly affected when the bowls of God's wrath are poured out (16:2–8).

The proclamation of the gospel is carried out in the world by the people of God; they are symbolised here by an angel (= messenger). The angel calls in a **loud voice** so that everyone can hear, repent, believe, and live. This gospel proclamation is itself a sign of the impending end of all things (Mark 13:10; Matt 24:14).

8 When that End comes, and the Lord returns in judgment, then the time for repentance will be at an end. Then the great whore **Babylon**, the great city, will be destroyed. This is the first time in Revelation that the great city is named.

Babylon is people in deliberate rebellion against God; it is the powers of evil and injustice and brutality, the political systems and rulers and governments which ignore God and subvert his will. Babylon is science and technology used in the service of oppression and dehumanisation and murder; it is the perversion of the media; it is the false philosophies and 'isms' which seek to distort all moral values. Babylon is child abuse, rape, injustice, selfishness, conspicuous consumption, exploitation, greed, and materialism. Babylon is where we live.

In John's day, everyone knew that 'Babylon' was a code name for Rome. Babylon-Rome is guilty before God, because it has drawn the whole world into idolatry. It has caused **all nations** to **drink** the intoxicating **wine** of worship of false gods and idols. In biblical terms, such worship is **fornication** (Jer 3:8,9;13:27). Fornicators inherit, not the kingdom of God, but only the **wrath** of God (1 Cor 6:9,10; Eph 5:3–6).

Thus, in a very compressed, even shorthand, way, the **second angel** announces that those who drink the **wine** of Babylon's **fornication** will surely drink the wine of God's **wrath** (see 14:10).

The 'good news' in this second announcement is that Babylon has indeed **fallen**. The description of Babylon's 'fall' comes only in chapters 17–19, but her doom is a *fait accompli.* Here is another example of how John had to work. When he received his revelation, he was outside the parameters of space and time. He saw everything 'at once'. But he can't report everything at once, so he says: First I saw this, then I saw that. When he saw Babylon, he saw her as **fallen**. But he reports the 'how' of her fall only in chapters 17 and 18, when he narrates the details of his third revelation (17:1–21:8).

From God's perspective, from the only point of view which matters, Babylon is **fallen**. That is her condition. Her citizens, the alcoholics, have had their supply cut off, as G.B. Caird puts it. Is there, perhaps, yet hope for their rehabilitation? Will they, at the last, turn to God and live? Nineveh repented. Even now God calls the people of Babylon, the great city, to himself.

Today, when you hear his voice,
do not harden your hearts. (Heb 6:7; Ps 95:7)

9 The second angel had spoken of the fate of the city; the message of the third angel is addressed to the individual. The fate of each rebel against God is announced with chilling clarity. They worshipped the beast instead of the Lamb; they bear the mark of the beast instead of that of the Lamb (13:4,15). These actions were depicted in verse 8 as 'drinking the wine of the wrath of the harlot's fornication'. Now, therefore, they will drink the wine of **God's wrath** (see Jer 51:7).

A powerful picture is used to portray the terribleness of this **wrath.** It is like wine which has had spices stirred into it to increase its potency. It is left **unmixed** in the sense that no water is added to tone down its bite. In plain language, unrepentant worshippers of the beast will feel the full undiluted force of **God's wrath.**

The false prophet (the second beast) had performed his signs and wonders in the presence of the beast (13:14), and deceived his followers. These followers of the beast will receive their punishment **in the presence** of the Christ whom they rejected, and in the presence of **the holy angels.**

The punishment of the worshippers of the beast is like that of the inhabitants of Sodom and Gomorrah: **fire and sulphur** (Gen 19:24). But unlike Sodom and Gomorrah, which were destroyed and that was the end of it, the punishment of the worshippers of the beast endures **forever and ever**. This is a liturgical phrase (for example, 4:9,10;19:3;22:5). It is a reminder of the worship of the Lamb, which continues day and night without stopping (4:8;7:15). This joyous activity contrasts grimly with the unending unrest and restlessness of those who **worship the beast and its image**, and who bear the **mark of its name.**

12 Those who refuse to worship God and the Lamb are heading for unimaginable disaster (14:14-20); those who worship God and the Lamb look forward to unimaginable blessedness (14:13; see Matt 25:34). The purpose of the third angel's announcement is not to give Christians an occasion for rubbing their hands with glee

(*Schadenfreude*, the Germans call it) over the fate of their enemies. Rather, as John says directly to his hearers, '*Here*, in this opposition between the worship of God and the worship of the beast, must come to the fore the resistance and staying-power **of the saints**'. They are people who keep the word of God and their faith in Jesus (20:4). John addresses all his hearers; he seeks from them a positive response (see 13:10).

13 In the first revelation (1:9 – 3:22), Jesus himself commanded John to write down what he saw and heard (1:11;2:1). Probably the unidentified **voice from heaven** is again the voice divine (see 10:4;21:5). John is told to write down a sacred beatitude or macarism, as such a message is sometimes called. The divine utterance is passed on to the hearers when it is read to the assembled worshippers. The hearers respond with a 'Yes!'. The NRSV has missed the liturgical character of this little dialogue:

God:	Blessed are the dead who die in the Lord.
Hearers:	Yes indeed (= we accept and affirm the statement).
Holy Spirit:	They will enjoy rest from their labours, for they take with them the record of their service.

The assurance of 'blessedness' is given to those who **from now on** — that is, from this time of crisis — die as Christians. This does not mean those who die because they are Christians, but simply those who die as they have lived: **in the Lord**, belonging to him, obeying him, confessing him, rejecting the beast and all his ways (see Rom 14:7–9). Such people have the promise of the **Spirit** that they will enjoy the Lord's eternal Sabbath, resting from the strenuous service which made them so weary and sometimes caused them pain. They are such a contrast to the worshippers of the beast, whose fate it is to have no rest, day or night, from their torment and punishment (14:11).

The **labours** of the blessed ones are not specified. We may assume the reference is to the service which Christians render to God through their fellow human beings. Such selfless service is often misunderstood and misinterpreted; it is often made the object of mockery and scorn; and Christians are often exploited and manipulated by those street-wise people who see Christians as naive, romantic fools. Sometimes Christians are so frustrated by it all that they are tempted to give up and join the worshippers of the beast, who have no such demands made on their time and energy and are accepted by the world. They belong.

But constant Christians, the Spirit promises, will **rest from their labours**, for the record of their faith and their service is known to God. He remembers their service to him, even if they themselves were not aware that they were doing it (note Matt 25:37,38). Especially their faithful witness to Christ and their confession to the Lamb bear fruit as God has promised. These fruits of their labours (see Rom 15:28) will become apparent when many believers stand before the throne of God at the side of those who spoke to them the word of God, the eternal gospel of the Lamb who was slain. Then these loyal witnesses will 'shine like the brightness of the firmament . . . like the stars forever and ever' (Dan 12:3).

The judgment of the wicked, 14:14–20

The heavenly worship of 14:1–5 produced a call to everyone to join the liturgy. The reverse of this call is a warning to those who ignore the worship of God in favour of worship of the beast (14:6–11). As is usual in Revelation, the outcome of heavenly liturgy is punishment for the rebellious and wicked (14:14–20), and safety and salvation for the faithful servants of God (14:13).

So the little scroll (10:1 – 14:20), which gave John's hearers a short version of the whole book of Revelation, ends as the big book ends, with an account of the final judgment of the unrighteous world (14:14–20, repeated in 19:11 – 20:15).

Following the pattern provided by Joel 3:13, John presents a matching pair of judgment narratives. The one is of a grain harvest, the other of a harvest of grapes. 'Harvest' as an image of judgment was familiar to both Jews and Christians (see Jer 51:33; Matt 3:12;13:30). But *who* are being harvested? Some commentators say that John is giving twin accounts of the judgment of the righteous. Others say the doublet narrates the judgment of the unrighteous. Others again say that the grain harvest (14:14–16) pictures the judgment of the righteous, while the grape harvest (14:17–20) tells of the judgment of the wicked.

The view taken in this commentary is that both accounts tell of the judgment of the unrighteous. Facts in favour of this view are:

1) Doublets, that is, matching accounts of the same scene, are not uncommon in Revelation (for example, 4:1–11;5:6–14;6:1–4;8:7–12;18:1–3;18:21–24).

2) When John tells of the fate of the wicked, he always makes sure to say something about the safety of the faithful. So here, 14:13 precedes the accounts of the fate of the unfaithful and rebellious (14:14–20). The same practice is evident in the narrative of 6:12–7:17, and especially 20:1–10 (see the commentary on those verses).

3) The passage in Joel on which Revelation 14:14-20 is modelled clearly speaks only of the judgment of the wicked (Joel 3:9–21, especially v 13; see Jer 51:33). The prophecy in Joel displays the same pattern of concern for the safety of the righteous in the midst of the judgment of the wicked.

4) In the corresponding narrative (19:11 – 20:15) John reports only the judgment of the unrighteous. The righteous do not come into judgment (see comments on 20:4–6). There is a line of thought in the New Testament which says that the return of Christ will not mean judgment for the suffering and afflicted people of God. Only the wicked are judged. This thought is articulated by Paul when he writes:

> All this is evidence that God's judgment is right, and as a result you will be counted worthy of the kingdom of God, for which you are suffering. God is just: He will pay back trouble to those who trouble you and give relief to you who are troubled, and to us as well. This will happen when the Lord Jesus is revealed from heaven in blazing fire with his powerful angels. He will punish those who do not know God and do not obey the gospel of our Lord Jesus. They will be

> punished with everlasting destruction and shut out from the presence of the Lord and from the majesty of his power on the day he comes to be glorified in his holy people and to be marvelled at among all those who have believed. (2 Thess 1:5–10 NIV)

a) The grain harvest, 14:14–16

14 John sees the **white cloud** of God's presence in judgment (see 1:7). **Seated** on the cloud is **one like the Son of Man**, coming as he promised 'in a cloud with power and great glory' (Luke 21:27). This figure is surely the Lord Jesus who had revealed himself to John in the opening revelation (1:9–20). It is Jesus Christ who wields his **sickle** and does the reaping. And yet in the parallel account (vv 17–20) an angel is reported to reap the harvest, while in 19:15 Christ is said to be the one who treads out the winepress.

It seems that we have here another instance of John presenting the person of Jesus as an angel (see 7:2;8:3;10:1–4). Never, of course, does he say that Jesus *is* an angel; he could not do that without contradicting his strong confession to Christ as true God. But John does follow the Old Testament lead and present the Lord in the form of an angel. Here John seems to be reflecting the strong Christian tradition which associated angels with the Lord's activities when he returns to 'judge the living and the dead' (see 2 Thess 1:7; Matt 24:31; and 13:39).

If **the one like the Son of Man** is to be understood here as Jesus in angel form, then the activities which John reports in 14:6–20 are performed by seven angels, matching the seven angels who blew the seven trumpets (8:2,6–9:21;11:15), and who pour out the seven bowls of God's wrath (15:1,7,16:1–21).

15 **Another angel**, the fifth in this group of seven, speaks with the authority of God himself. He is said to come from **the temple**, the sanctuary, which in Revelation is the place of God's presence (see Num 10:35,36), the place where the people of God assemble around the throne to worship him (see comments on 8:1–4 and 11:1,2).

Like Gabriel (Luke 1:19), this angel stands in the presence of God (see Exod 14:19; Num 14:14). When the angel speaks, it is as if God himself speaks (see Gen 16:7–14). Through this 'Angel of the Presence' God directs his Son to take his sickle and to begin reaping immediately, because the grain is dry enough for harvest. God is 'the Lord of the harvest' (Matt 9:38); he gives his Son the authority to harvest, that is, to judge the world, 'because he is the Son of Man' (John 5:25–30).

The **hour to reap has come.** John's gospel often speaks of 'the hour', the decisive time when God's glory will be revealed in and through his Son (for example, 2:4;7:6;12:23,27). The phrase is meant to indicate God's control over events which seem to be controlled by human agents such as Satan-filled Judas, and others. Here, the **hour** for reaping is of God's choosing. It is the day of judgment (John 5:28). God alone decides the day and date of this Day (Mark 13:32; Acts 1:7). Those who say they know the day or can calculate the day are liars and blasphemers, arrogating to themselves knowledge which God has chosen to reveal to no-one.

16 In obedience to his Father, Jesus wields his sickle, and reaps **the earth**. The **earth** is the home of those who oppose God and his people (17:2; see Isa 24:1–6). The **earth** is also the home of the second beast, the false prophet who deceives the 'inhabitants of the earth'. The earth itself is on God's side, however (12:16). The simple statement, 'The earth was reaped', means that judgment has taken place. This is described in more detail in the next verses.

b) The vintage, 14:17–20

The second narrative of the judgment of the wicked (that is, of those who worship the beast, 14:9–11), is introduced by the report of the entrance of **another angel** with a **sharp sickle**. This sixth angel comes from the **temple in heaven**, that is, from the presence of God himself. He is the agent and instrument of God and of the Lord Jesus to whom God has committed the judgment of the world. This fact is indicated by the report that yet **another angel** commands the sickle-bearer to start reaping.

The angel who gives the command comes **out from the altar** of incense, the place where the martyrs wait for vindication (6:9,10), and where the petitions of God's people are offered (8:1–5;11:1,2). As has been observed many times in this book, the worship of God's people brings both salvation and adverse judgment upon the earth (see commentary on 5:8 and 6:10). The angel who presides over the heavenly liturgy, and especially over the prayer-sacrifices of God's people, holds in his hands the power over the **fire** of judgment upon the worshippers of the beast (see 8:1–5). The angel who leads the heavenly liturgy is Jesus in angel form. It is he who commands the angel with the sharp sickle to act for him and to respond to the prayers and worship of God's people by reaping the grape harvest which is **ripe** to be reaped.

The strong New Testament tradition which links Jesus and the angels in the work of judgment is reflected in John's account of the judgment of the wicked (vv 14–19). In this account, Jesus and the angel who comes from the presence of God have interchangeable roles: In the story of the grain harvest (vv 14–16), Jesus wields the sickle at the command of the angel who comes from the sanctuary, that is, from the presence of God. In the story of the vintage (vv 17-19) the angel who comes from the presence of God wields the sickle at the command of Jesus.

The fact that Jesus and the 'angel from the Presence' perform identical functions is underscored by the way John structures his report of the two-act drama of judgment:

vv 14–16	vv 17–19
Jesus has a sickle.	The angel has a sickle.
The angel commands Jesus.	Jesus commands the angel.
Jesus reaps the harvest.	The angel reaps the harvest.

19 At the command, then, of Jesus, the seventh angel **swung his sickle over the earth**. Twice in verses 17 and 18 the sickle is emphatically described as being **sharp**. It would do the job it was designed to do, fully and efficiently. So the **vintage of the earth** was **gathered**

forthwith, and the angel hurled it **into the great winepress**, a vivid symbol for the very real **wrath of God** (see 19:15).

The picture in verse 19 seems to be taken from Isaiah 63:3–6, where the prophet portrays Yahweh's fearful judgment upon Edom. The description of the bloody carnage is traditional among writers of the time. John adapts it in order to highlight the contrast between the temporary distress of the holy city, the people of God, as they were trampled for 'forty-two months' (11:2), and the final and permanent fate of those very same enemies of God and his people.

No effort should be made, or need be made, to read any significance into the statement that **blood flowed** in a deep stream for **two hundred miles**. John's hearers are being reminded very graphically that God's wrath is a fearful thing; it reaches everywhere and everyone who refuses him worship. In the same vein, the phrase 'outside the city' is a reminder that God's punitive verdict involves exclusion from the city of God, the new Jerusalem. 'Outside' is the place of rejection and death, the place of the wicked (see Heb 13:11–13; Acts 7:58; Rev 22:15).

Where have we been? Where are we going?

John's account of the second revelation which he was granted (4:1 – 6:21) ends with one more septet, known as the 'bowl' septet. This is **the last** account of this kind; with the story of the emptying of the bowls the **wrath of God** reaches its end and its designated purpose.

But has not John already depicted the End, God's vindication of his people and his terrible judgment upon his enemies? He has. In fact, he has spoken of these things several times already, in the seal septet (6:1 – 8:1) and the trumpet septet (8:6 – 9:21,11:15). In keeping with the pattern of Revelation, John has been repeating variations on a theme, all the while building his symphony up to a climax of unimaginable power and glory (17:1–22:21).

The links joining the narratives of the second revelation (4:1 – 16:21) are twofold. First, John constantly reminds his hearers that heavenly worship is the context and source of the events which he narrates. Secondly, after the account of the opening of the seven seals by the Lamb, each major narrative segment involves the activities of seven angels (8:6 – 9:21;11:15;14:6–20;15:1 – 16:21).

The angels of 14:6–20 come from God's presence, speak for him, and act as his angels of judgment. Likewise the seven 'angels of the bowls' come from the presence of God, symbolised by the **temple of the tent of witness** (see Exod 25:9; Heb 8:5). This particular phrase takes John's hearers back to his introduction to the account of seven trumpet angels (8:1–5), as well as to the worship scene in chapter 5. The symbol of the 'golden bowls' is an allusion to the golden bowls which are the prayers of the saints (5:8;8:3).

The report of smoke filling the temple, and other evidences of God's powerful and glorious presence, recall the smoke of incense which are the prayers of the saints (8:1–5). Fuelled by fire from the altar, the golden censer called forth the terrifying sounds of God's presence (8:5).

Thus the bowl plagues are God's response to the prayers of Christians for God to vindicate himself and so to vindicate them. They are God's reply to the cry of the saints, 'How long, O Lord, how long?' (6:10).

WORSHIP: The victory song of acclamation, 15:1–4

15 Then I saw another portent in heaven, great and amazing: seven angels with seven plagues, which are the last, for with them the wrath of God is ended.

2 And I saw what appeared to be a sea of glass mixed with fire, and those who had conquered the beast and its image and the number of its name, standing beside the sea of glass with harps of God in their hands. 3 And they sing the song of Moses, the servant[u] of God, and the song of the Lamb:

'Great and amazing are your
deeds,
Lord God the Almighty!
Just and true are your ways,
King of the nations![v]
4 Lord, who will not fear
and glorify your name?
For you alone are holy.
All nations will come
and worship before you,
for your judgments have been
revealed.'

[u] Gk *slave*

[v] Other ancient authorities read *the ages*

Heavenly liturgy acknowledges God's majesty and his dominion over the whole historical process. It celebrates the victory of the Lamb who was slain, and the saving effects of his work. Worship is the means by which God draws his people into his work of salvation and judgment.

Heavenly worship preluded the opening of the seven-sealed book (4:1 – 5:11), and the blowing of the seven trumpets (8:1–5). Now, before the seven bowls are poured out — or rather, to set in motion the pouring out of the bowls — John reports another scene of heavenly worship.

The seven trumpet angels were participants in heavenly worship (see comments on 8:1). The seven bowl angels likewise participate in worship; their actions are an outcome of that worship. Their connection with worship is especially strong, since these bowl angels are priestly figures, serving in the temple (15:5,6; see 14:14–18).

1 The last time that John had reported that he saw something which he called a sign or **portent in heaven** was when he said he saw the church, symbolised by a woman clothed with the sun, and her mortal enemy, the great red dragon (12:1,3). What he now narrates is directly connected with the conflict between these two antagonists, for the pouring out of the bowls is God's reaction to the dragon's attack on God's people: the dragon 'poured water like a river out of his mouth after the woman, to sweep her away with the flood' (12:15).

The sign which John saw in heaven is superior to the previous two. Like all that God does (15:3), this sign is **great and amazing**. It consists of **seven angels with seven plagues**. This is the first of a great deal of 'Exodus' imagery in chapter 15. The **plagues** which God unleashed on Egypt as judgment upon her, and in order to provide freedom for his people, were designated 'signs' (Exod 10:1,2; Neh 9:10).

2 Participants in the heavenly liturgy are described as men and women who have come safely through the exodus from Egypt. They are the same ones who participate in the heavenly worship which John describes so movingly in chapters 4 and 5. They are the same one hundred and forty-four thousand who appeared with the Lamb on Mount Zion, accompanied by the music of the lyre (14:1–5). In short, they are the people of God, past, present, and future.

The links between the present report of heavenly worship and that in 5:8–14 are especially noteworthy. Both are visions of heavenly liturgy; both involve worship on the part of God's people; both speak of 'harps' (lyres) and 'golden bowls'; both report the singing of a 'new song'.

The worshipping community stands in heaven **beside the sea of glass**. The last time John spoke of this crystal-like sea (4:6), it was thought of as the heavenly counterpart to the Red Sea, viewed as the home of the powers who are opposed to God. The crossing of this sea (=Abyss, 13:1;20:1) was spoken of in terms of victory over the beast and his allies (for example, Ps 77:16–20;106:9).

Now the sea is said to be **mixed with fire**, suggesting God's holy wrath against all forms of sin and impurity, and his judging activity which thwarts the evildoer and brings the wicked to justice (Exod 14:24; 2 Thess 1:7). Repeatedly in Revelation John has shown that God uses evil as the instrument of its own destruction (for example, 8:8–11;9:11;17:16).

The **fire** might also point to the baptism of fire which God's people must experience in their journey to the promised land (1 Pet 4:12; Luke 12:49,50).

The people of God stand **beside the sea**. They have crossed the sea, and now stand on the farther shore. Their successful crossing is described in terms of conquest: **they have conquered the beast and its image and the number of its name**. In 13:11–18 John described the beast in terms of an image and a number. Probably a better translation of verse 2b is: '. . . and those who had conquered the beast, both its image and the number of its name'. The point is: no matter how you describe the beast, he has been overcome.

These victorious people have not defiled themselves with worship of false gods, worship of the beast, worship of the emperor. They have not compromised, but they have continued to be faithful witnesses to Jesus himself (14:12). They are 'virgins' (14:4,5). They have come out of the great ordeal, washed their robes and made them white in the blood of the Lamb (7:13,14). So John's hearers can visualise these people being led by the Lamb. He is a second Moses who brings them safely through the sea.

In short, a second Exodus, even greater than the first, has taken place. Wicked Pharaoh and all his hosts (= dragon, beasts, and followers) have been overcome; Israel (= the followers of the Lamb) stand safe on the other shore. They celebrate the God-given victory with the playing of God-given **harps** (better: 'lyres'). These musical instruments are **harps of God** in the sense that they produce perfect, powerful sounds, dedicated to service in the heavenly liturgy (see 1 Chron 16:42).

3,4 Like Israel of old, the new Israel celebrates the Exodus by standing on the farther shore and singing a new song (14:3). These servants of God **sing the song of Moses, the servant of God, and the song of the Lamb**. Perhaps a better translation is: 'They sing the song of Moses . . . that is, the song of the Lamb'. For John is speaking here not of two songs (one sung by Moses and one sung by the Lamb), but of one song: the one sung by the Lamb. Like a second Moses (see Luke 9:30,31) the Lamb has brought his followers safely through the sea (v 2), and now, like Moses after the crossing of the Red Sea, he leads his people in a song of victory and acclamation. The Lamb leads the worship of the people of God (see 8:1–5 and comments)!

The Old Testament records only two songs of Moses: a song of victory following the Red Sea crossing (Exod 15:1–18), and Moses' swan song (Deut 32:1-43). The song of the Lamb echoes both these songs of Moses, but the dominant theme is of a new and final Exodus, in keeping with its designation as a 'new song' (5:9;14:3).

The song is a psalm of praise accompanied, as usual with praise psalms, on the lyre (see 1 Chron 16:4,5;25:3; note especially Ps 33:2,3). Almost every word of the Lamb's song is drawn from the Old Testament, but always the reference is to God's acts in Christ. God's **deeds** are, like the sign which John saw in heaven (15:1), **great and amazing** (see 1 Chron 16:9; Ps 92:5; 118:23). People wondered at the beast and his marvels (13:3); God's acts in Christ, his acts of judgment and redemption, are far more wonderful and amazing, as the whole book of Revelation demonstrates. For the true **Lord God**, the Pantocrator or **Almighty** One is not the beast but God-in-Christ. He is the **King of the nations** by virtue of both creation and redemption. His **ways** are just (Ps 145:17) and true (Deut 32:4).

4 The two rhetorical questions which open the second part of the Lamb's song are drawn from Jeremiah 10:7 and Psalm 86:9. The expected answer to both questions is: No-one. All will **fear** the Lord and **glorify** his **name**; that is, they will glorify him, because the name stands for the whole person. Here again John gives his hearers a glimpse of the future seen from God's eternal present: God will be universally acknowledged as King and Lord of all (see Isa 2:2;66:19–21; Phil 2:9,10).

The song of the Lamb is one of the most carefully structured pieces of liturgy in the whole book of Revelation. This is illustrated by the way in which John expresses the reasons for the worship and praise. The reasons are given in three 'for' clauses:

For Thou alone art holy;
For all the nations will come and worship before Thee,
For Thy righteous acts have been revealed. (NASB)

First, God alone is holy, untouched by sin and all impurity. God is 'holy and awesome' says the psalmist (111:9). Therefore God alone is worthy of worship (see Rev 4:8–11).

Secondly, **all nations will come and worship before** him. Clearly, not all citizens of the great city will remain blind to God's holiness and greatness, and deaf to his call. Some will heed the witness of the church and turn to God (see 11:13).

Thirdly, God is worthy to be glorified and praised because his liberating verdict of acquittal, and his just condemnation of those who oppose the Lamb **have been revealed**. The prayers of the saints have been answered (6:9).

NARRATIVE: The seven angels and the seven bowls, 15:5 – 16:21

5 After this I looked, and the temple of the tent[w] **of**
witness in heaven was opened, 6 and out of the temple
came the seven angels with the seven plagues, robed in
pure bright linen,[x] **with golden sashes across their chests.**
7 Then one of the four living creatures gave the seven
angels seven golden bowls full of the wrath of God, who
lives forever and ever; 8 and the temple was filled with
smoke from the glory of God and from his power, and
no one could enter the temple until the seven plagues of
the seven angels were ended.
16 Then I heard a loud voice from the temple telling the
seven angels, 'Go and pour out on the earth the seven
bowls of the wrath of God.'

[2] So the first angel went and poured his bowl on the
earth, and a foul and painful sore came on those who
had the mark of the beast and who worshiped its image.
[3] The second angel poured his bowl into the sea, and it
became like the blood of a corpse, and every living thing
in the sea died.
[4] The third angel poured his bowl into the rivers and
the springs of water, and they became blood. [5] And I heard
the angel of the waters say,

'You are just, O Holy One, who
are and were,
for you have judged these
things;
[6] because they shed the blood of
saints and prophets,
you have given them blood to
drink.
It is what they deserve!'
[7] And I heard the altar respond,
'Yes, O Lord God, the Almighty,
your judgments are true and
just!'

[8] The fourth angel poured his bowl on the sun, and it
was allowed to scorch them with fire; [9] they were scorched
by the fierce heat, but they cursed the name of God, who
had authority over these plagues, and they did not repent
and give him glory.
[10] The fifth angel poured his bowl on the throne of the
beast, and its kingdom was plunged into darkness; people
gnawed their tongues in agony, [11] and cursed the God of
heaven because of their pains and sores, and they did
not repent of their deeds.
[12] The sixth angel poured his bowl on the great river
Euphrates, and its water was dried up in order to prepare
the way for the kings from the east. [13] And I saw three
foul spirits like frogs coming from the mouth of the
dragon, from the mouth of the beast, and from the mouth
of the false prophet. [14] These are demonic spirits,
performing signs, who go abroad to the kings of the whole
world, to assemble them for battle on the great day of
God the Almighty. [15] ('See, I am coming like a thief!

Blessed is the one who stays awake and is clothed,[y] not
going about naked and exposed to shame.') [16] And they
assembled them at the place that in Hebrew is called
Harmagedon.
[17] The seventh angel poured his bowl into the air,
and a loud voice came out of the temple, from the
throne, saying, 'It is done!' [18] And there came flashes
of lightning, rumblings, peals of thunder, and a violent
earthquake, such as had not occurred since people
were upon the earth, so violent was that earthquake.
[19] The great city was split into three parts, and the cities
of the nations fell. God remembered great Babylon
and gave her the wine-cup of the fury of his wrath.
[20] And every island fled away, and no mountains were
to be found; [21] and huge hailstones, each weighing
about a hundred pounds,[z] dropped from heaven on
people, until they cursed God for the plague of the
hail, so fearful was that plague.

[w] Or *tabernacle*

[x] Other ancient authorities read *stone*

[y] Gk *and keeps his robes*

[z] Gk *weighing about a talent*

The heavenly liturgy never ceases. John's focus is now on the actors and actions which flow like a stream out of heavenly worship. Once again John clearly demonstrates the involvement of the worshipping community in God's judging and saving actions. In so doing, the seer reminds his hearers that his narratives should be heard as variations on the one report of the one revelatory event (4:1 – 16:21). So in chapter 5 John describes the worshipping community as twenty-four elders who hold 'golden bowls full of incense, which are the prayers of the saints' (5:8). At the start of chapter 8, John tells of a priestly angel-figure (=Christ) who offers incense mixed with the 'prayers of the saints' (8:3). These prayers call forth the force of God's wrath (8:5). The subsequent story of the blowing of seven trumpets tells of God's wrath in action.

Now, in 15:5–8, John says that the golden bowls are full of the **wrath of God**. These same bowls are also full of the prayers of the saints (see 5:8). So the worshipping people of God, that maligned, weak, powerless people who keep the witness of Jesus and who refuse to follow the imperial cult, these worshipping people take part in God's judgment upon their enemies (20:4–6; see 1 Cor 6:2; 2 Thess 1:6–10).

Creation is also part of that worshipping community. It, too, participates in God's judging activities, as John indicates with his observation that the golden bowls were given to the angels by **one of the four living creatures** (see comments on 4:6–8).

5,6 John does not identify the **seven angels**, although they seem to be a definite group: '*the* seven angels'. Probably the seven bowl-angels are the same as the seven trumpet-angels (8:2,6). They are the heavenly counterparts of the angels of the seven churches (2:1 – 3:22). (See commentary on 1:20.) The proposal that the seven trumpet/bowl angels are the *alter ego* of the seven church-angels is most plausible in view of John's teaching that the church is intimately involved in God's judging and saving actions. The bowl-angels, it should be noted, are dressed in priestly robes, and they come out of the exposed **temple of the tent of witness.** This is where the church, the people of God, are at worship (11:1,2).

The dress of these seven angels vaguely resembles that of the risen Christ (see 1:13–19). The angels are clothed in **pure bright linen**, the characteristic dress of priests (Exod 39:27; Ezek 44:17). In fact, they are high priests, for they also wear golden sashes, symbols of kingship and high priesthood (see Exod 28:4,39; compare Rev 1:13). Their priestly character is further emphasised by John's notice that they come out of the open **tent of witness in heaven** (see 11:19;14:15). The 'tent of witness' is the name given to the tabernacle in the desert. It took its name from the witness to God's law which had been written on stone tablets and placed in the ark which was kept in the tent or tabernacle. This **tent of witness** was the focal place of God's presence among his people during the Exodus years.

The unusual phrase which John uses here — **the temple of the tent of witness** — probably means: 'the temple, that is, the tent of witness'. John is reminding his hearers of the intimate connection between the presence of the holy God among his people, the witness which his people give in their lives of worship, and their participation in the judging and saving activities of the God whose holy law is ignored at peril.

7,8 The **glory** and **power** of the God **who lives forever and ever** is signalled by the presence of **smoke** in the temple (see 1 Kings 8:10; Isa 6:4; 2 Chron 7:1-3). The temple is filled with the glory of God; the bowls which come from one of the four living creatures in the temple are filled with the **wrath of God**. The pouring out of the contents of the bowls, that is, the working out of God's wrath, is the inevitable divine response to the sin and wickedness of the beast and his worshippers.

The open temple reveals the glory and the **power** of God. His revelation of himself is always informative and performative: it describes, and it does what it describes (see Rom 1:18;3:21). His wrath will be poured out. The certainty of that fact is conveyed in the prophet's observation that **no-one could enter the temple** until the work of the seven bowl angels had reached its conclusion and goal. These angels are servants of God. The plagues which they unleash come with full divine sanction, for the angels who deliver these plagues come directly from the place of God's presence, from the temple, the place also where the worshipping people of God are gathered. This same truth was expressed already in 8:1–5, where the temple with its altar of incense and its worshipping community was the source of the trumpet-plagues.

John reports that **one of the four living creatures gave the seven angels seven golden bowls full of the wrath of God**. The fact that God acts through agents, even through 'nature', should not blind us to the truth that in the events which John describes in chapter 16 God is at work, to bless and to save, to punish and condemn, to build up and to throw down.

In the case of the **seven plagues of the seven angels**, the situation is clear: the angels and the plagues come from God. His judgments upon sin and evil and compromise and idolatry are being worked out.

Sometimes these judgments are impossible to decipher and discern. But when the judgment is complete, the smoke will clear, and God will be seen as God, the one **who lives forever and ever**, even after the last golden bowl has been poured out. And his people live with him.

The seven bowls, 16:1–21

Both the seven-trumpet cycle and the seven-bowl cycle draw on the account of the plagues of Egypt. So there are similarities between John's report of both septets. But there are some significant differences and some new emphases.

In the report of the bowl series the destruction caused by the trumpet cycle is intensified. Now not only a third of the earth is destroyed but all of the earth: the destruction is total. Furthermore, both the seal series and the trumpet series were interrupted after the sixth seal was opened or the sixth trumpet was blown. The blowing of the seventh trumpet (11:15) and the opening of the seventh seal (8:1) disclosed heavenly worship. The implication was that there is still an opportunity for repentance in response to the proclamation which is part of Christian public worship.

But with the pouring out of the golden bowls of God's wrath, the time for repentance has passed. The series moves inexorably to its climax, so that when the seventh bowl is poured out, a great voice straight out of the temple announces: It is done! Finished! There is no more. This same thought is expressed differently by the manner in which John relates these bowls of wrath to the Exodus event. The trumpet plagues, like the Egyptian plagues, *preceded* the Exodus of God's people. They were a call to repentance in the face of impending doom (the call goes to compromising Christians as well as to mocking unbelievers). The plagues of chapter 16, however, *follow* the Exodus event (see comments on 15:1–4); these plagues are part of the doom of God's enemies and unfaithful people, corresponding to the destruction of the Egyptians in the sea.

Finally, it should be noted that the first four trumpet judgments and the first four bowl judgments are in both cases directed to the natural order (earth, sea, rivers, sun). In the case of the trumpets, however, little mention is made of the effect the judgments have on people; the point is not ignored entirely, but it seems to be incidental. By way of contrast, in the bowl cycle God seems to be enlisting the natural order (earth, salt water, fresh water, sun) in the service of divine retribution against men and women who worship the beast. This is made quite clear in the case of the first, fourth, fifth, and seventh bowls: God's wrath is directed against the followers of the beast.

In short, there is a personal, flesh-and-blood dimension to the bowl judgments which was not so evident in the trumpet judgments. However, any differences between the two septets do not change the basic truth that both are speaking of God's acts of judgment. Both are like symphonic variations on the theme of the great Day of the Lord.

Formally, the 'bowl' reports follow a similar pattern:

1) The commissioning of all the angels (16:1), followed by
2) the action by each angel in turn (for example, 'went and poured out his bowl upon the earth . . .');
3) the extent and effects of the action (for example, 'and a foul and painful sore came . . .');
4) the reaction of the people (for example, 'but they cursed the name of God . . .').

a) The first three bowls, 16:1–4

1 All the bowls are poured out on the **earth**, that is, the world where people live, the disobedient people whom John customarily calls 'the inhabitants of the earth' (13:14;17:2; see Jer 10:25; Ps 69:24).

The wrath which is poured out is God's; the angels are his servants (see 19:10). The **loud voice** which commissions the seven angels is either the voice of God or it speaks for God himself, for it comes **from the temple** (see 16:17; Isa 66:6). The temple has been filled with smoke 'from the glory of God and his power', and declared to be out-of-bounds 'until the seven plagues of the seven angels were ended' (15:8). (For a discussion of the identity of **the seven angels** and the nature of the **seven bowls of the wrath of God**, see the comments on 8:2 and 15:1,6.)

2 The ancient Egyptian deities were associated with the earth, the waters above and below the earth, the sea, and the Pharaoh himself. It is probably not by accident that all but the seventh bowl deal with judgments which indicate that God's mighty arm rules domains which supposedly belong to other gods.

The **first** bowl is poured out on the **earth**. The word 'earth' is used here to mean the ground on which people stand and in which things grow (contrast verse 1). When God pours out his wrath on the **earth**, he is not punishing the earth, for it is on God's side (see 12:16). But the earth is God's instrument of punishment (see 12:12). When the angel empties the first **bowl**, a **sore** (abscess, boil) breaks out on the skin of those who **had the mark of the beast and worshipped its image** (see comments on 13:15–18). The parallel to the sixth Egyptian plague is obvious (Exod 9:9). Here the 'sore' comes first because it matches **the mark of the beast**.

The people of God, like Israel of old, are not afflicted with sores; they are under God's protection, having his seal (7:2,4). But the worshippers of the beast lack this seal and this protection (9:4), so they are vulnerable to deception by the second beast and to the consequent wrath of God. It is almost as if the **mark of the beast**, which people prized so highly, turns into a deadly beacon which attracts God's wrath and punishment. This dreadful irony would be in keeping with a saying which was well known to Jews and Christians alike: 'One is punished by the very things by which one sins' (Wisdom of Solomon 11:16).

3,4 There is further irony in the fact that the second and third angels pour their bowls into the **sea**, the **rivers**, and the underground sources of fresh water. These are thought to be the domain of the demonic and local deities. But God's long victorious arm extends even into the home of the enemy: the sea and the underworld (see Mark 3:27;4:39,40).

Yet another irony is to be recognised in the report that the salt and fresh waters turn to **blood**. The worshippers of the beast, who had gleefully 'shed the blood of saints and prophets' (16:6;11:10), are themselves required to drink **blood**. And unlike the blood which the Masai warrior drinks to receive life and strength, this blood, likened to **the blood of a corpse**, is deadly. Not just one third of the people die, as happened when the second angel blew his trumpet (8:9), but everyone dies: 'every living soul died, the things in the sea' is what John's Greek says literally.

There is no life without water, certainly not without the Water of Life (John 7:37,38). Followers of the beast had rejected the witness to the Lamb; they chose to live in Babylon, not realising that the water of life flowed not from Babylon but from the new Jerusalem, the throne of God and the Lamb (22:1,2).

b) WORSHIP: The victory song of acclamation (reprise), 16:5–7

The heavenly worship which had set in motion the pouring out of the bowls never ceases. It goes on day and night (4:8;7:15). Now it rises to a crescendo. Its similarity to the liturgy of 15:1–4 indicates that it is a continuation of that liturgy. It intensifies the action which is to follow.

One difference between the accounts of the two worship scenes is that 15:1–4 describes the worship of the 'conquerors' who have come unscathed through the sea, whereas the liturgy of 16:5–7 is led by creation (see 5:11–14), and is responded to by the people of God.

5 Creation is represented by **the angel of the waters**. In the religious literature of John's time, it was a common thought that the elements had angels assigned to look after them (see 7:1;14:18). The angels were said to protest when 'their' part of creation was exploited, polluted, or misused in any way.

Now, even though the salt water and the fresh water had been horribly polluted, the angel does not protest. Instead, the angel, on behalf of creation, recognises the justice of divine retribution, and sings: '**You are just, O Holy One, who are and were**'. The future element is omitted from the threefold divine title (see 1:8), and is replaced by the 'Holy One', as in the liturgy recorded in 11:17. God's holiness is a present, seen reality; he has come; there is no more waiting. His just judgments are in action.

6 The verdict and the punishment befit the sin (see comments on verses 3 and 4). God, it seems, works this way (see Rom 1:18–32): he allows people to reap the 'natural' harvest of their sins. How much blood have we had to drink (that is, how many deaths have there been) as a result of our abuse of nuclear energy, of genetic engineering, of scientific experimentation, of human resources?

The irony of this verse (shed blood — drink blood) is heightened by the final comment, but obscured in the English translation: **It is what they deserve**. The Greek says, in just two words: 'They are worthy'. The hearer immediately thinks of God and the Lamb, who are acclaimed by the heavenly liturgy as alone being 'worthy' because of the work of creation and redemption (4:11;5:9). Now the same heavenly liturgy declares someone else to be 'worthy', worthy not of universal worship but of death, because they worshipped the beast and shed the blood of others. They refused to worship the Lamb, who shed his own blood for others, for all (John 1:29; 2 Cor 5:15).

7 As in the liturgy recorded in 5:11–14, the church of God acts as a choir antiphonal to that of creation. **The altar** is the place of incense (8:2), from where comes the cry of the saints for God to vindicate himself and them (6:9), and where the worship of God's people takes place (11:1). God's people wait — wait for God to show the world that their foolishness was true wisdom, that their grasp of reality was not misplaced. As God acts to judge their enemies, they join creation's shout of acclamation of God's righteousness, justice, and the just punishments which he hands out to his enemies. God's nature as **true and just** is revealed in his refusal to let murderers and idolaters go unpunished (see 22:15).

c) NARRATIVE: The four last bowls, 16:8–21

8 The **fourth angel poured his bowl**, not on the earth or the water, but on the **sun**. Human beings have worshipped and venerated the **sun**, in all cultures and lands, including ancient Egypt. The Egyptians named the sun 'Universal Lord' and 'Lord of the Limit'. The sun, however, is a created body; it is not God. It has an important function in the old creation, but it will not be needed in the new (21:23;22:5). It joins the sea and darkness on the list of anti-God things which in the new creation shall be 'no more'.

When the wrath of God is poured out upon the sun, its heat is not diminished but intensified. The god turns on its worshippers and scorches them. That seems to be God's way of working: people are punished by their own gods (see comments on 15:2 and 9:1). What shall we say of our worship of the automobile and industrial production? The ozone layer is depleted and the sun begins to scorch. But even that is only a symbol of the impending wrath of God which is poured out on a rebellious and arrogant humanity.

Christians will not be spared the effects of the ravage of the ozone layer; but they are and will be protected from the fierce **fire** of God's wrath. Because they are sheltered by the Lamb, divine wrath does not strike them nor scorch them in any way (7:16,17; see Isa 49:10). For, as the prophet Jeremiah confessed:

> Blessed are those who trust in the LORD,
>   and rest their confidence upon him.
> They shall be like a tree planted by the waterside,
>   that stretches its root along the stream.
> When the heat comes it has nothing to fear;
>   its spreading foliage stays green.
> In a year of drought it feels no care,
>   and does not cease to bear fruit. (Jer 17:7,8)

9 Those who suffered the searing heat of the sun at least recognised that the **plagues** came from the hand of God; sadly, however, they did not acknowledge the cause: their own sin. Instead, they showed their true colours and their true allegiance by blaspheming God. This activity is characteristic of the beast and his followers (13:1,5,6;17:3).

The bowl septet represents a climax in John's account of his second great revelation (4:1 – 16:21). Likewise, the human reaction to the divine actions which John describes is climactic. Now people are not merely desperate (6:15–17), or impenitent (9:20,21). Now they do what their master the beast himself does (13:5,6): they blaspheme (**curse**) the God of heaven whose call to repentance they reject.

Their refusal to **repent** is signalled by their refusal to give God the **glory**. This is the primal sin, this refusal to honour God or to give him thanks, and the desire to give his honour and glory to another (see Rom 1:18-25). Repentance begins and ends with giving glory, all glory, to God (see 11:13).

In summary: the pouring out of the bowls does not bring about repentance. Instead, it exposes the true followers of the beast. Paul's words in Romans are especially appropriate as commentary:

> You have a hard and stubborn heart. Therefore you are making your own punishment even greater on the Day when God's wrath and right judgments will be revealed . . . Some people are selfish and reject what is right, in order to do what is wrong. On them God will pour his wrath and anger. (Rom 2:5,8 TEV)

10,11 When the **fifth angel** pours out his **bowl**, God's righteous wrath catches up with all the ungodly social and political structures which have claimed so many followers and existed in deliberate opposition to God. Satan's **throne**, which he shares with the beast, is the symbolic antithesis of God's throne, which he shares with the Lamb (7:15–17).

For the people of Israel, languishing in the servitude of Egypt, Satan's throne was the kingdom of Pharaoh. The living Pharaoh was called the 'Good God'; the dead

Pharaoh was called the 'Great God'. For Israel, the exodus from Egypt was not simply a political or economic necessity. It was a theological necessity: Israel could not continue to serve a false god.

In John's heavenly geography, the **throne** of Satan and the beast was located at Pergamum (2:13). This city was the provincial capital and the administrative centre of the imperial cult in the Roman province of Asia. Pergamum was a suitable symbolic location for the throne of the beast, for it was a microcosm of the beast's kingdom, which is the cultured world organised in opposition to God and his people.

Both Paul and John teach that those who live in active rebellion against God are living in self-chosen darkness, while those who faithfully follow Christ live in the light (Eph 4:8–18; 1 John 2:10,11). In keeping with the biblical thought that God confirms stubborn people in their sin, and makes them suffer their self-imposed punishment, the pouring out of the fifth bowl is said to plunge the world of the beast into **darkness**. More accurately, the beast's kingdom became darkened. That is its constant condition: it is darkened, deprived of all light. Inevitably, then, it must and will die. It is headed for destruction (see 17:8,11; 19:17–21).

Christians do not live in darkness (1 Thess 5:4,5); they are 'children of light' (Eph 5:8–14). Darkness or night is excluded from the new Jerusalem; it shall be 'no more' (21:25). Night is the time of the demonic (John 13:30); **darkness** is the sign of chaos. A darkened kingdom is a demonic, chaotic, dying kingdom. And it stands under judgment. As the ninth Egyptian plague suggested (Exod 10:21–23), darkness signals the coming of death and destruction; indeed, darkness is, in Scripture, considered to be part of the judgment (for example, Matt 8:12;25:30).

There is something about darkness which makes us afraid. The darkness which God imposes as judgment is bad enough; but combined with the sores which he inflicted (16:2) and the burns caused by the sun before darkness fell (16:8), it causes followers of the beast intolerable fear and pain: they chew **their tongues in agony**.

Again John tells his hearers (see v 9), that this act of divine punishment is final: there is no sign of repentance. Instead, the sufferers show who and whose they really are. They curse the God of heaven, blaming him for their **pains and sores**, as if they were innocent. They do not **repent**. There is no sadder sentence in Scripture.

12 A clear parallel exists between the judgment of the sixth **bowl** and the sixth trumpet (9:13–19). When the sixth trumpet was sounded, the four angels at the Euphrates were released to lead a huge demonic army in an invasion to kill one third of all people. When the sixth bowl was poured out on the **great river Euphrates**, its waters were **dried up**. When God 'dries up' waters he is proceeding to fulfil his goals (see Exod 14:21; Joshua 3:16; 2 Kings 2:8,14). When he 'dried up' the waters of the Red Sea and of the Jordan, he was making a way for his people; he was acting for their salvation. Here God 'dries up' the Euphrates for the purpose of destroying the kingdom of the beast, beginning with Babylon. Judgment of all enemies and the removal of all evil is the negative side of the work of salvation.

That is why John says that God prepares **the way for the kings from the east**, who come to destroy Babylon (17:16). Just as John the Baptist 'prepared the way' for the Coming One who would establish the kingdom of God (and in so doing destroy the kingdom of Satan, Matt 3:3;12:28), so God prepares the way for the kings who will destroy the kingdom of the dragon and the beast. These kings come **from the east**. They probably reflect the Romans' almost pathological fear of invasion from the Parthians, and represent the inevitable destruction of evil by evil, under God's direction (see comments on 9:13–19).

13,14 Although the writing is on the wall (Dan 5:24–28), Satan is too arrogant and too stupid to read it. The attack on the followers of the beast, the citizens of Babylon, is at hand (for comments on the significance of 'Babylon' see commentary on 14:8). Babylon's destruction is certain, and yet the anti-God, the unholy trinity of **dragon, beast**, and **false prophet** still tries to enlist new followers and organise opposition to God (for comments on the 'unholy trinity' see commentary on 13:1–18).

In the twentieth century, lying propaganda was only too well practised by Goebbels in Nazi Germany. From his mouth, as from the **mouth** of the unholy trinity, lies flowed like a foul breath. This lying and deceiving activity is **demonic** activity. John says that the rotten breath which comes out of their mouths is **like frogs**. It is a good comparison, because, for the Jews, frogs were unclean (Lev 11:10–12), and in Iranian religion, frogs were thought to be agents of an evil spirit who was a key figure in the final battle of history.

14,16 The **demonic spirits** try to gain new recruits for the armies of the unholy trinity by performing all sorts of **signs** and wonders (see 13:13,14). And they manage to persuade the **kings of the whole world** to gather together for the final battle, the showdown against God and his people (see Ps 2:1–6,10–12). The demonic spirits assembled the kings and their armies at **the place that in Hebrew is called Harmagedon**, that is, the mountain of Megido.

There is no 'mountain of Megido' on the map, and no-one has been able to locate it geographically. All attempts to do so will fail, for it is not a place but the symbol of an event — or better, a non-event. Because, despite all the huffing and puffing, there is no battle (see 20:7–10). There is no battle because it has already been fought and won at Calvary and the empty tomb. The message just hasn't got through to Satan yet; he doesn't know that his teeth have been drawn; he thinks he still has a chance of reversing Calvary.

The verb which is translated 'gather' or 'assemble' is often used in the gospel of Matthew to speak of people being 'gathered' for judgment. This judgment consists of a sorting-out process: the good from the bad, the tares from the wheat, the sheep from the goats, the chaff from the wheat (Matt 3:12;13:30,48;25:32). Often the ones who do the 'gathering' are the angels, whom John designates as God's agents and servants (Rev 1:1;19:10). Here John says that the demonic spirits, unwitting servants and agents of God, gather the kings and their armies for battle.

But there is no battle. There is only judgment and destruction (see 20:7–10). For the assembly takes place

on the great day of God the Almighty. The enemies gather in order to fight and defeat God. But as far as God is concerned, they gather only to make it 'more convenient' (if one may so speak) for God to destroy them. This is God's day; he chooses the day; he is in control. In the Scriptures, the 'Day of the Lord' is the day of his public triumph, the day on which salvation is effected and revealed for all of God's people. It is also the day when his wrath is revealed against all those who persist in their rebellious opposition to the kingdom of God, and insist on continuing to pay their membership fees in the kingdom of the beast (see Isa 2:12; Jer 46:10; Amos 5:18–20; Rev 6:16,17).

15 It is important that Christians remember just whose is 'the great day'. The enemies of God like to give the impression that it is their day, that there is a final battle to be fought, and that ultimate victory is inevitably theirs. But John's hearers have to keep in mind what John has been saying throughout his book: power and honour and glory and salvation and victory belong to God alone. It is not obvious — there is no power and glory and victory to be seen in the slain Lamb — but it is true nonetheless: the Day is God's day; the victory is his.

So, in a dramatic intervention into John's narrative, the Lord directly addresses his worshipping people through the voice of the lector. He warns them of the dangers of compromise, of switching allegiance. He encourages them to be alert, watchful, faithful. The beatitude is not a direct command ('Wake up!'), but a call to the hearers to examine themselves, each one ('Am I awake?').

Contrary to the wishful thinking of many Christians, the church will not be caught up to heaven before the end. Instead, it will be here on earth, right in the thick of things. That is surely the tenor of the 'blessings' spoken over those servants who, when the Lord comes, are found faithfully carrying out their tasks, serving God by serving his people and the world (see Matt 24:45 – 25:30; Luke 12:35–48).

Again, contrary to many who want to construct Last Day calendars, the end will be sudden and unexpected.

Jesus likens his **coming** to the stealthy invasion of a **thief** (a thief doesn't send a fax!). Those who know the thief (the Lord) is coming at any time will stay awake, fully clothed, ready for action.

Failure to keep careful watch could mean that one is caught with one's pants down—worse, in fact, one is caught without any pants on at all. One's genitals are exposed (**exposed to shame**). The cultural reference here is to the custom of sleeping naked; the theological reference is to being exposed before God's judgment, naked and without any protective covering (see Gen 3:8–11).

The need for watchfulness, wakefulness, and being properly dressed with the robes of Christ's righteousness, is a constant refrain in the New Testament (see Matt 22:1–14;24:36–25:13; Rom 13:11–14). Being asleep and being caught naked is a sure sign of rejection by God.

What does it mean to watch, to be ready, dressed and alert? Not pious inactivity in one's Sunday best. But living, working, serving in the world in obedience to God's will, getting your hands wet while you dry the tears of others, getting your hands dirty in the service of God, while at the same time keeping yourself clean from the polluting influences of the beast and his followers. Watching and waiting for the Lord means activity, not idle guessing games about when the Lord might come.

17,18 Bowls had been poured on the earth, on the waters above and below the earth, and on the sun. Each of these were thought to be the domain of the deities. But God's long arm reaches also into those places (16:2–5). The last **bowl** is poured **into the air**, which was commonly thought to be the sphere of activity of the powers of evil and the demonic (see Eph 2:2). So God is attacking and defeating the powers of evil on their home ground.

In the domain of the **air** God is present as Judge. He announces his presence and effects his judgment by word and by action. The spoken word, uttered in a **loud voice** by God himself ('out of the temple, from the throne', see 16:1), consists in Greek of only one word: **'It is done!'** John's hearers would immediately think of a similar cry from the Lamb on the cross: 'It is finished' (John 19:30). Both cries proclaim that judgment is completed (15:1) and the salvation of God has been accomplished (11:17,18;21:6).

19 The **lightning, thunder,** and **earthquake** of unprecedented magnitude not only signal God's presence, but they are also instruments of his judgment upon a sinful world. The **earthquake** was so violent that **the great city was split into three parts**. The 'great city' (see 11:8) is a powerful symbol of structured evil: human beings in organised opposition to God, people in rebellion against God. The 'great city' represents all human arrogance and pride in human achievements. The 'great city' is Babylon, Sodom, Nineveh, Egypt, Rome. It is the social base of the kingdom of the beast; it is the antithesis of the new Jerusalem. The 'great city' is post-Christian Australia which refuses to hear God's word and repent. It is materialism and idolatry in all its forms; it is trust in scientific and technological 'progress' at the expense of humanity and peace.

God will utterly destroy the **great city**, and with her all **cities of the nations** who follow her example. The reference to the city being **split into three parts** is a way of expressing the complete destruction of the city as a political and economic entity.

Thus God 'remembers' Babylon. God's 'remembering' is always effective. Sometimes, as in the case of Noah, God's 'remembering' produces deliverance and salvation (Gen 8:1); sometimes, as in the case of Babylon, it effects destruction. No wonder the psalmist prays: 'Remember not the sins of my youth' (Ps 25:7). For the unrepentant and rebellious, it is a fearful thing to be 'remembered' by the Lord.

When the Lord **remembered** Babylon he **gave her the wine-cup of the fury of his wrath**. In the whole book of Revelation there is no stronger expression of the devastating nature of God's punitive judgments. Babylon (=Rome) had made all the nations drunk with the wine of the imperial cult (14:8). So they had to drink the cup of God's wrath (14:10). Now Babylon must drink that same cup to the very last drop. Chapters 17 and 18 give a drop by drop account of the drinking of that cup.

20,21 The destruction of Babylon, that is, of all human structures which oppose God and his people, means that the earth and life as we know it came to an end. John reports that the islands **fled away** and the **mountains** were no more. The disappearance of the mountains meant that sailors and travellers had no fixed point by which to find their way; they were lost.

And what of the worshippers of the beast? A hailstorm, far more terrifying than the Egyptian plagues, devastated the people. Thus is answered the question asked when the opening of the sixth seal brought on the great day of the wrath of God and the Lamb: 'Who is able to stand?' (6:12–17). The answer is: those who worship the beast, that is, the inhabitants of Babylon, will not stand. Only those who follow the Lamb and dwell on Mount Zion in the new Jerusalem can stand.

The worshippers of the beast are like their ancestors, Pharaoh and his people. Despite all of God's plagues, they remain stubborn. They refuse to repent. They blaspheme (**curse**) God with their last breath. This is a sad refrain which runs throughout chapter 16: people refuse to repent. 'God has given men [and women] the terrible responsibility of being able to lock their hearts against him' (Barclay).

Chapters 17 and 18 describe in detail the destruction of the great city at the hands of the ones whom the city worshipped: the beast and his followers. Evil always destroys itself; wickedness is by nature self-destructive.

Where have we been? Where are we going?

In his account of the second revelation which God had given him (4:1–16:21), John had portrayed the state and fate of the worshippers of God and the worshippers of the beast. He did this in a series of scenes which were complete in themselves, but which lacked detail.

In the last of these scenes, the bowl septet, God had announced that there was nothing more to come: 'It is done', he said (16:17). Not unexpectedly, then, the account of the third revelation (17:1 – 21:8) contains no further septet. Instead, John gives a detailed description of the fate of the participants in the drama which he has narrated in the previous chapters.

It is important to bear in mind that one completely misses the point if one understands Revelation as a linear, chronological exposition (see the comments on pages 14-16). The narratives which are recorded in the third and fourth revelations (17:1 – 21:8;21:9 – 22:9) are detailed descriptions of things which John has already described in previous scenes and septets. Indeed, the subject matter of chapters 10–16 is the same as that of chapters 17–22, except in reverse order.

Two figures form the link between the second revelation (4:1 – 16:21) and the third (17:1 – 21:8). One of the seven bowl-angels from chapters 15 and 16 invites John to view the judgment of Babylon, the whore (chs 17,18). The same angel is also John's guide when he views the other city, the city of God, the new Jerusalem (chs 21,22).

The other link is 'Babylon'. In 16:19 John reported that God 'remembered' Babylon in order to make her drink the cup of God's wrath. Chapters 17 and 18 tell of this terrible 'remembering' on God's part.

Chapter 17 shows how Babylon was made to experience God's wrath. Chapter 18, with its unexpected worship scene of lamentation (vv 9–19), confirms the reality of God's judgment upon Babylon, and holds out no hope for the inhabitants. The Hallelujah Chorus of 19:1–10 has the double function of underscoring the finality of God's punitive judgment, and of introducing the final narrative of God's acts of judgment and salvation.

THIRD REVELATION, 17:1–21:8

Throughout his book, John has insisted that a glorious future awaits the faithful, that is, those who refuse to worship the emperor or any god, person, or power structure. In chapters 12 to 14 John has exposed the unholy trinity which is active behind the political, economic, and religious institutions, structures, and persons.

In the remaining chapters of Revelation, John details the divine punishment of the followers of the dragon and the beasts. He tells, too, of God's judgment upon the unholy trinity. He speaks also of the salvation of the worshippers of the blessed Trinity.

In the narratives of the previous revelation (4:1–16:21), John has spoken of the basic enmity and opposition which exists between the followers of the Lamb and the followers of the dragon. John has also referred to the cities to which these two groups belong. But he has not developed the symbol of the great city Babylon as a parody and antitype of the great city of God, the new Jerusalem. Nor has John filled out the parallel symbol of the beast's whore as a parody and antitype of the Lamb's bride.

Now, however, in twin visions, John explicitly draws out the parallels and contrasts between the two cities. He speaks, first, of fallen Babylon, the whore of the beast. He includes the laments and celebrations connected with her destruction (17:1 – 19:10). Then he narrates the vision of new Jerusalem, the bride of Christ (21:9 – 22:9). A comparison of the introductions (17:1–3;21:9,10) and the conclusions (19:9,10;22:6–9) to these twin narratives clearly establishes the deliberately patterned similarities and contrast between these two cities or two women.

The 'city', like 'the desert', is an ambiguous symbol in Scripture. On the one hand, the city is a symbol of human rebellion against God; of human efforts to replace God with a god made in the creatures' image; of people in structured and organised opposition to God. This 'city' is always by definition completely at odds with itself; it never achieves the coherence and unity of purpose which it so desperately desires. Instead, the 'city' is a symbol of alienation, human isolation, impersonalness, and dehumanisation.

This 'city' has been called various names: Babylon is a biblical favourite. Other names are Nineveh, Egypt, Sodom and Gomorrah, and even Jerusalem. Paul calls this city 'the flesh'; John calls it 'the world'. In Revelation the 'city' is often called 'the inhabitants of the earth' or 'those who worship the beast and its mark'. In John's day, the city which best represented 'the city' was Rome and the empire.

On the other hand, the 'city' also symbolises the new context of human existence, created by God's new creative activity. In this new environment, God is at work providing meaning, wholeness, and purpose to all of human life. He gives life sense and direction. He gives people a new way of looking at reality; he makes it possible for them to see things as they really are, that is, as he sees them.

The citizens of this 'city' are marked with God's own seal. They are being shaped to conform to the image and likeness of the Son of God himself. The inhabitants of this city do not oppose God and his will; on the contrary, through their acts of worship they actually participate in the unfolding of God's purposes for the universe, and in the carrying out of his acts of condemnation and of salvation.

This 'city' is likewise known by various names: Jerusalem is a biblical favourite. The New Testament calls it, among other things, the body of Christ, the saints, the people of God, Mount Zion.

These two cities — the city of God and the city of Satan — are antipodes. You cannot be a citizen of both cities. Saint Augustine, who spent twenty years of his life in Babylon, was speaking from experience, as well as reflecting the main thrust of Revelation, when he wrote in his essay, *The City of God*:

> We see, then, that the two cities were created by two kinds of love: the earthly city was created by self-love reaching the point of contempt for God, the Heavenly City by the love of God carried as far as contempt for self. In fact, the earthly city glories in itself, the Heavenly City glories in the Lord.

Revelation's purpose is to unfold the dynamics which operate in both cities, dynamics which are still at work today. It is necessary today to be aware of the polarisation between the two cities. Blurring of the borders, moving from one pole to the other, is as dangerous today as it was when John first recorded his revelations.

Compromise is still the great temptation facing Christians.

'Woe to those who sit complacently in Zion', cried the prophet Amos many years ago. The warning is always necessary. For as long as this world lasts, Zion, the new Jerusalem, is to be found right in the middle of Babylon (see 2:13 and comments there). The borders between the two cities are invisible. Only the wise, discerning, Spirit-filled and faithful Christian knows exactly where the boundaries are.

NARRATIVE: The whore Babylon and the beast, 17:1–6

**17 Then one of the seven angels who had the seven bowls
came and said to me, 'Come, I will show you the judgment
of the great whore who is seated on many waters, 2 with
whom the kings of the earth have committed fornication,
and with the wine of whose fornication the inhabitants
of the earth have become drunk.' 3 So he carried me away
in the spirit[a] into a wilderness, and I saw a woman sitting
on a scarlet beast that was full of blasphemous names,
and it had seven heads and ten horns. 4 The woman was
clothed in purple and scarlet, and adorned with gold and
jewels and pearls, holding in her hand a golden cup full
of abominations and the impurities of her fornication;
5 and on her forehead was written a name, a mystery:
'Babylon the great, mother of whores and of earth's
abominations.' 6 And I saw that the woman was drunk with
the blood of the saints and the blood of the witnesses to
Jesus.**

When I saw her, I was greatly amazed.

[a] Or *in the Spirit*

1 John's new revelation (17:1 – 21:8) is introduced by **one of the seven angels who had the seven bowls**. This

angel invites John to observe the **judgment** which God carries out on the whore called 'Babylon the great' (17:5). A **great whore** is the symbol of a great city which is in turn the symbol of great wickedness. The Jewish prophetic tradition commonly pictured a city as a woman (for example, Isa 37:22;66:7–14; Ezekiel 16), including the thought of woman as prostitute (for example, Isa 23:13–18; Nahum 3:1–7). Today other symbols would be just as potent and probably more telling.

The woman whom John sees is **seated on many waters**. In 17:15 this phrase is said to refer to 'peoples and multitudes and nations and languages'. So the whore-city is not one place. It represents all people who live in active and organised rebellion against God. Elsewhere in Revelation, John calls the citizens of the whore-city 'the inhabitants of the earth' (see commentary on 13:8).

2 Furthermore, the whore-city has implicated every aspect of human life and thought and culture in her wickedness. The **kings of the earth**, representing the power structures of the world and its cultures, and **the inhabitants of the earth**, representing all peoples and communities with their values and inner dynamics — all these together have made an idol of the whore-city. They have **become drunk** from drinking the **wine** of her **fornication** (see 14:8).

3 To get a good look at this whore-city, John needs to be in a safe place, and in a place where his view will not be coloured or distorted. So the Spirit takes John in prophetic mode to the desert or **wilderness**, a place where no people are living.

The wilderness stands in direct contrast to the city. The irony of the location is that, whereas for John the wilderness is a place of safety (see 12:14) and clarity of vision, for the city the wilderness is a sign of what she will become: a place of desolation, a haunt of every unclean demon, spirit, bird, and beast (18:2; see 17:16).

From his place in the **wilderness** John is empowered by the Spirit to see the city in its true colours. What follows is his report.

John sees the whore seated **on a scarlet beast**, the same beast which he described in 13:1. Variations on his description of the beast are: its **scarlet** colour, suggesting royalty (and perhaps kinship with his master, the great red dragon, 12:3), and its covering of **blasphemous names** (contrast 13:1, where the names cover only the beast's head). The variations are not significant. John's concern is that his hearers see the relationship between the city and the beast: they are a unit, as horse and rider are a unit.

4 John's report focuses on the woman, the whore who symbolised the city. She is dressed like a successful prostitute, in all the trappings of wealth and nobility. She personifies political power and economic prosperity. Only the ruling classes in Rome were permitted to wear **purple**; **scarlet** signified wealth, as did the wearing of **jewels and pearls**. The reference to **gold** probably means that she used gold paint for cosmetic purposes: she was a painted whore.

The whole picture suggests luxury and prosperity. Gorgeous. Attractive. Quite unlike that other city, the new Jerusalem, whose only adornment is the 'righteous deeds of the saints' and whose only dress is 'fine linen, bright and pure' (19:8).

Jesus, John had told his hearers, holds in his **hand** the saints of God, the people of the seven churches. The whore holds in her **hand** a **golden cup**. Its contents stand in horrible contrast to the brilliant outward appearance of the one who holds the cup: it is **full of abominations and the impurities of her fornication**. The cup's contents show who she really is. Unlike the new Jerusalem, who is holy, this whore-city is unclean, full of **impurities**.

She is an abomination in the sight of God, for she fostered and practised **fornication**. The word 'fornication' and 'harlot' both come from a Greek root *porn-*. We know about this whore: she practises her trade in many bookshops and video outlets. Behind all fornication lies the sin of idolatry: the will of a human being is placed above the will of God; a person becomes your idol, or you become your own god. For Jews and Christians alike, idolatry was the abomination above all **abominations** (see Mark 13:14).

5 Finally the whore-city is given a name: she is **'Babylon the great, mother of whores and of earth's abominations'.** This **name** is **written** on her **forehead**, perhaps in imitation of Roman prostitutes who wrote their name on the headband which women wore. But more likely they did so in satanic imitation of the people of God, who have the name of the Father and of the Lamb written on their foreheads (14:1).

The name is said to be a **mystery** or 'secret' (TEV). It's not really much of a secret. Every Jew and Christian knew that 'Babylon' was a code-name for Rome, just as everyone knew the supposedly secret name for Rome among the Romans: *Amor* (*Roma* spelt backwards). *Amor* is a Latin word which means 'love'. Babylon-Rome is a prostitute. 'What kind of love is that?' John would ask his hearers.

6 Babylon-Rome was a drunken whore, intoxicated by the blood of **the saints** and **witnesses to Jesus** whom she had either put to death or driven to death. The splendour that was Rome is the symbol, not of power and wealth and influence in the abstract, but quite concretely, of imperial power, imperial persuasion, and the imperial cult. For John as a pastor, the problem was not wealth and economic or political power as such, but the exercise of it in such a way that people were oppressed, treated unjustly, persecuted, and murdered. The enormous power of Rome extended into every corner of her empire. It supported imperial idolatry and the harassment not only of Christians, but of anyone who seemed unwilling to conform.

John's response to the gaudy spectacle which the harlot-city presented is, he admits, one of amazement, great amazement in fact. He comes dangerously close to joining the worshippers of the beast who follow him in amazement (13:3;17:8).

DIALOGUE NARRATIVE: The explanation of the 'mystery', 17:7–18

[7] **But the angel said to me, 'Why are you so amazed? I will tell you the mystery of the woman, and of the beast with seven heads and ten horns that carries her.** [8] **The beast**

**that you saw was, and is not, and is about to ascend from
the bottomless pit and go to destruction. And the
inhabitants of the earth, whose names have not been
written in the book of life from the foundation of the
world, will be amazed when they see the beast, because it
was and is not and is to come.**
9 **'This calls for a mind that has wisdom: the seven heads
are seven mountains on which the woman is seated; also,
they are seven kings,** 10 **of whom five have fallen, one is
living, and the other has not yet come; and when he comes,
he must remain only a little while.** 11 **As for the beast that
was and is not, it is an eighth but it belongs to the seven,
and it goes to destruction.** 12 **And the ten horns that you
saw are ten kings who have not yet received a kingdom,
but they are to receive authority as kings for one hour,
together with the beast.** 13 **These are united in yielding
their power and authority to the beast;** 14 **they will make
war on the Lamb, and the Lamb will conquer them, for
he is Lord of lords and King of kings, and those with him
are called and chosen and faithful.'**
15 **And he said to me, 'The waters that you saw, where
the whore is seated, are peoples and multitudes and
nations and languages.** 16 **And the ten horns that you saw,
they and the beast will hate the whore; they will make her
desolate and naked; they will devour her flesh and burn
her up with fire.** 17 **For God has put it into their hearts to
carry out his purpose by agreeing to give their kingdom
to the beast, until the words of God will be fulfilled.** 18 **The
woman you saw is the great city that rules over the kings
of the earth.'**

Every now and again in Revelation John uses a special method of helping his hearers to grasp the meaning of a scene which he has described. He reports on a conversation or dialogue which he had with a heavenly being, usually an angel-guide (see comments on pages 105-6). He has just told his hearers about a very attractive woman. She is real, for symbols always convey important realities. Christians must know exactly who she is and on whose side she is. So John conveys his message in the form of a dialogue with an angel-guide.

7 John's report of his own amazed response to the alluring woman is more than just a literary device, as some have claimed, to enable John to explain the **mystery of the woman, and of the beast with seven heads and ten horns that carries her**. No. John is being honest with his people. He was dazzled; he was almost taken in. He is human; he is a Christian who can be and is tempted just as his hearers are. Twice in this book he tells us that he tried to direct his worship to the wrong person (19:10;22:8).

In the present case, John is saved from falling into the sin of idolatry by his angel-guide, who, as so often in this book, reminds John and his hearers to trust their ears more than their eyes. What John saw he explains and interprets in his narratives. John's words, together with the liturgy of heavenly worship, make sense out of what he saw.

8 Who is the woman? Who is the beast? John answers the questions by reporting what the angel told him (in vv 8–18). In essence the angel said that the woman and the beast are Rome. The basic premise is that Rome is not the great mother, the source of all blessings, but she is the great whore, the source of all wickedness (17:5). Ultimately, she is the mother of death, not life. She devours her friends and will herself be destroyed by her friends (17:16). The very foundations of her existence are cracked and flawed.

But 'Rome', it should be remembered, is a symbol with many faces. 'Rome' is the city; she is the goddess Roma; she is the empire spanning the Mediterranean world; she is the emperor, the imperial cult, and the myth. 'Rome' includes also the goddess Artemis, who was venerated as the 'mother of maidens', but who, with the religious prostitution which was associated with her cult, could easily qualify for the title of 'mother of whores' (17:5).

In short, 'Rome' is an historical city, person, and power, as well as being a symbolic and theological entity.

First, John characterises **the beast**. Twice he says that the beast **was and is not and is to come** (or: **is about to ascend from the bottomless pit**). One thing is clear: the beast is a parody of the true God, who 'is, was, and is to come' (1:4,8;4:8). Another point, which is not so clear, is that the beast is a travesty of Jesus Christ, who said: 'I am . . . the living one; I died, and behold I am alive (1:17,18). The beast, too, appeared to be mortally wounded, and then he revived. The Nero legend has probably influenced the language which John is using here (see 13:3 and comments).

Two things, however, reveal the polar difference between the Lamb and the beast. The latter is described as one who is 'always ascending' (a better translation than **about to ascend**). His nature is that he always comes out of the depths of chaos, from the abyss of sin and evil.

The Lamb, by way of contrast, stands always with his church, while at the same time he stands before the throne of God (2:1;7:9). His place of origin is the throne of the holy God, the temple of the living God, heaven.

Secondly, the Lamb is acknowledged and confessed as the one who lived, died, rose again, and now lives forevermore (1:5,18), whereas the beast is said to have lived, died, revived, and now is heading for **destruction**. This is a crucial point for John's hearers to grasp. Characteristic of the beast is that he is going to destruction! Only a fool would follow such a one.

But the bemused and dazzled **inhabitants of the earth** are too blind to see the true nature of the beast (see Eph 4:18; 2 Cor 4:4). The phrase, 'inhabitants of the earth', is John's usual way of speaking of human beings in rebellion against God. They have on them the fatal mark of the beast (19:20). They show by their blind allegiance to the beast that their names are not **written in the book of life** which has been in existence **from the foundation of the world** (see comments on 13:8).

Much of the material in these verses (vv 7–14) is a repetition of 13:1–8. This is another indication that chapters 17–22 are a detailed exposition of previous narratives, rather than a linear, chronological sequential addition to that which has been described previously.

9 In chapter 13 John had warned his hearers that in order to grasp what was being said about the beast, they would need minds that have **wisdom** (13:8). He wasn't saying that they had to be on the ball politically, or good at arithmetic, or abreast of current affairs, or even intellectually smart. Everybody knew that **seven mountains** or hills was Rome's trademark. Every year Romans celebrated their special festival which was known as the 'Seven Hills Festival'.

So when the angelic commentator explained to John that the **seven heads** of the beast are **seven mountains on which the woman** named 'Babylon' **is seated**, you didn't have to be a genius to work out that the seven-headed beast is Rome. The **wisdom** required was the spiritual insight, a gift of God's Spirit (1 Cor 2:14–16), to see through the glorious facade of imperial Rome to the demonic anti-Christ forces at work, forces which are totally opposed to God and his people.

The angel's additional comment, **also they are seven kings**, clarifies the symbols which are in danger of becoming a little mixed up in John's mind. So:

> *The woman* = Babylon = Rome the city, as a social and economic force.
>
> *The beast* = seven kings = Roman emperors, as political and religious figures.

The image of a woman riding on the seven-headed beast and sitting on seven mountains is a potent symbol of the inseparability of Rome, the empire, the emperors, and the forces of evil.

10 The angel's description of the seven kings — **five have fallen, one is living, and the other has not yet come** — suggests that the angel wants John and his hearers to view the emperors corporately. Much as we say, 'The king is dead; long live the king!', so the emperors succeed each other, and always 'the emperor' reigns. So the angel describes 'the emperor' as one who was and is and is to come. This description matches that of the beast (17:8), the demonic power which both symbolises and controls 'the emperor'. Both beast and emperor, then, are parodies of the true God, about whom Christians confess that he alone is the one 'who is and who was and who is to come' (1:8).

The number seven, the traditional number of the Deity, and in Revelation the number of completeness, adds to the suggestion of parody.

In short, the angel is saying that the seven-headed beast is the Roman imperial power which set itself in opposition to God, and which in the Roman provinces, if not in Rome, was worshipped as 'God and Lord'.

Since 'the time is near' (1:3;12:12) for the end of the present creation, it is not surprising that the angel says that the end of the imperial power is near: when the last emperor comes, the showdown with God will be **only a little while** off. Already we live in the time of the 'sixth'; so the End is near indeed.

Readers should be aware that not all commentators agree with the interpretation given here, that is, that the number seven is a schematic representation of the complete number of Roman emperors, and of the rulers and powers who oppose God. They are all included — no matter how many there were or are — in the symbol of the beast.

Instead of following this interpretation, efforts are made to actually match the angel's 'seven' with seven historical emperors. The full list of Roman emperors up to Hadrian is:

44 BC–?	Julius Caesar	69 AD	Vitellius
31 BC–14 AD	Augustus	69–9 AD	Vespasian
14–37 AD	Tiberius	79–81 AD	Titus
37–41 AD	Gaius (Caligula)	81–96 AD	Domitian
41–54 AD	Claudius	96–98 AD	Nerva
54–68 AD	Nero	98–117 AD	Trajan
68–69 AD	Galba	117–138 AD	Hadrian
69 AD	Otho		

Counting six from Julius gives Nero as the Caesar who was **living** at the time when John wrote his report. The persecution of Christians (AD 64-65) is over, and Nero's reign is nearing its end. John, with genuine prophetic knowledge, sees the imminent violent demise of Nero (9 June 68).

Alternatively, counting six from Augustus gives Galba as the reigning emperor when John wrote. Nero is already one of those who **have fallen**.

Either alternative means that Revelation was written before AD 70, that is, before the destruction of the temple at Jerusalem (see comments on 1:9 and 11:1-4).

Perhaps a proper understanding of this difficult passage involves recognising that John combined a glimpse into the future with historical data, and used the familiar schematic 'seven' form to present the whole picture of Roman imperial rule.

One thing is certain: John and his hearers knew who was the reigning emperor; they knew his name. It seems that the angel's concern was that John and his hearers recognised *what* the reigning emperor represented. They had to see that the imperial power was, in the final analysis, demonic. Behind it stood the **beast**.

11 The **beast** is once again described as one **that was and is not . . . and it goes to destruction** (see 17:8). 'Heading for destruction' is characteristic of the beast, just as 'I am alive' is characteristic of the Lamb, whom the beast opposes (17:14).

The **beast** is further described as an **eighth** and yet as belonging to the **seven** kings. This is a complication to an already complicated symbolism. The simplest explanation seems to be as follows: the beast's seven heads are the Roman imperial power, symbolised also by seven kings. But these seven kings are not the full expression of the beast. The whole is bigger than the sum of its parts; the symbol is always more than that which it symbolises.

The beast **belongs to the seven**, yet it is an **eighth**. Roman imperial power, the imperial cult, imperial war-mongering, the temple cults of deities such as Artemis — all are manifestations of the beast, but you must not think that you have seen all of the beast when you've seen imperial Rome. There is still more of him. This 'still more' is summed up in the symbol of **an eighth** king (see NIV: 'The beast . . . is an eighth king. He belongs to the seven, and is going to his destruction.').

12 There is truly still more of the beast. He not only has seven heads, but also **ten horns** (see Dan 7:7). These horns represent **ten kings**. This may be a precise number; more likely it is symbolic, representing fullness. The angel's point is that there are other powers besides Rome, powers waiting in the wings as it were. **They have not yet received a kingdom**, that is, God has not yet brought them to power for his purposes (see 17:17). But at the right time, and for a very brief period in the story of the old creation ('for one hour') God will give them royal authority, an authority that they will share with **the beast**.

13 In fact, these kings will unanimously agree to throw in their lot with the beast. They will do this freely, without any coercion. The word which is translated as 'united' is an old technical term for the oneness of heart and mind which kindly gods brought about within a city or among nations. In the present case, the concord and unanimity is said to be brought about by God (17:17)!

They unite in order to oppose God; *God* unites them in order to destroy them, after they have destroyed the whore-city which is Babylon-Rome. Thus once again John's hearers are reminded of twin truths: 1) evil must be gathered and focused before it is destroyed; and 2) evil is self-destructive.

14 The forces of evil unite and gather to **make war on the Lamb**. But there is no war — there never is, for the Lamb has already conquered them (3:21;16:14.16). The Lamb has conquered, he conquers, and he **will conquer** all his enemies, **for he is Lord of lords and King of kings**. This is the name written on the Lamb's robe and thigh, according to the fuller account of the same confrontation in 19:11-21.

According to the Greek version of Daniel 4:37, the humbled king Nebuchadnezzar of Babylon acknowledged Daniel's God as 'Lord of lords and King of kings'. This is one of several instances in chapter 17 where John uses the language of the prophet Daniel when speaking of the beast with seven heads and ten horns (for example, Dan 2:37,47;3:2;4:27,33,37; 7:3,7,20,24). Here he confesses that a title which in Daniel is given to God is properly ascribed to the Lamb, who conquers all opposing powers just as God brought Nebuchadnezzar, king of Babylon, to his knees.

Remember: this King of kings and Lord of lords is the Lamb Who Was Slain. His victory was won on the cross. It was his faithful witness and the shedding of his blood which made him conqueror over the kings of the earth (1:5).

With the Lamb, and sharing his victory, are his **faithful** people. They are not frontline troops; 'they follow in his train', as Reginald Heber phrased it. They did not choose to be his, but he **called** them and chose them (John 15:16;

Rom 8:28–30; Gal 4:9). These **called and chosen** ones are also conquerors — 'super-conquerors' Paul calls them (Rom 8:37) — in the blood of the Lamb. They are kings and heirs of the kingdom, joint heirs with Christ, provided that they join him in his **faithful** witness (Rev 12:11), and in his obedience in suffering, even unto death (Rom 8:17; Rev 3:10).

15 The beast and his coalition partners are heading for destruction (v 11); but before they are destroyed, God has a job for them to do: they are to destroy the whore-city. John had seen her 'seated on many waters' (v 1). John's angel-guide explains now that these **waters** represent all the people of the earth over which the harlot city exercises control. Out from among these people the followers of the Lamb have been chosen and called (v 14). So the Lamb has his 'great multitude that no-one could count, from every nation, from all tribes and peoples and languages' (7:9), but so does the beast and his mistress, the great city Babylon-Rome.

16 The logic of evil is that it 'cannot preserve order but only consume it' (Goldsworthy). God condemns evil to self-destruction. So John's angel-guide points out to him that the kings of the earth, those same kings over which the harlot-city exercises control (v 18), and who form the foundation of her power and prosperity — these now join with the **beast** in hating the **whore**. Thieves fall out. Evil eventually reverts to chaos. C.S. Lewis's picture, in *The Screwtape Letters*, of the senior devil licking his lips at the thought of devouring the luckless junior devil is a humorous version of what John speaks of here.

The beast and the nations, headed by the ten kings, will 'desertify' Babylon, turn her into a desert, depopulate her, so that she will cease to be a 'great city' (v 18). They will strip her of her gaudy garments, the purple and the scarlet, the jewels and pearls, all the marks of luxury and riches. And they will leave her utterly destitute, **naked**, a shame to behold, deprived of every resource. She will become, in fact, as Jesus saw the church at Laodicea to be. Her only hope would be to 'buy from [Jesus] gold refined by fire, that [she] may be rich, and white garments to clothe [her] and to keep the shame of [her] nakedness from being seen' (3:17,18). John's hearers would catch the warning in this subtle parallel: unless you repent, your end will be as the end of the harlot-city.

The enemies of Babylon eat her flesh bit by bit. This is a metaphor for total destruction (see Ps 27:2). They will punish her with the same punishment which Jewish law prescribed for a whore: death by burning (Lev 21:9; see Gen 38:24).

Much of the angel's language here is taken from Ezekiel's description of another 'great city' which played the harlot: Jerusalem (Ezek 23:22–35). This, together with the allusions to Jesus' words to Laodicea (3:17,18), is a solemn reminder to all Christians that they actually live in Babylon. If they do not want to share her fate, they have to ensure that although they live in Babylon, they never become part of her (see 3:13; Rom 12:1–3).

17 The agents of Satan carry out the will of God. There is only one King of kings and Lord of lords. All enemies of God can only do that which God 'gives' them to do (see commentary on 6:2 and 13:5). They **carry out his purpose** without knowing it, and certainly without wanting to do so. But they do. A more literal translation of verse 17 brings out this truth: 'For God has given into their hearts to do his mind, both to do one mind and to give their kingdom to the beast, until the words of God will be fulfilled'. Their unanimity and singleness of purpose and action is precisely what God has in mind. Together they destroy the whore-city; together they themselves will be destroyed (19:17-21). So the **words of God**, spoken by his faithful prophets also in this book (19:9;21:5;22:6), **will be fulfilled**.

18 Finally, the angel articulates what everyone by now knows: the **woman** who is seated on many waters (v 1) and on the scarlet beast (v 3), is Rome, the city built on seven hills (v 9), the **great city that rules over the kings of the earth** and over all the nations of the earth over which the kings rule (v 15). This clear identification is like calling out the full name of the prisoner for execution. The crimes, the charges, the verdict, and the execution of the criminal are described in chapter 18.

NARRATIVE (continued): The fall of Babylon, 18:1–8

18 After this I saw another angel coming down from heaven, having great authority; and the earth was made bright with his splendor. 2 He called out with a mighty voice,

'Fallen, fallen is Babylon the
great!
It has become a dwelling place
of demons,
a haunt of every foul and hateful
bird,
a haunt of every foul and hateful
beast.[b]
3 For all the nations have drunk[c]
of the wine of the wrath of her
fornication,
and the kings of the earth have
committed fornication with
her,
and the merchants of the earth
have grown rich from the
power[d] of her luxury.'

4 Then I heard another voice from heaven saying,

'Come out of her, my people,
so that you do not take part in
her sins,
and so that you do not share
in her plagues;
5 for her sins are heaped high as
heaven,
and God has remembered her
iniquities.
6 Render to her as she herself has
rendered,
and repay her double for her
deeds;
mix a double draught for her in
the cup she mixed.

7 As she glorified herself and lived
luxuriously,
so give her a like measure of
torment and grief.
Since in her heart she says,
'I rule as a queen;
I am no widow,
and I will never see grief,'
8 therefore her plagues will come in
a single day —
pestilence and mourning and
famine —
and she will be burned with fire;
for mighty is the Lord God who
judges her.'

[b] Some ancient authorities lack *a haunt of every foul and hateful beast*

[c] Other ancient authorities read *she has made all nations drink*

Chapter 18 has two points of focus: the power, wealth, and splendour of Rome, and the justice of God. Picture a courtroom. The judge is God. The charges are laid by God's suffering people against the defendant, Rome ('Babylon'). The charge? Corruption leading to idolatry (18:8) and murder (18:24; see 16:6), all in the interest of furthering her own military might, economic influence, and the extravagant tastes of her citizens (18:7). We know Babylon's fate (14:8). Here John describes what happens to her, through the eyes of her so-called friends and trading partners. They weep and lament her fallen state, while Christians rejoice that at last God has demonstrated his just judgments for the world to see (19:1–8).

The language which John uses to describe Babylon's end is not so much that of the courtroom, but of what is known as a 'dirge' or 'lament'. John borrows phrases and pictures from Old Testament prophecies of the fall of Babylon and Tyre (for example, Isa 13:21; 23:1-16;34:11–14; Zeph 2:14,15; Jer 50:8–10). In particular, John seems to have been influenced, in his choice of words, by the dirges sung for Tyre by two different groups of mourners (Ezek 26:15-18;27:28-36).

He seems, too, to have drawn on a list of goods from various trading partners of Tyre, as he describes Rome's imports (Ezek 27:12–24). (Refer to Rev 18:11–13.)

The whole account of the events surrounding the judgment and destruction of Babylon-Rome is told offstage, as it were. We do not 'see' the events; we are only told of them. We learn of them from the reactions of those who witnessed them and were affected by them.

Chapter 18 is neatly arranged into an A B C B' A' pattern thus:

A	1–3	Fallen is Babylon!
B	4–8	Address to God's people: Come out of her!
C	9–19	Laments of her allies and trading partners
B'	20	Address to God's people: Rejoice, you are vindicated!
A'	21–24	Fallen is Babylon!

a) Fallen is Babylon! 18:1–3

1 In Revelation, the dragon, the beasts, and all evil ascend from the sea (=the Abyss) and the earth, whereas God's agents and the new Jerusalem descend from heaven. John's story of the fall of Babylon opens with his account of the descent **from heaven** of **another angel**, that is, one other than the seven bowl-angels. John's interpreter and guide was one of the bowl-angels.

To describe this 'other' **angel** John draws on Ezekiel's description of the glory of the Lord (Ezek 43:2). So impressive is this angel that he could well be taken as an angelic representation of Christ (see commentary on 8:3,4 and 7:2,3). This angel has **great authority**, as do Christ and God (12:10;16:9), who demonstrate their authority by conquering the dragon. Furthermore, always in Revelation, splendid brightness is associated only with Christ or God (for example 1:6;4:9;5:12,13). Finally, Jesus' voice is loud like a trumpet (see 1:10;4:1) and like the sound of many waters (1:15). Perhaps John did want his hearers to see in this **angel** the person of Jesus himself.

2 The angel-Christ announces the fall of **Babylon the great**. The language he uses is reminiscent of that used to announce the capture of ancient Babylon by Cyrus, king of Persia.

Fallen, fallen is Babylon;
and all the images of her gods
lie shattered on the ground. (Isa 21:9)

Here, however, Jesus is speaking of Rome, the whore-city, which represents all human habitations which are organised in arrogant disregard of God and his will and purposes for humankind. The verb which Jesus uses ('fallen') is in the past tense: in the past Babylon fell, as all Babylons fall, and will fall; always her condition is: she has fallen. God always triumphs over all opposition. The fall of all who rebel against God is inevitable; it is only a matter of time.

Rome's destruction is total. The only inhabitants of the land on which the city once stood are the creatures whom Old Testament writers traditionally associated with the desert: **demons** or unclean spirits, and loathsome and unclean birds and animals (see Isa 13:19–22; Mark 1:12,13). In John's world, people knew firsthand of the battle between creeping desert and cultivated land, between chaos and order. To say that a place had become 'desert' was to say that it was totally lost, gone, destroyed, vanished without a trace (like Sodom and Gomorrah, Isa 1:9; and see especially Isaiah 13:19–22; 2 Peter 2:6).

The site of Babylon-Rome becomes the permanent home (**dwelling place**) of unclean (**foul**) things. It stands in contrast to the holy city in which nothing unclean or **foul** is to be found (22:8;22:15).

3 Why has Rome suffered this fate? Because she has been a rich and powerful courtesan, associating with the people of the empire for her own benefit. Her economic allies don't see that she is exploiting them; they have, in fact, **grown rich from the power of her luxury**. Rome was guilty of self-indulgence and arrogance and irresponsible exercise of power. The fat cats grew fatter at the expense of the townsfolk and rural workers.

Her allies were content, because they benefited from Rome's exploitation of the poor and the working classes. For the ordinary subjects of Rome, the famous *Pax Romana* ('Roman peace') was nothing more than a system of economic exploitation. As the image of the harlot astride the beast (17:9,10) indicates, Roman life and culture rode on the back of Roman military might.

The poor, the workers, the peasants, and the people in the provinces gave Rome far more than she gave them. But they were seduced by her propaganda, dazzled by her harlot glory. So they drank **the wine** of the passion (**wrath**) of her **fornication**. As usual in Revelation, **fornication** refers to idolatry (for example, 2:14,20).

Rome is the 'mother of harlots and of the abominations of the earth' (17:5). The beautiful golden cup, symbolising Rome's wealth and splendour, offers corruption, religious and moral corruption, to those who drink from it. The 'Rome peace', the intoxicating wine which the people of the empire drank, was a delusion. It induced a false sense of well-being and of gratitude to the emperor. For the so-called blessings which he brought to his subjects he was hailed as God and Saviour and Lord. The further you went from Rome, the more the emperor was idolised and deified.

So Rome's false religion was the worst of all; it absolutised Rome's claims on her subjects, and dressed up her exploitation of them in the clothes of religious loyalty. Thus Rome's economic exploitation, and the corrupting influence of the religious observations which she encouraged, went hand in hand.

Jesus offers here a powerful critique of Rome, the 'great city'. Have we forgotten it?

b) Come out, my people! 18:4–8

4 From the time of Abram (Gen 12:1) and the slavery in Egypt (Exod 3:18), God's **people** have been called to separate themselves from the unbelieving and impure (see 2 Cor 6:14–7:1; Eph 5:11; 1 Tim 5:22). Once more God, through a **voice from heaven**, calls upon his people to get out of the great city. Peaceful coexistence, compromise, and toleration are impossible. Those who want to identify themselves with the great city will inevitably **take part in her sins** and will, in turn, suffer with her the **plagues** which will come upon her because of her sins (see 16:1–21). In other words, partnership in sin means partnership in punishment.

Christians, then, have to live in the great city (see 2:13), but they must never become conformists, obedient, unquestioning due-paying citizens of that city (see Rom 12:1–3). John's description of Rome could well have come as a shock to John's hearers, and the call to 'come out of her' could well have been a demanding challenge to them to think through their enslavement in the chains of culture. Christians at Thyatira, for example, would surely have seen in the prophetess Jezebel a kind of local representative of the harlot Rome. Jezebel encouraged Christians to participate without qualms in the commercial life of the city, and to take part in the religious observances which were bound up with the economic life of Thyatira. Through Jezebel, Rome's blasphemous mix of economics and idolatry threatened to worm its way into the life of the church.

Thyatiras are everywhere today. Jezebels, too, abound. Our besetting sin is compromise, willing acceptance of the values and morality and priorities of our society. Australian Christians have been so keen to prove that they are Australians that they run the risk of being Australian but not Christian. What we should want is to be both, without compromise: Australian and Christian.

5 Rome is destroyed because her **sins** have grown like the tower of Babel; one sin adheres to the other until the obscene heap touches **heaven**. Sin is not a fun thing, a peccadillo, a slip to be dismissed with a shrug. Sin destroys Babylon. The city is destroyed because God **remembered** her (16:19) and **her iniquities**. When God 'remembers' it is always effective remembering, bringing either destruction or salvation to those whom he 'remembers' (see Gen 8:1;19:29; Ps 25:7;79:8; Luke 23:42).

6 God, through the heavenly voice, now calls upon unnamed agents, probably angelic agents of punishment like the seven-bowl angels, to carry out God's punishment of Babylon-Rome according to the ancient law known as *lex talionis*. Basically, this law said that the punishment is to fit the crime. The divine sentence upon Rome is that the punishment shall be **double**, meaning that it shall be carried out in full, with no remissions for 'good behaviour' or for any other reason. The punishment shall consist of a working out to the bitter end of the consequences of her sins (see Rom 1:25–31).

7,8 Rome, then — Rome who flaunted her power, who basked in the 'glory that was Rome', who thought of herself as the Eternal City, who believed as an article of faith that she would never fall, who ruled like a **queen** over an empire which would last forever — Rome, who boasted that she was mistress of the world (see Isa 47:7,8), who didn't know what it was to lose a battle, to wear widow's weeds, to go into mourning, to bend the knee before a conquering king — Rome, who trusted in her own resources, who exploited all nations in her power, and especially her provinces, for her own pleasure, who felt that she lacked nothing — Rome receives a **measure of torment and grief** to match her arrogance and pride.

Suddenly (**in a single day**; see verses 10,16,19) she experiences three **plagues**: death (**pestilence**), **mourning and famine**. Here is a total reversal of her situation. John reported, when the fourth seal was opened (6:7,8), that Death and Hades were given authority by God 'to kill with sword, famine, and pestilence'. Here 'sword' is replaced by 'mourning', but the sense is the same: the sword causes mourning among the survivors.

But in the case of Babylon-Rome, even the survivors won't survive! For the great city **will be burned with fire**. Destruction by fire is the common biblical way of speaking of God's punitive judgment (for example, Amos 1:4; 2 Thess 1:8; Rev 14:10). Smoke rising up from a burning city was seen by friend and foe alike as a sign and symbol of its doom (see Gen 19:28).

So Rome, the mighty city, is sentenced by the **mighty** one, the **Lord God**. It is worth noting that the sentence is carried out by Rome's allies, the provincial rulers who had lived off her, and whom Rome had exploited for her own selfish ends (see 17:16–18).

WORSHIP: The laments of Babylon's allies, 18:9-19

**9 And the kings of the earth, who committed fornication
and lived in luxury with her, will weep and wail over her
when they see the smoke of her burning; 10 they will stand
far off, in fear of her torment, and say,**

'Alas, alas, the great city,
Babylon, the mighty city!
For in one hour your judgment
has come.'

**11 And the merchants of the earth weep and mourn for
her, since no one buys their cargo anymore, 12 cargo of
gold, silver, jewels and pearls, fine linen, purple, silk and
scarlet, all kinds of scented wood, all articles of ivory, all
articles of costly wood, bronze, iron, and marble,
13 cinnamon, spice, incense, myrrh, frankincense, wine,
olive oil, choice flour and wheat, cattle and sheep, horses
and chariots, slaves — and human lives.**[e]

14 'The fruit for which your soul
longed
has gone from you,
and all your dainties and your
splendor
are lost to you,
never to be found again!'

**15 The merchants of these wares, who gained wealth from
her, will stand far off, in fear of her torment, weeping
and mourning aloud,**

16 'Alas, alas, the great city,
clothed in fine linen,
in purple and scarlet,
adorned with gold,
with jewels, and with pearls!
17 For in one hour all this wealth has
been laid waste!'

**And all shipmasters and seafarers, sailors and all whose
trade is on the sea, stood far off 18 and cried out as they
saw the smoke of her burning,**

'What city was like the great
city?'

[19] **And they threw dust on their heads, as they wept and mourned, crying out,**

'Alas, alas, the great city,
where all who had ships at sea
grew rich by her wealth!
For in one hour she has been laid waste.

' Or *chariots, and human bodies and souls*

Throughout Revelation John speaks of true worship, worship of God and the Lamb, and false worship, worship of the dragon and the beast. Often in the reports of his revelations he has described the scene of worship around the throne of God. But he has never described the worship of the followers of the beast.

In 18:9–19 John does, for the first and only time, describe the worship of the counter-community. Ironically, the worship he describes is a series of laments. There is no joy.

Israel knew of lamentation as part of worship, especially in times of political crises such as war, oppression, and destruction of a city or sanctuary (for example, Pss 44;74;79;80; Jer 14). Lamentations were accompanied by fasting and various penitential actions such as mourning, putting on sackcloth (Isa 22:12), throwing dust on the head (Neh 9:1), gestures of humiliation and supplication, and 'weeping before the Lord' (Deut 1:45).

These features of worship are present in the laments of the allies of fallen Babylon. They weep and wail, and they throw dust on their heads as they cry: 'Alas! Alas! the great city'.

But one fundamental difference is to be noted between the worship of the people of God and that of the people of the beast. Even in their lamentations, God's people have hope of rescue and deliverance. In the past God had guided, preserved, and delivered his people; he would do so again. So the laments of the people of God end in praise, expressions of hope, and rejoicing (for example, Pss 80:18,19;79:13). This same combination is present in the lamentation recorded in the worship scene of Revelation 6:9–11;7:9–12 (see comments on those verses).

For those who worship the beast there can be only hopeless lamentation. For they, like the beast, are headed for destruction (17:8,11). In a final ironic touch, John records that the only worshippers who do any rejoicing and praising of their God are the saints of God, as they celebrate the vindication and salvation which are theirs in the defeat of all who threaten their health and wholeness and salvation (18:20;19:1–9).

Three groups of worshippers take part in the lamentation over the fallen Babylon: kings (18:9,10), merchants (18:11–17a), and the merchant marine (18:17b–19). Each lament is introduced with a double 'Alas!' (18:10,16,19), and concluded with the observation that the city's destruction has been accomplished in 'one hour' (18:10b,17a,19b).

a) The lament of the kings, 18:9,10

The **kings of the earth** who **weep and wail over** Rome are its trading partners, the leaders of provinces who shared in Rome's idolatry and benefited from its economic exploitation of others. In Revelation the phrase 'the kings of the earth' is a stock phrase, modelled on Psalm 2:2 and Ezek 27:33, to refer to the ruling classes in general (for example, Rev 1:5;6:15;17:2;19:19;21:24). It includes client kings who placed their kingdoms under Rome's umbrella, as well as local ruling classes who had been coerced or coopted by Rome into sharing its political muscle. In the Roman province of Asia the 'kings of the earth' would be the local aristocracy or city councillors, who used Roman authority to prop up their own position in society. These aristocrats of the cities of the empire invested in trading enterprises with Rome. As Rome prospered, so did they.

It is understandable, then, that these 'kings of the earth' lament the destruction of Rome's *might*, whereas others bewail the loss of its *wealth* (vv 17,19). Political power means economic advantage. As long as Rome ruled so did their prosperity increase. But only they benefited. The poor remained poor, while the gap between rich and poor widened. It is a familiar scenario.

These ruling classes (**kings**) see the **smoke of [Rome's] luxury**, and realise that their future has gone up in smoke. Babylon-Rome is finished, and so are they. Now these kings, who slept with Rome and couldn't get close enough to her, **stand far off**; they dissociate themselves from her (see Matt 26:58;27:55). When things go wrong, then you really learn who your friends are. Rome's 'friends' are horrified by her torture, but they do not come to her rescue. They have worries of their own. In trembling amazement they lament the sudden end of such a **great** and **mighty city**. '*Your* judgment', they say, 'has come in one hour'. They continue to distance themselves. But too late, too late! These **kings of the earth** also stand under judgment; they, too, are condemned for their participation in the great city's arrogance, pride, and self-indulgent luxury, and their rebellion against God (19:19–21).

Do not be deceived; God is not mocked,
for you reap whatever you sow. (Gal 6:7)

b) The merchants, 18:11–17a

These verses form the centrepiece of the report of the laments over Rome. In the account of Rome's destruction, John wants his hearers to learn and take to heart the truth that all the imported wealth which typified the degeneracy of Rome will be destroyed with the city. If Christians of the province of Asia were directly involved in Rome's sins, it would be in this economic area, for perhaps many of them actually did business with Rome.

There are kings and kings, merchants and merchants. John speaks of 'kings of the earth', 'merchants of the earth', and 'inhabitants of the earth' (13:14). They have this in common that they all serve the beast who comes from the earth (13:11). They are all 'of the earth', not 'of heaven'.

11 The **merchants of the earth** are 'the big international import-export wholesale merchants whose profits rose through Rome's exploitation of the provinces' (Krodel). They formed themselves into trading companies and consortiums. As they grew more and more wealthy, they wielded more and more economic and political clout.

These merchants **weep and mourn** for Rome, not because they feel any sympathy for the city, but because they feel sorry for themselves. With Rome gone, their major market has gone. Who will now **buy their cargo**? And what a 'cargo' of luxury goods! Nothing is more indicative of the decadence of Rome than the list of twenty-eight items in verses 12 and 13. The list follows closely a similar one recorded in Ezekiel 27:12–24, where the forty foreign products in which Tyre traded are listed. John's list is the most comprehensive listing of Rome's maritime imports which is available in any literature from the time — and even it gives only a selection of imports.

12 **Gold** from the state-owned mines in Spain was, according to Roman authors of John's day, *the* symbol of the moral mire in which Rome wallowed. It shared this doubtful honour with **silver**, which was also mined in Spain. People of Rome used **gold** and **silver** for anything from shoe buckles to bathtubs.

Jewels (literally: 'precious stones') came mainly from India. Roman matrons dripped with jewels; men wore jewelled rings; many banqueters drank from cups inlaid with precious stones. **Pearls** came from the Persian Gulf (if you wanted the best); the bulk came from India. The extravagant use of **pearls** and jewellery imported from India infuriated local economists, who blamed women especially for the loss of Roman currency to India (which was outside the empire).

The listing of **fine linen, purple, silk**, and **scarlet**, alternates kinds of cloth (linen, silk) with cloth dyes (purple, scarlet). **Fine linen** was at this time in the process of replacing wool as the staple material for clothing. The best was imported from Egypt, Spain, and Asia Minor. **Silk**, which the Romans thought grew on trees, was imported at huge expense from China. None of this would have helped Rome's balance of trade payments.

Silk, linen, and woollen clothing were all dyed **purple**. This dye has been called 'the most enduring status symbol of the ancient world'. Thousands of shellfish were needed to make a small quantity of purple dye. A Roman historian and social critic named Pliny observed that since both pearls and purple dye came from shellfish, this poor creature was the greatest single source of moral corruption and luxury in Rome!

Scarlet came from an insect parasite of a certain kind of oak which grew in Asia Minor. It was a costly status symbol.

It is not clear whether John next lists **all kinds of scented wood**, or 'all articles made of scented wood'. The wood in question came from a citrus tree which grew along the north African coast. Tabletops made of one piece of citrus wood were highly prized and very costly. The record price paid for one table made of citrus wood was enough to buy a large estate. Pliny, the Roman historian and social critic, notes that when Roman women were accused of extravagance because they imported pearls and jewels, they simply pointed to their husbands' mania for citrus-wood tables.

For over two thousand years now, elephants have been slaughtered for their **ivory**. When John wrote, the Syrian elephant was almost extinct. Rome traded in ivory from north Africa, where it was in short supply, and from India. **Articles of ivory** included anything from chairs to combs to dice and statues. Other items were made from **costly wood** such as ebony, maple, cedar, and cyprus. Wood-veneering was a recent innovation.

Corinthian and Spanish **bronze** was used for works of arts (for example, statuettes) or household furniture, especially lampstands and banqueting couches. From Spain and Pontus came implements of **iron** and steel, such as cutlery, swords, and other armaments. **Marble** was imported from Africa, Egypt, and Greece. Caesar Augustus boasted that he had found Rome brick and left it marble.

13 The list now shifts to spices and food. **Cinnamon** probably came from south Asia via southern Arabian middlemen. Cinnamon was used as perfume, medicine, and as condiment in wine. It was expensive. **Spice** from south India, **incense** from various eastern sources, **myrrh** from the Yemen and Somalia, and **frankincense** from southern Arabia, are all aromatic spices and ointments used in perfumes. These hugely expensive spices were used in vast quantities at the funerals of the rich.

Wine was imported from Sicily and Spain. From Spain and north Africa came large quantities of **olive oil**. These two commodities (wine and olive oil) were, like **wheat**, staple items in the diet of the one million citizens of Rome. Wheat was imported mainly from Africa and Egypt. Thousands of ships must have been involved in this operation of keeping up the supply of wheat to Rome. In times of shortage, the provinces had to give Rome first go — and there often were shortages (see 6:5,6).

The provinces also had to supply wheat to Rome as a tax-in-kind. Rome survived, even if the provinces died. Much of the grain which was supplied to Rome was distributed as a dole, available to those who possessed a government-issued inscribed tile, equivalent to a modern dole card (see 2:17). Wheat, wine, and olive oil were for everyone. **Fine flour** was only for those who could afford this luxury item. The finest of fine flour came from north Africa.

In John's day the Roman aristocracy had acquired large cattle and sheep stations or farms. Cattle were used mainly as work animals, or for milk. **Sheep** were kept for meat, but mainly for wool. Both cattle and sheep were probably imported for breeding purposes to improve the local strains.

Horses and chariots raced in the circuses, but 'chariots' here refers to the big four-wheeled carriages which were used by the rich for city travel or on their farms. These carriages were imported from Gaul (France). **Horses** came from the imperial stud farms in Spain and Cappadocia.

The last cargo is **slaves**. Prisoners of war usually became slaves. Foundlings and unwanted children ended up as slaves. Apart from these two sources, the most important source for slaves was Asia Minor. Perhaps John's hearers had experienced the loss of a family member to the slave-traders, often through kidnapping, although sometimes desperate people sold themselves into slavery.

The literal translation of the Greek word here rendered as 'slaves' is 'bodies'. In the market, slaves were simply 'bodies'. In God's sight, however, they are **human** beings (see Ezek 27:13). This final note is a comment on the slave trade and on the whole list. The life of the 'great city' rests on contempt for the life of others.

Babylon-Rome, the great city, exists still today in many forms and places. Anti-Slavery International, the world's oldest human rights organisation, estimates that more than a hundred million people around the world still suffer as slaves. The figure includes an estimate for child labour.

14 The heavenly voice comments unfavourably on the goods listed (18:12,13). The goods exemplify a love of luxury. The ripe **fruit** symbolises Rome's compulsive consumption of goods; the **dainties** and **splendour** suggest the self-indulgent opulence and the showy display of wealth. In the Greek, there is a play on words which is hard to express in English; closest is the NEB, which translates: 'all the glitter and the glamour is lost'. The bottom line, however, is that as a result of God's act of destruction all the 'glory that was Rome' is gone, **never to be found again**.

15 The **merchants**, who had a vested interest in maintaining the military power and economic domination of Rome, continue their lament over the fallen city. Like the 'kings of the earth' they **stand far off**, in awe at Babylon's destruction. They weep and mourn for the city (but actually for themselves, because their prime source of wealth is gone).

16 The merchants' description of the great city's wealth matches John's description of the harlot-city in 17:4:

> The woman was clothed in purple and scarlet, and adorned with gold and jewels and pearls.

The addition of **fine linen** to the merchants' description of the **great city** serves to link it with the list of imports in verses 12 and 13. All six articles in verse 16 occur in the list of luxury cargoes in verse 12. Obviously John wants his hearers to make the connection between the expensive attire of the prostitute and the luxury of the city.

Rome's luxury imports are like the extravagant lifestyle of a classy whore: it is maintained at the expense of her clients. Rome's clients were 'the kings of the earth' (17:2;18:3), that is, the local provincial rulers. But who actually footed the bill? The people of the empire. The money which Rome wasted on luxury items imported from all over the world came from booty, plunder, and taxation of the provinces. Rome lived on the pig's back at the expense of her subjects.

17 A select few benefited from Rome's craving for conspicuous consumption. Among these elite were the merchants. They could hardly believe that the destruction of the great city could happen so suddenly, and be accomplished so quickly (**in one hour**). Their concern, however, is not for people but for the loss of so much **wealth**.

c) The shipping industry, 18:17b–19

The third group who profited from Rome's insatiable demand for luxury goods, and her exploitation of her subjects, were all those associated with the maritime transport industry. The ship captains (**shipmasters**) and all in the coastal trade (**seafarers**), the sailors, and generally all who earned their living in connection with sea transport — all keep their distance from the **burning** city, and lament her destruction. 'There has never been a city like this great city', they wail (see Ezek 27:32).

In Revelation 13:4 John had recorded the shout of acclamation with which the worshippers of the beast greeted their lord: 'Who is like the beast?', they asked. The implied answer is: 'No-one'. This acclamation was accorded the beast in perverse parody of Old Testament acclamations of God (for example Exod 15:11; Ps 89:6).

'Worship of that which is 'not God' releases demonic powers' (Sweet). It also releases the wrath of God. It is because of the pouring out of divine wrath that 'Babylon the great' becomes 'Babylon the fallen'. 'Who is like the beast?' 'What city was like the great city?' The similarity between the two liturgical questions is an admission of the fact that if Babylon is fallen, the destruction of the beast cannot be far behind. The city rides on the back of the beast. The two stand or fall together.

Rome was regarded by its adoring citizens as a city without peer. Marcus Aurelius Martialis, a Roman poet and commentator on urban social life who lived at the time when Revelation was written, praised Rome as 'the goddess of the lands and nations, to which nothing is equal, and nothing second'.

The maritime community engages in the normal ritual for mourning the dead: they throw **dust on their heads**, they weep and wail. But like the merchants (vv 11–17a), their thoughts are not for the city but for themselves. They even mention their bosses, those who **had ships at sea** and **grew rich by her wealth**. Everyone, shipowners and ship captains and sailors, all sink or swim together.

In describing the great city's lifestyle, John wrote from the point of view of Rome's partners in crime: the ruling classes and the business tycoons. That John's presentation hits the nail on the head is shown by comparing it with a speech made by a man called Aelius Aristides. He came from Smyrna (see 2:8–11) and gave his speech before the imperial court about seventy-five years after John wrote. He said:

> Here [to Rome] is brought from every land and sea all the crops of the seasons and the produce of each land, river, lake, as well as of the arts of the Greeks and barbarians, so that if someone should wish to view all these things, he must either see them by travelling over the whole world or be in this city . . . So many merchants' ships arrive here, conveying every kind of goods from every people every hour and every day, so that the city is like a factory common to the whole earth. It is possible to see so many cargoes from India and even from Arabia Felix, if you wish, that one imagines that for the future the trees are left bare for the people there and that they must come here to beg for their own produce if they need anything. Again there can be seen clothing from Babylon and ornaments from the barbarian world beyond . . . Your farmlands are Egypt, Syria, and all of Africa which is cultivated. The arrivals and departures of the ships never stop, so that one would express admiration not only for

> the harbour, but even for the sea . . . Whatever one does not see here, is not a thing which has existed or exists, so that it is not easy to decide which has the greater superiority, the city in regard to present day cities, or the empire in regard to the empires which have gone before. (*P. Aelius Aristides: The Complete Works,* 26:11–13)

Why does John take so much care to present this perspective? Because it could easily have been that of some or many of his hearers (for example, in Thyatria or Laodicea). No doubt some of them were business people; others probably were closely involved with the Roman economic and political system. None of these Christians, John says, should be in the company of those who mourn for Babylon.

It is worth noting that the political and economic critique in chapter 18 is not addressed to the government or the marketplace or the CBD but to Christians at worship. Fear of 'mixing politics and religion' should not deter pastors from helping their people to see the corruption and oppression and injustices in political and economic systems. John made no bones about it. His critique of Rome matches and even surpasses similar critiques by his secular contemporaries.

The call to God's people: Rejoice! 18:20

20 **Rejoice over her, O heaven,**
you saints and apostles and
prophets!
For God has given judgment for
you against her.'

John's own perspective is not that of the people of the earth (vv 9,11), nor of the people of the sea (v 17), both of which places are the domain of the beast (13:1,11). His perspective is that of **heaven** (see 19:1-3). In 'heaven' Rome's victims rejoice in the triumph of God over the great city's exploitation of her people and the oppression of God's people in her midst.

In vivid contrast to the mourning and wailing which filled the previous verses, the inhabitants of **heaven** are called upon to **rejoice**. This heavenly company is defined as **saints** and **apostles** and **prophets**. The **saints** are the people of God; they are built upon the foundation of the seminal witnesses to Jesus, the **apostles and prophets** (see 17:6; Eph 2:20). In short, the call is for the church to rejoice over the destruction of the great city.

Why might God's people rejoice in this situation? Because they hate civilisation and human culture? No. Because they think urban life is essentially evil? No. Christians rejoice because 'God has passed sentence on the great city on the basis of the sentence which she passed on them', as verse 20b could be paraphrased. Salvation and vindication for God's people always involve rejection of those who rejected God's people. When God says yes to his people, he says no to those who harass and trouble his people. When God takes his people to a place of eternal safety, he makes sure there are no enemies who can threaten that safety.

The 'inhabitants of the earth' had rejoiced when the two witnesses (=the church) had been killed, and their bodies left to rot in the street of the city (11:8,10). They danced and celebrated in the streets. Behind them stood Satan, who blasphemes God and those who dwell in heaven (13:6). In the court of public opinion, and sometimes in the law courts, Christians were and are obliged time after time to defend themselves against all sorts of trumped up charges, petty niggles and jibes, mockery and scorn, even victimisation and discrimination, because they refuse to compromise, they refuse to take the easy road and try to please everyone, they refuse to give up their allegiance to God and the Lamb.

As they take this stand, they quietly appeal their case to a higher court, the only one that matters, the throne of God (see 1 Cor 4:1–5). Sometimes, when the strife is fierce and the warfare long, they cannot refrain from crying aloud:

> Sovereign Lord, holy and true, how long will it be before you judge and avenge our blood on the inhabitants of the earth? (Rev 6:10)

They pray this prayer in faith, surrounded by a faithless and unbelieving people (2:13), knowing that Jesus made them a promise:

> Will not God grant justice to his chosen ones who cry to him day and night? Will he delay long in helping them? I tell you, he will quickly grant justice to them. And yet, when the Son of Man comes, will he find faith on earth? (Luke 18:7,8)

An enacted parable and commentary of Babylon's fall, 18:21–24

21 **Then a mighty angel took up a stone like a great millstone and threw it into the sea saying,**

'With such violence Babylon the
great city
will be thrown down,
and will be found no more;
22 **and the sound of harpists and**
minstrels and of flutists and
trumpeters
will be heard in you no more;
and an artisan of any trade
will be found in you no more;
and the sound of the millstone
will be heard in you no more;
23 **and the light of a lamp**
will shine in you no more;
and the voice of bridegroom and
bride
will be heard in you no more;
for your merchants were the
magnates of the earth,
and all nations were deceived by
your sorcery.
24 **And in you[f] was found the blood**
of prophets and of saints,
and of all who have been
slaughtered on earth.'

[f] Gk *her*

21 The prophet Jeremiah once told Seraiah to read aloud the prophet's written sentence on Babylon, tie a stone to the document, and throw it into the Euphrates.

As he did so, he was to say: 'Thus shall Babylon sink, to rise no more, because of the disasters that I am bringing on her' (Jer 51:59–64). In a similar way, the action of **a mighty angel** symbolically confirms the prophetic word of 18:1–8. This is the third and last time that 'a mighty angel' is said to be active. In 5:2 he was not identified; in 10:1 he seemed to be the Lord Jesus in the form of an angel; here he is not identified.

The **mighty angel** threw a **millstone** into the **sea**, the home of the beast, and announced that as surely as the stone disappeared into the water's depths so surely shall Babylon be destroyed and disappear, 'never to be found again' (v 14).

The city's total desolation is emphasised at the end of chapter 18 just as it was at the beginning. In 18:1,2 Babylon's 'desertification' was portrayed in terms of its being taken over by repulsive, unclean, demonic beasts. In 18:21–24 the same truth is presented in terms of Babylon being overwhelmed by total silence and total darkness (see Jer 25:10; Ezek 26:13). Hiroshima writ large.

22 The dreadful silence which grips a city which is no longer a city is described in terms of the absence of the ordinary. There is no music and there are no musicians to make music: no instrumentalists, no singers. Only silence. There are no religious festivals, no worship, no feasts, no funerals, and no games at which harps and flutes and trumpets would be heard. Only silence.

Furthermore, there are no sounds of the workaday world. Not a sound from the carpenter and stonemason and other craftspersons. The millstone which grinds the corn is silent. On the air there float no longer the happy sounds of a wedding feast. Nothing. Silence.

23 Perhaps more frightening, however, is the absence of **light**. Total silence, total darkness, total devastation. The great city has been returned to the silence and darkness of primeval chaos (see Jer 4:23-26). Chapters 19 and 20 will reveal that all of the old creation has to be so treated before the unveiling of the new creation and the new great city of God, which is eternally a **bride** (21:2), and in which there is always music (for example, 4:7–15) and light perpetual (21:23–25).

When the Lord Jesus was crucified, the legal reason for his execution was nailed to his cross. In verses 23 and 24 the mighty angel, who speaks for God himself, gives the reason for Babylon's destruction: her evil influence was total, so her destruction is total. The charges against the whore-city known as Babylon are three in number. First, the merchants who did business with her were 'the honoured of the earth' (Isa 23:8), but they used their wealth and their economic and political clout to benefit only themselves and the elite of Rome.

Secondly, Rome herself had made the earth drunk with her idolatry and wicked practices (see 17:2). She had tricked her people, **deceived** them, hypnotised them, so that they really thought that she was the eternal city.

Thirdly, and worst of all, Babylon-Rome was 'drunk with the blood of the saints and the blood of the witnesses to Jesus' (17:6). These Christian martyrs share a sad solidarity with all the innocent victims of Rome's inhumane policies. Rome rides on a beast (17:3); the beast has a bear's hug and lion's teeth (13:2). The famous 'Rome peace', as even Roman writers admitted, was achieved through violence, maintained through constant war, and protected by repressing all public dissent. Rome shed a lot of innocent blood. Up to the time of John's writing, only a small amount of that blood belonged to Christians. But ahead lay a time when the church would be planted in blood as rice is planted in a flooded paddy.

In summary: the mighty angel draws lines connecting the great city's affluence, its self-deification, and its military and political brutality. The evils of Rome came to a head in its oppression of Christians. Here what was implicit in Rome's imperial policies, became explicit: Rome saw herself as supreme ruler, lord of life and death. The emperor personified this belief. The great city stood, then, in direct conflict with God himself. Such confrontation can and will end in only one way: destruction for the blasphemer.

For this reason the fall of the great city is most often portrayed in Revelation as retributive justice for the oppression and death of Christians (for example, 16:6;18:6,24;19:2). But this is not the whole story. God's judgment falls upon the great city because of her slaughter of innocents everywhere, including babies born and unborn (9:21;18:24), her idolatrous arrogance (18:7), and her sheer greed, pandered to at the expense of people (18:7,13,24).

WORSHIP: The hallelujah liturgy, 19:1–8

19 After this I heard what seemed to be the loud voice of a great multitude in heaven, saying,
'Hallelujah!
Salvation and glory and power to our God,
2 **for his judgments are true and just;**
he has judged the great whore
who corrupted the earth with her fornication,
and he has avenged on her the blood of his servants.'[g]
3 **Once more they said,**
'Hallelujah!
The smoke goes up from her forever and ever.'
4 **And the twenty-four elders and the four living creatures fell down and worshiped God who is seated on the throne, saying,**
'Amen. Hallelujah!'
5 **And from the throne came a voice saying,**
'Praise our God,
all you his servants,[g]
and all who fear him,
small and great.'
6 **Then I heard what seemed to be the voice of a great multitude, like the sound of many waters and like the sound of mighty thunderpeals, crying out,**
'Hallelujah!
For the Lord our God
the Almighty reigns.

7 **Let us rejoice and exult**
and give him the glory,

for the marriage of the Lamb has
come,
and his bride has made herself
ready;
8 **to her it has been granted to be**
clothed
with fine linen, bright and
pure' —
for the fine linen is the righteous deeds of the saints.

[g] Gk *slaves*

The liturgy recorded here serves, as is usual in Revelation, a double function. On the one hand, it is a response to God's activity which was narrated in chapter 18. It is a reminder that worship celebrates both God's saving actions and his acts of vindication. On the other hand, this heavenly worship introduces, and provides the dynamic for, the last great scenes of the third revelation (17:1 – 21:8), beginning with the return of Christ to judgment and concluding with the unveiling of the new creation, including the new Jerusalem, the bride of the Lamb. (For comments on the function of heavenly worship in Revelation see pages 95-7.)

Four 'hallelujahs' serve to guide John's hearers as they participate in the heavenly worship, which is a response to the summons given in 18:20: 'Rejoice over her, O heaven, you saints and apostles and prophets!' Three laments had been sung over Babylon by those who worshipped her (18:10,16,19). Now those who worship God and the Lamb respond to God's destruction of Babylon and his preservation of his people with four shouts of 'Hallelujah'.

1 The first 'hallelujah' is shouted in a **loud voice** by **a great multitude in heaven**. John has already used a contracted version of this phrase twice before (11:15;12:10) to speak of the redeemed people of God at worship. This **great multitude** of Christian people begin their worship with a shout of **Hallelujah!**

'Hallelujah' means 'Praise Yah[weh]!'. The word occurs for the first time in the New Testament here. This fact is noteworthy in view of the Jewish tradition about the use of 'hallelujah' as a shout of triumph in response to God's destruction of the wicked. One rabbi, for example, commenting on Psalm 104:35, noted that

> from the beginning of the book [of Psalms] up to this point there are 103 psalms, and none of them contains the Hallelujah; yet when it comes to the destruction of the wicked . . . then we say: 'Praise my soul, praise the Lord, Hallelujah!'.

The so-called 'Hallel Psalms' (Psalms 113–118) were associated in particular with the commemoration of the Passover (see Matt 26:30). This celebration remembered God's triumph over the Egyptian tyrant, and Israel's liberation from Egyptian oppression. It is fitting, then, that when the redeemed people of God celebrate the defeat of the tyrant Babylon-Rome, they do so with shouts of **Hallelujah!** The liberated people of God know that **salvation** is *God's* activity (7:10); it embraces all dimensions of individual, corporate, and cosmic existence. **Salvation** means victory; **Hallelujah!** is a victory shout. **Salvation** means healing, wholeness, liberation, room to move, rescue from a narrow place, deliverance from oppression, forgiveness.

God's saving actions are demonstrations of his **glory** and of his **power** (see Eph 1:19–23). The imperial cult, which did so much to unify the people of the empire, celebrated the glory and power of the saviour-emperor. But in the language of confession and worship, Christians proclaim the emperor's power and glory to be nothing in the light of the glorious judging and saving activity of **our God**.

2 Why? Because God's **judgments** are **true and just** (see 15:3;16:7). God has reversed the great city's judgment against the Christian, reversed it in a higher court. In so doing he has shown that he is the true judge, and that his **judgments** are **just**. With God, justice will in the end not only be seen to be done, but it will be done. The **great whore** Babylon-Rome has been tried and found guilty on two counts (see the charges recorded in 18:23,24).

First, Babylon-Rome **corrupted** everyone she touched ('the earth') with her wicked, self-serving, and idolatrous lifestyle, described in the language of the Old Testament prophets as **fornication** (see comments on 14:8;17:2;18:3,23).

Secondly, the **great whore** oppressed and killed the **servants** of God, a common name in Revelation for the people of God (for example, 1:1;2:20;7:3). Since God's **servants** are, in Revelation, God's agents (see 1:1), any attack on a Christian because he or she is a Christian is an attack on God himself. This is a lesson which the apostle Paul learnt on the road to Damascus. He was persecuting the 'disciples of the Lord' (Acts 9:1), and in so doing he was persecuting the Lord himself (Acts 9:4: 'Saul, Saul, why do you persecute me?').

The killing of a human being is, according to Old Testament law, punishable with death, on the grounds that murder is an attack on the image of God himself (Gen 9:6; Exod 21:12). Such wilful shedding of **blood** does not go unavenged, as the punishment of the harlot Babylon demonstrates (see 18:6,20,24). Such punishment is, on the one hand, vindication of those whom the great city had judged guilty and put to death; on the other hand, it is God's victory over the arrogant and complacent enemy (see 18:7), who has waged war on God by attacking his people. In Revelation, to judge is to conquer.

3,4 The antiphonal response to the Hallelujah song of verses 1 and 2 is a **Hallelujah** chorus, sung first by the choir of the heavenly church and creation (vv 3,4), and then by the whole worshipping community in heaven and on earth (v 5).

The first response celebrates pointedly the fact that God's victory over the harlot-city is full, complete, and final. In terrible parallel to the prayer-incense of the saints (5:8;8:4), the **smoke** of Babylon's destruction just keeps on rising from her. There is no hope of restoration or recovery. The great harlot-city is judged, conquered, destroyed, finished (Isa 34:8–10).

The second antiphonal response is a simple **'Amen. Hallelujah!'**. The 'Amen' is a petition that the condemnation and destruction of the great city, celebrated in the heavenly worship, may in fact come to pass. It means: 'May it be so!', looking to the future.

Hallelujah!, added to the prayer of 'Amen', expresses the confidence of those who worship that God's actions are so certain that what has been prayed for is already done.

The responses of **Amen. Hallelujah!** are sung by the **twenty-four elders and the four living creatures**. They are the heavenly representatives of the whole people of God and of all creation (see comments on 4:4–10). As usual when the **twenty-four elders** worship, they prostrate themselves and worship the one who sits on the **throne** (for example, 4:10;5:14;11:16). This is the last time the elders and the living creatures are named in the book of Revelation.

5 Finally, all who in Revelation are said to be on God's side are called to join in the great hymn of praise. The unidentified **voice** is probably the same voice which spoke from 'the midst of the four living creatures' when the third seal was opened (6:6). This collective voice of creation invites all of God's people to **'Praise our God'**. This phrase corresponds in meaning to 'Hallelujah' (see Pss 104:1;105:1;106:1). John likes a bit of variation. So the creatures invite the heavenly multitude and those on earth to repeat their hallelujahs.

In worship, boundaries are crossed. Socio-economic boundaries (see 11:16); ethnic and national boundaries (see 7:9); the boundaries of time and space. As John's hearers listen to the report of the revelations he received, they actually join with the heavenly choir in praise of God (see 5:11–14;8:3–5).

6 The worshippers on earth join in with gusto. With a mighty roar, like a waterfall or like rolling thunder, the people of God in Montreal and Moscow and Madang and Melbourne, in grass-roofed churches and great cathedrals, the beggar, the peasant, the media magnate, and the prime minister — the people of God 'small and great' join their voices with 'angels and archangels and all the company of heaven', and sing: **'Hallelujah!'**

The reason for the shout of praise is given with a glance backwards and forwards. First, God is praised because he has defeated and sentenced to destruction the arrogance of earthly empire. He has taken his power and begun to reign — or better, he is *seen* to have begun his reign. Despite the claims of human and demonic pretenders, God always has been ruler of the universe. But now the community of earth and heaven celebrates that the reign of the **Almighty** is manifest for all to see; his eternal kingship is actualised and concretised in the judgment of Babylon-Rome. He has begun his reign (see 11:7).

7,8 The song of the people of God and of the heavenly worshippers also looks forward. Hallelujahs are to be sung, Christians are to **rejoice and exult** (see Matt 5:12) and give God the **glory** because their future has arrived: the wedding feast of the **Lamb**. It is an old tradition this, the portrayal of the people of God (old or new Israel) as the bride, and God or Christ as the bridegroom (for example, Hos 2:14–20; John 3:29; Eph 5:25–33).

The **bride has made herself ready** for the marriage by dressing herself with **righteous deeds**. But these deeds are themselves gifts of the Lamb, prepared by him beforehand to be the bride's way of life (Eph 2:10). Or, as the church itself here confesses, the Lamb gave his bride her clothing of **righteous deeds**. They are like **fine linen, bright and pure** wedding finery. Paul expresses a similar thought in Ephesians 5:25–33.

The attractive woman named 'Babylon' was also clothed in **fine linen** (18:16). But she was a whore, not a virgin bride. There is no way that her dress could be described as **bright and pure**, for the grounds on which she was sentenced to death were her fornication and her bloody hands (19:2).

NARRATIVE DIALOGUE: John and the angel-guide, 19:9,10

9 And the angel said[h] to me, 'Write this: Blessed are those who are invited to the marriage supper of the Lamb.' And he said to me, 'These are true words of God.'
10 Then I fell down at his feet to worship him, but he said to me, 'You must not do that! I am a fellow servant[i] with you and your comrades[j] who hold the testimony of Jesus.[k]

Worship God! For the testimony of Jesus[k] is the spirit of prophecy.'

[h] Gk *he said*

[i] Gk *slave*

[j] Gk *brothers*

[k] Or *to Jesus*

John occasionally inserts one of these episodes into his basic pattern of worship and narrative, to tell his hearers of his own response, or to provide a link between one scene and another, or to report that he had been told to write down verbatim a particularly important statement (see 5:1–5;7:13–17).

The little episode which John records runs as follows:

	John		**The Angel**
9a	He says to me	9b	Write: Blessed . . .
9c	He says to me	9d	These are the true . . .
10a	And I fell . . .		
10b	He says to me	10c	Worship God!

9 The redeemed community is both the bride of Christ and the wedding guests (see Matt 22:1–14). They have been called to the **marriage supper of the Lamb**, and they have, by the grace of God, accepted the invitation.

John is directly commanded by an unidentified voice, presumably that of his angel-guide, to write down a divine word of blessing. The last time that John reported that he had been pointedly commanded to write down some particular words of God, was in 14:13, where an unidentified voice from heaven told John to record the beatitude concerning those who die in the Lord.

The point in the giving of a specific command to write seems to be that the words are especially important. Here their importance is related to the fact that the statement about the blessedness of those who have been invited to the wedding festivities is at the same time an indirect invitation to those who have not yet responded to the gospel invitation, 'Come!' The great city has been known to repent! (see Jonah chapter 3).

The fate of those who decline the invitation has been described in 18:1–24, and will be described again in 19:17–21, while the destiny of those who share in God's great wedding party is described in 21:1 – 22:7. That report closes, as does the present one, with the assurance that the words which John has written down in describing what he has seen are the **true**, reliable, and trustworthy **words of God** (see 19:11, the vision of Christ).

10 Worship has been the context, the dynamic, the beginning and end of all the actions which John has reported in his narratives. Every now and again John has recorded scenes of worship of God and the Lamb. Always he has made it clear that God alone is to be worshipped. He never describes the worship of the beast, except for the ironic account of worship which consists only of lamentations over fallen Babylon (18:9–19).

So it is with a sense of amazement that John's hearers would have heard the public confession of his own weakness. He admits that he was so overwhelmed by the scenes which his angelic guide had led him through that he mistook the agent for the Master, the servant of God for God himself. John could have pleaded a sense of confusion. In a number of instances John saw or heard an angelic figure who was really Christ. He might have offered that as an excuse or a justification for his attempt to worship the angel.

Instead, he reports what happened without any embroidery or attempts to rationalise the situation. His report is terse and to the point: I, John, the servant of God who have warned you so often against worshipping the parody of God, the unholy trinity, I actually prostrated myself before a **fellow servant**, the angel who had explained to me various aspects of what I saw. It's so easy to fall into idolatry!

John records the angel's rebuke, so that his hearers will get the message: the angel is no different from the prophet; both are messengers; both must obey the command: **'Worship God!'** No-one — not an angel, not an emperor — no-one must receive the homage and worship which is due to God who sits on the throne and to the Lamb who was slain.

John and his **comrades**, his fellow prophets, are described by the angel as those who hold to the **testimony of Jesus**, which in turn is said to be the **spirit of prophecy**, or perhaps the 'Spirit which inspires prophecy'. The **testimony of Jesus** to which John and his fellow prophets bear witness is the witness which Jesus in his life and work bore to God's plans and purposes, particularly in chapters 2 and 3 of Revelation. The parallel with 22:9 suggests that **the comrades who hold the testimony of Jesus** are Christian prophets, who are themselves spokespersons and symbols of the church as a prophetic community (see 11:3–12).

The angel instructs John in how God works with his word. The Spirit of God takes the **testimony of Jesus**, which is the word of God, and places it in the mouths of Christian prophets (see John 16:12–15). The close connection between the **testimony of Jesus** (=Word of God) and the **Spirit of prophecy** (the commonest rabbinic expression for the Holy Spirit) undergirds the command to **'Worship God!'** It introduces a trinitarian dimension to this little dialogue which ends the report of the worship scene (19:1–8; see 1:4,5).

The **testimony of Jesus**, the Word of God (19:13), points hearers to God. Since prophecy inspired by the Spirit is nothing more nor less than proclamation of the revelation of Jesus, Spirit-filled prophets will do as Jesus did: point people to God. To worship anyone other than God is to abandon one's prophetic calling. That this is always a possibility for Christians is attested by John himself when he, a prophet, wanted to worship an angel. Angels are fellow servants of John and of all who hold fast to Jesus' witness to God's judging and saving work.

Where have we been? Where are we going?

The people of God live their lives in the light of eternity. They know that their destiny and end is not an event or a thing but a person. Jesus Christ, the one in whom they have their beginning, is also the goal of their existence.

Christians are also aware, often painfully aware, that there ought to be a correlation between their present lives and the future which comes to them from Christ. Christians believe that they do have a future, that the future is worth living for and even, if necessary, dying for.

At the end of this world's history God will clear the decks. He will judge, sentence, and punish those people and powers who opposed him in this life. He will get rid of all sin and evil and uncleanness. The old will go so that the new can be revealed in all its glory. The 'new' means the new heaven and the new earth which God even now is creating, and which he will reveal for all to see in all its beauty at the end of this present world's existence.

In worship, Christians celebrate these realities which lie in the future. By means of worship, which is essentially praise of God, Christians cross the boundaries of time and space and enter God's eternal present. There, in God's presence and present, the worshipping community participates in God's creating activity; they create and shape the new world. This new world cannot come into being without the destruction of the old. So worship is the context and the dynamic not only for God's new-creating actions, but also for his work of destruction and punishment.

Throughout Revelation, John has spoken of God's saving and punishing actions, actions which we usually think of as coming at the end of history. He has reported judgment scenes (for example, in chapter 14), terrible scenes of destruction (for example, chapter 18), as well as scenes of Christians living in safety (for example, chapter 7). All of these scenes have been narrated within the brackets, as it were, of heavenly worship.

In 19:1–8 John told of yet another worship scene, one which is the Christian's response to God's destruction of

Babylon and at the same time the dynamic for the events described in 19:11 – 21:2. With this worship scene, John is reminding his hearers (who are themselves at worship) that the boundaries of time and space are broken. This is happening in God's time and space, not ours. Worship transports you to that same heavenly sphere.

In 19:11 – 21:2 John describes events which we place at the end of history. He speaks of Christ's return; a gruesome banquet; the binding of Satan and his release in order to collect his forces; the reign of the saints in glory; the last judgment; and the descent of new Jerusalem. Most of these scenes are introduced with the words: 'Then I saw . . .'

It is that word 'then' (literally: 'and') which epitomises the problems associated with the interpretation of the last chapters of Revelation. Those who believe that Revelation gives a chronological overview of world history at least remain consistent when they come to the last chapters: they treat these scenes as events which happen in chronological order.

Others recognise that in chapters 1–18 John repeats himself; the 'end' has come on several occasions (for example, 14:14–20;16:17–21), and therefore Revelation should not be treated as a chronicle of events. It is like a spiral, or a big painting which John sometimes describes in its wholeness and sometimes only in parts. But when they come to the last chapters of Revelation, these same commentators insist that John is presenting a calendar of end-time events: first this happens, then that, then that.

Such interpretations of the final chapters of Revelation create more difficulties than they solve. Proof of this lies in the profusion of differing interpretations, and the great differences of opinion even among those who follow the same basic line.

Far preferable is to treat these final chapters in the same way as we have treated the rest of the book (see comments in the Introduction, pages 17-19). Throughout the book, and now also at the end, John gives his hearers a view of end-time realities from a heavenly (that is, God's) perspective. He urges his hearers to put on God's glasses, to see things as God sees them. To do so, they must join in worship, listen to John's reports of his four revelations, and then respond in the only possible way: with praise to God, that is, with worship of him who sits on the throne.

So in 19:11 – 21:2 John narrates what he saw by filling in details of many of the things which he had already told his hearers about. He saw the end-times events 'in a moment, in the twinkling of an eye'. But he can't describe them in a moment. He needs time. So he tells first of this action of God; then he tells of something else he saw. Gradually he puts the whole picture together. The 'time' is not in what John saw, but in his narrating of what he saw.

The coming of Christ in glory (the Parousia), 19:11–16

11 Then I saw heaven opened, and there was a white horse! Its rider is called Faithful and True, and in righteousness he judges and makes war. 12 His eyes are like a flame of fire, and on his head are many diadems; and he has a name inscribed that no one knows but himself. 13 He is clothed in a robe dipped in[l] blood, and his name is called The Word of God. 14 And the armies of heaven, wearing fine linen, white and pure, were following him on white horses. 15 From his mouth comes a sharp sword with which to strike down the nations, and he will rule[m] them with a rod of iron; he will tread the winepress of the fury of the wrath of God the Almighty. 16 On his robe and on his thigh he has a name inscribed, 'King of kings and Lord of lords.'

[l] Other ancient authorities read *sprinkled with*

[m] Or *will shepherd*

11 An open door in heaven enabled John to have a clear view of the heavenly throne-room when he received his second revelation (4:1 – 16:21).

If there is no 'opening' there is no revelation and no action. So, for example, the narrative of the defeat of Satan in heaven by Michael-Christ is preceded by the notice that the temple of God in heaven was opened (11:19). Likewise, when the 'seven bowls of God's wrath' are to be poured out on earth (16:1–21), another 'opening' precedes the action: 'the temple of the tent of witness in heaven was opened' (15:5). Heavenly action requires a heavenly 'opening'.

The most dramatic 'opening' is described in 19:11, when John reports that he **saw heaven** 'wide open' (NEB). Heaven is opened, not so that John can be taken 'in the Spirit' into heaven, but in order for the Judge and King, Jesus Christ, to be revealed (see Acts 7:56). John is still in the 'desert', the place to which the Spirit took him in order to view the destruction of God's enemies from the place of safety God has provided for his church (17:1–3;12:14).

So in these last scenes of the third revelation (17:1 – 21:8) the coming together of heaven and earth, actualised throughout Revelation in the scenes of worship, is now narrated in detail. Earthly and heavenly reality are revealed to be one and the same reality. The unity of heaven and earth, under the rule of the one who sits on the throne and the Lamb, is revealed for all to see, whether they welcome the view or not. Heaven is wide open. Take a good look, Christian. And be warned or be comforted, as the case may be.

The first thing John said that he saw on the first occasion when heaven opened for him was a throne (4:2); it was a white throne (20:11). The first thing John says he saw on the last occasion that heaven opened for him was a horse, a **white horse**. White is the colour of victory. The horse is the mount of kings and generals; Roman generals rode a **white horse** in their victory processions through Rome. Clearly the **rider** of the white horse which John saw is a conquering king.

The **rider**, not the horse, is the true focus of attention. He is Jesus Christ. Here is the person and event celebrated in Christian worship and received in anticipation in the eucharist. Look at him! John draws on images from earlier descriptions in order to describe Christ in all his glory, the victorious judge and ruler of all.

The names by which Jesus is known are **Faithful and True**. Nobody gave him these names; they are self-designations. He told the Laodiceans that he is 'the faithful and true witness' (3:14; see 1:5). He is true to the word that he has given to his church; indeed, he is the content of the faithful and true words of God which are given to John and authenticated by God himself (21:5;22:6).

The Lord's very appearance in this end-time scene is proof that he is a faithful and true witness. He keeps his promises to his people (for example, John 14:3; Acts 1:11). His faithfulness is also demonstrated in this, that he obtains justice for his oppressed and maligned people (Isa 11:4). At the same time he carries out his righteous judgments by making **war** on the beast and all his followers

(17:14), including the compromising Christians in John's congregations (2:16).

So the rider on the white horse is Jesus Christ, conquering general and Supreme Court judge. This is not the first time in Revelation that John has combined legal and military language to speak of Christ (see 2:16 and 12:1–5 and comments).

12 Jesus' eyes are like **a flame of fire** (see 1:14). The description emphasises Jesus' role as judge of the church and of the world. As he warned the Thyatirans, his laser-beam eyes enable him to see the actual situation of Christians, and to know their true allegiance (2:18). To judge is to expose; to expose is to judge.

The **many diadems** that Christ wears on his head symbolise his unlimited power as conquering king and supreme judge of all. It is a reminder of Christ's ultimate superiority over the satanic powers whose authority is symbolised by seven or ten diadems (12:3;13:1). Once again, as often in Revelation, Jesus Christ is shown to be the reality of which the dragon and the beasts are only cheap copies, parodies, poor imitations.

The idea of the copycat nature of all demonic powers is continued with the reference to a **name** which only the rider himself knows. The beast from the sea (13:17) and the woman who rides that scarlet beast (17:5) both have a mysterious name, again in imitation of Christ.

The unknowableness of Christ's **name** suggests the mystery of his person: he comes from heaven (19:11); he is not of the earth. Since John expressly tells his hearers that Jesus' name is known only to **himself**, it borders on blasphemy to think that we might be able even to guess at what this unknowable name might be.

13 Christ wears the bloody garments of the divine warrior of Isaiah 63:1–3, but the blood is not the blood of his enemies. It is his own blood, the blood of the Lamb who was slain. In this blood, that is, by his death, he has conquered. Once again, we are reminded of John's 'theology of opposites': Christ conquers by being himself killed; the anti-Christ (Satan, beast, Babylon, Rome, and all modern equivalents) conquers by killing others.

Christ's peace was established by his own death (see Eph 2:14–18); the anti-Christ's peace — in John's day the famous *Pax Romana* — was accomplished by shedding the blood of others.

So Jesus Christ redefines. He reveals reality to be the very opposite of what Satan says it is. In our Lord's sacred dictionary of salvation, 'to conquer' means 'to give up your life'; 'victory' means 'a cross'; a 'Lion' means a 'Lamb'; 'to rule' is 'to serve'.

The initial description of the returning Christ closes as it began, with a reference to his martyr (=witness) character. 'Faithful' and 'true' are characteristic of John's prophecy, which are the words of Christ himself (21:5;22:6). But they are also said to be words of God (1:1,2) to which Jesus bears witness. So it is not surprising that the **name** by which he has been, and still is, **called** is **The Word of God**.

In Jesus Christ, word of God and action of God come together: he embodies God's word in his acts of salvation and judgment, just as he bore faithful witness to God in all he said, especially in the face of death (1 Tim 6:13). The focus here is on God's word as being what is called a 'performative utterance', that is, it does what it says. God speaks, and it is done (see Ps 33:9). So Christ as **The Word of God** is the complete agent of God's purposes in both salvation and in judgment.

14 The returning Christ is accompanied by **the armies of heaven**. These could be the angelic armies whom Jesus said would attend him and be actively involved in the judgment (for example, Matt 13:41; Mark 13:27). More likely, John is echoing Paul, who confessed that Jesus would return 'with all his saints' (1 Thess 3:13). The **armies** are the church of God in heaven, the 'prophets and saints' (18:24), described also as 'called and chosen and faithful' (17:14).

The **fine linen, white and pure,** which the members of the salvation army wear, are the clothes which the bride of Christ (=the church) wears for the marriage of the Lamb (19:8). The linen is **white** because these people have dyed their clothes in the blood of the Lamb (7:14).

In sum: the **armies of heaven** are the one hundred and forty-four thousand of 7:1–8 who follow the Lamb wherever he goes (14:1–5), and who bear faithful witness to him. They ride **white horses** because they, too, have conquered by the death of Christ and by their witness to that victory even to the point of their own death (12:11).

For the **armies of heaven** there is no final battle, even though the armies of Satan gather for battle in fearful array (19:19–21;20:7–10). The victory belongs to the Lamb alone, and he has already achieved it by that action which bloodied his clothing: the cross (see Col 1:14;2:15).

15 In his description of the royal Christ riding at the head of his armies, John continues to draw on images he used earlier in Revelation. Like the messianic king depicted in Isaiah 11:4, Christ has in his **mouth** a **sharp sword**, symbolising the lethal nature of his word of judgment, and the saving nature of his word of grace and forgiveness (see 1:16;2:12;19:10; Hosea 6:1–5).

In his prophetic proclamation to the Christians at Pergamum (2:12–17), Jesus had warned that he would wage war against the Nicolaitans, the champions of accommodation and compromise. He would fight against them, Jesus said, 'with the sword of my mouth' (2:16). Having conquered all opponents and all **the nations** with his word of judgment and his word of grace, Christ will rule (or 'shepherd') them with **a rod of iron** (see Ps 2:9; Rev 12:5;2:27 and comments there). Part of Christ's ruling activity is passing sentence on his enemies. Those who shed the blood of God's people (11:2) — and all innocent blood, for that matter (18:24) — will themselves be trampled under foot in the **winepress of the fury of the wrath of God the Almighty** (see 14:19,20). This divine wrath is also the wrath of the Lamb (6:16,17). This truth must be maintained against those who refuse to believe in any other Christ than the 'gentle Jesus meek and mild' of Sunday school.

Those who tormented God's faithful witnesses because they were faithful witnesses will themselves be tormented as they experience the **fury of the wrath of God** (see 14:10). In a powerful, awful picture, John combines the image of a winepress with that of drinking from a wine cup: he speaks not just of the **fury** of God, but of the **fury** of his **wrath**. That was the same cup, the hearer will recall, which Babylon had to drink (16:19). This is yet another reminder that John has described the judging and condemning activities of Christ several times already (for example, 6:12-17;11:17,18;14:8–20). What John gives his hearers in chapters 19 and 20 are not reports of further judging and saving events, in addition to the events which he has already reported. Rather, he gives them (and us) further, more detailed *reports* of the same events that he has already described in earlier chapters of Revelation.

16 Christ's judging activity is all carried out, not by means of a final, cosmic battle, but simply by the power of his name, The Word of God. There can be no battle, for who can stand against the one who is called **'King of kings and Lord of lords'**? The Roman emperor was often given this title, and sometimes he claimed this title for himself. But as usual, like all persons and powers who think they can replace God, the emperor is only aping God. He is not God (see Deut 10:17).

The royal title ('King of kings and Lord of lords') is **inscribed** or embroidered (?) on the **robe** dipped in blood (19:13). This is a perpetual reminder of how he came to be worthy of being acclaimed as king (see 5:9-14). It is also a reminder of what kind of king Christ is: he rules, as John the Evangelist teaches, from the cross. So by his *action* (the 'robe dipped in blood' = his work of atonement) Christ demonstrates his worthiness to receive the title of 'King of kings and Lord of lords'.

Not only in his *actions* but also in his *person* Jesus is worthy of the royal title above all titles. This truth is indicated by the fact that the title is written on **his thigh**. In Old Testament anthropology, the **thigh** is regarded as the part of a person which, in terms of power and vitality, is the seat of life for the whole personality. It is also the source of life for those produced by the 'thigh'. Since a name reveals the nature of the one who bears the name, and since the **thigh** symbolises the essence and life of a person, what better way of confessing that Christ is the cosmic king than by writing on his **thigh** the title, 'King of kings and Lord of lords'?

Many many people are curious — and the curiosity is understandable — about what the end of history will be like, how it will end, and when it will end. John's report in 19:11–16 is a gentle reminder that the end, like the beginning, is God-in-Christ. Instead of getting caught up in guessing games about the when and what and how of the end, and reading Revelation as if it answered *those* questions, we should listen to John as the Spirit speaks through him, and focus on the *who*: Jesus Christ. It is to him that the Spirit always bears witness (John 15:26; 1 John 5:6–12).

The 'other' feast: The defeat of the beast, 19:17–21

17 Then I saw an angel standing in the sun, and with a loud voice he called to all the birds that fly in midheaven, 'Come, gather for the great supper of God,
18 to eat the flesh of kings, the flesh of captains, the flesh of the mighty, the flesh of horses and their riders — flesh of all, both free and slave, both small and great.'
19 Then I saw the beast and the kings of the earth with their armies gathered to make war against the rider on the horse and against his army.
20 And the beast was captured, and with it the false prophet who had performed in its presence the signs by which he deceived those who had received the mark of the beast and those who worshipped its image. These two were thrown alive into the lake of fire that burns with sulfur.
21 And the rest were killed by the sword of the rider on the horse, the sword that came from his mouth; and all the birds were gorged with their flesh.

17,18 The 'then' with which verse 17 begins is misleading: it suggests the idea of 'the next thing I saw (after the previous happening)'. What John wants to convey is, rather: 'Another detail I want to tell you about in the scene I saw from my vantage point in the "desert" is . . .' John saw everything 'at once', because he was outside of time and space; he was 'in the Spirit'. But he can't tell everything 'at once'. So he follows more or less an orderly line, with some doubling for effect. He has told of the appearance of the glorious Judge and King, accompanied by the 'armies of heaven'. Next (19:17–21), he will tell of the destruction of the two beasts of chapter 13, together with the 'kings of the earth' who were their willing accomplices (see 17:12–14). He will tell of the capture, imprisonment, and final judgment of the dragon and his followers, and the resurrection and reign of the saints (20:1–10).

In reporting these dramatic end-time events, John seems to have been heavily influenced by his favourite Old Testament prophet, Isaiah. The following analysis reveals the parallels:

	Isaiah 24:1 – 27:1		**Revelation 19:19 – 20:10**
24:1–22	Day of the Lord; judgment of heavenly and human powers	19:19 – 20:3	Punishment of rebellious humans and of Satan
24:23; 25:6–9	Reign of God; messianic banquet	20:4–6	Reign of God, Christ, and saints (=messianic banquet; see 19:9)
26:14–19	Resurrection of righteous; no resurrection for the wicked	20:4–6	Resurrection of righteous; no resurrection of the wicked
26:10–21	Punishment of 'inhabitants of the earth' (by fire? 26:11)	20:9	'Gog and Magog' destroyed by fire
26:1,11, 12;27:2–4	Enemies destroyed because they are attacking Jerusalem	20:7–9	'Gog and Magog' destroyed because they are attacking 'the beloved city'
27:1	Punishment of Leviathan the serpent	20:10	Punishment of Satan (=Leviathan [12:3,4] or serpent [20:2])

(Based on J. Webb Mealy, *After the Thousand Years*, p 100)

In particular, it is clear that behind John's words in 19:19 – 20:3 lies the prophetic oracle recorded in Isaiah 24:21,23 (NIV):

> In that day the LORD will punish the powers in the heavens above and the kings on the earth below.
> They will be herded together like prisoners bound in a dungeon;
> they will be shut up in prison and be punished after many days.
> The moon will be abashed, the sun ashamed; for the LORD Almighty will reign on Mount Zion and in Jerusalem, and before its elders, gloriously.

At the end of the hallelujah chorus which celebrated the victory of the Lamb and the fall of Babylon, those who were invited to the wedding feast of the Lamb were said to be 'blessed' (19:7–9). Now another invitation to a feast goes out, a feast which God provides. But the people who are present at the feast are far from blessed, for they will in fact be the food which is eaten at the grisly **supper of God**. Clearly, John's hearers are meant to see this supper as an awful contrast to the 'supper of the Lamb', at which Christians are both the guests and the bride of the Lamb (19:7–9).

The invitation to the **supper of God** is issued by **an angel** who stands **in** or on **the sun**. That is a position of glory, appropriate to such a divine agent; it is also the highest point in the sky. From there, **all the birds that fly in midheaven** can hear the angel's invitation (see the eagle of 8:13). These **birds** are most likely carrion birds, vultures, unclean because of their contact with dead bodies. It is fitting that these unclean birds (see 18:2) are invited to feed on the corpses of the unclean people who have gathered to fight against Christ. Evil devours itself.

Those who provide food for the vultures come from the whole range of humanity (see Ezek 39:17–20) and creatures: from rulers, generals, national heroes, business tycoons, and cavalrymen and their horses, to all kinds of 'little' people from all economic and social strata (see 6:15–17).

It is worth noting that the angel calls the feast **the great supper of God**. God himself prepares this feast as punishment for those who refuse to worship him, just as the marriage supper of the Lamb is prepared by God for those who do worship him (19:9).

It is also noteworthy that the invitation to attend the **great supper of God** is issued *before* the armies of evil gather to do battle against the rider on the white horse (19:19). It's like a football team issuing invitations to its premiership dinner before grand final day. But whereas the football team would be taking a chance and even indulging in an act of bravado, with God there is no question of chance, no whistling in the dark, no 'maybe'.

The decisive battle against all the forces of sin and evil has been fought and won. The issue was decided with the birth, life, death, resurrection, and enthronement of the Son of God, the Lord Jesus Christ.

19,20 Those who rebel against Christ and who gather for battle against him and **his army** have been described in verse 18 as **kings** . . . **captains** . . . **the mighty** . . . **riders** . . . **all, both free and slave, both small and great**. Now John identifies the leaders of the rebellion. At this point his attention is focused on recounting *their* fate.

The commander-in-chief of the rebel armies is the **beast** who rises from the sea to make war on the two witnesses (11:7,8), the people of God. This beast is the agent of Satan, the great red dragon (12:3,4). He represents all political and economic powers which work in blatant opposition to God. His tool is the whore Babylon; she rides on his back (17:3). The beast is supported in his opposition to God and his people by **the kings of the earth with their armies** (see Ps 2:2; Rev 16:12,14;18:9 and comments there).

This great army of enemies **gathered to make war against the rider on the horse and against his army** of Christian people who faithfully confess him and worship him in defiance of pressure to worship the beast. The evil army gathers for battle, but, as usual in Revelation, *there is no battle.* In a last act of evil stupidity, the rebel armies gather only to make it easy – to speak as a human – for God to deal with them. There is no battle. Despite all the hype, there is no battle of Armageddon (see 16:14,16). Instead, he who is The Word of God judges, sentences, and executes his enemies.

The beast and his partner **the false prophet** were **captured**. The **false prophet** is the second beast of 13:11–18 (see commentary). His deceiving days are over. All the **signs** and miracles in the world won't save him.

The two beasts are not killed, unlike their followers, who were killed and who provided food for the vultures (v 21). Instead, the two beasts are **thrown alive** into a familiar environment: water. But, as often happens in Revelation, their own environment is used by God against them, to torment them. The water into which they are thrown is **the lake of fire that burns with sulfur**. They are thrown into hell, not merely into Hades, the place of the dead. They are thrown into hell.

In hell the two beasts, so John will report later, are joined by the devil (20:10), by Death, Hades, and all those whose names are not written in the book of life (20:14,15). John calls the **lake of fire** the 'second death' (20:14), which signifies, negatively, exclusion from eternal life in the presence of God, and positively, torment unending.

21 As non-human powers, the two beasts are not said to die; they are **thrown alive** into the **lake of fire**, and so experience eternally the 'second death'. With human beings, the pattern is different: first death, then punishment or blessedness. John reflects this pattern when he tells of the fate of **the rest**, that is, those who 'did not repent of the works of their hands or give up worshipping demons . . . and did not repent of their sorceries or their fornication or their thefts' (9:20,21). He says that they were **killed**. Their judgment has begun; they have passed stage one, as it were. Stage two will be described when John tells of the fate of the third being in the unholy trinity, the dragon (20:1–3;7–10). Then he will finish the account of the judgment and fate of the followers of the beasts and the dragon (20:11–15). Their fate is likewise the 'second death'.

The followers of the beast were **killed by the sword** of the Word of God. It is a dynamic and effective word which slays those who deliberately and consistently reject the witness of Christ and his faithful people (see 2 Cor 2:15,16; John 3:36). The reality of this death is emphasised by John's concluding note, that the vultures **were gorged** with the **flesh** of those who had been judged and killed by the powerful **sword of the rider on the horse**. These people did not repent when they had the opportunity (16:9,11); now the day of repentance has passed. They have been killed by the Word; all that remains is divine wrath and fury, which the unrepentant have stored up for themselves 'on the day of wrath, when God's righteous judgment will be revealed' (Rom 2:4,5,8,9).

The end of Satan and his followers, 20:1–3,7–10

20 Then I saw an angel coming down from heaven, holding in his hand the key to the bottomless pit and a great chain. [2] He seized the dragon, that ancient serpent, who is the Devil and Satan, and bound him for a thousand years, [3] and threw him into the pit, and locked and sealed it over him, so that he would deceive the nations no more, until the thousand years were ended. After that he must be let out for a little while.

The two beasts who make up two-thirds of the unholy trinity revealed in chapters 12 and 13 have been forcibly captured, judged, and consigned to the place of torment, called the 'second death' (19:19,20;20:14). The key figure, the first in the unholy trinity, has yet to be dealt with — although John's hearers will recall that his fate has already been described in 12:7–12. But now John, as he tells of God clearing away all that must be cleared away in order to reveal his new creation, describes in detail the fate of the great enemy of God and his people, and of the evil army which he heads. We have met this army before, in 9:1–11;16:13–16, and 19:19. We already know its fate. John's focus is the fate of the dragon.

John divides into two parts his account of the judgment and destruction of the dragon (20:1–3,7-10), somewhat like what he is doing in his account of the judgment and destruction of the followers of the dragon (19:21;20:5a,11–15). Between the two parts of the account of the fate of the dragon, John inserts a statement on the fate of God's people. John often does this in Revelation: when he is speaking of the pouring out of God's wrath and punishment upon the enemies of God, he makes a point of assuring faithful Christians that they are safe. The unfaithful followers of the Lamb, the compromisers, had better tremble and repent before it is too late. But the faithful ones, far from being the objects of God's judgment, never come into judgment. Instead, they actually participate in God's judgment of, and victory over, his enemies.

1 Once again, and for the last time in Revelation, John reports that he saw an angelic representation of the Lord Jesus. He had introduced himself to John as the one who 'has the keys of Death and Hades' (1:18). He was dead, but is now alive and lives forever. By his death and resurrection he broke the power of sin and death and Satan (1:18; Heb 2:14,15). He invaded the Abyss, the **bottomless pit**, the home of the demonic, and conquered it. So he holds the **key** not only to Death and Hades, but also to the Abyss. In 9:1 John reports that a 'star' from heaven was *given* by God the key to the bottomless pit. Jesus, however, himself has and holds the key, which means, in this context, that he possesses ultimate power and authority (see Matt 16:19).

The angelic Christ holds not only a **key** but also a **great chain**, or, more exactly, a great manacle, like modern handcuffs (see Jude 6).

2,3 With the same effortless ease with which he had captured the beast and the false prophet (=the second beast, 19:20), Christ grabbed and held on to the **dragon**, who in 12:3 is described as 'great' and 'red'. He is the primeval enemy who shows up in various guises and under different aliases. He is known as Leviathan or Rahab (Job 26:12,13; Ps 74:13,14). He is also the **ancient serpent**, the deceiver of humankind, who operates through his front man, the second beast, the false prophet (19:20).

Other names by which the dragon is known are the **Devil and Satan**. He is the accuser or slanderer of human beings. But since Christ's victory, nobody can sustain a single charge against God's people; nobody can rightly accuse; nobody can condemn (Rom 8:33-39). All charges have been dismissed, and the prosecutor has been thrown out of the heavenly court (Rev 12:7–9).

Satan has been thrown out of heaven; now John reports that he saw him thrown out of earth and returned to his own place, the Abyss or **pit**, which is then **locked and sealed**. So Satan is truly impotent: he is manacled, locked up, and sealed into the Abyss, awaiting final destruction. With his two henchmen, the beasts, permanently out of action (19:19), Satan cannot even get others to work for him. This is truly the end. Satan is finished. No longer can he do what he is best at doing: deceiving people (see 12:9; John 8:44).

So John responds to a major question which all Christians ask: Does Satan belong to the ultimate or the penultimate? The answer is clear: Satan does not and will not have the last word. Satan is a creature, and he, too, is judged by God. John begins his description of God's act of judgment by reporting that Christ seized the devil, bound him, and kept him under lock and key, *incommunicado.* He stays that way, John says, **for a thousand years**.

It is truly folly to insist on a literal understanding of this number, when all around are symbols: bottomless pit, a chain to bind a demon, a key to the pit. What might **one thousand years** symbolise? It seems to be suggesting God's time, complete time, ideal time, a different quality of time.

This thought is suggested by Psalm 90:4 which points out that our time is maybe seventy or eighty years (Ps 90:10), whereas God's time is one thousand years — and that's just one day!

Even clearer is the discussion in 2 Peter 3:8–13. The context comprises teaching about the end of the old creation and the unveiling of the new. The sacred writer remarks that 'with the Lord one day is like a thousand years, and a thousand years are like one day' (3:8). God has a unique relationship to time. He is Lord of time; all time is at his disposal. He alone conceives, surveys, and controls the endless line of time. Time is a variable; God is unvariable. 'One thousand years' is inadequate human language for God's 'time' or God's 'eternity'.

John gives two other clues to the meaning of **one thousand years**. First, in 11:18 he speaks of the *kairos,* the time set by God for the judgment of the dead, the vindication of God's people, and the destruction of those who destroy the earth. The expression 'one thousand years' is another way of speaking of God's *kairos,* God's 'time'.

Secondly, during the period of **one thousand years** the saints are said to reign with Christ (20:4,6). They are also said to reign with Christ 'forever and ever' (22:6). How long is 'one thousand years'? It is 'forever and ever'.

The closest we come now to experiencing God's time and space is in Christian worship. By means of worship we break out of the boundaries created by time and space. Heaven and earth come together in liturgy. Liturgy creates its own sense of time, its own rhythm. Liturgy enables us to participate in God's time, and to thumb our noses at those who, like the Roman emperors, thought that calendars should begin on their birthday.

Dietrich Bonhoeffer understood the meaning of **one thousand years**. During his imprisonment at the hands of the leaders of the 'thousand-years Reich', Bonhoeffer marked the movement of time by observing the liturgical year. Thus he confessed that God, not the beast, rules human history and determines human destiny. He lived in God's time.

Satan, then, is held bound in the locked and sealed bottomless pit, awaiting judgment and execution at the King's pleasure. The point is that God is in complete control, and Satan is totally helpless and impotent. He is finished.

No longer is Satan able to deceive **the nations of the earth**. These are the 'inhabitants of the earth' (6:10;8:13;13:7,8), the men and women who had been deceived by the false prophet (= the second beast), and been persuaded to receive the mark of the beast and to worship its image (19:20). They are the people who had been deceived by the 'sorcery' of the city which rode on the back of the beast, the whore-city Babylon (18:23). Lies and deceit are the stock-in-trade of the dragon and his servants.

These **nations** had gathered at the grisly banquet of God, and they had been 'slain with the sword' (19:21). John has not yet described their final fate. So far in the narrative they are in the place of the dead (Hades); John will describe their final judgment and punishment in a double judgment scene (20:7–10 and 20:11–15).

The 'bottomless pit' or Abyss into which Satan is thrown is part of the larger underworld prison in which 'the dead', that is, the unrepentant nations who follow the beast, are held (see Isa 24:21,22). The nations are quickly undeceived: their god joins them in their state of helplessness. To think that we put our trust in *this* one! The reason, then, that Satan can no longer deceive the nations is that he is imprisoned along with them. He is in chains, powerless even in that prison to do any harm.

Such inability to deceive lasts as long as the **thousand years** last. When he is released or **let out for a little while**, Satan's powers of deception will be exercised for one last time (20:8). As usual, no good will come of it, for his followers will follow him to destruction. He will be destroyed, and they with him.

Why, then, 'must' Satan be released? This is a divine 'must'. When Jesus suffered and died, he did so in obedience to God's will, in fulfilment of God's plan of salvation (for example, Matt 16:21;26:24; Acts 17:3). (See comments on 1:1.)

If the people of God are to have full and eternal salvation, then all threats to their peace and safety and well-being must be removed. Satan 'must' be released in order that God's saving will is done. Satan is released so that he can deceive his followers once more, trick them into following him to destruction. Satan is released in order to gather his followers for judgment.

As usual, in the end the forces of evil bring about their own destruction. They gather themselves to make it 'simpler' (if one may so speak) for God to destroy them.

The resurrection and reign of the righteous, 20:4–6

4 Then I saw thrones, and those seated on them were given authority to judge. I also saw the souls of those who had been beheaded for their testimony to Jesus[n] **and for the word of God. They had not worshiped the beast or its image and had not received its mark on their foreheads or their hands. They came to life and reigned with Christ a thousand years. 5 (The rest of the dead did not come to life until the thousand years were ended.)**

This is the first resurrection. [6] Blessed and holy are those who share in the first resurrection. Over these the second death has no power, but they will be priests of God and of Christ, and they will reign with him a thousand years.

[a] Or *for the testimony of Jesus*

The book of Revelation is meant to be a warning for lax Christians who want to compromise, sell out to the culture, and worship the beast instead of God. But it is also meant to comfort and assure those who 'hold the testimony of Jesus' and worship God (19:10).

It is John's habit, when he speaks of God's terrible judgment on the wicked, to quickly reassure his faithful people that they need not be afraid. They are safe. In fact, by means of their faithful confession and worship, they rule and judge with God.

So, before the opening of the seals (6:1–17) John reports his view of the worshipping people of God, safe and sound in the heavenly throne-room. And when the sixth seal has been opened, and God's judgments are filling the world with terror (6:12–17), John again assures his people by telling them about the sealed one hundred and forty-four thousand: they are safe (7:1–17). The same pattern is followed before and after the 'harvest' scenes of judgment in chapter 14. The narrative begins with the people of the Lamb safe and sound on Mount Zion, and it ends with the same worshipping community safe on God's side of the sea of glass mixed with fire (15:1–4).

Once more John follows the same pattern. He is speaking of the fearful final fate of all who deserve God's punitive judgment (19:17 – 20:15). Such judgment and punishment are necessary if Christians are to experience full and final salvation. But it is still very frightening. So John interrupts his account of the destruction of the great enemy, the dragon, to make two very important points: 1) the faithful, witnessing people of God are safe; and 2) the boot is on the other foot now. Instead of being hounded, harried, persecuted, and even killed, Christians are ruling with Christ, judging instead of being judged and condemned by the agents and followers of the dragon.

4 A literal translation of the opening words of verse 4 is: 'And I saw thrones. And they sat on them . . .' The first thing John says he saw in his second revelation (4:1 – 16:20) was a throne (4:2). Now he reports that when he is shown the situation of God's people from God's perspective, the first thing that strikes him is **thrones**. The reference is probably to the twenty-four thrones upon which are seated the elders, 'dressed in white robes, with golden crowns on their heads' (4:4). These elders symbolise the worshipping people of God, viewed from the heavenly perspective.

To his faithful worshipping community, God gives the **authority to judge**. That is, they participate in Christ's reign as kings and judges (see Matt 19:28; Luke 22:30; 1 Cor 6:2,3). In particular, John reminds his hearers that they join God in judgment upon the old enemy, Satan.

An alternative translation of the phrase, 'judgment was committed to them', is: 'judgment was given for them', meaning that they were vindicated. The judge found in their favour and against their persecutors and accusers (see Dan 7:22). They received justice from God, these people who had so often been refused justice in earthly courts.

This second translation and interpretation is to be preferred, in view of the words which immediately follow. All of verse 4 provides a headache or two for translators. A fairly literal translation runs as follows:

> And I saw thrones. And they sat on them. And judgment was given to [or: for] them, both the souls [= people] who had been beheaded because of the testimony of Jesus and because of the word of God, and those who did not worship the beast nor its image and did not take [or: receive] the mark upon the forehead and upon their hand. And they came alive and reigned with Christ for a thousand years.

Here John describes the people of God in their totality. But he distinguishes between two groups: the martyrs (v 4b) and the other faithful Christians who refused to worship the beast (v 4c). Both these groups sit on thrones; both reign with Christ.

Victory over the beast and over Satan is especially sweet for the martyrs. These are the ones who come out of the great tribulation (7:14). The beast killed them (13:7,15); fallen Babylon shed their blood (18:24). But they died in the Lord. They are blessed (14:13). They had been **beheaded** because they maintained the witness which Jesus himself had made before God and the world. Like Jesus, they were faithful to the **word of God**.

The phrase, 'the testimony of Jesus and the word of God', is better translated as: 'the testimony of Jesus, that is, the word of God'. The expression seems to have been used in John's community as a kind of shorthand for the Christian faith. John himself uses it to characterise the prophetic content of his book (1:2;19:10).

The faithfulness of the saints enthroned in heaven was demonstrated in their refusal to embrace the false view of reality offered by the **beast**. In them there had been a correlation between baptism and life (see Col 3:1–4). They had steadfastly refused to worship **the beast or his image, and had not received its mark on their foreheads or their hands** (see comments on 13:15–18). In short, they had worshipped God and the Lamb, and declined, even to the point of death, to acknowledge any claims of the beast.

These faithful witnesses come **to life** (see 11:11) and, as John has already said, they reign. But he adds a further thought: they reign **with Christ**. They had shared his testimony; they were faithful even unto death; they worshipped him despite pressure to conform to what most others in the culture were doing, that is, worship the beast. To them Christ gives, as he has promised, a place with him on his throne, just as he himself conquered and sat down with his Father on his throne (3:21; see 2:26,27;22:5).

They reign **for a thousand years**. Just as Satan's fate is entirely in God's hands, so also the people of God rule at God's pleasure, in God's time, called here a 'thousand years' (see comments on 20:2). In 22:5 this reign of a thousand years is said to be 'forever and ever'. In short, the coming of Christ (19:11–16) ushers in judgment for the wicked, and vindication and salvation for his people.

They, his servants (22:3), rule as kings and live as priests forever and ever, or, as John puts it here, **for a thousand years**.

5 Verse 5 contains two explanatory notes concerning the coming to life of the dead. The word which John uses is not the usual one for 'resurrection'; it simply means 'to live' or 'to come to life'. John's first comment is about the coming to life of **the rest of the dead**, that is, those who had been killed when the two beasts were thrown into the lake of fire which is the 'second death'. What about these people who are not included on the roll of faithful witnesses, those who *had* worshipped the beast, and who *did* bear his mark? They had given Christians an especially hard time, for Christians had to live and work and play among them.

What happens to these people? John's response is that they will be dealt with when the dragon is dealt with, that is, when the **one thousand years** is completed or fulfilled — in other words, when God wants judgment to come to them, in his time. John reports God's judgment upon Satan and his followers in 20:7–15.

The 'coming to life' of the enemies of God and his people is a coming to life for the purpose of being judged. John does not call it a 'resurrection'. He reserves the word 'resurrection' for believers only. The enthronement and ruling and judging which John has described in verse 4 is, he explains, **the first resurrection**.

The phrase 'the first resurrection' has been greatly misunderstood. In striving to understand it, we must bear several key points in mind. 1) In Scripture, the phrase 'the first' can mean, and often does mean, 'the first of several', implying a second and a third and so forth. However, 'the first' often has the very important meaning of 'the first and only'.

So, for example, Jesus is called God's 'first-born Son' and God's 'only-begotten Son' (for example, Heb 1:6;11:17; John 3:16). Another example: Jesus urged his disciples to 'seek first the kingdom of God' (Matt 6:33). The context in Matthew makes it clear that the kingdom of God is not one thing among many things that we seek after. Rather, the kingdom of God is to be the *only* thing to which we dedicate our lives.

So when John says that the reign of the saints 'after' the return of Christ is 'the first resurrection', it does not necessarily follow that he means to imply a second resurrection. He might well mean 'the first and only resurrection'. That this is in fact what John means is proven by the second factor to be considered.

2) According to verse 6, those who share in the 'first resurrection' are **blessed** and **holy**. They are **holy** because they have been washed and cleansed and made holy by Christ (see Eph 5:25–27). They are **blessed** because they are delivered from the **second death**. Careful note must be taken of the fact that here John presents the **second death** as a grim alternative to the **first resurrection**. He never talks about a 'first death' or a 'second resurrection'. The alternatives are: *either* the first resurrection *or* the second death.

This important either/or needs to be explored further. In Scripture there is one line of teaching which says that everyone, Christian and unbeliever, must appear before the judgment seat of God (for example, Rom 14:10; 2 Cor 5:10). There is, however, another line of teaching (also in Scripture) which says that whereas unbelievers will face divine judgment and punishment, believers will not come to judgment, but will pass from death to life (for example, John 3:18,36;5:24).

The prophet John, in Revelation, seems to follow this second line of teaching. In so doing, he is following the lead of the prophet Isaiah. In Isaiah chapter 26 the prophet speaks of the wicked, whom he calls 'the inhabitants of the earth'. This is John's favourite phrase for the people who harass Christians, pressure them, and try to get them to deny Christ and to worship the beast (for example, 12:10;17:2). These 'inhabitants of the earth', Isaiah teaches, will not be raised; they will be judged (26:14). The righteous, however, will be raised, and this resurrection will be their vindication and their salvation. Through their resurrection they receive back the lives which were wrongly taken from them (Isa 26:19).

Isaiah, then, teaches that resurrection is not a means by which all parties involved are brought to judgment, but a means by which the righteous are vindicated and liberated. Don't then speak of 'resurrection' when you speak about the wicked; the wicked are judged and punished. The righteous are not judged and punished, but resurrected and vindicated and saved. Thus spake Isaiah.

The influence which Isaiah 26 has had on John's thinking is apparent. The continuation of the prophecy in chapter 27 makes the influence even clearer:

> On that day the LORD will punish
> with his cruel sword, his mighty and powerful sword,
> Leviathan that twisting sea-serpent,
> that writhing serpent Leviathan,
> and slay the monster of the deep. (Isa 27:1 NEB)

Leviathan is the dragon, Satan, the devil. (See further the comments on 19:17,18 for Isaiah's influence on John's report of end-time events.)

To sum up: John sees an either/or situation:

either	first resurrection	*or*	second death
	no judgment		judgment
	no second death		no first resurrection

Followers of the Lamb share in the first (and only) resurrection; they do not come into judgment, and they do not experience the second death. Followers of the dragon do not share in the first (and only) resurrection; they come into judgment; and they suffer the second death, along with their lord the Dragon.

6 To be part of the first resurrection, which involves vindication and salvation for God's people, means that those concerned are **holy** and **blessed**. Their holiness is God's gift in Christ, not a native holiness; their blessedness lies, negatively, in the fact that they are delivered from the **second death**, that is, from being thrown into the lake of fire, and so sharing the fate of the dragon, the two beasts, and their followers (20:14;21:8). Positively, these faithful people of God are **blessed** in that **they will be priests of God and of Christ** (see 5:9,10),and they will rule with Christ for a **thousand years**, that is, at God's good pleasure, in his 'time' which has a perspective and an intensity which we cannot imagine. We can get an inkling of this kind of 'divine time' when we consider the patience of God. Saint Augustine said that 'God is patient because he is eternal'. Certainly God's patience with us has a quality which in us is entirely lacking. Think of God's patience with the people of Noah's day (1 Pet 3:20). It is significant that in 2 Peter the matter of God's patience is taught in connection with the statement that a thousand years are as but a day in God's sight (2 Pet 3:9). Thank God that his time is not our time! Otherwise he would have lost patience with us long ago. God's patience, like his time, is not limited as ours is limited. Likewise, the reign of God's people is limited only by the limits which the eternal God places on it. They reign at the King's command and at the King's pleasure (Rev 22:5).

When the saints rule in the new heaven and new earth (21:1–4;22:5), then the true nature of God's people will be revealed for all to see. Already now they are a 'royal priesthood, a holy nation' (1 Pet 2:9), but it is not at all evident to the eyes of anyone who does not have faith. When Christ comes, the true nature of the church will be unveiled. As kings, God's people will be free from the attempted dominion of all human and demonic powers which now cause them so much pain and worry (see Rom 8:18–25). As **priests of God and of Christ** (note the inseparable connection!), they serve God in his temple day and night (21:22;22:3).

The true people of God are a worshipping community of kings and priests. From this worshipping community there flow streams of living water, water which offers life to the nations (see John 7:37–39; Rev 22:1–3).

The destruction of the dragon (continued), 20:7–10

7 When the thousand years are ended, Satan will be released from his prison 8 and will come out to deceive the nations at the four corners of the earth, Gog and

Magog, in order to gather them for battle; they are as numerous as the sands of the sea. [9] They marched up over the breadth of the earth and surrounded the camp of the saints and the beloved city. And fire came down from heaven[o] and consumed them. [10] And the devil who had deceived them was thrown into the lake of fire and sulfur, where the beast and the false prophet were, and they will be tormented day and night forever and ever.

[o] Other ancient authorities read *from God, out of heaven,* or *out of heaven from God*

John has encouraged his hearers by assuring them that God's faithful people are safe from all the accusations and threats of their accuser, Satan; and they are safe from God's punitive judgment on the dragon and his followers, the 'inhabitants of the earth' (20:4–6). Now he picks up the thread of the story that he began in 20:1–3. Satan had been locked up, ready for final punishment.

John describes this final divine action by drawing on the oracles of the prophet Ezekiel, chapters 38 and 39. The prophet speaks of 'Gog of Magog'. Gog is the epitome of evil. God raises him up and then destroys him, as a demonstration of divine sovereign power and might. In Ezekiel's report, the focus is entirely on God. Gog is 'little more than a stage prop', as one commentator aptly remarks.

After the time of Ezekiel, Jewish tradition changed 'Gog of Magog' to **Gog and Magog**, symbols of the ultimate enemies of God's people. They are not historical nations; nor are they a modern military power about whom John supposedly 'prophesied'. John is a pastor, writing for his people then and there. What pastoral goal would John have achieved by telling his people about Saddam Hussein or Uncle Sam? Such 'prophecy' would serve no pastoral purpose; it could, in fact, have drawn John's hearers away from facing up to the realities of their own situation.

Gog and Magog are symbols of evil. They are the hordes, the bands of hell (see 9:1–11,13–19). As usual in Revelation, evil is named before it is destroyed. Symbols are by far the most effective way of exposing reality. Against this background, read 20:7–10.

7 Whenever **the thousand years** of Satan's imprisonment are ended, that is, when the 'time' which God has appointed has been filled up, **Satan will be released** (for comments on 'a thousand years' see commentary on 20:2). Once again it is important to bear in mind that John is not giving a chronological account of end-time events: first this, then that. When John was given this revelation, he was outside space and time, beyond history. But when he comes to report what he saw, he must write in some sort of order. What he is attempting here is to portray as vividly as possible the final judgment and destruction of Satan. In particular, he wants to show how, ultimately, Satan and evil are themselves self-destructive.

8 So Satan is released from the prison in which God had placed him, released only so that he can go about his typical task of deceiving **the nations**. By so doing he involves them in his fate. The **nations** are the 'rest of the dead' (19:21;20:5) who have been deceived by Satan and who share his confinement (see comments on 20:3). When John now says that these nations are **at the four corners** of the earth, he is not contradicting himself. He is simply reflecting the Old Testament view that the outer edges of the earth are the entrances to the place of the dead. We are to visualise the hordes of unrepentant 'inhabitants of the earth' just waiting to climb out and afflict God's people once more.

In 7:1–3, when speaking of the intrinsic safety of God's people, John had described the **four corners of the earth** as the boundaries of the cosmos. Four angels guarded the entrances to the underworld, and restrained the armies of destruction until the 'sealing' of God's people had been accomplished.

Now these armies of evil, these **nations** who followed the dragon and the beast, clamber out of the place where they had been confined. Here is the final irony. The followers of the unholy trinity are still blind and stupid. They think that they are backing a winner, that Satan will triumph in the end. So they follow him, despite the fact that God has exposed him as a sham and a fraud, as a creature who is as impotent and helpless as they are in the face of God's terrible wrath and judgment. Their god has clay feet.

This foolish army is called **Gog and Magog** (see comments above). The name suggests evil and universality. 'Gog and Magog' was a favourite epithet among Jewish writers when they spoke of the nations who combined to attack Israel. The rabbis identified 'Gog and Magog' as the 'nations' who are referred to in Psalm 2, a psalm which frequently influences John's choice of images and language.

The army of the Lamb is huge, too big to count (7:9), and it draws its soldiers from 'every nation, from all tribes and peoples and languages' (7:9; see 5:11-13). Since Satan tries to copy God in everything, it is not surprising that his army is also enormous: 'two hundred million', John says (9:16), including soldiers from 'every tribe and people and language and nation' (13:7; see 17:15).

Now John says that the hordes of Satan, like the promised descendants of Abraham (Gen 12:2;17:4), are **as numerous as the sands of the sea**. They, like Satan himself, must be judged by God if God's people are truly to experience liberation, salvation, and vindication.

9 So they gather for battle. John gives his hearers yet another description of forces gathering for battle against the Lamb and his armies (9:1-11;16:13-16;19:19–21). In awful array they march over the earth and surround the **camp of the saints**. This **camp** is also known as **the beloved city**. The pilgrim church is said to be a camp; but it is also the eternal **city**, the new Jerusalem. It exists in deliberate contrast to its counter-image, the great city Babylon, which is heading for destruction, just like its builder, Satan (17:8,11).

You won't find this battlefield, this camp, this city, on any map. To search for it is to completely mishear John's message. Look again at the picture: Satan has assembled all his hordes for a mighty attack on the people of God. God actually 'released' Satan so that he could do just that: gather his armies (20:7). Is God in the end unfaithful? Are God's people ultimately at risk? Unsafe? Will Satan win finally? The answer is given in the report of an event which would be almost comical if it weren't so serious.

Satan gathers his mighty army for battle — *and there is no battle*. How can there be a battle?

The strife is o'er, the battle done;
Now is the Victor's triumph won;
O let the song of praise be sung.
Alleluia!

Instead of reporting a mighty battle, John simply tells how God deals with this wicked, perverse, and ultimately stupid enemy. It is almost as if God lets Satan gather his followers together so that God can deal with them all together. In a series of short sentences, John records the fate of Satan and his army. The army is **consumed** by **fire** (see Ezek 38:22;39:6), a fate reserved for those who oppose God and his people (2 Kings 1:10; see Luke 9:54). So God keeps his promise: 'On that day I will seek to destroy all the nations that come against Jerusalem' (Zech 12:9).

10 The devil's prime attribute is that of deceiver. Moffatt and NEB translate correctly: 'their seducer', which is better than 'who had deceived them' (NRSV,NIV,TEV). He joins the other two members of the unholy trinity, **the beast and the false prophet**, in **the lake of fire and sulfur**, which is also called 'the second death' (20:14). There they endure continual torment. The language used to describe their chronic condition is liturgical: **forever and ever** is a phrase used by the people of God in connection with worship and their life with the Lamb (for example, 4:10;22:5). God's people worship him **day and night** (4:8). Their life of service is full, complete, and unending. In fearful contrast, the torment of Satan is likewise full, complete, and unending.

The end of the present creation, 20:11

11 **Then I saw a great white throne and the one who sat on it; the earth and the heaven fled from his presence, and no place was found for them.**

The phrase with which John introduces the next stage of his report ('Then I saw') is literally 'And I saw'. He does not mean to signal a sequence of events, one following another. When he had his revelation, he was outside of time and space. The sequence is in the order of the *report*, not of the events which he is reporting. So the 'then' of the translation means: 'The next thing I will tell you about is . . .'

The **great white throne** which caught John's eye is the same one which John saw in the throne-room scene in chapter 4. John's hearers would also have been reminded of the thrones in the earlier report of the saints of God in heaven, sitting as kings, ruling and judging with Christ (20:4–6). Certainly John wants to focus on the **throne**. The Greek of verse 11 reads simply and starkly: 'And I saw a throne, great, white . . .'

The heavenly **throne** has been a constant, dominant image throughout the book of Revelation, symbolising God's sovereign and judicial power and presence; it is the locus and focus of worship (for example, 4:2-10; 5:11–13;6:16;8:3;19:4). The description of the throne as 'great' and 'white' serves to emphasise the glory and holiness of **the one who sat upon it**. Usually in Revelation the one who sits on the throne is God the Father (for example, 4:2,9;5:1,7,13;7:10). There is no reason here to think otherwise.

Before the holy grandeur of God, **the earth and the heaven**, corrupted by evil and sin, flee and vanish forever. They are destroyed, or, as John puts it, **no place was found for them** (see 6:14; Dan 2:35; 2 Pet 3:7,10,12).

The present order vanishes in order to make way for the new; the old creation loses its place to the new, just as Babylon must be removed so that the new Jerusalem can be unveiled and revealed in all its glory.

The image etched on one's mind is of everything cleared away except the great white throne, standing there in awesome splendour. What a sight! Before that throne will appear all those whom John calls 'the inhabitants of the earth'. Their 'place' has gone. Now they will go to their eternal place, the one reserved for all those who in this life refused to worship before the **great white throne**.

The judgment of the dead, 20:12–15

[12] **And I saw the dead, great and small, standing before the throne, and books were opened. Also another book was opened, the book of life. And the dead were judged**

according to their works, as recorded in the books. [13] And the sea gave up the dead that were in it, Death and Hades gave up the dead that were in them, and all were judged according to what they had done. [14] Then Death and Hades were thrown into the lake of fire. This is the second death, the lake of fire; [15] and anyone whose name was not found written in the book of life was thrown into the lake of fire.

There is considerable debate among commentators as to whether John is speaking in these verses of a 'general' judgment (one which includes believers and unbelievers) or of a judgment of unbelievers only. The view taken in this commentary is that in 20:12–15 John is speaking only of a judgment of unbelievers (see discussion in the commentary on 20:5). Although Scripture does speak of a 'general' judgment, John speaks of a 'resurrection' for believers and 'judgment' for unbelievers.

In 19:17–21 John had said that the followers of the beast had been killed by God. But he had not spoken of their final fate. In 20:5, when speaking about the people of God and their resurrection, John had made the point that the followers of the beast whom God had killed would not have a part in the resurrection.

In 20:7–10 John had described, briefly, the gathering of the enemies of God and his people, and God's judgment upon them. The followers of the dragon were destroyed by fire (20:9; see 20:15).

In 20:11–15 John offers a parallel account of the same judgment, but in more detail and using the image of a royal court room. He describes the judgment of those who are variously called 'the inhabitants of the earth', 'the nations', or the citizens of 'the great city'.

John often works with doublets (see comments on page 127). This double judgment report (20:7–10;11–15) matches the double report in 14:14–16 and 14:17–20.

12,13 **Before the throne**, the great white throne which John had described in verse 11, stand all **the dead**. These are the followers of the beast who had been killed by God, awaiting final judgment (19:17-21). These **dead** are not raised; they do not experience resurrection. Such a happy event is reserved, in Revelation, only for the blessed people of God. These **dead** will be judged. Their sentence and punishment will be 'the second death'. For them there is no resurrection and joy in the presence of God for evermore.

The totality of the number of the **dead** is indicated by the phrase 'great and small'. This simply means all those who belong to the category of 'dead'. The completeness and extensiveness of this assembling of the 'dead' is further indicated by the observation that all three power bases of the beast and the demonic — the **sea**, **Death**, and **Hades**, all had to give up **the dead in them**. The **sea** is the home of the beast (13:1) and his followers. The beast certainly was not safe from God's searching judgment (19:17–20), neither are his followers and worshippers: the **sea**, their home and fortress, must give them up. Likewise **Death**, the terrible tyrant, had to give up its subjects, as did **Hades**, the place of the dead.

In short, no rebel, no unbeliever, no worshipper of the beast, was excused or spared in this judgment. They were hauled out of all their so-called places of safety. They stood naked and unprotected before God. They might call upon heaven and earth and sea and Death and Hades to defend and protect them, but their cries would be in vain, for these things themselves are heading for destruction (v 14).

The **dead** are to be judged. So **books were opened**. Once, when king Ahasuerus of Persia could not get to sleep, he asked a courtier to read to him from 'the book of records, the annals' (Esth 6:1;2:23). It was normal for kings to keep a record of the activities of their subjects. When a citizen appeared in court, then the books were consulted (see Dan 7:10). This practice seems to have shaped John's report at this point: the **books** which were opened in heaven contained the record of each person's **works**, that is, **what they had done**.

The thought that God judges people according to their works is a common one throughout the Scriptures (see Ps 62:12; Jer 17:10; Matt 25:31–46; Rom 2:6; 1 Pet 1:17). It is a sobering thought, this, one which Christians should announce now in clear terms to all who will listen. God's judgment is on the basis of works. The critical question is: *whose* works count before God? Yours or Christ's?

The **book of life** is also open before God. This book belongs to the Lamb (13:8). All whose names are in it belong to him; his obedience covers their disobedience; his righteousness is given to them, while he took upon himself their unrighteousness (2 Cor 5:21; Gal 3:13). His power within them produces holiness. Those who reject God's 'blessed exchange' of righteousness for unrighteousness (see Phil 3:9), can only plead their own righteousness — and that is woefully inadequate. Indeed, the very idea that one could plead one's own righteousness is an offence to the holy God. What righteousness can a sinner plead, apart from Christ's gifted righteousness?

14,15 The **book of life** has the last word. If a person's name is not in that book, it means that that person rejected God's gracious call and invitation to come to the marriage of the Lamb. They were too involved with the things of this life to worry about ultimates (see Matt 22:1–14; Rev 19:7–9).

Those whose names were not **found written in the book of life** have no hope of life; all they have in front of them is the **second death**, which is the absence of eternal life. The reason for this judgment is not that the Lamb did not shed his blood for them. He did (2 Cor 5:15). It is not that the Lamb did not want them to have eternal life. He did (1 Tim 2:4). The cause is their own stubborn refusal to listen to God and his people's testimony to Jesus, the Lamb (see John 3:16–21;31–36). They loved darkness more than the light; they chose to worship the beast instead of the Lamb. Those who refuse to gather around the throne in worship of God and the Lamb, will have no joy when they are compelled to stand before that throne in the end.

John's report of God's judgment of the wicked and the last enemies of God's people is remarkably subdued and low-keyed. In three words he gives their fate. They are thrown into **the lake of fire**, which is also known as the **second death** (see 19:20 and comments there, as well as the comments on 20:5).

Into the **lake of fire** are thrown **Death** and **Hades**. They try to terrorise people with their ugly threats. They like to act as if they are ultimates. But Christ broke the bars of Hades; he has the key. In the last judgment Hades has to give up its dead (20:13), as does also **Death**, the king of Hades. Death, as Saint Paul says, is the last enemy. With Hades gone, the sea 'no more' (21:1), and Death destroyed, the final threats to the peace and well-being of the people of God are removed. The citizens of the new Jerusalem are forever safe (see 1 Cor 15:26,54–57).

With everything of the old creation cleared away, the way is now open for the revelation or unveiling of the new heaven and new earth, and in particular, of the alternative city, the opposite to Babylon the fallen city. We await the story of the new Jerusalem, the people of God.

The new creation and the new Jerusalem, 21:1,2

21 Then I saw a new heaven and a new earth; for the first heaven and the first earth had passed away, and the sea was no more. [2] And I saw the holy city, the new Jerusalem, coming down out of heaven from God, prepared as a bride adorned for her husband.

In several brief sentences John had reported the end of the old creation (20:11). He matches that brevity when he tells of the unveiling of the new creation. The reason for this brevity is that his focus is not now on the people of the new creation. He will speak about them in his report of the fourth revelation (21:9 – 22:9). For now he is content to report the appearance of the new creation and the new Jerusalem.

It is important to remember that John is still in God's time and space; he is reporting the things that happen in the 'thousand years' which make up the 'forever and ever' of eternity (see comments on 20:2).

1 For the last time in the series of reports which began in 19:11, and for the last time in the book, John introduces his narrative with the words: 'And I saw . . .' What he **saw** was **a new heaven and a new earth**. 'Heaven' could mean here simply 'sky' (as in 6:14 and perhaps 20:11). The focus is on God's creation of new structures, a new environment for human existence, one which matches the new nature of the redeemed and liberated people of God.

Especially the **earth** is affirmed as having a place in God's future. The earth is abused and exploited by 'the inhabitants of the earth' (see commentary on 13:8). Yet the earth is always on the side of God and his people (for example 12:16). Now it is designated the locus of the new Jerusalem which comes down from heaven.

The old boundaries which defined and determined the old orders (**the first heaven and the first earth**) have gone. In particular, **the sea** no longer exists. The **sea** symbolises evil chaotic powers, all that is anti-God, anti-Christ, anti-creation. The **sea** is the place of the beast (13:10), and the home of the demonic. The **sea** is one of seven evils which John specifically says are *not* a part of the new creation (see 21:4,22,23,25;22:3,5).

2 The old structures and the old rebellious powers are gone. But God has been creating a new human community who are to live in the new environment he has brought into being. In sharp contrast to the old, rebellious community ('Babylon') which dominated and exploited the old creation and worshipped the beast, the new community (**the holy city, the new Jerusalem**) fits perfectly into the new creation.

Characteristic of this new community is that its origin is heavenly: it comes down **out of heaven from God**. God himself has made her **holy**, washed her, cleansed her, dressed her as **a bride adorned for her husband**, the Lamb (see 19:7,8; Eph 5:25–32). The people of God are his own creation. He chose them, called them, justified them, and glorified them (Rom 8:28–30). Out of those who were 'not his people' God has created his very own people, his signet ring, his own workmanship and possession (Hos 2:23; Eph 1:14;2:10,21,22).

It is worth noting that John does not report a 'rapture' of the church. The only one in Revelation who is 'caught up to heaven' is the Messiah (12:5). In the case of God's people, the movement is the opposite of 'rapture'. Their citizenship always has been in heaven (Phil 3:20); their liturgical service always has been heavenly. Their worship has always transcended the boundaries between earth and heaven. Not surprisingly, then, in the new creation the people of God come down from their home in heaven to earth. Heaven and earth are joined as one. As we shall see, what joins them is, as always, worship of God.

This worship is described, for the last time in Revelation, in the final verses of John's report of his third revelation (21:3–8).

WORSHIP: The liturgy of divine self-presentation, 21:3–8

3 **And I heard a loud voice from the throne saying,**
'See, the home[p] of God is among
mortals.
He will dwell[p] with them as their
God;[q]
they will be his peoples,[r]
and God himself will be with
them;[s]
4 **he will wipe every tear from their**
eyes.
Death will be no more;
mourning and crying and pain will
be no more,
for the first things have passed
away.'
5 **And the one who was seated on the throne said, 'See,**
I am making all things new.' Also he said, 'Write this, for
these words are trustworthy and true.' 6 **Then he said to**
me, 'It is done! I am the Alpha and the Omega, the
beginning and the end. To the thirsty I will give water as a
gift from the spring of the water of life. 7 **Those who**
conquer will inherit these things, and I will be their God
and they will be my children. 8 **But as for the cowardly,**
the faithless,[t] the polluted, the murderers, the fornicators,
the sorcerers, the idolaters, and all liars, their place will

be in the lake that burns with fire and sulfur, which is the second death.'

[p] Gk *tabernacle*

[q] Other ancient authorities lack *as their God*

[r] Other ancient authorities read *people*

[s] Other ancient authorities add *and be their God*

[t] Or *the unbelieving*

John concludes his account of God's judging and saving (= destroying and creating) activities with a reminder that it all takes place in the context of worship. Worship in heaven never ceases. Always God is being praised and acknowledged as God by his people in heaven and on earth. The worship scene which John now describes not only concludes the narrative of the third revelation, but also serves as an introduction and a dynamic for the narrative of the final revelation (21:9 – 22:9).

The first and fourth revelations are both about the state of the church (1:9 – 3:22;21:9 – 22:9). Both revelations begin with a liturgy in which God himself participates directly. The only time God is said to speak in Revelation is in 1:8 and 21:5–8. In both cases, the context is liturgical.

The structure of the last liturgical scene is as follows:

- vv 3,4 Liturgical chant by the worshippers
- 5–8 Liturgical response by God
  - v 5a Declaration: 'I am making new all things'
  - 5b Command to John to write: validation of declaration
  - 6a Declaration: It is done
  - 6b Divine self-presentation
    - v7 promise
    - 8 threat

a) The liturgical chant, 21:3,4

3 The **loud voice from the throne** which John heard is not identified. As in 19:5 (another worship scene), the **voice** might well be the collective voice of the four living creatures, leading the worship (see 4:8,9;6:6).

With an attention-getting 'See!', the worshipping community celebrates the fact that God has made his tabernacle, his dwelling place, among his people. This was not news, even in the old creation. God always did dwell among his people. But the important thing now is that this is characteristic of the new reality: God **will dwell with them**. So God provides the context, the 'temple', in which he is worshipped (see 11:1,2;22:3).

This announcement by the worshipping community forms the closure of a long story. The story began with God tabernacling among his people during the Exodus experience (Lev 26:11). It continued with God's promise to David, when David wanted to build a house for the Lord, that God would build *him* a house which would last forever (2 Sam 7:1–16; see Luke 1:32,33). A further chapter was written when God tabernacled among his people in the person of his Son, Jesus Christ (John 1:14;2:19–22), and then called the people of the Messiah to form his body, the new temple of the living God (1 Cor 3:16,17; 2 Cor 6:14-18).

The conclusion and the climax of the long story come in the new creation, where the new Exodus of the people of God ends in the new Jerusalem, where there is no temple except for God himself and the Lamb (21:22).

The plural, 'peoples', is not to be understood as suggesting some kind of universal salvation (this is excluded by 21:8,9). Rather, the plural points to the great diversity of those who conquer and who will inherit the things which God has promised. They are an ecumenical community, drawn from all nations (see 21:24–27).

4 The worshipping community confesses that Immanuel ('God with us', Matt 1:18;28:20) has caused the old structures and powers to pass away (21:1). If God's people are truly to experience salvation and life in its fullness, all the powers which threaten their safety and security must be destroyed.

As God's people celebrate their salvation, they rehearse briefly the events of judgment which John has described in the previous narrative. They sing of the absence of the **sea**, the home of the demonic, and the symbol of all that is evil.

They sing of the absence of **death**, that great enemy which threatens and scares us, and causes us such heartache and even dread. Death, like Babylon (18:9-19), is **no more**; it has no place on the new earth (see Isa 25:7). The worshipping community underlines the truth of this confession concerning the death of death by affirming that **mourning and crying and pain will be no more**. The Christian community borrows the beautiful language of the prophet Isaiah; it speaks of God as mother, drying the tears of her weeping child (Isa 25:8; Rev 7:17).

The total effect of these 'no mores' in chapters 18-22 — no more Babylon (18:21), no more deceiving of the world by Satan (20:3), no more sea (21:1), no more curse (22:3), no more night (22:5) — the total effect is to underscore a fundamental truth: **the first things**, the things which are so much part and parcel of the present existence, **have passed away**. All this comes as a result of the victory of the Lamb. His conquest through the cross is God's full and final answer to the problem of evil and suffering.

b) The divine liturgical response, 21:5–8

For the second and last time in Revelation, God himself speaks directly, not through an agent. John couches the divine response in the form of liturgical narrative, with John as the narrator and God as the sole speaker:

	John		**God**
5	And he who sat . . . said:	5b	New I am making all things
5c	And he said:	5d	Write . . .
6a	And he said to me:	6b–8	It is done. To the thirsty . . .

God's liturgical response to the celebration and acclamation of the worshipping community matches that of the opening liturgy (1:4–8). Indeed, 21:6–8 is an expansion of God's word in 1:8.

God is described, as usual in Revelation, as the one who sits on the throne (for example, 5:1,7;6:16;7:10). God alone is Lord and King. The throne symbolises his power base, as it were. From this place, the place where his creation worships him, God makes a series of declarations which sum up the central message of the book of Revelation.

5 First, God speaks the power-laden, dynamic, creative words: 'Look, *new* I am making all things!' If you want a single-sentence summary of all that John has reported, here you have it.

As God's spokesperson, John has offered Christian people an alternative view of reality. One view, the natural human view, is that the emperor is lord; Artemis is supreme; Rome is invincible and eternal. Life in 'the great city' is the only way to go. Pluralism and compromise are the only realistic options for Christians who want to make it in this world.

The alternative view — the world according to God — is the one which sees reality as it is. This view sees the copycat nature of all human, earthly power structures. It sees Satan and the demonic lurking behind all persons and authorities who in their rebellion are parodies of God and the Lamb.

The reality is that, since the cross ('the Lamb who was slain'!), God is creating **all things new**. The old is being dismantled, unmasked, stripped of its power (=judgment), and the new is being put in its place (=salvation).

The best example in Revelation of this old/new, destruction/new creation, judgment/salvation pattern is in 18:1–24 and 21:9 – 22:9. John contrasts the destruction or judgment of the great city Babylon (the parody), with the revelation or salvation of the great city Jerusalem (the reality).

God says: 'I *am* making new all things'. This is a present fact. God, through his judging and saving activity, *is* making new all things. Christians are the only ones who see this and know it to be true. Indeed, through their worship they share in it (see commentary on 5:8 and 6:10). In the end, everyone will see it, for better or for worse. The church is called to be seen to be part of the new, the visible sign of God's activity in the world. 'A kind of sacrament', is how Vatican II described the church in the world.

God follows his statement concerning his creative activity with a command which is addressed directly to

John. John is to **write** the words which God has just spoken. They, like the personal Word of God, are powerful, faithful, and genuine (see 19:11). Thus God legitimates and validates his own statement about making all things new. You can rely on it, even though there is not much evidence for it at present. Trust what your ears hear, not what your eyes see!

6a Finally, God continues to address John directly, and assures his prophet that the work of judgment and salvation is finished. The removal of the old and the creation of the new have been completed successfully: **It is done**!

A literal translation of God's words reads: 'They have happened'. In view of the announcement in 16:17 that the *destruction* of Babylon is complete and finished, we do well to recognise the deliberate parallel and contrast between the fate of the two cities (Babylon and Jerusalem), and interpret God's announcement to mean that the creation of the new world and the new Jerusalem *has been completed.* The future of God's people is assured.

c) Divine self-presentation 21:6b–8

Finally, as in some Psalms (for example, 81:5b–16), God introduces or presents himself to the worshipping community, and pronounces solemn words of promise and threat.

With a strong 'I am' (just like the 'I ams' of John's gospel) God introduces himself as the living God, the ground of his people's being, the aim and goal of their existence. 'The Beginning and the End' was a title commonly given in the Greek world to deities and semi-divine kings. The title was meant to emphasise cosmic sovereignty and lordship. God, however, claims the title for himself alone.

In the beginning, God . . . In the end, God. Our end is not a time or place or event, but a person. Our times are in God's hands. Our future comes to us with the compliments of our Lord Jesus Christ. To those who trust him and the Lamb, God gives two promises. First, to the

thirsty God promises to give, as an act of sheer grace, **water** from the **spring of the water of life**. This phrase, 'the water of life', is surely to be written: 'Water of Life', referring to the Lord Jesus himself (see John 7:37,38; Rev 22:1). Those who believe in him ('drink') will never thirst and never die.

Those who drink shall live forever;
'Tis a soul-renewing flood.
God is faithful; God will never
Break his covenant of blood,
Signed when our Redeemer died,
Sealed when He was glorified.

7 A second promise is addressed to those who, drinking continually from the Water of Life, that is, holding fast to the confession and faith of Jesus (19:10), **conquer** the dragon, the beast, and all enemies. They **conquer** just because they drink from the Water of Life. At the end of their earthly lives of faithfulness, even to the point of death, they receive their true heritage. This includes the fulfilment of the promises which, in chapters 2 and 3, Jesus gave to 'those who conquer'. But above all, their inheritance means that they are called — and actually are — **children of God**. 'Heaven', wrote one commentator at this point, 'is belonging to the family of God' (Caird).

The Greek of the second half of verse 7 is a quotation from 2 Samuel 7:14. It reads, literally: 'I shall be to him God and *he* will be to me son' (see NIV,RSV). In its laudable attempt to avoid what it calls 'linguistic sexism', the NRSV translation gives up two important truths. First, it conceals the connection between Jesus Christ, the Son of God, and Christian men and women as 'sons' of God. It is true that in Revelation God is never called the Christians' 'Father'; that name is reserved strictly for the relationship between God and Christ Jesus. Nevertheless, the whole New Testament witnesses to the truth that Christians are, in a special sense which reflects the Sonship of Christ, properly called 'sons of God'. Secondly, the NRSV translation gives up the truth that in biblical theology 'son' is not a synonym for 'child'. 'Son' denotes adult freedom and responsibility, not childish dependence (see John 8:31–36).

8 The last word which God speaks directly in Revelation is a threat, a warning directed especially to John's hearers who are tempted to compromise, to give up worship of God for worship of the beast, to exchange life in the new Jerusalem for the glittering lights of the great whore-city Babylon.

The list of people who will be excluded from the new Jerusalem begins with the **cowardly** and ends with the **liars**. It is no arbitrary listing. God begins by speaking of **cowards**. He is pointedly referring to those who buckle under pressure and compromise the faith. The **cowardly** are those who lead the retreat. They fear people more than they fear God; they hang on to this life, but they lose eternal life.

The **faithless** are Christians who lose faith, who fail to remain faithful to Christ and constant under pressure. The **polluted** are those who have participated in the polluting rituals of emperor worship or the worship of Artemis and other deities. They have drunk from the whore's 'cup full of abominations and the impurities of her fornication' (17:4). They are the opposite of the faithful followers of the Lamb 'who have not defiled themselves with women . . . in their mouth no lie was found; they are blameless' (14:4,5).

The **murderers** include those who shared directly or indirectly in Babylon's oppression and killing of enemy and citizen alike for economic or political advantage (see 18:24;17:6). Some commentators wonder if this can really refer to Christians. But why not? 'Murder' was, in John's day, often a specific reference to abortion. Furthermore, if 'murder' is understood as Scripture understands it — a lack of love, a refusal to love (1 John 3:15) — then **murder** is not unknown in Christian communities. Many Christians have acquiesced, and still do acquiesce and remain silent, in the face of political and systemic oppression, deprivation, and violence against the 'poor' of this world.

Fornicators include those who practise various forms of sexual promiscuity; here it includes also metaphorical **fornication** with the great whore-city, Babylon (17:4,18:3,9).

The **sorcerers** are those who practised magic, especially those who did so under the umbrella of religion. **Sorcerers** 'represented the broad spectrum of an international underground in Greco-Roman society, known to us through magical papyri, amulets, gems, and tablets with spells' (Krodel).

The Greek word which is here translated 'sorcerers' forms the base for the English word for drugs. The modern version of 'sorcerers' would be those who use drugs to induce pseudo-religious experiences, and even do these things in the name of Christ. More generally, God would today have in mind those who wear good-luck charms, those who put their faith in palmists and go to astrologists.

Idolaters are, plainly, those who give their allegiance to false gods.

> A god is that to which we look for all good, and in which we find refuge in every time of need . . . That to which your heart clings and entrusts itself, I say, is really your god. (Martin Luther)

The list closes with **liars**. Lies are, alas, the stock-in-trade of those who are leaders in politics and false religion. In the city which is ruled by him who is 'Faithful and True' (19:11), there cannot possibly be a place for **liars**. They have no part in the inheritance of the saints (21:7; Eph 5:5). Their proper **place** is with him who is the father of lies, the one whose characteristic work is to deceive (John 8:44; Rev 20:3). Liars belong with him in **the lake that burns with fire and sulfur, which is the second death** (see Rev 19:20;20:6,10 and comments there).

This is a blunt, almost brutal warning from God. Its purpose is to underline the seriousness of the sin of compromise and apostasy. The list 'highlights various ways of committing treason against God's empire' (Schüssler Fiorenza). In Christian circles, lists like this belonged in the context of baptism. Such lists spoke of the kind of things that baptismal candidates are to 'put off' as members of the new creation (for example, Eph 4:22-32; 1 Pet 2:1,11).

There is a basic contradiction involved in the claim to be a part of God's new creation, a citizen of the new

Jerusalem, and at the same time to persist in living as an enthusiastic citizen of the whore-city Babylon. God's warning is clear and unambiguous: I will not tolerate such a deliberate contradiction. Repent or perish (see 2:5, 14–16,22,23;3:3,19;22:15).

So ends the last report of heavenly worship in Revelation. It is not the last heavenly worship, for it continues 'without ceasing', 'day and night', 'forever and ever' (4:8;22:5). But this is John's last description of heavenly worship. The fact that God has the last word is a reminder that worship is a divine activity. Worship is performative, but always it is God who 'performs'. In the end, in the final analysis of what worship is and is not, we, John, the angels, the living creatures, John's hearers — all of us are servants. The wonder of liturgy is that in it and by it God serves us.

THE FOURTH REVELATION, 21:9 – 22:9

In the first revelation which John received (1:9 - 3:22), he recorded verbatim the Lord Jesus' view of the state of the church as it existed in seven cities in the Roman province of Asia. Jesus has 20/20 vision. He sees things as they really are. So his report on the state of the church in the world is a hundred per cent accurate.

The fourth revelation (21:9 – 22:9) is also a divine view of the state of the church. There are so many parallels between the first and fourth revelations, so many cross-references and allusions, that there can be no doubt that John meant them to be matching 'state of the church' reports. Compare, for example, 2:7 and 22:2; 2:28 and 22:16; 3:5 and 21:27; 3:11 and 22:7,10; 3:21 and 22:3.

In the third revelation (17:1 – 21:9) John had described in full one reality, and only mentioned another. The one reality of which John had spoken at length is 'the great city', Babylon, which tries to shape and control our present and our future. John showed clearly that although Babylon is a present reality, it has no future. It is doomed to be destroyed.

The other reality, the one John had only mentioned in his third revelation, is the direct antithesis of Babylon. This other reality is the new Jerusalem. Both these realities exist now. The new Jerusalem is not simply the Christian's ultimate destiny. It is a present reality, as real as is Babylon. The new Jerusalem exists right in the middle of human history, and in the middle of the great whore-city Babylon (see 2:13). The new Jerusalem, however, unlike Babylon, has a future. It is heading for glory.

The literary and theological connection and contrast between the two cities is brought out by the way in which John introduces his reports of the fate of the two cities. In both cases, John's angelic guide is **one of the seven angels who had the seven bowls** (17:1;21:9). This connection with the seven bowl-angels is a reminder to John's hearers that the narrative and worship described in chapters 15 and 16 are another way of recounting God's actions which are reported in chapters 17 to 22.

In 17:1 and 21:9 the bowl-angel speaks identical words of invitation: **Come, I will show you**. What John will be shown is dramatically different, and yet there are parallels. He will be shown women/cities. In chapters 17 and 18 he tells of being shown the whore who is fallen Babylon. In chapters 21 and 22 he is shown the bride, the new Jerusalem.

In both 17:3 and 21:10 John is said to be **in the Spirit** (see 1:10 and comments there). In both cases he specifies his location. He observed Babylon's destruction from the safety of 'the desert' (see 17:3 and comments). In the case of new Jerusalem which comes down from heaven, John's vantage point is that place where heaven and earth were thought to meet: **a great, high mountain**.

The mountain top provides the right kind of landscape for a revelation. Its height offers a vision of heaven and a broad perspective on earth. The great Chinese poet Han-Shan wrote:

> High, high from the summit of the peak,
> Whatever way I look, no limit in sight. (*Cold Mountain*, p 46)

At the end of his ministry, Moses experienced the revelatory nature of a mountain top (Deut 34:1–7). Jesus, the second Moses, had a similar experience at the start of his ministry (Matt 4:8).

Now the prophet John, the last of the biblical prophets, stands on his Pisgah and surveys for his people the city which Bernard of Cluny calls 'Jerusalem the golden . . . the home of God's elect'.

John does not identify the mountain on which he stands. Since he is outside of space and time, we may assume that the mountain is a symbol. And in view of the many echoes of Ezekiel 40–48 in these last chapters of Revelation, there is some warrant for assuming that the mountain upon which John stood was the same Mount Zion upon which the new Jerusalem descended and settled (see further the comments on 21:12).

With these fairly obvious hints, John signals to his hearers that they are to compare and contrast the two cities. It is not an academic exercise. The two cities exist now. Your citizenship now determines your eternal destiny. To live in Babylon is to tear up your Jerusalem passport. Here there is no such thing as dual citizenship.

NARRATIVE: The new Jerusalem, 21:9 – 22:5

9 Then one of the seven angels who had the seven bowls full of the seven last plagues came and said to me, 'Come, I will show you the bride, the wife of the Lamb.' 10 And in the spirit[u] he carried me away to a great, high mountain and showed me the holy city Jerusalem coming down out of heaven from God. 11 It has the glory of God and a radiance like a very rare jewel, like jasper, clear as crystal. 12 It has a great, high wall with twelve gates, and at the gates twelve angels, and on the gates are inscribed the names of the twelve tribes of the Israelites; 13 on the east three gates, on the north three gates, on the south three gates, and on the west three gates. 14 And the wall of the city has twelve foundations, and on them are the twelve names of the twelve apostles of the Lamb.

15 The angel[v] who talked to me had a measuring rod of gold to measure the city and its gates and walls. 16 The city lies foursquare, its length the same as its width; and he measured the city with his rod, fifteen hundred miles;[w] its length and width and height are equal. 17 He also measured its wall, one hundred forty-four cubits[x] by human measurement, which the angel was using. 18 The wall is built of jasper, while the city is pure gold, clear as glass. 19 The foundations of the wall of the city are adorned with every jewel; the first was jasper, the second sapphire, the third agate, the fourth emerald, 20 the fifth onyx, the sixth carnelian, the seventh chrysolite, the eighth beryl, the ninth topaz, the tenth chrysoprase, the eleventh jacinth, the twelfth amethyst. 21 And the twelve gates are twelve pearls, each of the gates is a single pearl, and the street of the city is pure gold, transparent as glass.

22 I saw no temple in the city, for its temple is the Lord God the Almighty and the Lamb. 23 And the city has no need of sun or moon to shine on it, for the glory of God is its light, and its lamp is the Lamb. 24 The nations will walk by its light, and the kings of the earth will bring their

glory into it. 25 Its gates will never be shut by day — and
there will be no night there. 26 People will bring into it
the glory and the honor of the nations. 27 But nothing
unclean will enter it, nor anyone who practices
abomination or falsehood, but only those who are written
in the Lamb's book of life.
22 Then the angel[y] showed me the river of the water of
life, bright as crystal, flowing from the throne of God
and of the Lamb 2 through the middle of the street of the
city. On either side of the river, is the tree of life[z] with its
twelve kinds of fruit, producing its fruit each month; and
the leaves of the tree are for the healing of the nations.
3 Nothing accursed will be found there any more. But the
throne of God and of the Lamb will be in it, and his
servants[a] will worship him; 4 they will see his face, and
his name will be on their foreheads. 5 And there will be
no more night; they need no light of lamp or sun, for the
Lord God will be their light, and they will reign forever
and ever.

[u] Or *in the Spirit*

[v] Gk *He*

[w] Gk *twelve thousand stadia*

[x] That is, almost seventy-five yards

[y] Gk *he*

[z] Or *the Lamb. ²In the middle of the street of the city, and on either side of the river, is the tree of life*

[a] Gk *slaves*

The angel had promised John that he would be shown 'the bride, the wife of the Lamb' (21:9). This redundant phrase serves to remind John and his hearers of two truths. First, they are about to see the woman who was briefly introduced in 19:7 and 21:2. She is the people of God. She wears the shining white bridal linen of 'the righteous deeds of the saints' (19:8). Secondly, they are not about to see a whore, who commits constant fornication with the beast and his agents (17:1–3). On the contrary, they will see a faithful wife, the wife of the Lamb.

The image of the bride/wife is not, however, developed further. Instead, John is shown a **city** called **Jerusalem**. A number of features characterise this city. First, a complementary pair: it is **holy** and it is **coming down from heaven**. The dominant feature of the new Jerusalem is that it is **holy**; this distinguishes Jerusalem sharply from its counter-image, the whore-city Babylon. What characterises Babylon is fornication, abominations, impurities (17:4,5), sins, plagues, and iniquities (18:4,5).

In short, Babylon symbolises all that is unholy, unclean, and impure. The new Jerusalem is **holy**. She is holy not because the community which comprises the city is innately holy, but because the Lamb has made it so (see 7:14;14:4;19:8; Eph 5:26,27).

Secondly, the holy city has a holy source and origin: it is seen to be **coming down out of heaven from God**. God built this city (Heb 11:10) through the powerful working of his Holy Spirit through the word of the apostles and prophets (see Eph 2:19–22). Since the church is God's creation, it is naturally characterised as **coming down from heaven**. That is a present and permanent characteristic of the new Jerusalem, the people of God.

To the Christians in Philadelphia Jesus promised to write upon those who conquer 'the name of the city of my God, the new Jerusalem that comes down from my God out of heaven' (3:12). This is a promise which Christ gives to a flesh-and-blood people living in human history. In the structures of existence which express eternal, divine realities, heaven comes down to earth in the worshipping community among whom God lives and rules. Every time the people of God worship God, there the new Jerusalem is **coming down out of heaven**. There heaven and earth are met together. Worship breaks the boundaries of space and time. It takes us into God's sphere of existence, and we see things as they really are.

11 The third and fourth characteristics of the holy city also form a complementary pair. The people of God, the city of God, **has the glory of God**. 'Glory' is God's very nature. Without God's **glory** the city would not exist; God's glory both creates and sustains the city. It is impossible here to avoid making the connection with Jesus Christ, who is himself the image and glory of God (1 Cor 2:8; 2 Cor 4:4–6). Christ is the source and sustainer of both creation and the church (Col 1:15–20).

So close is the connection between Christ and God's glory that on occasion in the New Testament he is even given the title The Glory (for example, Eph 1:17; James 2:1). In Christ the glory of God, which was present at creation (Heb 1:3) but lost by fallen humanity (Rom 3:23), is restored to members of the new creation, the new Jerusalem (2 Cor 3:18).

To say that the holy city, the holy people of God, **has the glory of God** is to say that Christian hope has turned to sight (Col 1:27; Rom 8:17,18,30).

Finally, the holy city possesses a **radiance** which John struggles to find words to describe adequately (reminiscent of Mark's efforts to describe the clothing of the transfigured Lord; Mark 9:3). The word translated as 'radiance' is rendered 'brightness' in Daniel 12:3, and 'stars' in Philippians 2:15, referring to the people of God. John is seeking to describe the glittering brilliance of a many-faceted gemstone.

The comparison with **jasper** recalls the vision of God seated on his throne. He was 'like jasper and carnelian' (4:3). Since the city **has the glory of God**, it is not surprising that in trying to describe this **glory** or **radiance**, John uses the same language which he used to describe God. The cleansed city perfectly mirrors the holiness and glory of God (see 2 Cor 3:18).

Lastly, John says that the city's jasper-like brightness is **clear as crystal**. Perhaps 'ice' would be a better translation. **Jasper** was used to designate any opaque precious stone. 'Clear as crystal' suggests transparency. The point, however, is not that the glory was transparent, but that it glittered, shimmered, reflected light as ice glitters and shimmers and reflects and refracts light.

12 So far John has described the nature of the heavenly city in terms of purity and holiness. He now describes the structure of the city (vv 12–14). His concentration on the **wall** of the city shows, as we shall see, that his emphasis is still on holiness and purity.

John describes the **wall** in exactly the same words which he used to describe the mountain from which he views the city: it is **great** and **high** (see 21:10). John seems to be indicating that the place where the new Jerusalem comes down to earth is in fact the place where John is standing. John, then, is no mere spectator. He is a participant in the life of the city. His subsequent act of measuring the city points in the same direction (see 11:1,2).

John is apparently influenced in his description of the new Jerusalem by the reports which Ezekiel gave of the new Jerusalem, in Ezekiel 40–48. Ezekiel says that he was transported 'by the hand of Yahweh' (= the Holy Spirit) to Israel, where he was 'set down upon a very high mountain, on which was a structure like a city'. The most imposing feature of this structure is its wall, which was ten feet thick (Ezek 40:1–5). John, too, focuses immediately on the walls of the new Jerusalem; indeed, he does not at first describe the city as such; first he describes the **wall**.

John's description, like that of Ezekiel, is organised around two axes. The wall is of imposing height, and it serves to set the city off from its surroundings. Every ancient city had a **wall** for purposes of safety and security and defence. Walls were also status symbols. They added to the prestige of the city. But walls were also thought to serve as a means of separation; true status was founded on the idea that a careful distinction and separation was made between the pure and the impure.

In view of the context which emphasises purity and holiness, it is best to take the **wall** of the holy city as symbolising the separation of the holy from the unholy, the clean from the unclean (see 21:27;22:14,15, and note especially Ezekiel 42:20).

The **wall** has **twelve gates** which are 'never shut by day' (21:25), but they are guarded by twelve angels. The thought of an angelic gatekeeper is unusual in Jewish and Christian literature, but it is not wholly foreign. John seems to be combining two themes here. At the east of the garden of Eden God placed the cherubim 'to guard the way to the tree of life' (Gen 3:24; see Ezek 28:14). Cherubim also had the duty to protect sacred places (1 Kings 6:23–36;8:6,7), in particular the holy things, such as the Ark (Exod 25:20;37:9). Since the new Jerusalem in its entirety is the Holy of Holies in which is located the throne of God (= the Ark), it is fitting that angels stand guard over the entrances to the garden-city in which is found the tree of life, and in which 'nothing accursed will be found' (Rev 22:2,3). Their purpose is to control who goes in and out: those who 'wash their robes' may come and go freely; all unclean persons are excluded (22:14,15).

Upon the twelve **gates** are **inscribed the names of the twelve tribes of the Israelites** (see Ezek 48:31–34). The faithful in Israel, the true descendants of Abraham (Rom 4:13; Gal 3:29), have an inheritance and portion in the eternal community of heaven. The fact that there are twelve gates, three on each side of the city, announces open access to all who have the right to go out and come in, that is, all 'those who are written in the Lamb's book of life' (21:27).

13 John describes the location of the gates in a strange order: east, north, south, west. He seems to be following Ezekiel's report of the measuring of the temple area (Ezek 42:16–20; see Rev 21:15–17). It is not clear, however, why Ezekiel followed the order he did. Perhaps he started with the east because the solar east was the direction which the temple faced (Ezek 43:1–5;47:1), and from which direction God came to enter the sanctuary (Ezek 44:1–3). West came last because it was 'the dark west', the 'least honoured direction'.

14 The **wall of the city** is divided by gates into twelve sections. Each section of the **wall** is seen to rest upon huge blocks of stone which form **twelve foundations** in all. On these are inscribed the twelve **names of the twelve apostles of the Lamb**. Three 'twelves' in one verse ensure that John's hearers do not miss the importance and significance of the number: it matches the threefold repetition of 'twelve' in connection with the gates (vv 12,13). The two sets of twelve together make up the twenty-four who represent the whole worshipping people of God of both the old and new covenants (see 4:1–11; 7:1–12).

The **twelve apostles of the Lamb** have their names written on the foundation stones. According to New Testament writers, the Twelve were the patriarchs of the new Israel of God (Matt 19:28; Luke 22:30), and they form the foundation of God's holy temple (Eph 2:20). The apostles bore 'the testimony of Jesus'. To have this testimony as a foundation is to rest on the Word of God himself.

15 The bowl-angel who was John's guide was responsible not only for carrying out God's judgments, but also for ensuring the safety and security of God's people. He demonstrates the total protection under which the city from heaven exists by measuring it in all its parts: **the city and its gates and walls**. When John measured the temple, he was instructed to leave some of it unmeasured and therefore unprotected (11:1,2). But now the angel measures everything, and so signals that all of the city is under God's protection.

The angel uses a golden **measuring rod** which measures in human terms things which are in fact beyond human measure (see v 17). We have to do here with that which is 'coming down out of heaven from God' (21:10); we are in God's time and space, the new heaven and earth. For this new existence you need new means of measurement of both time ('one thousand years') and space ('one hundred and forty-four cubits', 21:17).

16 First the angel measures the **city**. It proves to be a perfect cube. Like the Holy of Holies of Solomon's temple (1 Kings 6:20), the city's length and breadth and height are equal. Thus the city is a fitting symbol of God's presence. No temple is needed in this city, 'for its temple is the Lord God Almighty and the Lamb' (21:22). Translating the image into 'people' terms, the new Jerusalem is a square of the twelve thousand in each tribe of Israel (7:4–8) which together make up the one hundred and forty-four thousand, the symbol of the whole people of God ('twelve thousand stadia' is the Greek behind the English **fifteen hundred miles**). Put simply, the angel finds that there is room for all; all who should be in the city are in the city.

17 The central architectural feature of the city from heaven is the **wall**; it is mentioned six times in these verses, and is the first feature which John describes (21:12). John conceives of the **wall** as being divided into two parts: the foundation or base, and the upper structure in general (not including the foundation as such).

The **wall** reflects the perfection of the city; it is **one hundred and forty-four cubits**. A cubit was about half a metre. A wall seventy-two metres high was a good-sized wall. But John says his mountain was 'great and high', and he says the same thing about the wall (21:10,12). Seventy-two metres is not a 'great and high' mountain. Furthermore, a wall seventy-two metres high hardly matches the height of the city (fifteen hundred miles). Perhaps the wall was fifteen hundred miles high, and its base was seventy-two metres wide. Hardly. Such a wall needs a much broader base.

Clearly, the **one hundred and forty-four cubits** is symbolic. It is the square of twelve. The wall is just right for its job of protecting God's people and keeping out those who would defile the city (21:27). John does not, by the way, tell us the height of the gates (see v 15).

18 John proceeds to describe the wall, the city, the foundations, and the gates respectively. The **wall** is not just studded with **jasper**; it is actually built of jasper. Since God is enthroned in jasper-like splendour (4:3;21:11), and since God's throne is in the middle of the city (22:1), and the throne is where God's people gather for worship (4:10;22:3), it is clear that the wall of jasper signifies God's holy and glorious presence which surrounds and fills his people. It permeates and controls and transfigures their lives for time and eternity. The **wall**, that symbol of God's glory and holiness, serves as a line of demarcation between holy and unholy. It sets God's people apart from others.

The **city** itself, and its streets (v 21), are **pure gold**. Gold heads the list of extravagant imports of the great city (18:12). That wicked city, the counter-image of the new Jerusalem, was 'adorned with gold' (17:4). Roman authors and social critics regarded **gold** as the central symbol of Rome's moral degeneration. It is disconcerting, then, to hear that the new Jerusalem, the antithesis of the bejewelled and painted prostitute city, is made of **pure gold**.

But this is no ordinary gold; in fact, it is no gold which we know. Probably a better translation of the Greek is:

'The city is gold, clear like clear glass' (see Moffatt). In verse 21 the gold is described as being like glass that you can see through. In short, the gold of which the city and its street is made is transparent. The light of God's holiness and glory shines in and around and through the city, so there is no need for any light-source other than God himself. His presence is symbolised by the throne within the city (22:3–5) and the radiant jasper wall without (21:18).

19,20 The jasper wall rests on **foundations** which have been decorated, permanently, each with a precious stone (see Isa 54:11,12). The list of gems which John records corresponds to no known list in biblical or other literature.

The stones cannot be correlated conclusively with particular tribes, apostles, zodiacal signs, or geographical directions. Nothing can be deduced unequivocally from the colour of the stones, their names, or the sequence in which they are listed. Gemologists are not even sure about the identity of some of the stones.

All that can be said with confidence is that the stones symbolise the presence of God, and the divine origin of the city, which is the new people of God living in the new paradise of God.

Ezekiel the prophet included in his lament over the fate of the king of Tyre a list of the precious stones which adorned the king's garments (Ezek 28:11–19). His lament describes the fall of the king of Tyre in terms of the downfall of the first man who lived in Eden, a garden of God which was planted on the mountain of God. The royal adornments are described as follows:

> You were in Eden, the garden of God;
> every precious stone was your covering,
> carnelian, chrysolite, and moonstone,
> beryl, onyx, and jasper,
> sapphire, turquoise, and emerald;
> and worked in gold were your settings
> and your engravings. (Ezek 28:13)

This translation is from the Hebrew text. The Greek text, which is thought to be older than the Hebrew at this point, actually lists twelve stones and precious metals, instead of the nine given here.

It seems that, in describing the new city of God which is set in Paradise (2:7;22:1–3), John used the language of Ezekiel's lament over the king of Tyre. In that lament, the king is addressed as the first human being. A contrast is drawn between his first and his later state. It is not improbable that the lament over the king of Tyre did indeed influence John's language, for the new Jerusalem is clearly the counter-image of the whore-city Babylon. John had told the story of the fall of Babylon by using, in part, the language of the doom oracles against Tyre (see comments on page 286-7).

Certainly the twelve stones of the new Jerusalem are a reminder of the jewellery with which the whore Babylon was adorned (Rev 17:4;18:12,16). Although John obviously wants his hearers to be conscious of the polar differences between Babylon and New Jerusalem, we should be careful not to exaggerate the contrasts between the external appearance of the two cities.

Outwardly, Babylon is the attractive woman who mimics the new Jerusalem. The beast who dresses and adorns Babylon knows exactly what the new Jerusalem looks like. For us, however, the new city of God is hidden beneath the ordinariness and humbleness of the Christian life on earth. It is easy even for Christians to mistake Babylon's reality for ultimate reality. That is why we must trust our ears (=believe what God says about his holy people), and not our eyes.

Some commentators suggest that, in portraying the jewels of the new Jerusalem, John is drawing on the description of the High Priest's breastplate (Exod 28:17–21). This breastplate had twelve precious stones, one for each of the twelve tribes of Israel. John, it is said, transforms the image by referring the twelve stones to the twelve apostles who represent God's new high priests at worship (22:3).

But John's point is that there are two lots of twelve, totalling twenty-four. The twelve tribes are the gates, and the twelve apostles are the foundations. In this imagery, the twelve apostles do not replace the twelve patriarchs of Israel.

It seems preferable to conclude that John describes the bejewelled foundation stones in language borrowed from Ezekiel 28. In so doing he enhances the parallel and contrast with gaudy Babylon.

Jasper, which came from Egypt, was an opaque, impure variety of quartz, found in colours of red, yellow, green, and black. **Sapphire** was a clear deep-blue stone; hardness: 9. It was imported from India. **Agate** has opaque or translucent stripes or layers in various shades of white, grey, yellow, red, brown, or blue. When agate is cut horizontally it is known as **onyx**. **Emerald** was a crystal stone, a deep-green variety of **beryl**, which was a yellow, green, or bluish transparent crystal; hardness: 8. **Carnelian** was a blood-red gem; **chrysolite**, a silicate of magnesium and iron, was a rare gem, golden yellow in colour; hardness: 6.5–7. **Topaz** was a clear gem, usually yellow in colour; hardness: 8. **Chrysoprase** was a crystal whose nickel impurities gave it a grass-green tone; **jacinth** has not been identified with certainty. Possibly it was the same as the **amethyst**, which is a rare variety of quartz, so hard that it scratches glass.

21 Each of the **twelve gates** of the new Jerusalem is made of **a single pearl** (see Isa 54:12b). Evidence from rabbinic writings, dated several centuries after John wrote, indicates that there was a tradition which associated pearls with the gates of new Jerusalem. One rabbi wrote:

> The Holy One, blessed be He, will in the time to come bring precious stones which are thirty [cubits] by thirty, and He will cut out from them [openings] ten by twenty, and will set them up in the gates of Jerusalem.

It is not certain that John knew or used this tradition. Perhaps he was influenced by Isaiah's promises to Jerusalem, and he took the word 'jewel' (Is 54:12b) to mean 'pearl'. What *is* clear is that the city's adornments are magnificent, even down to the gates themselves. Pliny, the Roman historian, said that 'the first place and the topmost rank among all things of price is held by pearls'.

John concludes this part of his description of the new Jerusalem by saying something about **the street of the city** (see 11:8;22:2; always the singular, 'street', is used). Many of the great cities of Asia Minor and Greece had a broad main street, for processions, commerce, and public discourse. The central thoroughfare, the Champs Elysées of the new Jerusalem, is made out of **gold**, clear as **glass** which you can see through. Ordinary ancient glass was cloudy; only the rarest and most expensive was transparent. The main street was made out of the same material as the city itself: transparent gold (21:18). There is, apparently, a point in the process of treating the metal at which gold becomes translucent.

In verses 18–21 John has described a beautiful city, a bride-city, dressed and adorned for her wedding (see 21:2,9). Thus the new Jerusalem, as the adorned bride, is the antitype of the adorned harlot-city Babylon (17:4;18:16). Outwardly there is little difference between the two cities; the splendid attire of the harlot is not in itself a sign of wickedness.

The difference between the two cities is a matter of inward character and purpose. Bejewelled Babylon entices people to become involved in an evil system (see Ezek 16:8–18); the equally bejewelled Jerusalem draws people to its glory in order to worship the true God.

The image of the bride dressed in white linen (19:8) and adorned with gold, precious stones, and pearls (21:18–21), reflects contemporary wedding customs among royalty and the affluent. Pliny the Roman historian tells of a betrothal banquet at which the bride was 'covered with emeralds and pearls interlaced alternately, and shining all over her head, ears, neck, and fingers'. Archaeologists have discovered a Roman necklace made of precious stones interspersed with pearls. We are reminded that the precious stones of the foundation of new Jerusalem, interspersed with the pearls of the gates, form a beautiful bridal necklace.

So John's hearers are reminded that the city, the new Jerusalem, is not a structure but a people. Her fine linen, given to her by the Lamb (19:8; see 3:4,5), and her adornments, also given to her by Christ (21:2; see Eph 5:25–27), are emblems of her faithfulness and holy conduct as she 'conquered', that is, as she overcame the attractions of the whore-city Babylon, the beast, and the dragon. The 'city' is a metaphor for the people of God.

John has been looking at the city from a distance (21:9–21). He has described it as a whole, its structure and dimensions. He has been walking with his angel-guide, gradually approaching the city. First they examined the wall, 'measured' it, and described it in some detail. For quite a time the wall was the central focus. Then the pearly gates came into view; then the magnificent golden main mall.

22 Now, in 21:22–27, John walks even further into the city. He takes in the urban sights and sounds. As he does so, he describes what he sees. But he notices that something is missing in this new Jerusalem: there is **no temple**.

The stated reason for this absence of the central symbol of God's presence among his people, comes as a surprise and serves as a warning. The description of the city as a perfect cube, like the Holy of Holies (21:16), might have led John's hearers to conclude that they, the worshipping people of God, actually form the temple (see 21:16 and comments).

In fact, however, it is **the Lord God the Almighty and the Lamb** who form the **temple** (literally: 'the inner sanctuary of the temple'). The people of God are 'temple' only because, and insofar as, they do what they should do in the temple of **God the Almighty**: worship him as his servants (see 22:3:11:1). True worship and true temple begins and ends with God and the Lamb, not with us. A temple is a temple, not because people worship there, but because God is present there (see 2:1). The liturgy of the eucharist is a constant reminder of this fact.

23 Since the city 'has the glory of God' (21:11), and since he who is the Light (John 1:9; 1 John 2:8) is enthroned in the heart of the city, the city is full of light. The transparent nature of the structures and wall allow the light of God's glory and holiness (21:10,11) to fill it through and through (see 2 Cor 3:18;4:6). There is glory, glory everywhere. So in the community of God, the holy people of God, there is fulfilled the promise which God made through his prophet Isaiah:

> The sun shall no longer be your light by day,
> nor for brightness shall the moon give
> light to you by night;

> but the Lord will be your everlasting light,
> and your God will be your glory. (60:19)

John's point is that, with such divine light and glory filling the city of God, **sun** and **moon** are redundant, irrelevant, obsolete. What a blow to those who think that sun and moon and other heavenly lights control human destiny!

24-26 God had made a further promise through Isaiah:

> Nations shall come to your light,
> and kings to the brightness of your dawn . . .
> the abundance of the sea shall be brought to you,
> the wealth of the nations shall come to you. (60:3,5)

Since there is only light always in the city, there is no **night** — that time of dark deeds and demonic activity (see John 13:27–30). During the perpetual **day** there is never need to **shut** the **gates**. Angel-guards see to it that the unclean remain outside. All enemies who could threaten God's people have been consigned to their proper place in the 'lake of fire'.

For every true citizen of new Jerusalem there are no travel restrictions. They may enter freely. And what a procession! The beautiful bejewelled city, shining like a golden beacon on Mount Zion (14:1), attracts people from all the nations (see Matt 8:11). Their coming is reminiscent, in a way, of the wise men following the beacon-star to Jerusalem, first, and then to Bethlehem, so that they could worship the Christ-child.

And just as those first Gentile worshippers brought their gifts (Matt 2:11), so the **kings of the earth** and all **people** will bring into the new Jerusalem their treasures, their gifts, all that is good and true in their cultures, all that can be offered in worship of God and used in his service. John calls all this the **glory and honour of the nations**. It seems that some church people, who reject every aspect of culture (especially when missionising in a foreign culture), are in for a big surprise!

The church is supposed to model and prefigure this final great in-gathering, show that it is happening already now. The church does this when it opens its doors and welcomes people of all nations without partiality (Jas 2:1). It models God's future when it claims all that is good and true in our cultures, claims them all for the service of

God and his creation. Where they have been demonised, the church consecrates them anew to God.

Why should we let the devil, that great red dragon, make use of the good things of culture and creation and manipulate their use for his own evil ends, as if they were his by right? The Lamb is Lord, and God is Pantocrator, ruler of all. Why on earth, then, should Christians let the devil have all the good tunes?

27 Excluded from the city, of course, is anything which is **unclean** (Isa 52:1), or anyone who shares the **abominations** of the harlot-city (Rev 17:3–6). As John has said already several times, the people of God are the ones who **are written in the Lamb's book of life** (see 3:5;13:8;20:12). They have come through the great ordeal and washed their robes in the blood of the Lamb. 'For this reason they are before the throne of God, and worship him day and night within his temple' (7:14,15).

The implied contrast between the harlot-city Babylon and the bride-city Jerusalem should not be overlooked. Babylon symbolises the concentrated political and economic power of the nations. New Jerusalem, too, attracts the nations' wealth and splendour. But whereas Babylon misuses its military might and economic resources to corrupt and destroy the earth, the new Jerusalem is God's creation (Heb 11:10) and God's promise of new life, health, and freedom for the earth (see Rom 8:21). In this city, 'throne' is not a symbol of exploitation and oppression, but of peace and eternal life. This theme is taken up in the final section of John's story of new Jerusalem.

22:1,2 As John moved further into the city, his attention was captured by the **throne of God**, the central feature of this city. Once again, as he has done repeatedly in Revelation, John describes what is happening around the throne (see 4:1-11;5:1-13; 19:1-8).

The connection of this last section of the account of the fourth revelation (22:1–5) with the first chapters of Revelation is demonstrated by the way in which John reports the fulfilment of the promises given to the faithful members of the churches of Asia. For example, 'the conquerors' were promised that they would eat of the tree of life and not be harmed by the second death (2:7,11; see 22:2 and 21:8); they would receive a new name and see God's face (2:17;3:5,12; see 22:4); and they would rule over the nations (2:26;3:21; see 22:5).

These parallels are a reminder to John's hearers that there is an intimate relationship and continuity between the flesh-and-blood faithful members of the churches in Asia and the heavenly new Jerusalem. The same people are involved. The difference is one of perspective, of time and space and sphere of existence. The reality, however, is one.

John next reports that his angelic guide, the bowl-angel, had shown him **a river of the water of life**. This river, like the divine radiance of the city proper, is crystal-clear. The source of the river is **the throne of God and of the Lamb**. From this throne the river flows right down the middle of the great main street (21:21).

The unique phrase, 'the throne of God and of the Lamb', is another pointer to a fulfilled promise. In 3:21 Jesus had promised 'the conqueror' a place with him on his throne. This corresponds to the truth that Christ has conquered and sits with his Father on his throne.

The phrase ('the throne of God and of the Lamb') also confirms the rightness of the heavenly liturgy which John reports throughout the book. Worship is always led by, and offered to, 'him who sits on the throne' and 'the Lamb who was slain' (4:8–11;5:11–13; see 22:3).

John's reference to the **river of the water of life** seems to be an echo of the Genesis account of the garden of Eden. It suggests that the new Jerusalem is a garden-city. From this it would be incorrect, however, to argue that, according to Revelation, humankind is finally restored to a lost paradise. If this were so, it would mean that God has ignored the way human history has travelled since the founding of the first city. History tells of kings and their kingdoms; of the building and rebuilding of temples; of the calls of prophets, urging cities to repent; and of Jesus weeping over stubborn Jerusalem. The movement of history has been from a single person to two to a multiplying of people, so that a growing community is formed. 'City' is the proper end and goal of human history.

God built the new Jerusalem (Heb 11:10,16). The city is a work of art; it stands in contrast to the other city, Babylon, the city which people built. As a work of divine art, the new Jerusalem, the city of the new creation, reflects God's appreciation of things beautiful. In the beginning, God the master architect and builder (Heb 11:10) pronounced his creative work 'good'. That is, it was suited to its purpose, and it was beautiful. It was functionally and aesthetically 'good'.

Human beings have been gifted by God with artistic skills. The descendants of Cain began the arts of music and metal working (Gen 4:21,22). The care for craftsmanship and precision is found in the working of Aaron's vestments (Exod 28), in the temple of Solomon (2 Chr 3,4) and the temple in Ezekiel's vision (Ezek 40–42).

In the new Jerusalem, everything is under the lordship of the Lamb: nations bring to the city their cultural treasures and riches (21:26). In this city, not in a garden paradise, redeemed humanity finds its purpose and destiny.

In Ezekiel's vision, the presence of the river meant that 'everything will live where the river goes' (Ezek 47:9). In Revelation, God sends out streams of water which mean life for his people. This contrasts with the activities of Satan. He spews out of his mouth a flood of water in an attempt to destroy the people of God (12:15).

The water from Satan means death; the water from God means life.

The fact that the river flows from the **throne of God and the Lamb** emphasises the trinitarian nature of the God who gives light and life to the city. In John 7:37-39 Jesus invites the thirsty to come to him and to drink (= to believe in him). The evangelist explains that the living water which flows from Christ is the Spirit (see Ezek 47:12).

The invitation recorded in John 7:37 is repeated in Revelation 22:17; this invitation is given by 'the Spirit and the bride'. The Holy Spirit, we confess, proceeds from the Father and the Son; he is the Lord and giver of life. The image of living water is the perfect symbol of the life-giving work of the Creator Spirit. It is also the perfect symbol of the purifying work of the Spirit. He is the 'Spirit of holiness'; he makes his people clean through the washing of water with the word (Eph 5:26; 2 Thess 2:13). In the new Jerusalem, the cleansing Spirit is always present to sanctify the people of God (Zech 13:1).

Another image which seems to stem from the Genesis account of creation is that of the **tree of life** (Gen 2:9). The first tree of life offered immortality to those who ate from it (Gen 3:22). Sin kept human beings from that tree. The second tree of life gives abundant, eternal life to those who eat of it. All the holy people of God may eat of it, constantly and continually. It bears fruit the whole year round.

The tree of life was also a familiar urban image, associated with the temples of Artemis. The tree of life in Artemis's temple was a place of salvation and asylum for criminals; their crimes went unpunished. Perhaps John is contrasting the beast with the Lamb, and showing how once again the beast parodies the Lamb and his work.

The tree of life was used in the Wisdom literature of the Old Testament to signify that which gives life and wholeness. Wisdom itself, which was active in creation, is a tree of life (Prov 3:18). Likewise, obedience to the law of God, and charitable use of the tongue, is a tree of life (Prov 11:30;15:4). Hope realised is a tree of life to those who have hope (Prov 13:12). In short, access to 'the tree of life' meant access to life in its fullness. It is hard to know whether John had this thought in mind when he spoke of the 'tree of life'. Perhaps he did. It certainly fits his general flow of thought.

This **tree of life** provides fruit to eat; but its leaves, too, are of value: they heal. Like the pawpaw or papaya tree, which provides food and medicinal leaves for the people of the South Pacific, so too the tree of life provides nourishment and healing for Jerusalem. The imagery of a tree which bears fruit prolifically, and whose leaves have therapeutic qualities, is taken from Ezekiel 47:12. The healing leaves of this wonderful tree are for all – for **the nations**, John says. Since the tree of life and the river of the water of life are both located within the city, John must be speaking here of that which nourishes and sustains the people of God in the new Jerusalem both now and forever.

The early Christians had fine instincts when they related the tree of life to the tree of the cross (see 2:7 and comments).

> Come to Calvary's holy mountain,
> sinners ruined by the fall;
> Here a pure and healing fountain
> flows to you, to me, to all
> in a full perpetual tide
> opened when our Saviour died.

3 Since Christ by his death on the tree 'became a curse for us 'in order that in Christ Jesus the blessing of Abraham might come to the Gentiles' (Gal 3:13,14), there is nothing **accursed** in the city. Originally, the word which is translated 'accursed' referred to something which is devoted or dedicated to a deity. That original meaning would make good sense here: in the new Jerusalem there is nothing which is dedicated or devoted to a 'deity' such as the emperor or Roma or any other false god.

However, the translation 'accursed' is also appropriate (and to be preferred) in the context. It reflects the Old Testament thought of setting someone apart, handing them over to God for destruction (see Exod 22:20, NIV note; Deut 13:12–17, NIV note). The Greek word which John uses here (*katathema*) is a variant of the word *anathema*, which Paul uses in 1 Corinthians 16:22. It seems that in the early church the *anathema* had the purpose of excluding the unworthy from sharing in the eucharist. Possibly John's thought here, in this book of worship, is to indicate that in the worship of the new Jerusalem, all who deserve to be handed over to God for judgment are by definition excluded from the community of God. So there will no longer be a need to speak the *anathema*: all who deserve to have it spoken over them will have received it; all who exclude themselves by their persistent unbelief and rebellion are excluded.

Here again is an example of the way in which Christian worship, including the practice of excluding the unrepentant from the Lord's supper, is a foretaste and anticipation of the world to come. Indeed, Christian worship on earth is already a participation in heavenly worship; the difference between now and the time after our Lord's return is that now we don't *see* what is happening; we believe it. Eventually, faith will turn to sight.

Instead of the **curse**, there is only the **throne of God and the Lamb** (see 22:21), around which the people of God — known throughout Revelation as 'the **servants** of God' — gather to serve him. The word 'serve' may be translated as **worship**, provided that worship is understood as the total life of the people of God, as confessed in Deuteronomy 10:12 and Romans 12:1–3. Worship of God is service of God; service of God (and of his people) is worship of God. Jesus reminded the devil himself of this connection between worship and service when he rejected the tempter's revelation and promise of a universal kingship: 'Worship the Lord your God and serve only him' (Matt 4:10).

4 Those who worship God by serving him body and soul, live continually in his presence. It used to be that the high priest, the one who had the name of God written on his forehead (Exod 28:36–38), went into the presence of God once a year, on the great Day of Atonement. But now, in the new covenant, all the people of God are priests before him; all bear his name on their foreheads (Rev 7:3;14:1).

All God's people are given the promise that they will live with him and talk with him as man and woman did in the beginning. They shall see him face to face, and they shall not die in doing so. This hope of seeing God is the highest hope of God's people (see Pss 27:4;42:2; Isa 52:8;60:2). It is a sure promise given by Jesus to the pure in heart (Matt 5:8; see 1 John 3:2).

5 The account of John's view of the new Jerusalem closes with a summary of all that has been said in 21:1 to 22:4. All evil is gone: **there will be no more night** (see 21:25). The old is gone for good: **they need no lamp or**

light or sun (see 21:23); and, as the Aaronic blessing says, the Lord God will shine on them (a better translation than: **the Lord God will be their light**).

The liturgical flavour of the verse carries to the last phrase: **forever and ever** the people of God will participate in the rule of God and the Lamb. Thus the new creation replaces the old. The first creation began with men and women commissioned to exercise responsible rule (Gen 1:28–30). The story of the new creation concludes with God's people exercising kingly rule. It will never be abused or distorted (as it was in the first creation), for God's people live and rule with Christ, and will do so **forever and ever** (20:6).

And so is fulfilled the last promise given to all members of the churches to whom John wrote:

> To the one who conquers I will give a place with me on my throne, just as I myself conquered and sat down with my Father on his throne. (3:21)

CONCLUDING DIALOGUE NARRATIVE: John and the angel-guide, 22:6–9

6 **And he said to me, 'These words are trustworthy and true, for the Lord, the God of the spirits of the prophets, has sent his angel to show his servants**[a] **what must soon take place.'**

7 **'See, I am coming soon! Blessed is the one who keeps the words of the prophecy of this book.'**

8 **I, John, am the one who heard and saw these things. And when I heard and saw them, I fell down to worship at the feet of the angel who showed them to me;** 9 **but he said to me, 'You must not do that! I am a fellow servant**[b] **with you and your comrades**[c] **the prophets, and with those who keep the words of this book. Worship God!'**

[a] Gk slaves

[b] Gk slave

[c] Gk brothers

John concludes his report of the vision of the new Jerusalem, the bride of the Lamb, in much the same way as he concluded his report of the destruction of Babylon and the various responses to that great act of divine judgment.

Thus he repeats the affirmation concerning the trustworthiness of the revelation (19:9;22:6). He tells again of his attempt to worship the angel-guide (19:9;22:6), and of the angel's rebuke and command to 'Worship God!' (19:10;22:9). In both reports the narratives are couched in the form of a dialogue between John and his angel-guide (see comments on page 105-6).

The dialogue which John records in 22:6–9 runs as follows:

	John		The angel
6a	And he said to me . . .	6b,7	These words . . . of this book
8	I, John, am he . . . And when I heard and saw, I worshipped.		
9a	But he said to me;	9b	Worship God!

6 John's guide repeats the assurance, given in 19:9 and again in 21:5 by God himself, that the revelation which John has received can be trusted. It is a wholly reliable view of reality, for it is the view of him who is himself Faithful and True (19:11). Even though God speaks only twice directly in Revelation (1:8;21:5), the revelations have their origin in him. This fact is emphasised by the angel when he repeats the original statement about the chain of communication of the revelations (see 1:1).

In the opening verse of Revelation, John had confessed that it is the Lord God himself who inspires the prophets: he is **the God of the spirits of the prophets**. The 'spirits of the prophets' are the prophets themselves. They are subject to the Spirit who inspires all prophecy and all prophets (see 1 Cor 14:32; 1 Pet 1:10–12). Prophets are not autonomous. If they are genuine, they come from God and serve only God. Self-serving prophets are by definition false prophets. The rebellious Jezebel called herself a prophet (2:20), but the obedient John never gives himself that appellation. In his own eyes he is a servant, like his fellow prophets

(1:1;22:9), including Paul (Rom 1:1), James (James 1:1), and Peter (2 Peter 1:1). John received his revelations through the agency of yet another servant of God, an **angel** (22:9). The revelations concern **what must soon take place** (see 1:1 and comments). The 'soon' in this statement, and in the phrase 'I am coming soon', should not focus exclusively on the time factor ('without delay'). The emphasis is on the thought of 'the right time', the ordained time, the time appointed by God.

7 It is not clear whom John actually heard speak the promise, 'I am coming soon', and who pronounced the following beatitude. Elsewhere in Revelation, the declaration that he is coming quickly or soon is explicitly attributed to Jesus. Perhaps Jesus himself spoke to John at this point, and that is why John was confused about whom he should worship (v 9). On the other hand, it is perhaps more likely that John's angel-guide said all that John recorded in verses 6 and 7. He is functioning as a prophet, like John and his brothers, and as a prophet he speaks words which are really utterances of Jesus. This, too, could well have caused John to confuse the angel, who speaks the words on behalf of Jesus, with Jesus himself. So he worshipped him.

To the promise that Jesus is **coming** at his own determined time — and so will answer the prayers of those who pray: 'Come, Lord Jesus!' — there is attached a solemn beatitude, a blessing, pronounced upon those who are holding fast to the **words of the prophecy of this book**. This beatitude, the sixth in Revelation, parallels the first, which was directed to the one who read the book in public and to those who hear and hold the things written in 'the prophecy' (1:3). The beatitude says that they are blessed who keep on doing that which the book of Revelation enjoins: worship God and not the beast. That was, in fact, happening right then, as Christian people, gathered in worship, listened to the word of God as it came to them from Jesus via John via the lector.

Through his angel Jesus declares that John's words are those of a true prophet: they are **prophecy**. They are the genuine and trustworthy word of God to his people. They warn, comfort, judge, threaten, promise, and give salvation to all who believe (see 2 Tim 3:16,17).

8 At the beginning of the book, and again at the end, John makes a point of identifying himself as the human agent whom God used to transmit the divine prophetic word. He solemnly attests that he did actually have the experiences and see the things which he says he experienced and saw. He **heard** and **saw** them. These two verbs are the two used most frequently to describe John's involvement in the scenes and events which he describes in Revelation.

John's response to having heard and seen all **these things** was to prostrate himself in worship before **the angel who had showed them** to him.

We misunderstand Revelation if we say: 'For the second time John attempts to worship the angel'. There is no time element involved here; what John saw and heard and did was outside of time and space. What we should say is: 'For the second time John *reports* that he tried to worship his angel-guide (see 19:10). John's repetition of his report of the incident is a device he uses to imprint on his hearers' memory the truth that the new Jerusalem, the fruit of God's saving action, is the counter-image of fallen Babylon, the object of God's judging action. So marvellous is this pair of revelations that John is tempted to worship the one who showed them to him on God's behalf, that is the bowl-angel (see 17:1–3;21:9,10).

In rejecting John's attempt to worship him, the angel demonstrates by his very words the truth of what he says: he is not God, and therefore he is not to be worshipped. He is simply a **fellow servant** of John's, of the prophet leaders of the congregations (the 'angels' of the churches), and of those who hear and **keep the words of this book**.

The angel himself refuses false worship and urges John to worship God (see 19:10). Thus the revelation of the new Jerusalem ends, as did the revelation of the fall of Babylon, with an admonition to true worship. This has been the signature tune of the whole book.

THE EPILOGUE: 22:10–21

10 And he said to me, 'Do not seal up the words of the
prophecy of this book, for the time is near. 11 Let the
evildoer still do evil, and the filthy still be filthy, and the
righteous still do right, and the holy still be holy.'
12 'See, I am coming soon; my reward is with me, to
repay according to everyone's work. 13 I am the Alpha
and the Omega, the first and the last, the beginning and
the end.'
14 Blessed are those who wash their robes,[d] so that they
will have the right to the tree of life and may enter the
city by the gates. 15 Outside are the dogs and sorcerers
and fornicators and murderers and idolaters, and
everyone who loves and practices falsehood.
16 'It is I, Jesus, who sent my angel to you with this
testimony for the churches. I am the root and the
descendant of David, the bright morning star.' 17 The
Spirit and the bride say,

'Come.'

And let everyone who hears say,

'Come.'

And let everyone who is thirsty

come.

Let anyone who wishes take the

water of life as a gift.

18 I warn everyone who hears the words of the prophecy
of this book: if anyone adds to them, God will add to that
person the plagues described in this book; 19 if anyone
takes away from the words of the book of this prophecy,
God will take away that person's share in the tree of life
and in the holy city, which are described in this book.
20 The one who testifies to these things says, 'Surely I
am coming soon.'

Amen. Come, Lord Jesus!

21 The grace of the Lord Jesus be with all the saints.
Amen.[e]

[d] Other ancient authorities read *do his commandments*

[e] Other ancient authorities lack *all*; others lack *the saints*; others lack *Amen*

In his introduction to Revelation John had combined a 'letter' form with a 'worship' or liturgical form. In so doing, he emphasised the fact that he was writing something to be read in a worship setting.

The epilogue or conclusion of Revelation is more strongly liturgical, and less like the usual end of a letter. John records something like a liturgical dialogue, which involves the lector (public reader) in a dialogue with the worshippers who listen to Revelation being read in the church service. The lector speaks sometimes for John, sometimes for Jesus, and sometimes for the angel-guide. It is not always possible to determine exactly for whom the lector is speaking. But that is not as important as recognising the liturgical nature of these last verses of this book of worship.

a) Divine self-introduction and final charge 22:10–16

Although there is much to be said in favour of treating verses 10–16 as an alternating dialogue between Jesus and John's angel-guide, the view taken in this commentary is that all of these verses are a self-introduction on the part of Jesus, and a final set of admonitions concerning John's recording of his revelations. Thus this last scene matches the opening one, where God introduces himself, Jesus appears to John, and the prophet is instructed to 'write what you see' (1:11). Since the command to write clearly came from Jesus, it is assumed that the command not to **seal up the words of the prophecy of this book** also came from Jesus himself.

Once again the prophetic character of John's words are affirmed (22:6,7). To unseal a book is to disclose its contents and to set in motion God's acts of judgment and salvation (contrast 10:4 and see comments there and on 5:1,2).

What John has recorded in this book is not to be sealed, because **the time is near**, that is, God's judging and saving activity in human history is already operative; indeed, it is at work in the worship activity of God's people. Words of healing and blessing are spoken on and by the citizens of new Jerusalem; words of judgment and condemnation are spoken on the unrepentant citizens of fallen Babylon.

Or, to speak plainly: God is here and now at work judging wicked individuals and societies, warning compromising Christians, threatening the rebellious, encouraging the faithful, and blessing those who 'conquer'. God's agent in all this is his worshipping community, who by the very act of worship make history and topple idols from their throne, create a new 'world', and sort out who is who before God. This happens in worship, because human worship is led by God himself, it is centred on him, and receives from him its life-or-death power in the world.

11 The two kinds of people who make up the human race are the inhabitants of the two cities, Babylon and new Jerusalem. They are described in terms of clean and unclean, pure and impure, nearness to or distance from God (see Matt 13:47-50;25:32). The line of demarcation exists now (see John 3:36). The **evildoer** and the morally **filthy** persons are warned that they cannot, dare not, presume on God's patience; they cannot assume that God will keep on extending his time of patience (see Rom 2:4,5). God's invitation does indeed go out right until the End (see 22:17), but no-one knows when this End will be. God forces, compels, no-one. Those who choose, deliberately and persistently, to do evil and promote filthiness and uncleanness, will be treated as evildoers and filthy people when the judging Christ comes at his appointed time. All we know about that time is that it is 'soon'.

Only a fool will think that he or she can outguess God (Matt 24:48–51). The wise person, the obedient servant, the **righteous** and **holy** people of God, will think of Christ's 'soon' as 'now': they will continue to **do right** and to be **holy** in their conduct (Isa 56:1; Dan 12:10; 2 Pet 3:11–18; Rom 13:11–14).

12 So when the judging Christ comes, bringing with him the appropriate wage (**reward**) due to each, his faithful people will not come into judgment, as he has said in 20:11–15. But those who did not give him the worship due to his holy name will receive the appropriate wage or **reward**. The wages which sin pays is death, says Paul (Rom 6:23). Christians, lest they become puffed up with pride and so lose their 'reward', should remember how Paul finishes the sentence: 'The wages of sin is death, but the free gift of God is eternal life in Christ Jesus our Lord' (Rom 6:23). The saints' 'work' is the fine linen of righteousness which the Lamb has *given* them to wear (21:8; Eph 2:10;5:25).

13 The Christ who is judge, the one who gives out appropriate sentences, claims for himself the divine titles by which God had identified himself in the opening liturgical sentences (1:8). Jesus Christ is and does what only God is and does (Mark 2:6–12) because he is 'very God of very God, of one substance with the Father', and to him God has committed all judgment (John 5:22).

The three pairs of divine titles all point to the one reality: in the beginning was the Word . . . in the end is the Word. **Alpha and Omega**, the first and last letters of the Greek alphabet, remind John's hearers that Christ embraces the whole of history, the start and the end and all in between. **First and last** emphasises the truth that Jesus Christ is the centre of history; from him all history gets to make sense and to have meaning and purpose (see 1:7). **The beginning and the end** affirms that Christ is the genesis, source, and author of existence. He is also its goal, the purpose of human history. Who can deny that *this* Christ, even this Lamb who was slain, is both worthy and able to judge the world?

14,15 Jesus speaks the last (the seventh) beatitude or blessing in Revelation. His pronouncement is a declaration of salvation which is followed (in verse 15) by a declaration of judgment. The two statements in verses 14 and 15 do what Christ said he would do in verse 12, while in verse 13 he established his credentials, as it were, for acting as judge. These verses are simply a summary of everything that has been narrated in the story of the two cities in 17:1 – 22:9.

The declaration of blessedness is couched in the language which has been used to describe some of the leading characteristics of the garden-city Jerusalem. She is a bride, dressed in **robes** which have been washed white in the blood of the Lamb (7:14; 19:7,8). These citizens have the inalienable **right** of access to the **tree of life** with its twelve kinds of fruit (22:2). This **right** is one not deserved or earned; it is given by judicial decree of Christ.

As redeemed, washed, and forgiven people, the citizens of the new Jerusalem **may enter the city by the gates**. Since there is no other means of entry to the city than by the gates, the seemingly superfluous statement serves to underline the fact that the citizens of new Jerusalem have complete freedom: they may come and go freely, unhindered, unchallenged by the angelic guardians of the city's gates (21:12).

Although some of the imagery is taken from the story of the garden, the image of city reminds all Christians that the community which began with Adam and Eve finds its destiny fulfilled not in a garden with two inhabitants and a sneaky serpent who has open access, but in a city with a population which cannot be numbered, and into which nothing deceitful can enter and from which all unholiness is excluded.

Outside the city, in the eerie desolation which is all that is left of the memory of fallen Babylon (18:2,3,21-23), is the place for those who stand under God's judgment. They are described in six phrases (see 21:8). For the Jews, **dogs** were not pets but street scavengers, hateful and hated (they only added to poor Lazarus's misery, Luke 16:21). When used of people, 'dogs' meant evildoers (22:11), unclean persons (Deut 23:17,18 JB), godless people, the wicked (see Ps 22:16,20; Phil 3:2). **Sorcerers, fornicators, murderers**, and **idolaters** are all listed in 21:9 as having a place, together with Satan and the beasts, in the lake of fire. The last in the list recorded in 21:9 is here expanded as **everyone who loves and practices falsehood**. Aristotle, the Greek philosopher, once remarked that 'a good mind loves the truth, a bad one loves falsehood'. The apostle Paul said that truth is to be done in love (Eph 4:15). He also reminded his readers that the speaking of the truth at all times is something which Christians must make a high priority if they want to maintain the unity which God has granted them in

Christ (Eph 4:25). He warned that those who love and do the lie have no 'inheritance in the kingdom of Christ and of God' (Eph 5:5; see Gal 5:20,21).

16 As John's prophecy comes to its conclusion, Jesus more and more 'takes over'. His has been the voice behind various angelic voices in this book. He now puts his stamp of approval and authentication on the angel who had been his agent and mouthpiece in the last two revelations (17:1 – 21:9 and 21:10 – 22:5). Jesus calls the angel 'my angel'. That which 'the Lord God of the spirits of the prophets' was said to have done, that is, 'sent his angel' (22:6), Jesus here says he himself has done. The angel is thus God's messenger and also the messenger of Jesus. The words of the angel, the words of God, and the words of Jesus are interchangeable. All are faithful and true because all are word of God.

The angel was sent 'to you' (plural). Although John was the immediate recipient of the revelations, they were intended for all John's fellow prophets. In particular they were intended for the churches in the Roman province of Asia (1:1,11;22:6). So the book has come full circle. John returns to the theme which he introduced programatically in the first verse of Revelation:

> The revelation of Jesus Christ, which God gave him to show his servants what must soon take place; he made it known by sending his angel to his servant John. (1:1)

John's hearers are reminded that the revelations which John received are no private unveilings; they are God's word to all the churches.

Jesus has identified the angel, and certified that the angel is his very own. Now the Lord identifies himself. He uses his 'human' name, as it were: he is simply **Jesus** (see 1:2).

The Lord Jesus reminds his worshippers that he is the Lamb who was slain. The Lamb is the Lion of the tribe of Judah, and the Root of David (5:5). He is also the **bright morning star** (see 2:28). In this Lamb is fulfilled the messianic prophecies of Isaiah, and the fourth oracle of Balaam the prophet (Num 24:17). Jesus is the star Venus, the sign of sovereignty and victory over the nations. What king David accomplished for Israel, the Son of David accomplishes to the nth degree for all his people of all times and places (see Luke 1:31–33).

b) The closing sentences, 22:17–21

In 22:8 John had brought his hearers down to earth, so to speak, after he had drawn to a close his reports on the revelations which God had given him. The lector had spoken in John's name: 'I, John, the one hearing and seeing these things . . .'

But now, just when things seem to be winding down, the worshippers hear the dramatic declaration: 'I, Jesus, sent my messenger . . . I am the root and offspring of David . . .' When the lector spoke these words in front of the congregation, the effect must have been electrifying, for the oral performance of this book served to actualise Jesus' presence among his people. The prophet John stands in the place of Jesus; through John's words Jesus is present among his people. The lector stands in the place of John; through his reading of John's words both John and Jesus join in the worship.

They must have had lengthy worship services in those days. Very likely the service began with the opening eight verses of Revelation, and then proceeded with interaction between reader and congregation to the end of the book and the end of the worship service.

The usual service of worship included the celebration of the eucharist. This sacrament looks back to the death of Christ, 'the Lamb who was slain', and forward to the banquet with him in heaven ('Blessed are those invited to the marriage supper of the Lamb'). Revelation is a dramatic portrayal of Christ's coming to judgment and salvation; the eucharist celebrates these actions. What the book does in narrative, worship centred on the eucharist does in ritual.

Although the connection between narrative and worship has been evident throughout Revelation, it is particularly clear in the last verses of the book, where almost every element has a parallel in the eucharistic celebrations of the church.

In a writing called *The Didache* or *Teaching of the Twelve Apostles*, which is dated to about fifty or sixty years after Revelation was written, the outline of a very early eucharistic service is given:

> Thanksgivings are spoken over the cup and the bread, including thanks to God 'for the Holy Vine of David . . . which you made known to us through Jesus'. A clear statement is made concerning who may participate and who may not: 'But let none eat or drink . . . except those who have been baptised in the Lord's name. For concerning this also the Lord said: "Give not that which is holy to the dogs".'
>
> The confession is made that God 'tabernacles' with his people, and he provides spiritual food and drink.
>
> The concluding eucharistic prayer ends with the words: 'Let grace come and let this world pass away. Hosannah to the God of David. If any one is holy, let him come! If anyone is not, let him repent! *Marana tha* ['Our Lord, come!]. Amen.'

Some of the obvious correlations between this account and the last verses of Revelation are: the reference to David; only some are worthy to participate in the eucharist; the ones who are excluded are compared to 'dogs'; a drink of life is promised; some are invited to 'Come!'; the Lord is confessed as the one who is to come; and the service closes with 'Amen'.

The parallels between this early eucharistic liturgy and the last verses of Revelation are sufficiently close to warrant the conclusion that John intended his book to be part of the worship of the church. This worship normally concluded with the celebration of the eucharist.

17 Twice Jesus had said, through his angel and directly, in the last verses of Revelation, that he was coming 'soon' (22:7,12). At his own appointed time he will come. The **bride** of Christ, that is, the community of worshipping Christians in heaven and on earth (19:7,8), is led by the **Spirit** to respond to Christ's announcement with a cry and a plea: **'Come'**! Christians, together with all of creation, are like little children standing on tiptoe waiting for the king's procession to arrive (Rom 8:19,23). They wait for it with patient impatience, praying earnestly for the Lord's coming. They are joined and assisted in their prayers by the **Spirit** of God (Rom 8:22–27).

John then urges all those who are listening to the reading of his book to make the cry and petition of the bride and Spirit their very own. Each listener is to echo the cry: **'Come'**! The immediate reference and focus of this prayer is to Christ's coming in the eucharist, where the Lord's death is proclaimed 'until he comes' (1 Cor 11:26).

The liturgy continues with the issuing of a pair of matching invitations, addressed by the lector to those who are about to participate in the eucharist, the supper of the Lamb. The invitation takes up the promise of God himself: 'To the thirsty I will give water as a gift from the spring of the water of life' (21:6). The Lord's supper is a 'foretaste of the feast to come'. At the table of the Lord the food is provided by Christ himself. The hungry are fed: they eat and are satisfied. The thirsty drink: they drink and their thirst is quenched. So at the conclusion of the meal, God's people quite rightly give thanks for the heavenly food with which they have been fed. They praise God for refreshing them through the healing power of the gift of life. They pray for the strengthening in them of this gift.

18,19 In a direct reference to the ending of the book of Daniel (Dan 12:4,9), John makes it clear that his book is not to be kept secret but is to be heard. And then he adds a solemn exhortation, intended to preserve the wholeness and integrity of the written revelation. The exhortation covers two eventualities: taking away something from the book, or adding something to the book. To do either is to violate the integrity of John's prophetic work.

Twice John insists on the written text (**described** = 'written'), and twice John speaks of **this book**, implying that it is a finished product. The warning is addressed to individual Christians, the same ones to whom the invitation of verse 17 is addressed. John speaks directly to **everyone who hears**, that is, to the members of the congregations in the Roman province of Asia, who take part in the worship services in which this book is read.

John's warning is concerned with the wilful distortion of the prophetic message. John has been careful to insist that the **words of the prophecy of this book** are not his, but they enjoy the threefold inspiration of God, Christ, and the Spirit (1:1-3;22:6,8,9,16,18). What John has written is the authoritative word of the Triune God. Those who truly have 'an ear' will 'listen to what the Spirit is saying to the churches' (2:7,11,17, and so forth).

The warning is an extremely solemn one, matching the seriousness of the sin. To pervert or distort God's word — and to do so deliberately and persistently — is to deny God; it brings upon the offender the judgment of God. As usual in Revelation, the punishment fits the crime. If anyone **adds** to the book, to them God will **add** the plagues; if anyone **takes away** from the book, from them God will **take away** their **share in the tree of life and in the holy city** (see 22:1-5). This 'share' is granted as a gift only to those who hold faithfully to 'the testimony of Jesus' which is the same thing as faithfully keeping 'the words of this book' (see 19:10 and 22:9).

What John does here is bring together the tree of life, the holy city, and the book. So he unites the whole Bible, from Genesis to the end of Revelation. The early Christians were fully aware of this, and deliberately set Revelation as the last book of the Bible. Clearly, they also intended John's warnings about tampering with the contents to be extended to cover not just Revelation but the whole Bible (='book').

What John does in verses 18 and 19 was common practice in ancient times: it was a kind of copyright protection device. When the Greek translation of the Hebrew Old Testament was completed, it was read aloud to an assembly of the Jewish community. They approved it, and then instructed the translators to pronounce a curse 'upon anyone who should make any alteration either by adding or changing in any way whatever any of the words which had been written, or making any omission'.

Soon after John's day there arose false teachers who altered the text of the gospels or the epistles to fit their own teachings. The second-century heretic Marcion, for example, rejected the Old Testament and denied the humanity of Christ. To make Luke's gospel more compatible with his views, he removed from the gospel all references to the Jewish background of Jesus.

By using the familiar 'warning' formula, John is echoing Deuteronomy 4:1–4, and claiming for his book the full authority of the 'word of God and the testimony of Jesus' (Rev 1:2).

20 In the opening liturgy (1:5), Jesus had been confessed as 'the faithful witness'. Now at the end of the worship service he bears approving testimony to the contents of the book and to the worship event which the book has brought about. To the prayer and cry, 'Come!' (22:17), Jesus responds with the reassuring words: **'Surely I am coming soon'**.

The word which is translated 'surely' has the idea of indicating the acceptance of a statement which has just been made (for example, 14:13;16:7). The word looks backward; it is a reply to a word or action which is assumed already to have taken place. In this case, Jesus' 'surely' is a response to the prayer of the worshipping community (22:17). In effect Jesus says: 'Your prayer has been heard; it has been effective; I am on my way'.

The liturgical response of the worshipping community (see 1:7) is a simple but profound **'Amen'**. In Revelation, 'Amen' expresses a conviction concerning the certain experience of something in the future (see 1:6;5:14;7:12;19:4). Here the people of God articulate their desire and certainty about the coming of the Lord Jesus.

The 'Amen' of the community is followed by a phrase which in Aramatic is rendered *Maran atha* (see 1 Cor 16:22, footnote). The same phrase occurs in the eucharistic prayer of the early Christian liturgy. It translates as: **Come, Lord [Jesus]!** This liturgical shout expresses in compact form all the hopes and longings of the faithful people of God.

O Son of God, we wait for Thee,
We long for Thine appearing;
We know Thou sittest on the throne,

And we Thy name are bearing.
Who trusts in Thee
May joyful be,
And see Thee, Lord, descending
To bring us bliss unending.

21 The book, and the worship service, closes as it began (1:4): with the benediction. The words, 'the saints. Amen', were probably not in the original manuscript. In any case, the last words which John's hearers hear are words which convey the free, undeserved love and favour of God, **the grace of the Lord Jesus**.

> This grace of Christ our Lord, for mind and heart and life, the writer prays may rest with those who read this Commentary, that they may be led into deeper knowledge of him who is our life.
>
> The writer asks the reader to pray that this grace of Christ may rest in forgiveness and love upon him who has now finished his task of commenting on this book, whose hidden meanings must far transcend our knowledge and our expectations.
>
> May He (He alone can) open our eyes to see the shining towers of the Heavenly Jerusalem; may He unseal our ears to hear the heavenly music to which it is being built; may He bind us by His love to that sweet service and citizenship which is perfect freedom, and bring us to that spiritual city which is full of divine enchantments. (Bishop Carpenter, concluding his commentary on Revelation, 1897)

FURTHER READING

Readers who would like to have a 'second opinion', or who want to deepen their understanding of Revelation, have a goodly number of helpful commentaries available to them. None of the following requires a knowledge of Greek.

Boring, Eugene M. *Revelation: Interpretation,* John Knox Press, Louisville, 1989.

A fine resource for the preacher.

Caird, George B A. *A Commentary on the Revelation of St John the Divine,* A & C Black, London, 1966.

An older commentary which broke new ground and has influenced many others. Caird sees the forest as well as the trees.

Krodel, Gerhard A. *Revelation,* Augsburg, Minneapolis, 1989.

Based on the text of the RSV, this commentary identifies the underlying structure of Revelation, and brings out the major themes, especially that of worship.

Lilje, Hanns. *The Last Book of the Bible: The Meaning of the Revelation of St John,* translated by Olive Wyon, Muhlenberg Press, Philadelphia, 1957.

A reflective commentary by a bishop who lived through the bestiality of Hitler's Third Reich.

Morris, Leon. *The Revelation of St John,* William B. Eerdmans, Grand Rapids, 1969.

A sound, sober commentary based on the Authorised (King James) Version.

Mounce, Robert H. *The Book of Revelation,* William B. Eerdmans, Grand Rapids, 1977.

A thorough treatment, based on the American Standard Version (1901).

Schüssler Fiorenza, Elisabeth. *Revelation: Vision of a Just World*, Fortress Press, Minneapolis, 1991.

Not so much a commentary as an extended essay on the structure and themes of Revelation.

Sweet, John P M. *Revelation*, Westminster Press, Philadelphia, 1979.

Brief notes and discussion often include original references to literature which other commentators have overlooked.

Wilcock, Michael. *The Message of Revelation*, Inter-Varsity Press, Leicester, 1975.

Helpful for its overviews, and its reflections on the relevance of Revelation for the 1990s.

Two older commentaries in English which have influenced several generations of commentators are:

Charles, R H A. *A Critical and Exegetical Commentary on the Revelation of St John*, 2 volumes, Charles Scribner's Sons, New York, 1920.

Swete, H B. *The Apocalypse of St John*, MacMillan, London, 1906.

Both these commentaries work with the Greek text.

Of the many published studies on various facets of Revelation, the following will be especially helpful to the readers of this commentary:

Aune, David E. *Prophecy in Early Christianity and the Ancient Mediterranean World*, William B. Eerdmans, Grand Rapids, 1983.

Boesak, Allan A. *Comfort and Protest: The Apocalypse from a South African Perspective*, The Westminister Press, Philadelphia, 1987.

Farrer, Austin. *A Rebirth of Images*, Dacre Press, Westminster, 1949.

Goldsworthy, Graeme. *The Gospel in Revelation*, Paternoster Press, Exeter, 1984.

Hemer, Colin J. *The Letters to the Seven Churches of Asia in their Local Setting*, JSOT Press, Sheffield, 1986.

Price, S R F. *Rituals and Power: The Roman Imperial Cult in Asia Minor*, Cambridge University Press, Cambridge, 1984.

Rissi, Mathias. *The Future of the World*, SCM Press, London, 1972.

Rowland, Christopher. *Revelation*, Epworth Press, London, 1993.

Thompson, Leonard L. *The Book of Revelation: Apocalypse and Empire*, Oxford University Press, Oxford, 1990.

Since the manuscript for this book was completed, three studies of particular usefulness to readers of this commentary have been published:

Bauckham, Richard. *The Theology of the Book of Revelation*, Cambridge University Press, Cambridge, 1993.

Kleinig, John W. *The Lord's Song: The Basis, Function and Significance of Choral Music in Chronicles*, JSOT Supplement Series 156, Sheffield Academic Press, Sheffield, 1993.

Metzger, Bruce M. *Breaking the Code: Understanding the Book of Revelation*, Abingdon Press, Nashville, 1993.

www.ingramcontent.com/pod-product-compliance
Lightning Source LLC
LaVergne TN
LVHW020522100826
845148LV00010B/1314

* 9 7 8 1 5 5 6 3 5 4 3 9 7 *